BLACKSTONE

The Care Standards Act 2000

BLACKSTONE'S GUIDE TO

The Care Standards
Act 2000

Philip Engelman and Paul Spencer

Barristers, Cloisters, Temple EC4Y 7AA

OXFORD
UNIVERSITY PRESS

OXFORD
UNIVERSITY PRESS

Great Clarendon Street, Oxford OX2 6DP

Oxford University Press is a department of the University of Oxford.
It furthers the University's objective of excellence in research, scholarship,
and education by publishing worldwide in

Oxford New York

Auckland Bangkok Buenos Aires Cape Town Chennai
Dar es Salaam Delhi Hong Kong Istanbul Karachi Kolkata
Kuala Lumpur Madrid Melbourne Mexico City Mumbai Nairobi
São Paulo Shanghai Taipei Tokyo Toronto

with an associated company in Berlin

Oxford is a registered trade mark of Oxford University Press
in the UK and in certain other countries

Published in the United States
by Oxford University Press Inc., New York

© Philip Engelman and Paul Spencer 2003

The moral rights of the authors have been asserted

Crown copyright material is reproduced under
Class Licence Number C01P0000148 with the permission
of HMSO and the Queen's Printer for Scotland

Database right Oxford University Press (maker)

First published 2003

British Library Cataloguing in Publication Data

Data available

Library of Congress Cataloging in Publication Data

Data available

ISBN 1–84174285–6

1 3 5 7 9 10 8 6 4 2

Typeset in Times
by Cambrian Typesetters, Frimley, Surrey
Printed in Great Britain
on acid-free paper by
Antony Rowe Ltd, Chippenham

Contents—Summary

Contents

Preface

The Care Standards Act 2000 has transformed the provision of social care law, changing it almost beyond recognition. There have been dramatic changes not only in the law, but also in the procedure. The provisions of the Act impact on a whole range of social care providers who were not previously regulated.

This book has been produced to aid practitioners, providers, those who work in care, nursing and child care sectors, and those who police the regulatory aspects of the 2000 Act for the Commission and Assembly. The aim of the book is therefore to assist those involved in this area of law to understand more deeply the relevance and effect of this Act, the Regulations and the Standards and apply it with confidence in a legal and social care setting.

We are indebted to our editor Annabel Macris, Nicola Freshwater, Rebecca Allen and Michelle Thompson for their tireless assistance with the preparation of the text and other invaluable work behind the scenes, much of which has passed unnoticed.

There are others who have helped and expressed ideas and whilst we do not mention them individually, we thank them.

We should also like to thank David O'Sullivan and Carolyn Pearson for their research and assistance.

This book has been a long time in gestation and there are a number of people who have contributed to the development of our thinking in this area.

Paul's thanks go to Shasa Behzadi for her tolerance and encouragement over a long period of time.

Any inaccuracies in the text can, of course, only be attributed to ourselves. We have stated the law as of 1 April 2003. Since there are frequent amendments, we advise the reader to refer to the relevant websites (a list of them is given at Appendix 5).

Philip Engelman
Paul Spencer
July 2003

TABLE OF CASES

TABLE OF PRIMARY LEGISLATION

TABLE OF SECONDARY LEGISLATION

1

INTRODUCTION

1.1 INTRODUCTION

On 20 July 2000 the Care Standards Act 2000 ('the 2000 Act') was passed into law by Parliament. From 1 April 2002 the old system of registration and regulation of residential care and nursing homes under the Registered Homes Act 1984 ceased. The National Care Standards Commission ('the Commission') in England and the National Assembly for Wales took over the registration of care homes, children's homes and a wide number of other agencies, clinics and day care centres.

In Wales the National Assembly for Wales ('the Assembly') delegated registration and regulation to two non-departmental public bodies, the Social Services Inspectorate for Wales and the Care Standards Inspectorate for Wales, both accountable to the Assembly. Those two organizations regulate and support the delivery of personal social services and support to children, young people, older people, their carers and people with learning difficulties, mental health problems, physical and sensory disabilities, and they operate along similar lines to those of the Commission in England. A more thorough overview of the Commission and the Assembly is provided later in this introductory chapter.

Many former inspectors and their supporting staff transferred from local authority registration and inspection units or health authorities to the Commission and the non-departmental public bodies in Wales shortly before the commencement of the Act on 1 April 2002. Subject to the delay in implementation of certain regulations and standards, the following services are now or shortly will be regulated under the 2000 Act:

- children's homes,
- independent hospitals,
- independent clinics,
- care homes,
- residential family centres,
- independent medical agencies,
- domiciliary care agencies,
- fostering agencies,
- nursing agencies, and
- voluntary adoption agencies.

In addition, the 2000 Act provides for the regulation and inspection of local authority fostering and adoption services.

The Act establishes a General Social Care Council (and its Welsh equivalent) with the specific and welcome purpose of making provision for the registration, regulation and training of care and other staff, who will now be called social care workers. It establishes a Children's Commissioner for Wales who will have important powers to safeguard and promote the rights and welfare of children in Wales. Regrettably, England has no equivalent post, though the Climbié inquiry is likely to recommend that such an office be set up. The Act also makes provision for the registration, regulation and training of those providing childminding or day care to the under-eights as well as making provision for the protection of children and vulnerable adults. Finally, it amends the law relating to children looked after in schools and colleges.

The breadth and scale of the changes brought about by the 2000 Act are significant. The Act and the accompanying regulations and National Minimum Standards are daunting, running, as they do, to several thousand pages.

The 2000 Act repeals the whole of the Registered Homes Act 1984 ('the 1984 Act') and the Nurses Agencies Act 1957. It makes consequent repeals and amendments to a variety of Acts of Parliament, including amendments to the Children Act 1989, recognizing the exceptional vulnerability of children.

The purpose of this book is to provide a guide to the 2000 Act and its dramatic effect on the provision of social care in the 21st century. It is anticipated that the Act will come into force fully in April 2003.

1.2 WHITE PAPER—MODERNIZING SOCIAL SERVICES

In November 1998, as a prelude to the Care Standards Bill, the Secretary of State for Health published a White Paper entitled *Modernizing Social Services: Promoting independence; Improving protection; Raising standards* (Cm 4169).

In the Foreword the then Secretary of State, the Rt Hon Frank Dobson MP, said:

This White Paper spells out what the Government proposes to do to modernise social services, in line with our proposals for the NHS and for improving public health and reducing health inequalities which we have already published. We are determined to have a system of health and social care which is convenient to use, can respond quickly to emergencies and provides top quality services.

The proposals were expressed to be the embodiment of 'the third way' advocated by New Labour. It was expressed thus in chapter 1 of the White Paper:

... our third way for social care moves the focus away from who provides the care, and places it firmly on the quality of services experienced by individuals and their carers and families ...

The White Paper recognized the problems in social service provision for adults, noting that in April 1993 (see the National Health Service and Community Care Act 1990) social services responsibilities for people needing long-term care had expanded and would continue to increase significantly. Until that time, people who lived in independent residential or nursing homes were funded through the Department of Social Security without any real regulation. The new Act entrusts this responsibility to social services, who are charged with the responsibility of carrying out an assessment of the care needs of the individual concerned, and ensuring that the care being provided meets that person's needs. The view was taken in the White Paper that, despite earlier reforms, 'social services need direction if they are to serve adults better'. The new scheme was to have as its objective the promotion of independence. Wide-ranging domiciliary care regulations and standards came fully into force in April 2003, extending protection to tens of thousands of people previously outside regulation or protection. The task of policing this unenviably falls to the Commission and the Assembly and it has to be hoped that they will rise to this difficult challenge, thereby ensuring that the quality of personal care and support received by people living in their own homes is maintained.

In relation to children, the Government's stated aims were:

- to ensure that children are protected from sexual, physical and emotional abuse and from neglect.
- to raise the quality of care of children in care so that it is as close as possible to the care provided by loving and responsible parents.
- to improve the life chances of children in care, and of others ('children in need') who need social services support, in particular through improving their health and education and support after they leave care.

It was rightly recognized that there was particular concern concerning failures in the regulatory safeguards around residential children's homes and schools and in the arrangements for monitoring of foster care. There were also failures in the safeguards concerning the appointment or retention of people in work with children. The Government recognized that too many children were placed a long way from their homes, which sometimes led to a failure to ensure that they were properly monitored. The lack of effective monitoring of prospective care staff for children's homes sometimes acted as a magnet to those who sought to physically and mentally abuse young children, highlighted by many inquiries and police investigations such as Operation Goldfinch in Wales and Operation Ore in England.

The regulatory reforms proposed for children were as follows:

- A new independent regulatory system, ending the situation where the local authority is both the purchaser and the inspector.
- Full powers of inspection and enforcement for all children's homes, including homes run by local authorities.
- New protections in services not currently covered: small children's homes, mainstream and special boarding schools accommodating any child for over 295 days a year, residential family centres, independent fostering agencies and some specialist establishments providing therapeutic support.
- The requirement to follow regulations and new national minimum standards, thereby replacing the inconsistencies of the old system with a uniform set of criteria. An overview of these provisions appears below.

In relation to care services, the White Paper identified the following issues:

The existing arrangements for regulating care services have developed in a piece-meal fashion. Responsibilities for regulating the various services for adults and children are divided between Local Authorities, Health Authorities and the Department of Health essentially ... Other services—notably Council's own care homes, small children's homes and domiciliary care ... are not subject to any regulation ...

The old system led to a number of problems, specifically a lack of coherence leading to complaints by providers and others. Responsibilities were previously split between different authorities and different professional disciplines (social services professionals on the one hand, and mostly professional nurses on the other). This meant that there was no effective scrutiny of nursing care in residential homes or social care in nursing homes. Vocal concern was also expressed about a lack of consistency and unfairness in the policing of the old system. Previously there were 150 local authorities and 100 health authorities in England. Standards varied from one area to another, creating uncertainty for both providers and service users. For instance, different approaches were taken by registration and inspection units and health authorities to room sizes, training and number of staff as well as the permitted number of residents to be accommodated in a home. That was a particular problem which resulted in much criticism because it affected the financial viability of many former registered services. Whilst the Government recognized that the Social Services Inspectorate had done valuable work in assessing local authorities' regulatory work, it wanted a clear national approach.

The Government identified four modes of solving the above-mentioned problems:

- Create Commissions for Care Standards, with independent regional authorities responsible solely for the regulation of care services. They would be non-

departmental public bodies accountable to the Secretary of State in England
and to the Assembly in Wales.
- Introduce new statutory regulation for services not currently covered, including domiciliary care and small children's homes.
- Introduce mandatory national minimum standards.
- Improve the way in which registration and inspection are carried out.

All care homes, whether run by private organizations, local authorities or organizations established by Royal Charter or Act of Parliament would, the Government decided, be registered and regulated. In respect of domiciliary care, which had previously escaped registration and regulation, after extensive lobbying it was decided to bring that service under the regulatory umbrella too. We welcome the extensive regulations and standards covering domiciliary care agencies which came into force in April 2003. A rigorous system of regulation of children's homes is extended to any variety of children's home, ie whether local authority or privately run, voluntary or small, private children's homes. The same approach was to be taken to residential family centres and independent fostering agencies, as recommended by the Burgner Report and the Children's Safeguards Review. Welfare aspects of boarding schools, whether independent (which are currently subject to inspection by local authorities) or local authority run, are now regulated under the new system.

In respect of minimum standards the Government's objective was to introduce consistency in regulation, as well as reducing duplicated bureaucracy. It suggested that there would be three levels at which standards would be set:

- Some standards will be set firmly in legislation, and those would be non-negotiable (an example in the current system is the requirement that the person in charge of a nursing home (an establishment) must be a registered nurse or medical practitioner).
- The standards would be spelt out at national level, for example, clear procedures governing the contents of detailed records, their retention and the requirement that they be available for inspection.
- Some of the standards will allow for interpretation by the Commission/Assembly who will be able to define their own requirements within the limits of the national standards, an example being the timescales within which specific below-standard accommodation must be upgraded. This may not now occur as the Government has recently announced that the environmental standards may not be mandatory.

It was also an objective of the standards to ensure that uniform standards be developed for both residential and nursing home care so that an integrated approach can be taken 'with common standards for all care homes, differing only in matters relating to the nursing care needs of those in nursing homes ...'.

A vast number of detailed national minimum standards have been prepared by the

Government and by the National Assembly in Wales under s 23 of the 2000 Act. Those who were charged with policing the new regime had hoped that all the standards would become requirements. That will not now be the case.

The White Paper then moved on to the problem of social care and social workers. It observed that:

- 80 per cent of this large workforce, working with very vulnerable people, had no recognized qualifications or training.
- There were no national mechanisms to set and enforce standards, practice and conduct. Health care professions have had such mechanisms for many years. A General Social Care Council has been established and will set up a comprehensive register of social care workers, introduce new qualifications (a degree in social work) and enforce standards of conduct and practice. All of this is to be welcomed, though there is much criticism, some of it deserved, about how this will be funded.

The Government proposed registration, training and the taking of enforcement action against those who were in breach of the codes of conduct and practice, and setting up a new system to meet those challenges.

The White Paper also emphasized the importance of partnership, particularly between the many bodies that make up the modern NHS and local authorities. However, this 'partnership' is not brought forward in the 2000 Act. It is likely that this issue will surface in a new NHS Bill and, presumably, further local authority powers.

Finally, the White Paper dealt with the modernization of social services and local government, so as to provide the most effective method of delivering social care. Once again, this did not find its way into the 2000 Act, although more social services and local authority legislation is anticipated in order to bring this objective into effect.

1.3 NATIONAL CARE STANDARDS COMMISSION AND NATIONAL ASSEMBLY FOR WALES

The Commission is an independent body which acts under the direction of the Secretary of State for Health. The Commission's headquarters are in Newcastle and it is divided into nine regional commissions in England with a further 71 area offices. It replaces the old inspection system and procedures operated by some 230 local and health authorities. The Commission's stated aim is to 'pioneer a national approach to inspection that places service users firmly at the heart of its operations … and … ensuring that care services are run in accordance with national minimum standards … to ensure … consistent quality of service, welfare and protection for vulnerable people across England …'.

In Wales, the Assembly oversees the Social Services Inspectorate Wales and the

Care Standards Inspectorate for Wales. The individual commission areas each register and supervise establishments and agencies in their geographical area. The Commission's stated intention is to enforce the uniform provision governing the registration and regulation of establishments, agencies and other bodies under its control. Whilst the Commission is 'independent' of government it acts under guidance issued by the Department of Health under s 6, enforces the regulations issued under s 22 and the standards under s 23 of the 2000 Act.

The Commission is required to keep the Secretary of State informed as to how services are being provided, with a view to improving their quality. By this method it is hoped that there will be uniformity in the policing of establishments and agencies.

The provision of care in Wales is supervised by the Assembly. Through its Health and Social Services Committee the Assembly oversees those vulnerable individuals who receive personal care or related support. The Social Services Inspectorate is divided into three areas: services governing adults and resources; issues relating to children and family services, and the inspection unit. Again, all these bodies are formally accountable to the Assembly.

A Commission for Health Improvement (see www.chi.nhs.uk) has been established in order to assist the National Commission in the provision of services.

1.4 ESTABLISHMENTS AND AGENCIES

In order to bring the diverse services referred to at 1.1 above under the umbrella of the 2000 Act, new terminology is adopted as follows. Children's homes, independent (ie non-NHS) hospitals, independent clinics, independent medical agencies, care homes (both residential and nursing), residential family centres, domiciliary care agencies (ie an undertaking providing personal care to people in their own homes), fostering agencies, nurses agencies and voluntary adoption agencies all now lie within the remit of the Commission and the Assembly under the umbrella definition of an 'establishment' or 'agency'. Thus the concept of 'premises' which was relevant to the registration of, for example, residential care homes, nursing homes and children's homes, no longer has any real place in the new legislation. These services are principally described in ss 1–4 of the 2000 Act. For convenience the term 'establishments' will be used below.

1.5 REGISTRATION

All establishments (save for voluntary adoption agencies) must be registered by the Commission or the Assembly. It is now mandatory that the services listed above register and ss 11–19 together with their accompanying regulations set out the requirements to be met and the procedure to be followed. Registration is the process of formally approving persons and organizations to carry on an establishment or agency. The Commission and the Assembly will consider the 'fitness' criteria in determining whether a person, organization or service is suitable to be registered.

Having received the application form, the Commission and the Assembly will consider it with a view to determining the fitness of the applicant, the fitness of the premises and the fitness of the services and facilities being offered. An applicant or organization will not obtain registration for a prospective service, unless he or it satisfies the national minimum standards and complies with the registration regulations and requirements. The Commission has produced a helpful and detailed application pack. It has a useful registration route-finder, which should be carefully studied and followed by those seeking registration. If granted unconditionally, an application will be recorded by the issue of a certificate of registration ('the certificate').

If the application for registration is refused or is granted subject to non-agreed conditions, then an appeal process can be triggered by the dissatisfied applicant. Initially an applicant will have a right to make written representations to the Commission/Assembly and if those representations are not successful the applicant has a right to make a written and/or oral appeal to the Care Standards Tribunal.

However, it is clear that any person who carries on or manages an establishment or agency, whatever its description, must register. An establishment or agency must register the person who carries on the service, ie have a registered owner/proprietor and manager. The requirements to register are contained in Pt II of the Act from s 15 onwards, but regulations made under s 22 require the appointment of a registered manager in addition to the above requirements. Running an unregistered service is, as before, a criminal offence.

The Commission/Assembly charges a fee according to the type of service applying for registration. In England the scale of charges is set out in the National Care Standards Commission (Fees and Frequency of Inspections) Regulations 2001, SI 2001/3980, or is available on their website at www.carestandards.org.uk. In Wales the level of charges can be viewed by visiting the Assembly's website at www.wales.gov.uk. Once a service is registered it becomes liable to pay an annual fee, or a further fee where there is a change in provider or manager.

Thus registration will be:

- granted if all the fitness criteria are met and no conditions are made;
- approved with conditions if criteria are met with the conditions required;
- refused if any of the fitness criteria are not met;
- varied if any of the conditions of registration need to be changed;
- cancelled if any of the fitness criteria, regulations or minimum standards are not maintained.

Further, a certificate will be cancelled where there has been a breach of any of the criminal offences set out in the Act or the regulations; or where there has been cancellation by an urgent order granted by the magistrates' court where the justices are satisfied that there is a serious risk to a person's life, health or well-being.

1.5.1 Fitness

The 'concept of fitness' underpins the registration process. By reference to it, the Commission/Assembly determines whether the applicant is suitable to run a regulated service. The Commission/Assembly will require verification of identity, qualifications, detailed employment records, health and business standing, evidence of completion of a criminal record check, and consider whether the applicant is, in light of his application, someone who is 'trustworthy', has 'integrity', is 'upright', 'honourable' and 'truthful'. The concept of fitness is covered in greater detail in chapter 3.

1.5.2 Cancellation

There is, as before, a cancellation procedure which can be undertaken by the usual 'slow' route. The emergency procedure for cancellation is set out in ss 20 and 79K. Where the 'slow' procedure for cancellation is followed, the holder of the certificate is given notice of the proposal to cancel his registration, and an opportunity to make written representations against any such notice of proposal is permitted. It is usual that the residents will not be removed from what is now the establishment or agency until the appeal process has been exhausted. Under the urgent procedure an application can be made to a justice of the peace without notice. However, a district judge or justice of the peace in the magistrates' court now has power under s 20(2) to hear submissions from the registered person, establishment or agency if that is deemed appropriate. It is suggested that unless there is a compelling reason for not informing the registered service or manager of the application to be made, it or he should be notified. Failure to do so may be a breach of the Human Rights Act 1998 or may render the Commission or Assembly liable to other challenge such as in the Administrative Court and/or for a private law claim for any loss that flows.

1.5.3 Appeal

The decision of the Commission/Assembly to refuse, or to impose conditions or to cancel registration gives a right of appeal to the Care Standards Tribunal, presided over by the President, HH Judge Pearl. An appeal also lies to the Tribunal from a decision of the justice under the emergency cancellation procedure.

1.5.4 Regulations and standards

The appropriate Minister is given wide powers to make regulations under s 22 setting out the requirements for registration and detailed matters of operation. The Minister is also empowered to 'prepare and publish statements of national minimum standards (ss 22–23) applicable to establishment or agencies'. Those standards, (referred to in later chapters) set out minimum standards that the Minister deems appropriate and are to be kept under review and be amended from time to time where necessary.

The standards have had or will have a great impact upon all establishments and agencies. The Government has made it clear that it will review all the standards in the first three years of operation and any changes considered appropriate will be made. Some of the standards have already been the subject of statutory guidance issued by the Commission. The Government has been forced to respond to the disquiet being expressed about the number of small to medium-sized care homes that have closed over the last few years. It has proposed further amendments to certain standards in an attempt to address some of the criticisms levelled at it. The environmental requirements will not now, it appears, be mandatory. However, the relevant standards are to be taken into account:

- in the making of any decision by the registration authority;
- in any proceedings in respect of the urgent cancellation;
- in the proceedings on an appeal to the Tribunal against such a decision;
- in any proceedings for an offence under the regulations.

1.5.5 Offences

A significant number of offences are created under the Act and the accompanying regulations. It is, for example, an offence to run an unregistered service (s 11), to fail to comply with any conditions imposed on registration (s 24) or to knowingly make a statement in the application for registration which is false or misleading in a material respect (s 27).

It will be an offence for any establishment 'without reasonable excuse' to fail to comply with any condition being in force in respect of that establishment, but the corporate body or person accused may have a defence under the objective criteria set out in the test.

It will also be an offence to breach any of the regulations made under the Act.

New offences are created, such as the false description of establishments.

The ambit of those potentially liable in respect of such offences is extended to companies where it can be established that an offence has been committed 'with the consent or connivance of, or to be attributable to any neglect on the part of' any director, manager or secretary of the company or any person acting or purporting to act in that capacity.

1.5.6 Inspection

The powers of inspectors are substantially increased. For example, a person 'who carries on or manages' the relevant establishment is under a duty to supply information when requested to do so by the registration authority.

There are wide new powers under s 32 permitting an inspector to enter and inspect any premises and seize and remove any document or material which the inspector believes may show evidence of a failure to comply with a condition or requirement. Obstructing an inspector is a criminal offence.

1.5.7 Annual returns

There are now provisions for regulations to be made in respect of the provision of an annual return to the registration authority under s 33. These will impose an onerous burden on those registered. However, it was thought that those most vulnerable needed such protection, though it is difficult to see what action could reasonably be taken in most cases as many of those currently registered are operating either at a loss or are making no more than a minimal trading profit.

1.5.8 Register

A register is to be kept by the Commission/Assembly under s 35 and copies of that register should be made available 'for inspection at all reasonable times' or for copying (s 36).

1.6 PUBLIC SERVICE/OFFICERS

Where functions are discharged by a local authority, such as adoption under the Adoption Act 1976 or fostering under the Children Act 1989, then both the Commission and the Assembly are given extensive powers. The former may advise the Minister on any matters connected with local authority functions; the latter may request information or inspect local authority premises used for the discharge of the relevant functions and associated powers. Local authorities may be liable to conviction for the offence or offences of failing to comply with the regulation or standard. Annual returns and an annual fee will be payable.

1.6.1 Social workers and social care workers

Part IV and ss 54–70 of the Act deal with the position of social workers, social care workers and the Councils (the General Social Care Council in England and the Care Council for Wales). A social care worker is anyone employed at or by or running a children's home, care home, residential family centre, domiciliary care, fostering or voluntary adoption agency. The General Social Care Council is mandated to improve public protection, raise professional standards and (in England) create a well-trained, effective and accountable social care workforce. The Welsh equivalent is the Welsh Council which follows similar criteria. These Councils are required to maintain an up-to-date register of social workers and social care workers. Codes of Conduct and Practice for Social Care Workers are in the process of being finalized.

There will be specific requirements governing education and training and a Code of Conduct and Practice relating to this area is now near completion. The Councils will be able to suspend or remove social care workers from the register. Detailed provisions are made as to the qualifications, training and post-qualification training of social care workers. The Central Council for Education and Training in Social Work is abolished and provision is made for the setting up of new training.

Readers may find it useful to visit the Councils' websites: www.gscc.org.uk and www.ccwales.org.uk.

1.6.2 Children's Commissioner for Wales

A Children's Commissioner for Wales is established with the object of protecting children who are the recipients of 'regulated children's services in Wales'. The Commissioner has wide powers to review and monitor the operation of arrangements for children and to report on their effectiveness or otherwise. The Commissioner is required to ensure that proper action is taken where, amongst other things, a criminal offence has been committed or the health or safety of children is endangered.

1.6.3 Childminders/children's day care

On 1 September 2001 the Office for Standards in Education (Ofsted) took over responsibility for the regulation of childminding and day care to the under-eights in England. The application form, various guidance on national standards, the protocol and the framework for the regulation of day care and childminding is helpfully set out on Ofsted's website at www.ofsted.gov.uk.

1.7 CONCLUSION

Thus a substantial change in the care industry is brought about by the 2000 Act. Responsibility for the registration and inspection of an estimated 40,000 care services in England transferred to the Commission on 1 April 2002. Delivery of social care affects well over a million people in England and Wales, and provides employment for many thousands. When the Domiciliary Care Regulations 2002, SI 2002/3214, came into force on 1 April 2003, thousands of other services or agencies providing personal care which were previously not policed became subject to registration and formal inspection.

As described above, a number of diverse institutions and establishments are now brought under a single umbrella, to which a uniform procedure is to be applied. Other welcome developments are being co-ordinated at local and national levels. An example of this is the Memorandum of Understanding set up between the Health and Safety Executive, the Local Government Association and the Commission on how they will work together to regulate and enforce health and safety matters in care homes and establishments in England. The Memorandum of Understanding recognizes the demarcation of responsibility which it is envisaged will lead to a more effective inspection and enforcement regime. All those in the care industry, whether as providers, receivers or administrators, will be concerned with the workings of the 2000 Act.

The Commission and the Assembly aim to pioneer a national approach to the registration and inspection of establishments and agencies to ensure that national minimum standards are consistently met and that the welfare and protection of those who are vulnerable is maintained. This is a mammoth task and the benchmarks that the Commission and the Assembly have set themselves are high. The chapters that follow will look at specific Parts of the Act, and the relevant regulations and standards.

On 19 April 2002 the Secretary of State for Health, Alan Milburn, announced that he would establish two new inspectorates: the Commission for Healthcare Audit and Inspection (CHAI) and the Commission for Social Care Inspection (CSCI), both non-departmental bodies. On 12 March 2003 the Health and Social Care (Community Health and Standards) Bill was introduced into Parliament which, if enacted, will establish the CHAI and the CSCI.

It is proposed that the CSCI will take over responsibility for social care functions currently carried out by the Commission, the work of the Social Services Inspectorate (SSI) and the Joint Review Team of the Audit Commission and the SSI. CHAI will take over the independent health care work presently undertaken by the Commission, the work of the Mental Health Act Commission and the NHS value for money work of the Audit Commission. These proposals are significant and those wishing to find out further information about the changes may find it useful to visit the Commission's website at www.carestandards.org.uk and read the statements of purpose of these two bodies.

2

THE NATIONAL CARE STANDARDS COMMISSION AND THE NATIONAL ASSEMBLY FOR WALES

2.1 THE COMMISSION

2.1.1 The role of the Commission

Section 6 establishes the Commission as an executive non-departmental body-corporate exercising functions bestowed upon it by the 2000 Act. The Commission acts in accordance with directions and guidance given by the Secretary of State for Health. In the foreword to the Department of Health's guide, *The Care Standards Act 2000: A Guide for Registered Services Providers,* Jackie Smith, Minister of State said:

This landmark legislation has created the N.C.S.C., a powerful body dedicated to raising standards of care, and has taken another important step towards ensuring that the most vulnerable people in our community are carefully protected ...

The Commission's website describes the Commission as having 'some independence' from the Department of Health, operating with its own independent Chair, Chief Executive and Board. If it has any independence from the Executive, in our view that is limited. The Commission will be set targets and those targets will be monitored by Department of Health ministers, with a view to improving the care provided to vulnerable children and adults.

From its headquarters in Newcastle, the Commission oversees eight regional offices and 71 area offices. The 71 area offices take over the day-to-day inspection and related work previously carried out by 150 local and 95 health authorities. The Commission's inspectors and their counterparts in Wales have a considerable job ahead of them in coming to terms with the detailed and lengthy regulations and standards that cover the wide number and variety of services now regulated.

2.1.1.1 *Scope and functions*
From 1 April 2002, the Commission became the Registration Authority in England (s 5) and will inspect all registered services as well as local authority fostering and adoption services, boarding schools, further education colleges providing residential accommodation to under-18s and residential special schools.

2.1.1.2 *Part II services*
The Commission is required to keep the Secretary of State 'informed' about Pt II services (establishments and agencies, but not those for medical or psychiatric treatment or listed services as defined in s 2) and in particular to express views on the availability and quality of services provided (see s 7 and para 8 of the Code of Practice for Board Members of the Commission). It is well documented that a considerable number of residential care homes have closed in recent years. Providers have complained, with some justification, that they have been regulated in an unstructured and non-uniform way. Rightly or wrongly this has led to accusations of bias and unfairness in the policing of care homes. Given the new regime introduced by the Act providers are now, it is said, faced with uniform criteria and regulation. Whilst uniform National Standards are long overdue and welcome, it may be that this legislation will lead to further homes closing in England and Wales. Although fees paid have risen, those rises are modest. Providers are now faced with annual registration fees and a plethora of new regulations and standards that they are required to understand and which are going to have a profound effect on every aspect of their establishments or agencies. The authors suggest that the sheer number of provisions and standards are perplexing not only to providers, but also to officials at the Commission and the Assembly. In this case, the Commission and the Assembly must exercise their discretion carefully as to how the new regime is policed and enforced.

The Commission is required to encourage service users to improve the quality of Pt II services by publishing, for example, National Minimum Standards (see ss 7(2) and 23). As mentioned above, detailed standards are, for the first time, to be applied consistently across England and Wales. Inspectors are given wide inspection powers under ss 31 and 32 and it is hoped that the national uniform standards covering nursing and personal social care and other services will be applied uniformly from now on. Whilst there may initially be a 'softly, softly' approach by inspectors, providers should note that in relation to the provision of child services for example, the Commission and the Assembly are unlikely to countenance breaches such as running an unregistered children's home or employing care staff (social care workers) without proper police checks being undertaken. At the time of going to print, it still remains the position that the strict requirements governing police checks have not yet been fully implemented because of the staffing problems which have plagued the Bureau and have led to a significant backlog of unchecked applications.

The Commission is also required to publish information about Pt II services (s 7(3)) and to advise the Secretary of State on any changes that should be implemented in order to improve provision of Pt II services.

The Commission is to provide training so that those who provide services meet the detailed standards being issued under s 23. It is helpful that those standards are easily accessible from the Commission's and National Assembly's websites (www.carestandards.org.uk and www.wales.gov.uk). However, how small to medium size providers will deal with numerous standards, one running to 113 pages and currently accompanied by 27 regulations is not easy to say. Examples include the Care Homes for Younger Adults and Adult Placement National Minimum Standards, and the National Minimum Standards for Children's Homes, which is 71 pages long, with references to other material (with which providers will be expected to be familiar) and the regulations running to a further 27 pages.

A General Social Care Council is established in England (and in Wales, the Cyngor Gofal Cymru) to promote high standards of training, practice and conduct by social care workers. It is hoped that the Government and the Commission will be true to their word and take 'a cooperative and collaborative approach ... to get all Services up to a high standard ... looking at areas that need improv[ing], ... set[ting] an action plan and a realistic timetable ...'. It would be unfortunate if criminal proceedings and/or regulatory enforcement action were taken without inspectors recognizing the enormity of what providers are faced with. It has been suggested by some of those involved with the Commission at national level that only wilful misconduct ought to lead to enforcement action in the first 12 months.

2.1.1.3 *Administration*

The Commission will charge (annual) fees to cover the cost of registration, training and the like, subject to the approval of the Secretary of State (Sch 1, para 17). The current rates are set out in appendix 2 of the Department of Health's *Guide for Registered Service Providers.*

It is important to note that the Commission is required to abide by the nine principles set out in its Code of Practice entitled 'Public Service Delivery'. Providers should read these carefully. Where complaints are made, a provider may find it useful to view the conduct complained of against the background of these principles. To what extent the Care Standards Tribunal will take judicial notice of any breach of these principles is of course yet to be determined.

Subject to the power of the Secretary of State to issue directions under Sch 1, para 12(4), the Commission is empowered to appoint its own staff and regional directors, and to make provision for pay, pensions and compensation for loss of employment pursuant to Sch 1, paras 8, 9 and 12.

The Commission is required to prepare annual audited accounts and submit those for examination and certification to the Comptroller and Auditor General.

The Commission is also required to compile a report for the Secretary of State commenting on how it has exercised its functions during the year (s 6 and Sch 1, para 19). The Commission's Board is accountable to the Secretary of State for Health, the relationship being defined in the Commission's Management Statement. It will take enforcement action, but initially it may be slow to do so for the reasons touched upon above. In the Department of Health's *Guide for Registered Services Providers*, the following question is posed: What if services repeatedly fail? The use of the word 'repeatedly' suggests that providers will be given considerable latitude. Again, it appears that the Commission may permit a lengthy period of grace before initiating criminal or cancellation proceedings.

2.1.2 Conclusion

The principal functions of the Commission are, therefore, the regulation of social care services as well as private and voluntary health care services. The Commission takes over the regulatory functions previously exercised by the registration and inspection units of local authorities and health authorities. Thus, the Commission and its eight regional offices register, and the 71 area offices, inspect care homes, children's homes, private and voluntary hospitals and clinics, independent medical agencies, residential family centres, independent fostering agencies, voluntary adoption agencies, nurses' agencies and domiciliary care agencies. The area offices will further inspect and monitor boarding schools, further education colleges providing residential accommodation to the under-18s, residential special schools and local authority fostering and adoption agencies.

These establishments, bodies and institutions will be judged and regulated against the background of national minimum standards issued under s 23 and discussed in some detail below. The Commission, as stated on its website and in the various draft consultation documents that it has issued, proposes to carry out regular inspections and rigorously apply its enforcement powers in order that the quality of service provided to the vulnerable is improved. Now that consultation has ended, it is noted that in the final standards there is no increase in the number of inspections of care and children's homes, currently two per year. This is regrettable. The unannounced inspections were a valuable tool in rooting out poor care practice and it is to be hoped that the frequency of such inspections will increase. To what extent the Commission will be successful ultimately depends on whether it will have proper resources to implement and police the new regime. The commitment of national Government in ensuring that these aims are met is crucial. In late 2000 and early 2001 some Commission areas such as London struggled to fill inspector posts. The manner in which former local and health authority inspection staff were treated led to complaint, and some senior staff were not able to find commensurate posts and rates of pay. Retaining and recruiting key personnel is crucial to the prospects of success of this Act and enforcement generally.

In April 2002 Secretary of State Alan Milburn announced his intention to abolish the Commission in favour of a body to be called the Commission for Social Care Inspection. Certain Commissioners put a brave face on this announcement, but the headlines in the national press at the end of May 2002 ('The Case of the Disappearing NCSC') cannot have helped staff morale.

2.2 THE ASSEMBLY

In July 1999 the Government published its paper, *Regulation and Inspection of Social and Health Care Services in Wales—A Commission for Care Standards in Wales*. The recommendations contained in the paper have been substantially reflected in s 8 and elsewhere in the 2000 Act. The Assembly is the regulatory body that is charged with the duty of securing improvement of Pt II services in Wales. Many of the observations made about the Commission also apply to Wales. The Assembly has a helpful website and those looking for information are directed to it (www.wales.gov.uk). Accountability is encouraged in s 8(2) as it requires the Assembly to publicize information about Pt II services.

The Assembly has powers similar to those of the Commission. The Assembly will, via s 8(3), regulate providers through the Care Standards Inspectorate for Wales. The Act also enables the Assembly to make provision for any 'additional functions' specified by the Assembly to cover Pt II services. This was explained in the statement made by the Under-Secretary of State for Wales during Standing Committee G of the Bill at col 204.

Some features to note about the Assembly are:

- Its wide powers of appointment including the Chair and other members of the Council.
- It will provide training with a view to ensuring that the standards issued under s 23 are met and adhered to.
- A Care Council for Wales is established by s 54(1)(b) which will be known as the 'Welsh Council' or Cyngor Gofal Cymru.
- The Assembly will appoint the Council, which will be an independent statutory body of not more than 25 members.
- The Assembly has established the Care Standards Inspectorate for Wales with four main roles: registering appropriate services; inspecting; ensuring compliance with national minimum standards and dealing with complaints. Helpful and detailed standards and accompanying regulations have been produced with the Social Services Inspectorate for Wales which, under its Chief Inspector, makes provision of social services to users and carers throughout Wales.
- The Assembly will enable inspection of services including care homes for adults, children's homes, and local authority fostering and adoption services under Pt III of the Act and other agencies. The Care Standards Inspectorate for Wales has decided to have a lay assessor input in most inspections of care homes. This is to be welcomed, as it will add a degree of independent

assessment to the views and conclusions of the Inspectorate in any annual announced inspection.

• The Assembly will ensure that regulations and national minimum standards are met and that service is provided covering, amongst other things, quality of life, care and treatment, staffing, management, complaints and protections.

The Assembly envisages that its members will work with health care professionals, the Health and Social Services Committee and Social Care Group and others in local government to ensure that minimum standards are met and maintained. As with the Commission, the Care Standards Inspectorate for Wales recognizes that 'it will take time to build an approach that makes sure of a consistent minimum quality of service in Wales'. Objectives have been set against the context of 'Better Wales' (the Welsh Assembly's strategic plan), and focus on who should be permitted to provide services, the inspection of services to ensure compliance with minimum standards, and the means for dealing with complaints.

Various amendments have been made to Part IV of the 2000 Act and the role, review, and monitoring functions of the Assembly covering the Children's Commissioner in Wales. Readers are referred to the Children's Commissioner for Wales Act 2001 for the statute's full effect.

3

REGISTRATION AND CANCELLATION

3.1 INTRODUCTION

From 1 April 2002 the Commission, the Assembly, Her Majesty's Chief Inspectors for Schools (Ofsted), and Her Majesty's Chief Inspector of Education and Training in Wales (ESTYN) undertook the regulation of the following services:

- care homes (s 3(1)–(2)) where accommodation, nursing and/or personal care is provided to persons who are ill, have a mental disorder, who are disabled or infirm, or who are recovering alcoholics or drug addicts;
- children's homes (s 1) including community homes (Children Act 1989, Pt VI) (and if clause 104 of the Health and Social Care (Community Health Standards) Bill is enacted this will extend to cover children's homes providing secure accommodation), voluntary homes (Children Act 1989, Pt VII) and registered children's homes (Children Act 1989, Pt VIII);
- childminders (ss 79D(1)(a), (b) and 79F);
- day care centres (ss 79C, 79E(3) and 79F);
- domiciliary care agencies owned by an individual or organization;
- independent and local authority fostering agencies in accordance with ss 4(4) and 110;
- private and voluntary hospitals, including maternity hospitals, abortion clinics and acute hospitals;
- independent medical services which provide doctors to visit private patients;
- independent clinics or 'walk-in' medical centres run by wholly private doctors (this provision is likely to be amended by the Health and Social Care (Community Health Standards) Bill; clause 103 currently amends s 2(4) of the 2000 Act);

- mental health hospitals and hospices;
- various medical establishments providing Class 3B or 4 laser treatment, dialysis, endoscopy, IVF, oxygen treatment and intense light sources;
- nurses agencies (including those licensed by local authorities) and residential family centres will come under the Commission's umbrella, as will voluntary adoption agencies in April 2003;
- local authority adoption services;
- colleges of further education if they provide personal or nursery care to more than ten per cent of students who are resident and boarding schools providing (or arranging) accommodation for any child over 295 days per year.

3.1.1 The old system

The Care Standards Act 2000 heralds a wholesale change of the procedure and practice in respect of registration and cancellation. For example, under the Registered Homes Act 1984 and its accompanying regulations, providers were registered by local authorities or health authorities depending upon whether they provided Pt I or Pt II services. Many services such as small care homes were either not registered at all (including children's homes before 1 January 2001) or went substantially unsupervised under the Registered Homes Amendment Act 1991. Those who 'policed' the registered services in their area were required to carry out no more than two inspections per year, one announced and one unannounced. The application forms and the criteria applied in respect of registration varied quite markedly from one local or health authority to another. The enforcement of standards varied from area to area; part of that variation but by no means all of it arising out of budgetary constraints. The length and quality of inspections also varied. Some inspection units had detailed questionnaires requiring completion by a home owner prior to an announced inspection with those being followed up by the inspectors during their visit. Other inspection units had very short inspection forms. Inevitably the lack of uniformity led to a subjective approach being adopted by inspectors during inspections. This frequently led providers to express grievances, especially where it transpired that other homes were inspected differently in the same registration area.

3.1.2 The new system

The Care Standards Act 2000 and the new regulations and standards now apply to all services listed under 3.1 above, subject to implementation dates, making it a legal requirement to submit and be approved and registered to carry on a service. Subject to later ratification (for example, the regulations in respect of domiciliary care agencies), from 1 April 2002 no new service can operate without registration. If it does so a criminal offence is committed (see s 11(1)). The Commission has stated that it intends to carry out regular inspections. As before, there will certainly be two inspections per year. Whilst the various standards introduced are detailed, the

Secretary of State for Health, the Commission, the Secretary of State for Wales, the Assembly and all those who have been involved in consultation are to be commended for producing a single set of standards which are readily available to specific providers and can be easily downloaded from the Commission, Assembly or Department of Health websites. However, it remains a matter of concern that the standards are so detailed and long and inevitably will in part be subject to varying degrees of interpretation. Difficulties are already emerging over whether all the standards will be mandatory. On 24 July 2002 Alan Milburn announced that the 'environmental' standards for care homes would not be mandatory. On an earlier occasion Jackie Smith, Minister of State at the Department of Health, also suggested on Radio 4's 'Woman's Hour' that other standards would not be mandatory. If this is right, then inspectors will have a difficult time ahead, trying to keep abreast of these changes. If all the standards were mandatory then all those involved in this area would know where they stood.

However, what is important is that inspectors are clear and consistent in their interpretation of and approach to the regulations and applicable standards; there will in future be very little scope for providers and others to feign ignorance of what are minimum standards and requirements. Over time, it is hoped that the benchmark for standards will rise above the minimum level.

Whilst it is early days, the Commission and the Care Standards Inspectorate for Wales (CSIW) have made much of the fact that they are purportedly independent regulatory bodies. It is the view of the authors that if they are able to maintain this position and follow their respective stated aims to be fair in their approach to providers and others, and free from local and national political influence, that is to be welcomed.

All inspectors who have taken up positions with the Commission and CSIW and other bodies such as Ofsted and ESTYN have received training on the application of the new standards, including applying them in a uniform way to a particular service. Despite training, criticism continues from within the various services enforcing the Act, regulations and standards. Perhaps that is to be expected in an area now so detailed and complex, though over time it is to be hoped that any difficulties that may arise can be dealt with by auditing decisions and giving national guidance as to how they should be approached in the future.

From April 2004 it is envisaged that a number of significant changes will be brought about as a result of the Health and Social Care (Community Health Standards) Bill coming on to the statute book. In addition to establishing the framework for foundation hospitals, the Bill would establish the Commission for Social Care Inspection and the Commission for Healthcare Audit and Inspection. These Commissions will be non-departmental bodies which will take over a number of functions currently carried out by the Commission, for example the Commission for Social Care Inspection will register and inspect private, voluntary and public social care organizations. The Bill was tabled in the House of Commons on 12 March 2003.

3.2 REGISTRATION

Registration is the written application process leading (or not, as the case may be) to the formal approval of organizations and/or persons to 'carry on' the provision of social or health care services at an establishment or agency.

There is now a mandatory requirement to register under Pt II of the 2000 Act. Sections 11–19 and the information set out in the statutory procedure governing applications for registration and the requirements and procedure in respect of registration are extremely detailed. However, there are some points to note.

Section 11(2) requires an agency that has more than one premises and which carries out activities from more than one premises to submit a separate application for each. A person who wishes to manage more than one establishment or agency must make separate applications as required by s 12(4). However, at the time of going to print it is understood that this is the subject of detailed discussion at departmental level and regulations may be introduced minimizing the effect of this requirement.

Running an unregistered establishment or agency is an offence pursuant to s 11(1) and (5), addressed later in this chapter.

A person applying for registration under Pt II must provide the information requested and pay a fee. See s 12(1) and the National Care Standards Commission (Fees and Frequency of Inspections) Regulations 2001, SI 2001/3980.

An application for registration will be granted if the Commission or its counterpart determines that the applicant is fit, having satisfied them on such matters as:

- fitness to carry on or manage a service (see the decisions set out in *Encyclopedia of Social Services and Child Care Law*, Vol 3 and the decisions referred to below);
- fitness of premises (s 22(2)(c));
- whether there is available provision to secure the welfare of persons accommodated, including children placed by a fostering agency (s 22(2)(e));
- the number of persons employed;
- training or appointment of a manager;
- that the applicant has demonstrated a familiarity with the legislation and minimum standards;
- production and verification of identity;
- qualifications;
- financial standing;
- employment record;
- evidence of good character; and
- a Criminal Records Bureau disclosure check.

At the time of writing this chapter, the Secretary of State relaxed some of the requirements and deadlines for disclosure checks. Further information can be found in Pt V of the Police Act 1997, the Commission's *Guide to Criminal Records Bureau Checks* (revised on 31 March 2003), and the Criminal Records Bureau's own guidance obtainable from www.disclosure.gov.uk or www.crb.gov.uk. The Department of Health has produced a practical guide for individuals and organizations working with children and how they are affected by the Protection of Children Act 1999 and the Criminal Justice and Court Services Act 2000 which is available at www.doh.gov.uk.

The extent to which the Commission, the Assembly and others will take into account antecedents following a disclosure check (there are three levels of check: basic, standard and enhanced) with the Criminal Records Bureau is a moot point. Will a conviction for, say, possession of cannabis, now a Class C drug in certain parts of England, lead to questions concerning fitness of the applicant? What about a conviction for theft committed seven years previously where the applicant protests his innocence? The above list is not meant to be exhaustive but s 22 provides a helpful checklist that should be read in conjunction with the standards. Each case will depend on its own circumstances, but the authors suggest that a conviction for, say, possession of cannabis will not be significant. (Where, however, the applicant has a number of convictions for possession of cannabis, then that may raise the issue of whether cannabis is likely to be consumed at the establishment or agency and if so whether the vulnerable may be at risk from that.) Interestingly, the Commission does not deal with this issue in its *Guide to Criminal Records Bureau Checks*, although it does offer useful guidance to those who discover they have employed someone with a conviction or who have to assess whether to employ someone with a criminal record.

3.2.1 The registration procedure

Standard application packs have been produced by the Commission and the Assembly. A registration route-finder plan has been helpfully inserted on the inside cover of the application for registration pack. Those applying for registration should study the relevant route-finder plan with care. Thus, agency services are divided into four categories: domiciliary care agencies (for which use application forms 1 and 3), independent fostering agencies (use application forms 2 and 3), nurses agencies and voluntary adoption agencies (application form 3).

Applicants are also required to apply for a Criminal Records Bureau disclosure check by registering with the Bureau at PO Box 110, Liverpool, L3 622. A standard or enhanced level disclosure check should be requested if the applicant proposes to have 'regular contact with children or vulnerable adults' or is employed in a position 'caring for, training, supervising or being in sole charge of children or vulnerable adults'. Those who propose to work with children must also obtain a check from the Department for Education and Skills and the Department of Health confirming that they are not on the list of persons who are not permitted to work in that area. At the current time, it is known that there are significant delays in processing the checks.

The Secretary of State has expressed his concern about the significant backlog and resulting delay and some of the applications are now being sent abroad to be processed. As a result, and very regrettably, for a limited period there has been a relaxation of these rules. See the Commission's website for the latest information.

The Commission and the Assembly say that they will apply the 'fitness' criteria in determining whether a person, organization or service is suitable to be registered. The applicant's application will be used to check his fitness, the fitness of the premises, and fitness of services and facilities. It appears that the test that the Commission and the Assembly will use when assessing fitness will be by reference to the standards and to the previous registered homes decisions, including such cases as decision number 76, where the Registered Homes Tribunal said when defining the meaning of fit person that:

There is no statutory definition of a 'fit' or 'unfit' person. It is probably much easier to recognise the quality of fitness than to attempt to define it. However, the words 'trust', 'integrity', 'uprightness', 'honourable', and 'truthful' spring to mind. A fit person is one who can be trusted, in whom one has confidence, who acts according to high principles. It follows that a person will be unfit if he or she is untrustworthy or dishonest. The 1984 Act requires that a proprietor of a care home be such a fit person, since the elderly people in their care are often frail and vulnerable, and the person in control of them is in a powerful position to exploit that frailty. It is imperative that residents' well-being can be assured and that they must be protected from harm. It is a high standard that the law requires ...

In decision number 209 the Registered Homes Tribunal stated that:

Dictionaries turn up various synonyms for integrity and honesty: soundness, uprightness, accuracy, truth, sincerity, virtue, honour, being of good principle, probity, faith, straightforward, open, true, frank, trusty, reliable, genuine and so on. Trust goes to the very heart of the relationship which should exist between a proprietor and a manager, between the manager and the most vulnerable residents, between the manager and those vulnerable peoples' relatives, who trust the manager to look after and care for them. This is self-evident, since the welfare of those defenceless and susceptible residents are so much at the mercy of those who care for them. Any failure to exercise truth and honesty could have dire consequences for residents ... Local authorities are under a statutory duty to protect those who cannot protect themselves. They must be able to trust people who have been registered. They are able to make few visits to Homes generally, and must be able totally to rely on the veracity of records, accounts, statements, to which they are referred, for example, staffing rotas, accounts of accidents, medication—in short, on what the manager or her staff under her authority and control says or writes ...

It is clear from the decisions that fitness is not limited to the character of the applicant but also extends to management and care skills, qualifications and other factors which demonstrate good care practice. In decision number 110 the Registered Homes Tribunal stated that '... fitness ... in the sense used in the [1984] Act must imply more than competence at a job ...'. In decision number 289 the Tribunal stated that fitness must include considerations of the capacity of the registered person to carry out the requirements of the Act and regulations and comply with all conditions imposed on the certificate. Thus, the Commission or the Assembly in Wales may say that where an applicant has convictions for theft, especially where the factual circumstances of the offences(s) involve a breach of trust, then the applicant is likely to be deemed unfit. Those considering whether such a person ought to be registered will have to weigh carefully whether vulnerable residents may be put at risk in the light of the applicant's disclosed antecedents. Decision number 189 would appear to support that contention. In *R v Humberside CC, ex p Bogdal* [1992] 11 BMLR 46, Brooke J held that whilst a registered person could be fit to be involved in the carrying on of a home in a small way, he may be unfit to be involved in carrying on a home in others and that the registration authority had to 'be satisfied about the person who was carrying on the home in the sense that he or she would have control or direction of the home'. This would cover a person who was not involved in the day-to-day care being given at the home and the running of it. In decision number 114 the Registered Homes Tribunal held that the separation of a husband and his wife was an 'artificial and a temporary expedient' or device to distance himself from the running of the home. In that decision the appellant had been convicted of two counts of obtaining money by deception from the Department of Social Security. The Tribunal concluded that it and the registration authority had an 'over-riding responsibility to ensure that only persons of integrity are entrusted with the care of the elderly and vulnerable ... to ensure ... that there is no danger of residents being financially prejudiced ... [and] also to ensure that those running a home can be trusted in all matters ...'.

Section 13 of the 2000 Act deals with the grant or refusal of registration. Registration will be granted if the Commission and the Assembly are satisfied that the applicant has demonstrated that he will comply with the standards and requirements of regulations issued under s 22. The wording of the sections suggests that the burden remains upon the registration authority. The applicant will have to demonstrate compliance with the standards.

3.2.2 Conditions

The application for registration can be granted unconditionally or subject to any reasonable conditions the registration authority thinks fit (s 13(3)). The Commission and the Assembly have wide powers to vary, impose new, or remove conditions under s 13(5). Inevitably, the attachment of conditions is a subjective exercise, though it is envisaged that the registration authority will follow uniform and established criteria in its approach to the exercise of this statutory power. Where the Commission has concerns about an applicant or the proposed staffing level of an existing registered provider it may, for example, impose conditions over the number of staff required to work in a home. Any person affected by any condition may apply to the registration authority for the variation or removal of the same under s 15(1).

A person can also apply for cancellation of their registration under s 15(1)(b), but not where a notice of proposal to cancel registration has been served pursuant to ss

17(4)(a) and 19(3). Some guidance has been given on surrendering registration under the Registered Homes Act 1984 and the 2000 Act by the Court of Appeal in *Kowlessur v Suffolk Health Authority*, The Independent, 15 December 2000, and by Richards J in the High Court in *Alternative Futures v National Care Standards Commission* [2002] EWHC 3032, where the *Kowlessur* decision was reviewed.

Any person affected by a decision of the registration authority (which would include a decision in respect of a condition) has a right of appeal to the Commission and ultimately to the Care Standards Tribunal under s 21.

Any appellant will need to comply with the mandatory time limits. Section 21(2) says that no appeal against a decision or order may be brought more than 28 days after service of notice of the decision or order. The Care Standards Tribunal is at the time of going to print an extremely efficient tribunal which is hearing appeals quickly and giving rulings within ten days of the conclusion of an appeal. The process of appeal is, so long as the time limits and any directions are complied with, straightforward. Costs will only be awarded where a party has acted unreasonably (*Fun Camps Ltd v Ofsted* (2003) 124 EY). Those who wish to challenge a decision, especially a condition, will find the procedure 'user friendly', in particular the 'paper' appeal procedure which is dealt with in chapter 10. See 3.3 below for the notice of proposal procedure.

3.3 CANCELLATION

The registration authority can cancel the registration of an establishment or agency where:

- A person has been convicted of a relevant offence. For the purposes of s 14 a 'relevant offence' is one where there has been: a failure to comply with conditions (s 24); contravention of any regulation (s 25); giving a false description of an establishment or agency (s 26); providing a false statement in an application for registration (s 27); failure to display a certificate of registration (s 28); obstructing an inspector during a visit or inspection (s 31); contravening the regulations issued under s 9(2) of the Adoption Act 1976; any offence or breach of regulations made under the Children Act 1989 and any offence committed under the Registered Homes Act 1984 or its regulations.
- The person has been convicted of an offence in relation to the establishment or agency.
- On the ground that the establishment or agency has been carried on without compliance with the relevant requirements.
- On grounds specified by regulations.
- On the ground of 'unfitness' of the person or premises by reference to any of the above.

Section 17 sets out the registration procedure. The registration authority is required to give notice under s 17(2) of its intention to grant, grant subject to conditions or to refuse an application under s 17(3). A decision to refuse registration will be notified by a notice of proposal to refuse. Where a decision to cancel registration is taken, that decision is also notified by way of a notice of proposal to cancel registration pursuant to ss 15(2)(a), (b) and 17(4).

Where a notice of proposal is issued under s 17, any person affected by it is entitled to make representations to the registration authority. The Registered Homes Tribunal made it clear in decision number 182 that it expected the registration authority to present a clear, consistent and structured case supported by cogent and credible evidence. That requirement will continue under the new Act and in proceedings before the Care Standards Tribunal. Any representations must be made within 28 days of receipt of the notice. In the past, many local and health authorities permitted a person served with a notice to make oral representations to members of the Social Services or Health Service Committees. Section 18(1) says that any person affected may make written as opposed to oral representations. However, s 18(2) refers to any person making 'representations'. It is the view of the authors that those representations are limited to 'written' representations, but any procedure established by the registration authority will need to be compliant with the European Convention on Human Rights and general principles of fairness. Where a person or organization makes representations to the registration authority there is an issue as to who is to hear any submissions and representations made. This is a very important issue and a decision in respect of cancellation (or refusal of registration) will have serious repercussions. There is no authority on this issue as yet.

The registration authority is prevented from making a decision until the 28 day period has elapsed, unless any person served with a notice has indicated that he does not intend to make representations (s 18(2)(b)).

Following the conclusion of the representation stage, the registration authority is required to serve a notice of its decision in writing (s 19). Section 19(1) refers to the decision to grant an application for registration covering an establishment or agency either unconditionally or subject to conditions. Section 19(3) refers to the decision to adopt the proposal, ie the decision to refuse registration. The notice must comply with ss 19(4) and 21. If the decision is challenged, then the decision will not take effect until the appeal procedure (for which see s 21) has been exhausted. But see below for cases of urgency.

3.3.1 Urgent procedure for cancellation

Section 20 permits the registration authority to apply to the magistrates' court for an emergency closure of an establishment or agency or the imposition of an additional condition where it is demonstrated that there is 'a serious risk to a person's life, health or well-being …'. See the analogous provisions in s 79K in relation to children.

It is the view of the authors that s 20(2) entitles the magistrates to hear representations from the registered person, establishment or agency. The wording of s 20(2) states that 'an application under sub-section (1) *may*, if the Justice thinks fit, be made without notice'. The application can, in an appropriate case, and invariably has, before the 2000 Act, been made without notice. Whether this is Convention compliant (see in particular Art 1 of Protocol 1 and Art 6) remains to be determined. However, it is the view of the authors that failure to notify a registered person, establishment or agency of an emergency application is to result in a finding, if there is an appeal, that Convention rights have been infringed regardless of the correctness of the original decision. In a recent case involving a hospital consultant the Commission made an ex parte (on notice) application to the Bow Street Magistrates' Court seeking to attach a condition to the certificate of registration of a private hospital in London, preventing that consultant from practising at that hospital. Had the Commission's application been granted, the attachment of that condition would have had very serious ramifications for at least the consultant. The decision by the Commission to notify the consultant's solicitor of the proposed application, albeit on very short notice, is a decision that is welcomed and it is hoped that it will be followed in all cases, except where there is very good reason not to do so. Given the ramifications of an urgent order for cancellation being granted, s 21 envisages a fast track appeal procedure, for which see s 9, the relevant rules and the provisions of the Protection of Children Act 1999.

The Tribunal is in a position to hear appeals from an emergency cancellation case quickly and HHJ Pearl, President of the Care Standards Tribunal, is known to be committed to ensuring that those who feel aggrieved about an emergency closure order can have their appeal heard very soon after the magistrates' decision, with judgment handed down in less than ten days. In many cases the Tribunal may be willing to give an indication of its ruling after submissions have been made.

4

CARE HOMES

4.1 INTRODUCTION

A care home is defined in ss 3 and 121(9) of the 2000 Act as being one in which an establishment provides accommodation together with nursing or personal care to any person who is ill, has or has had a mental disorder, is disabled or infirm, or is or has been dependent on alcohol or drugs. Section 121(9) states that an establishment is not a care home unless the care provided includes assistance with bodily function, where such assistance is required. The above sections must be read in conjunction with the relevant regulations made pursuant to s 22. Regulation 3 of the Care Homes Regulations 2001, SI 2001/3965, excludes the following establishments from the definition of a care home:

- an NHS hospital in which nursing care is provided (but see reg 3(3)(i)(b));
- a university;
- a further education institution, as defined by s 91(3) of the Further and Higher Education Act 1992;
- a school; and
- certain other further educational establishments such as colleges or institutions which are in the nature of a college.

While a nursing home run by an NHS Trust will not require registration under s 3, a residential care home run by an NHS Trust does require registration as does any residential care home run in accordance with Pt III of the National Assistance Act 1948.

4.2 THE REGULATIONS

The primary regulations governing care homes in England are the Care Homes Regulations 2001 and in Wales the Care Homes (Wales) Regulations 2002, SI 2002/324(W37). There are separate regulations dealing with 'Young Adults' and 'Older People'. Whilst it is outside the scope of this chapter to deal fully with all these regulations, there are several matters worth noting.

The registered person is required to provide a written statement setting out the aims and objectives of the care home (reg 4 and Sch 1), the facilities and services provided (reg 4(1)(b)), as well as a statement addressing the matters listed in Sch 1. Schedule 1 to the Regulations requires the following information be included in the home's statement of purpose:

- the name and address of the registered provider and/or any registered manager;
- the relevant qualifications and experience of the registered provider/manager;
- the relevant qualifications and experience of staff;
- the organizational structure of the care home;
- the age, range and sex of the service users;
- the range of needs the care home can meet;
- whether nursing care is provided;
- criteria for admission to the care home;
- the arrangements for service users to engage in social activities, hobbies and leisure interests;
- arrangements for consultation about the operation of the home;
- fire precautions and associated emergency procedures;
- arrangements for religious attendance;
- arrangements that will be made for contact between residents and their relatives and friends;
- procedure for dealing with complaints;
- arrangements for dealing with reviews of a resident's care plan; and
- arrangements for respecting the privacy and dignity of the resident.

In Wales the Assembly has produced its own criteria. The regulations concerning children in care homes in Wales are dealt with in Pt VI of the Act, in the Care Homes (Wales) Regulations 2002 and elsewhere in the 2000 Act. See for example s 72 and the role and powers of the soon-to-be established Children's Commissioner for Wales. Since drafting this chapter amendments have been made to, amongst other sections, s 72 of the 2000 Act by s 1 of the Children's Commissioner for Wales Act 2001.

In addition to the above, the registered person is required under Pt 1 of the English regulations to provide the resident or his relative or next friend with a contract, the most recent inspection report, a summary of the complaints procedure established under reg 22 and the address and telephone number of the Commission (see reg 5(1)(a)–(f)).

Part II of the English regulations addresses the fitness of the registered provider/manager, appointment of the manager, general requirements and notification of offences. These minimum requirements mirror many of the minimum requirements set out elsewhere in analogous draft/final regulations issued in accordance with s 23 and referred to in this book. Part III includes provisions concerning the conduct of care homes requiring, amongst other things, the registered person to promote and make proper provision for health and welfare of service users, and generally make suitable arrangements to ensure that the care home is conducted in a manner that respects privacy, dignity and has due regard to sex, religious persuasion, racial origin, cultural and linguistic backgrounds, and any disability of any residential service user. Those welcome requirements appear in nearly every final set of regulations and standards produced by the Department of Health and the Assembly. These are important requirements and providers are at risk of refusal or cancellation if they are not properly set out and adhered to.

There are important requirements covering the recording, handling, safekeeping, safe administration and disposal of medicines (Pt III, para 13(2) and Sch 3(3)(i)) and a requirement to make suitable arrangements to provide proper training to prevent residents being harmed, abused or being placed at risk of harm or abuse (para 13(6)). The rationale behind much of these welcome requirements and standards is set out in summary form in the National Service Framework for Older People Executive Summary prepared by the DOH in March 2001 (available at www.doh.gov.uk/nsf/olderpeople.htm).

Any use of physical restraint is required to be fully recorded, including the nature of the restraint used. There are specific provisions governing the use of restraint of children (see Pt VI, reg 32(2); Sch 5, paras 6 and 10; and Sch 7, para 13). The registered person is required to make the resident's care plan or service user plan available to the resident and, as under the old Regulations, keep the care or service user plan under review and notify the resident of any revision to it (regs 14–15 and Schs 3 and 4).

Whilst the requirements in respect of room size will not come into effect until at least 2007 there are important requirements in reg 16(2)(a)–(n) covering:

- The provision of private telephone facilities.
- The provision of adequate furniture, bedding and other furnishings, including curtains and floor coverings.
- Permission should be granted to a resident to use his own furniture if he so chooses.
- Requirements concerning the regular laundering of linen and clothing.
- The provision of adequate facilities for service users, although adequate facilities are not described. Such facilities must be suitable for residents who are old, infirm or physically disabled.
- Provision of suitable and sufficient kitchen and other equipment.
- The provision in adequate quantities of suitable, wholesome and nutritious

food together with a requirement that such food be varied, properly prepared and available at suitable times.

- Satisfactory standards of hygiene in the care home.
- Importantly in respect of the provision of accommodation to older people, there is a requirement that the care home be kept free from offensive odours. This can be a particularly difficult care management issue and has frequently in the past been the subject of litigation before the Registered Homes Tribunal. It can now be pointed to as a breach and, if proved, a ground for a finding of unfitness.
- Suitable arrangements to engage the residents in local, social and community activities and requirements that a programme of activities be arranged by the care home.

Part III, reg 17 of and Schs 3 and 6 to the Regulations require detailed records be kept in the care home covering each resident. The records must be available for inspection. Providers frequently forget that such records should be readily accessible and known by staff. It has frequently been alleged in cancellation cases before the Registered Homes Tribunal that staff have no access to records because those records have been locked away.

4.2.1 Records to be maintained

The records to be maintained must include:

- the full name, address and date of birth of the resident;
- the date on which the resident entered the care home;
- details of the resident's general practitioner and details of all those who supervised the resident's welfare;
- the date on which the resident left the care home together with details of where the resident was transferred to;
- a full record of all medicines kept in the home for the resident and the date on which they were administered;
- a full record of any accident affecting a resident and of any other incident in the care home which was detrimental to the resident's health or welfare noting the nature, date and time of the accident or incident, whether medical treatment was required and the name of the person who was in charge of the care home at the time.

There are other requirements in respect of records and readers are referred to the full text of Schs 3 and 6 to the Regulations. Providers are strongly reminded to have in mind ss 31–32 of the Act, and the offences committed if the requirements therein are found to have been breached.

4.2.2 Requirements—premises

In Pt IV there are detailed requirements covering the premises. These govern:

- the suitability of the premises having regard to the aims and objectives set out in the statement of the care home's purpose;
- the location of the premises and whether that is appropriate to the needs of the service users (a care home in an isolated area may be refused registration if the Commission or the Assembly determine that the position of the care home is detrimental to the needs of the proposed residents);
- the requirement to have regard to the number of residents and their needs and to ensure that the physical design and layout of the premises meets the residents' needs;
- the requirement that premises be of sound construction and kept in a good state of repair both internally and externally;
- the requirement that equipment be maintained in good working order; and
- other requirements covering communal space, suitable facilities and storage which must be considered carefully by providers to ensure compliance (see Pt IV, reg 23(1)–(2)(a)–(e)).

4.2.3 Complaints

Providers should not underestimate the significance of the new requirements governing the complaints procedure. That requirement appears in several parts of the Regulations. See for example reg 17(2); reg 22; reg 26(4)(b); reg 37(g); Sch 1, para 14; Sch 4, para 11; Sch 5, para 16; and Sch 7, para 6. The complaints procedure is required to be appropriate to meet the needs of all residents. The provider or registered manager is required to ensure that any complaint made is fully investigated. By no later than 28 days after the date on which the complaint is made the provider/manager must inform the person who made the complaint of any action (if any) to be taken. A written copy of the complaint procedure must be provided to each resident or to any person acting on behalf of the resident if that person so requests. If the resident is blind or visually impaired a Braille copy of the complaints procedure is to be provided. In addition to these requirements, the complaints procedure must note the telephone number and address of the Commission or the Assembly. The registered person is required to supply to the Commission/Assembly, at its request, a statement containing a summary of the complaints made during the preceding 12 months and details of action taken in response. (regs 17, 23, 38(e) and Sch 1, para 14; Sch 3, para (i); Sch 4, para 11; Sch 5, para 15).

Under regs 24 and 26 the registered person is required to review at appropriate intervals whether the care provided at the home meets requirements. An appropriate interval is not defined in the Welsh Regulations or in Standard 4 of the Care Homes for Older People National Minimum Standards; however, a service user's plan must be reviewed in the home at least once a month under Standard 7. The registered provider will be able to argue that he is entitled to carry on the care home in a way that makes his care home financially viable (reg 25(1)). The registered person shall, if requested to do so by the Commission, provide detailed financial information concerning the following:

- the viability of the care home, including certified annual accounts;
- a reference from the bank expressing an opinion as to the registered person's financial status;
- information concerning the finances and financial resources of the care home;
- details of any connected or associated companies of the registered provider, certificates of insurance, and other records.

Where the registered provider is an individual but not in day-to-day charge of the care home he is required to visit the home in accordance with reg 26, such visits taking place at least once a month and being unannounced. The person carrying out the visit is required to interview (subject to the issue of consent and in private) residents, their representatives and other persons working at the care home, form an opinion of the standard of care being provided and prepare a written report. In addition the registered provider is required to inspect the premises, any record of events and any record of complaints, and prepare a full written report on the conduct of the care home. The registered provider must provide a copy of the report to the Commission, the registered manager and, where the registered provider is a partnership, to each of the partners.

4.2.4 Children

There is an additional layer of protection for children contained in Pt VI of the Care Home Regulations 2001, which should be read in conjunction with the Children's Homes Regulations 2001, SI 2001/3967, and the Care Homes for Younger Adults and Adult Placements National Minimum Standards published in December 2001. Those standards are extensive, running to some 100 pages and further appendices. The core requirements apply to all care homes providing accommodation, or nursing or personal care for adults aged between 18 and 65. There are supplementary standards covering young people aged between 16 and 17 who have or have had physical, sensory or learning disabilities, who suffer from autistic spectrum disorders, who have or have had a mental health or alcohol or substance abuse problem, or who have been diagnosed as suffering from HIV/AIDS illness or any complex multiple disability including deafness or blindness. Some of the standards are summarized at 4.3.2 below.

Part VII of the Care Homes Regulations 2001 contains miscellaneous provisions requiring the registered person to notify the Commission (without delay) of, amongst other things:

- the death of a resident;
- the provision of details concerning the circumstances of death;
- the outbreak of any infectious disease which is in the opinion of a GP sufficiently serious to be notified;
- any serious injury to a resident;
- details of any serious illness of a resident at a care home at which nursing is not provided;
- any event in the care home which adversely affects the well-being or safety of a service user, mirroring the old reg 14 of the 1984 Regulations;
- any instance of theft or burglary or accident in the care home; and
- any allegation of misconduct by a registered person (see reg 37(1)(a)–(g) generally).

The above provisions not only mirror, but supplement in important ways the duties previously placed on providers under the 1984 Regulations.

There are further important notification provisions set out under Pt VII. Where the registered provider, if he is an individual, or the registered manager proposes to be absent from the care home for a continuous period of 28 days or more, he is required to give notice of that absence to the Commission. Except in the case of emergency, the details of the proposed absence should be given to the Commission no later than one month before the proposed absence commences. The notice of absence must contain the following information:

- the length or expected length of the absence;
- the reason for the absence;
- what arrangements have been made for the running of the care home during the absence;
- the name, address and qualifications of the person who will be responsible for the care home during that absence; and
- in the case of the absence of the registered manager, the proposed arrangements for appointing another person, including the proposed date by which the appointment is to be made.

These are important requirements and should not be overlooked by providers and others involved in the care of the vulnerable.

Where the absence arises as a result of an emergency, the registered person is required to give notice of the absence within one week of its occurrence, specifying the matters set out above. Where the registered provider is an individual there are further requirements.

A registered person is required to give notice in writing to the Commission as soon as is practicable where any of the following events take place or is proposed to take place:

- a person other than the registered person carries on or manages the care home;
- a person ceases to carry on or manage the care home;

- where the registered person is an individual, he changes his name;
- where the registered provider is a partnership and there is a change in the membership of the partnership;
- where the registered provider is an organization and there is a change of name or address of the organization or change of director, manager, secretary or other similar officer of the organization;
- where there is a change of responsible individual;
- where the registered provider is an individual and a trustee in bankruptcy is appointed;
- where the registered provider is a company or partnership and a receiver, manager, liquidator or provisional liquidator is appointed; or
- where the premises of the care home are significantly altered or extended or additional premises are required.

There are additional miscellaneous requirements governing the termination arrangements of the residents' accommodation and the reasons given for that unless it is impracticable to do so. The requirements include a requirement to forthwith notify the Commission.

A contravention or failure to comply with any of the provisions of regs 4, 5, 11, 12(1)–(4), 13(1)–(4) and (6)–(8), 14, 15, 16(1), (2)(a)-(j) and (l)-(n) and (3), 17–26 and 37–40, is an offence. Proceedings cannot be brought by the Commission unless certain requirements are complied with. Where a notice is served on a registered person, that notice must specify the alleged contravention, the regulation breached and/or the alleged failure to comply with standards and what action is required to be taken to comply with the regulations and remedy the breach. The Commission is required to give the registered person up to three months to comply. Failure will result in enforcement action.

4.3 STANDARDS

4.3.1 Care Homes for Older People National Minimum Standards

The Government has published following the consultation minimum standards covering: choice of home (Standards 1–6); health and personal care (Standards 7–11); daily life and social activities (Standards 12–15); complaints and protection (Standards 16–18); environment (Standards 19–26); staffing (Standards 27–30) and management and administration (Standards 31–38).

It is beyond the scope of this book to look at those standards in any detail. Whilst the standards are to be welcomed, the length and complexity of them has been the subject of considerable debate with concern being expressed by providers and other organizations who represent their interests about their ability to comply. It is understood that there will be some flexibility about the enforcement of standards and the Secretary of State Alan Milburn announced on 24 July 2002 that the environmental standards (19–26) would not be mandatory. It appears that the Secretary of State has recognized the difficulties that providers face and is trying to ameliorate the very significant numbers of small to medium sized care homes that have either closed or are currently considering their positions.

Throughout the standards the Government refers to a number of minimum standards which 'cross-cut seams' and in terms of enforcement the Government has said that so far as the following minimum standards are concerned enforcement will centre on:

Focus on service users ... the key areas that most affect the quality of life experienced by service users, as well as physical standards ... Regulators will look for evidence that the facilities, resources, policies, activities and services of the home lead to positive outcomes for, and the active participation of, service users. Fitness for purpose ... the regulatory powers ... are designed to ensure that care home managers, staff and premises are 'fit for their purpose' ... Regulators will look for evidence that a home—whether providing a long-term placement, short-term rehabilitation, nursing care or other specialist service—is successful in achieving its stated aims and objectives.

Comprehensiveness. Life in a care home is made up of a range of services and facilities ... Regulators will consider how the total service package offered by the care home contributes to the overall personal and health care needs and preferences of service users, and how the home works with other services/professionals to ensure the individual's inclusion in the community.

Meeting assessed needs. In applying the standards, inspectors will look for evidence that care homes meet assessed needs of service users and that individuals' changing needs continue to be met. The assessment and service user plan ... should be based on the care management individual care plan and determination of registered nursing input ...

Quality services. The Government's modernizing agenda, including the new regulatory framework, aims to ensure greater assurance of quality services other than having to live with second best ... Regulators will seek evidence of a commitment to continuous improvement, quality services, support, accommodation and facilities which assure a good quality of life and health for service users.

Quality workforce. Competent, well-trained managers and staff are fundamental to achieving good quality care for service users ... Regulators will look for evidence that registered managers and staff achieve TOPSS requirements and comply with any Code of Practice published by the General Social Care Council ...

4.3.1.1 *Standards 1–6*

Standards 1–6 require the care home to produce a statement of purpose setting out its aims and objectives and, amongst other things, the range of facilities and services it offers to residents. The aim is to offer prospective residents a fully informed choice about whether the home is appropriate for their needs. For the first time, copies of the most recent inspection reports should be made available. It follows that critical inspection reports will result in residents or their representatives looking at alternative care homes.

Some concrete examples are given as to how a care home should meet its stated aims and objectives. Thus if a provider claims that it can meet the needs of a person with dementia, the provider will have to make it clear in the prospectus how that is achieved. If a care home says that it can cater for the needs of Muslim residents whose first language is not English then it ought to be able to offer and provide halal food, have links with a local mosque and be able to provide appropriate staff who can communicate with the resident.

There is provision under Standard 5 for a move to a care home on a trial basis. Standard 6 is directed at the provision of intermediate care.

4.3.1.2 *Standards 7–11*
The Government recognizes that it is not possible to issue minimum guidance covering every aspect of personal care. However, there is much emphasis on the assessment process and in particular the care plan for the individual resident is a crucial document which 'sets the standard'. There is a specific requirement that care must be delivered in accordance with the resident's service user plan. A resident is not permitted to go into a care home without a full assessment, except in an emergency (Standard 7). Care home owners are referred to detailed guidelines and publications at the introduction to Standards 7–11 and in the Bibliography.

4.3.1.3 *Standards 12–15*
These standards are directed at recognizing the differing social activities and lives that residents will wish to lead. Care home providers will have to ensure that those who want an active and organized social life are provided with it whilst those who want privacy from other residents are provided with that. Many homes tend to offer elderly residents dinner at about 5 or 5.15 pm. Standard 15 suggests that the provision of meals ought to be at flexible times, offering three full meals each day at not more than five hour intervals.

4.3.1.4 *Standards 16–18*
Standards 16–18 supplement the complaints provisions referred to earlier in this chapter, with a view to providing 'a robust and effective complaints procedure'. Care homes are encouraged to develop an 'open culture' so that those residents who are less able to complain feel that they are supported in making constructive suggestions regarding improvement. Inspectors are specifically required to look for evidence of an open culture. See also the requirements of Standard 33.   .

4.3.1.5 *Standards 19–26*
The environmental standards will not be mandatory. They are standards governing premises, shared facilities, lavatories and washing facilities, adaptations and equipment and other apparatus. Standard 21.3 suggests that there should be a ratio of one assisted bath to eight service users. Providers are encouraged to offer en suite facilities. It is surprising to the authors that the Secretary of State appears to take the view that Standard 26 should not be mandatory. Standard 26 requires that premises be kept clean, hygienic and free from offensive odours and that systems are in place to

control the spread of infection in accordance with health and safety statutory provisions (Food Safety (General Food Hygiene) Regulations 1995, SI 1995/1763) and other professional guidance.

4.3.1.6 *Standards 27–30*

The Government recognizes that it encountered great difficulty in drawing up the standards in respect of staffing. Registration and training will fall to others (see the General Social Care Council website at www.gscc.org.uk/about.htm), but a number of minimum standard targets are set for the years ahead. Standard 28, for example, requires a minimum ratio of 50 per cent of trained staff to be of NVQ Level 2 or equivalent by 2005. That 50 per cent will exclude the registered manager or care manager and, in homes providing nursing care, care staff who are registered nurses.

4.3.1.7 *Standards 31–38*

These standards set the benchmark of the qualities and qualifications expected of the person in day-to-day control at the care home. There are some onerous requirements. For example, Standard 38 requires the registered manager, so far as reasonably practicable, to be familiar with and ensure compliance with a whole plethora of legislation including the Health and Safety at Work Act 1974; the Management of Health and Safety at Work Regulations 1999, SI 1999/3242; the Workplace (Health, Safety and Welfare) Regulations 1992, SI 1992/3004; the Provision and Use of Work Equipment Regulations 1992, SI 1992/2932 and five other sets of complicated regulations. Many of those who are legally qualified will not be familiar with a number or all of these complex regulations and it is therefore difficult to see how small care homes can, with all the other burdens placed upon them, be expected to become familiar with these provisions. Training is, of course, the solution, but this can only be achieved at a cost and, given the breadth of the provisions, it is likely that this will be a substantial cost that providers simply cannot afford.

4.3.2 Care Homes for Younger Adults and Adult Placements National Minimum Standards

These standards include the additional standards for children aged between 16 and 17 who are service users in a care home. These standards specifically refer to the National Minimum Standards for Care Homes for Older People referred to above. The Government recognizes in its introduction to the standards that they are 'broad in scope' and that some of the standards concerning physical environment will be phased in. The standards do not apply to independent hospitals, hospices, clinics or establishments registered to take patients detained under the Mental Health Act 1983. Importantly, the standards do not seek to distinguish between small homes providing accommodation for fewer than four residents, and larger homes. The standards make clear that care homes should not accommodate children under the age of 16.

The standards seek to lay down minimum criteria governing:

- the choice of a home;
- individual needs and choices;
- lifestyle;
- personal and health care support;
- concerns, complaints and protection;
- environment;
- staffing and conduct; and
- management of the home.

Many of the standards are similar to the Care Homes for Older People National Minimum Standards, but these standards are considerably more detailed. Each of the headings is, as with the other standards, prefaced by an explanation. Again, the standards provide the benchmark for judging the quality of service provided to the residents. Inspectors are specifically directed to look for evidence that requirements are being met and that a good quality of life is enjoyed by residents. That evidence is to be found by inspectors through discussions with residents, their families and friends, staff and managers and others; observation of daily life in the care home; and very careful scrutiny of the written policies, procedures, and records. The involvement of the lay assessor in this process is seen as pivotal.

Because many of the standards mirror those referred to at 4.3.1 above we will touch upon only some of the National Minimum Standards for Younger Adults, those being supplementary standards for care homes accommodating young people aged between 16 and 17.

At the time of preparing this chapter no introductory guidance or rationale has yet been provided. The rationale seen in other standards is extremely helpful and it is to be hoped that the Department of Health will in due course prepare such information and not merely rely on the information provided in the main Care Homes for Younger Adults and Adult Placements National Minimum Standards. For example, Standard 41 requires that '[r]ecords, required by regulation for the protection of service users and for the effective and efficient running of the business are maintained, up-to-date and accurate', yet that requirement adds nothing to the very detailed requirement in respect of record-keeping already in place. If that is right, what is the purpose of Standard 41?

Some important standards to note include Standard 12 which directs staff to assist young residents to find and keep appropriate jobs or to continue their education and training and to take part in 'valued and fulfilling' activities. Standard 14 encourages staff to ensure that there is an appropriate range of leisure activities; Standard 23 is directed at concerns, complaints and protection, although, other than a general statement, there is nothing on dealing with bullying; and Standard 25 (which is described as an environmental standard and is therefore unlikely to be enforced for some time) requires each young resident to be provided with their own bedroom and sufficient usable floor space to meet their needs and lifestyle.

These very detailed regulations and standards are to be welcomed. They have been drafted after consultation and in conjunction with experts from many fields, with a view to protecting those who cannot protect themselves. However, the authors remain concerned that the sheer volume and complexity of the provisions and standards mean that it would be unrealistic to expect providers to be familiar with all their content. The authors fear that lack of familiarity may be used by some inspectors as an excuse to bring cancellation proceedings against providers who are not liked. If such a subjective approach is taken, which would be unfair and against the spirit of the new regime, the authors suggest that every care home in the country could be found to be in breach of some standard or other. It is to be hoped that the vast majority of inspectors will approach the difficult and onerous task of inspection in a balanced and even-handed way.

5

CHILD SERVICES

5.1 INTRODUCTION

Part VI of the Care Standards Act 2000 inserts Pt XA into the Children Act 1989. In England the onus of regulating and advising on childminding and day care passes to Her Majesty's Chief Inspector of Schools for England (HMCIS), under the superintendence of Ofsted and its Early Years Directorate. In Wales powers are exercised by the Assembly through Her Majesty's Chief Inspector of Education and Training in Wales (ESTYN). An amending s 79 is inserted into the Children Act in respect of England and Wales, but not Scotland.

The review of children's services addresses the following three broad aims, within the general theme of raising standards through regulation to achieve consistency, quality and best value:

- protection of children from sexual, physical and emotional abuse;
- raising the quality of care for children who are looked after, to a level as close as can be achieved to that provided by loving parents; and
- to improve life chances for children who are in care or otherwise in need of social services support, in particular by improving health, education and support on leaving care.

The content of the standards is not new to the child care sector, but the imposition of a national, consistent system with a more effective enforcement system is anticipated to bring about a much needed and substantial improvement in the quality of services for vulnerable children. Two of the three categories of children's services dealt with in this chapter, children's homes and day care, have been regulated for some time, largely as a reaction to concerns over poor, dangerous, and inappropriate practices. The third category, residential assessment centres, has not previously been the subject of a special regulatory scheme. Inclusion undoubtedly reflects the expansion of the independent family assessment sector of child care procedure, and the need to ensure consistent standards of assessment, reporting and therapeutic and rehabilitative support where children may have received inadequate parenting.

The importance of children and the recognition of their vulnerability in certain regions has led to an additional layer of protection in Wales. Under Pt V of the 2000 Act a Children's Commissioner is to be established. The Commissioner has extensive powers including powers to ensure proper action is taken where offences have been committed (s 73(3)(a)) or health and safety (s 73(3)(c)) endangered. The Commission has the same powers as the High Court (s 74(4)) to require the production of information and attendance of witnesses. All of these provisions are welcomed, it being hoped that those who are the most vulnerable in our society will now receive the full and proper protection they clearly deserve.

5.1.1 Definition

Of the 58,000 children who were in care in March 2000, a very small proportion, around 6,000, were living in children's residential homes rather than foster placements or placement with parents. For the purposes of registration and standards, an establishment providing care and accommodation wholly or mainly for children is a children's home, provided that it is not a health service or independent hospital or clinic, a residential family centre (see 5.4 below), a school (save for those falling within s 1(6)), or otherwise of a description excepted by regulations. The definition of a children's home contained in Pt 1 of the Act (see s 1(3)–(7)) is somewhat confusing. A children's home is not created simply by a child or children being cared for by parents, relatives or foster parents. For example, a school is a children's home if accommodation is provided and has been provided to at least one child for 295 days in each year of the two years preceding the date of inquiry, or if it is intended to accommodate or arrange to accommodate at least one child for more than 295 days per year.

5.2 CHILDREN'S HOMES NATIONAL MINIMUM STANDARDS

Before the coming into force of the 2000 Act, several different and unrelated registration systems applied to different categories of children's home. Private homes were bound by national regulations and local standards, community homes were subject to inspection against the same standards but were not required to register, and voluntary homes were subject to registration with and inspection by the Social Services Inspectorate under the authority of the Secretary of State for Health.

5.2.1 Introduction

In addition to the introduction of a single system of children's home registration for all categories, the Department of Health has published National Minimum Standards, which have applied since 1 April 2002. The standards expand upon the Children's Homes Regulations 2001, SI 2001/3967, and form part of a regulatory matrix encompassing those regulations and the relevant provisions of the Children Act 1989, in particular Pts VI–VIII. The standards are explicitly the minimum required to achieve adequacy, and are not a statement of best practice. All regulated premises must comply with minimum standards, and compliance will be taken into account by the Commission in any decision concerning registration, cancellation, variation or imposition of conditions, together with any other factors that appear reasonable and relevant. Each of the 37 standards, summarized below, is preceded by a statement of service-user outcome: these are set out in full in bold type in this chapter, together with observations on their applicability where appropriate as they represent a clear general summary of the document's child-centred objectives. The standards fall into eight categories: planning for care (1–7), quality of care (8–15), complaints and protection (16–20), care and control (21–22), environment (23–26), staffing (27–31), management and administration (32–35), and specific settings: secure accommodation and children under eight (36–37). There has been a lengthy consultation process concerning the scope and content of the regulations which apparently closed to contributions in September 2001.

5.2.2 The standards

5.2.2.1 Statement of the home's purpose

Children and young people are guided through and know what services they can expect from the home, how they will be cared for and who they are likely to share with, and a clear statement of how the home operates is available for others needing this information.

The statement of purpose must be reviewed annually by the registered provider and contains the information required by Sch 1 to the Children's Homes Regulations 2001. It should be readily available to children living in the home and to other people working in or visiting the home for whatever reason. Schedule 1 sets out 26 categories of information to be covered by the statement, including:

- aims and objectives;
- details of the registered provider;
- numbers and characteristics of the children accommodated;
- criteria for admission and emergency admission;
- policies on behaviour management and bullying; and
- specific arrangements for the promotion of the children's welfare and development.

Providers should not underestimate the importance of the information to be provided. If they are unable to provide this information properly, for example because the aims and objectives are wrongly directed at a different age group of children, they may find their application being refused. A separate Children's Guide is directed more specifically to the child's experience of living in the home, and contains information about contacting an independent advocate and making complaints.

5.2.2.2 *Placement plans*

The placement plan for each child sets out clearly the assessed needs of the child, the objectives of placement, how these are to be met by the registered provider on a day to day basis, the contribution to be made by the staff of the home, and how the effectiveness of the placement is to be assessed in relation to each major element of the plan.

The placement plan attempts to raise the formal recording of comprehensive arrangements for looked-after children up to a standard that social services authorities have repeatedly pressed for in order to achieve proper care planning in adult mental health and learning disability, and, more generally, to assist in future planning for the child in care. It is a single reference source for the day-to-day experience of the child including sections dealing with health, education, culture, religion, language, race, leisure and contact with family, friends and significant others. The plan must be monitored by the child's key worker in the home, with the child being consulted on selection or change of key worker.

5.2.2.3 *Reviews*

Children's needs, development and progress are reviewed regularly in the light of their care and progress at the home.

The registered manager is obliged to contribute to each child's placement plan review and child in care review, and to ensure that the child participates as far as is feasible in their review process. The registered manager must implement the agreed outcome of all reviews to meet the day-to-day care needs of the child.

5.2.2.4 *Contact*

Children are able to maintain constructive contact with their families, friends and other people who play a significant role in their lives.

This standard requires the home to facilitate all proper contact arrangements that are made for the child, pursuant to the Children Act 1989 and related secondary legislation and circulars. The frequency and duration of any contact should be set out clearly in the child's placement plan.

5.2.2.5 *Moving in and leaving the home*

Children are able to move into and leave the home in a planned and sensitive manner.

This requirement is principally directed at the provision of clear information, both orally and in writing, to the child. The child's key worker and any other staff involved in the process should ensure through discussion that the child has understood the information provided as fully as he or she is able. Children are encouraged to bring reassuring personal possessions with them when they move. It is important to note that a child should not be admitted as an emergency to a home that does not have emergency admission procedure among its stated functions in its statement of purpose.

5.2.2.6 Preparation for leaving care

Children receive care which helps to prepare them for and support them into adulthood.

Failure to give adequate support and help on leaving care is identified as one of the major failings of the care system. The Children (Leaving Care) Act 2000 now requires the registered manager to ensure that a comprehensive leaving care plan is prepared that is consistent with other plans and covers the widest possible range of information, including accommodation, education, support networks, understanding sexual and social relationships, and work on self-esteem and life skills. It is also a specific minimum objective that homes provide all children with the opportunity to develop the skills necessary for independent living. These objectives will be in the young person's placement plan and, where appropriate, their 'pathway' plan.

5.2.2.7 Support to individual children

Children receive individual support when they need it.

This standard has two principal aims: promoting social inclusion within the home by the registered person and other staff; and ensuring that easily accessible support networks are available to all children. The structure relies on the child's key worker, but explicitly states that children are entitled to contact any member of staff with personal concerns. In addition, each child must have at least one person independent of the home and the placing authority, who could be, for example, a befriender or mentor, an advocate or children's rights officer, or other independent visitor. Advice for children who have been abused or who are abusers, including involvement in prostitution, requires specific provision in each home and the inclusion of the individual child in planning a programme of support. Specific therapeutic techniques, as opposed to lay advice and support, are only to be used if fully specified in the child's placement plan and approved by the placing authority or, where there is no placing authority, the parent. Such techniques should only be employed if recognized as safe and effective, and undertaken by or under the supervision of an appropriately qualified practitioner. Standard 7.9 provides that children are 'supported to take controlled risks that are relevant and necessary to negotiating their place in the community'.

5.2.2.8 *Consultation*

Children are encouraged and supported to make decisions about their lives and to influence
the way the home is run.

Consultation relies on systems for sharing information, including written agreements, private interviews, key worker sessions, children's meetings and house meetings. All significant views expressed or discussions should be appropriately
recorded. Topics for consultation include: the operation of the home, the adequacy
of staff, space, furnishings and decoration; and privacy. Providers should note that
lack of consultation, or the failure to record it properly where it has taken place,
regularly used to feature in the grounds presented by registration and inspection
units in cancellation proceedings. It is the view of the authors that the Care
Standards Tribunal will take a robust stance in respect of any provider caught flout-
ing these standards.

5.2.2.9 *Privacy and confidentiality*

Children's privacy is respected and information is confidentially handled.

Privacy includes procedures for adults and other residents to adopt when entering a
resident's bedroom, access to a telephone and arrangements to pay in a convenient
and private place, and sensitivity to sex and gender issues. The registered person is
required to provide guidance where it appears to be necessary to protect the welfare
of a child or children to prevent breach of privacy policies, such as where a search of
a child's belongings is deemed necessary.

5.2.2.10 *Provision and preparation of meals*

Children enjoy healthy, nutritious meals that meet their dietary needs. They have opportunities to plan, shop for and prepare meals.

This standard is deemed a simple way to counteract institutionalization of children in
residential accommodation by encouraging the development of life skills necessary
for independent young adulthood. Cultural, ethnic, religious food issues and dietary
needs and choices must be taken into account. Menus, and the food served, form part
of the records of the home. Children should not be routinely excluded from meals,
which form part of the social life of the home. Children should be able to prepare
snacks or be provided with snacks and drinks at reasonable times. What is reasonable will need to be determined on an individual basis, depending on the needs of the
resident or resident group. Again, breach of this standard will be a serious issue and
could lead to enforcement action.

5.2.2.11 *Personal appearance, clothing, requisites and pocket money*

Children are encouraged and enabled to choose their own clothes and personal requisites and
have these needs fully met.

This standard promotes an important area of personal and/or religious or cultural identity expression and development. All clothing and personal requisites are for each child's exclusive use. Those registered will be encouraged to guide children to learn to manage their own finances.

5.2.2.12 General health care

Children live in a healthy environment and their health needs are identified and services are provided to meet them, and their good health is promoted.

There is an obvious need for all aspects of health management and promotion to be managed by a clear plan and regular developmental checks and appropriate advice. Written policy must include immunization and screening, nutrition and diet, exercise and rest, personal hygiene, sexual health, alcohol and smoking, HIV/AIDS and other blood-borne diseases. Discussion around illness and disability is encouraged.

5.2.2.13 Treatment and administration of medicines within the home

Children's health needs are met and their welfare is safeguarded by the home's policies and procedures for administering medicines and providing treatment.

All first aid and treatment of minor illness and the administration of medication must be undertaken by competent designated staff, for example a qualified first aider or UK Central Council for Nursing, Midwifery and Health Visiting (now Nursing and Midwifery Council) registered nurse. Full written records must be kept and regularly monitored, and permission for treatment must be kept on file. Children considered capable of self-medication must be helped to keep this away from other children, and prescribed medication must not be retained for the use of any other child. The registered provider must have and follow a written protocol, based on medical advice, on the provision of household medicines to children. The authors remind providers that breach of this requirement is taken very seriously and could lead to urgent cancellation or enforcement action. It is the experience of the authors that where there has been successful enforcement action, and nursing staff have been criticized in decisions, inspection units and health authorities have subsequently made complaints to the Nursing Midwifery Council. Under the new system the General Social Care Council and its equivalent in Wales will take disciplinary action against any social care worker implicated or involved in poor care practices.

5.2.2.14 Education

The education of children is actively promoted as valuable in itself as part of their preparation for adulthood.

This standard is supported by written policy and record-keeping. In addition to full access to appropriate educational facilities, space should be made available within the home which is suitable and conducive for study. Placement plans must foresee the likely course of the child's education including examinations, and plan for appropriate liaison with schools, careers services, employment agencies, and employers. Frequently used noisy rooms are likely to fall foul of this standard.

5.2.2.15 Leisure and activities

Children are able to pursue their particular interests, develop confidence in their skills and are supported and encouraged by staff to engage in leisure activities.

The registered person is responsible for allocating sufficient financial resources to fund leisure activities and trips. Birthdays and cultural and religious festivals should be prepared for and celebrated jointly by staff and children. Leisure interests should form part of the child's placement plan. Videos, internet access, computer games and access to other leisure materials and equipment should be available. Policies should be in place to ensure appropriate use. Children should be able to maintain friendships with children outside the home.

5.2.2.16 Complaints and representation

Any complaint will be addressed without delay and the complainant is kept informed of progress.

The standard requires consistent, effective and user-friendly complaints procedures, based on accessible information. The failure to have in place a proper complaints process and failure to deal with complaints has in the past frequently featured as a ground in cancellation cases. There is now greater emphasis on the complaints process, and those registered must ensure that there is a proper procedure and that it is followed.

5.2.2.17 Child protection procedures and training

The welfare of children is promoted, children are protected from abuse, and an appropriate response is made to any allegation or suspicion of abuse.

The importance of this standard cannot be overstated. The appropriate response requires, as a minimum, investigation.

5.2.2.18 Countering bullying

Children are protected from bullying.

An anti-bullying policy should be in place to protect the vulnerable from abuse. Failure by a provider to follow his written policy and procedure is likely to be taken extremely seriously by inspectors and other health care professionals.

5.2.2.19 Absence of a child without authority

Children who are absent without authority are protected in accordance with written guidance and responded to positively on return.

Registered providers/managers are aware that those who accommodate children with challenging needs must follow procedure. If a child absconds, it is likely that the police and health care professionals will be informed, and it will probably be a reportable incident in any event, as it affects the health and well-being of the resident. If, when the inspectors come to review the documentation concerning such an incident, they uncover deficiencies in the reporting and handling of the incident, they may well decide to undertake a more detailed examination of all the documents. That may lead to other deficiencies being uncovered with all the consequences that can flow from that including, in a glaring case, the service of a cancellation notice.

5.2.2.20 Notification of significant events

All significant events relating to the protection of children accommodated in the home are notified by the registered manager of the home to the appropriate authorities.

This standard, now a requirement, restates reg 14 of the Registered Care Homes Regulations 1984, SI 1984/1345. The Tribunal is unlikely to be impressed by submissions that Parliament intended a higher test when it abandoned the words 'any event affecting the well being', and replaced them with 'any significant event'. Is being drunk and disorderly or purchasing cannabis for personal use a 'significant event'? If providers are in any doubt they should protect themselves by reporting the matter immediately, following up any telephone call made by written correspondence, stating the view expressed by the National Care Standards Commission, the Care Standards Inspectorate for Wales (CSIW) or Commissioner for Wales official.

It is the experience of the authors that providers frequently overlooked the provisions of reg 14(1)(d) of the Registered Care Homes Regulations 1984 which required them to notify the registration authority of any incident affecting the well-being of any resident within 24 hours. The fact that a provider can reasonably demonstrate that, say, an allegation of assault or sexual abuse is untrue, is not a cogent reason for failing to notify.

5.2.2.21 Relationship with children

Children enjoy sound relationships with staff based on honesty and mutual respect.

5.2.2.22 Control, discipline and restraint

Children are assisted to develop socially acceptable behaviour through encouragement of acceptable behaviour and constructive staff response to inappropriate behaviour.

5.2.2.23 Location, design and size of the home

Children live in well-designed and pleasant homes providing sufficient space to meet their needs.

Prior to these provisions many registration authorities, particularly London ones (London Inspectors Children's Group, *Quality Care for Children* (GLA, revised 2000)) adopted uniform standards about room size and the sharing of rooms by children who are not siblings, etc. The new regime is expected to be rigorously enforced in time, however where providers are unhappy about any conditions imposed, provision is made for them to appeal. Whether the home meets the requirement is likely to feature in any inspection report. Where adverse comment is made by an inspector and that is corroborated by the lay assessor, a provider should not ignore this. These observations will feature in the published report that will be widely available on the internet and elsewhere.

5.2.2.24 *Accommodation*

Children enjoy homely accommodation, decorated, furnished and maintained to a high standard, providing adequate facilities for their use.

The authors repeat the comments made above. Providers are reminded that, in any enforcement action or appeal, the Tribunal may visit their premises during a cancellation appeal. A high standard of provision is expected to be the benchmark.

5.2.2.25 *Bathrooms and washing facilities*

Children's privacy is respected when washing.

It is the experience of the authors that those who hear cancellation appeals, particularly wing members, frequently ask detailed questions about how a resident's or child's privacy is safeguarded. Providers should expect no relaxation of this important requirement.

5.2.2.26 *Health, safety and security*

Children live in homes that provide physical safety and security.

Detailed written policies and procedures will be required and must be shown to be followed by providers if they are to be successful in their application for renewal of registration.

5.2.2.27 *Vetting of staff and visitors*

There is careful selection and vetting of all staff and volunteers working with children in the home and there is monitoring of visitors to prevent children being exposed to potential abusers.

There are already in place regulations prohibiting the recruitment of staff who have not been properly police checked and vetted. The authors continue to be surprised at the frequency with which these provisions are ignored by providers. They do so at their peril. Providers are reminded of the provisions contained in Pt VII governing the protection of children and vulnerable adults, the powers of the Commissioner in Wales (Pt IV) and the accompanying regulations. The second phase of Lord Laming's inquiry into the death of Victoria Climbié reinforced the importance of this and other requirements.

5.2.2.28 *Staff support*

Children are looked after by staff who are themselves supported and guided in safeguarding and promoting the children's welfare.

5.2.2.29 *Adequacy of staffing*

Children receive the care and services they need from competent staff.

The Commission or Assembly, whether through the Care Standards Inspectorate for Wales or otherwise, may in many applications make it a condition that a certain number of staff are employed at waking or night times. It is an important requirement that staff are properly trained to meet the needs of the resident group.

5.2.2.30 *Staffing policy*

Staff are sufficient in number, experience and qualification to meet the needs of the children.

Providers are referred to 5.2.2.29 above, the regulations, and chapter 6 below.

5.2.2.31 *Staff training*

Children are looked after by staff who are trained and competent to meet their needs.

Providers are increasingly faced with staff recruitment problems. This can be regional as well as pay related. Providers will need to ensure that properly qualified staff are recruited and retained. Providers are reminded of the ongoing need for training which is likely to become a formal requirement once the General Social Care Council, which began work on 1 October 2001, becomes fully operational from about 2004. For social workers these provisions may apply from 2003. Providers frequently forget that many training courses lead to certification that expires after three years or less.

5.2.2.32 *Monitoring by the person carrying on the home*

The person carrying on the home monitors the welfare of the children in the home.

Providers are reminded that the Commission will expect to see written evidence that this requirement is being followed at any announced or unannounced inspection.

5.2.2.33 *Monitoring of the operation of the home*

The care of children accommodated in the home is monitored and continually adapted in the light of information about how it is operating.

The authors refer to the observations set out at 5.2.2.32 above. This requirement will cover a plethora of issues ranging from the basic such as food likes and dislikes, to more difficult issues such as substance abuse, under-age sexual relations and the like. Providers are likely to be found wanting if they do no more than merely record the happening of an event. The Commission and its equivalent in Wales will expect to see evidence of a constructive policy being properly implemented to deal with any issue.

5.2.2.34 *Business management*

Children enjoy the stability of efficiently run homes.

Poorly run homes will, if warnings are ignored, face enforcement action. Providers are reminded that the Commission is also there to help and providers should not be afraid of seeking advice and assistance where problems are encountered. If a provider has been transparent about the difficulties it has faced, breach of these requirements may be explained or put in context if any enforcement proceedings are brought.

5.2.2.35 *Children's individual case files*

Children's needs, development and progress are recorded to reflect their individuality.

5.2.2.36 *Secure accommodation and refuges*

Children living in secure units or refuges receive the same measures to safeguard and promote their welfare as they should in other children's homes.

Whilst there is unlikely to be any different approach to interpretation for secure units or refuges, enforcement is likely to be dependent on manpower. The task that the Commission and the CSIW face is enormous. Commission staff are already complaining that form filling takes days, distracting them from the real task at hand, that of carrying out unannounced inspections and the like to ensure proper compliance with the new regime. It is the view of the authors that form filling alone (if at all) will not detect abuse or poor care practice.

5.2.2.37 *Accommodation of children aged under eight*

Any children aged under eight living in a children's home are looked after appropriately for their age.

5.3 CHILDMINDING AND DAY CARE

5.3.1 Definition

Sections 79A and 79B of the Children Act 1989 define a childminder and day care provider. A childminder looks after one or more children under eight years of age on domestic premises for reward. The definition of reward is not limited to money. A parent, relative, other person with parental responsibility, local authority, private or voluntary agency foster parent, is not acting as a childminder in relation to that child for the purposes of the section. Neither is a person childminding if they look after a child for the parents in the parents' home, or if, in addition to that child, another child of different parents is cared for wholly or mainly in the home of either of the parents (s 79A(4)). An exception has been introduced to cover domestic nannying arrangements, and permits nanny sharing without engaging the statutory scheme. The arrival of a second child in either family would seem to engage the need to register.

Day care is child care provided either day or night for periods of over two hours to children under eight years of age, but not on domestic premises (ie, not on premises used wholly or mainly as a domestic dwelling) (s 79A(6)-(8)). Schools, care homes, children's homes, hospitals, and residential family centres can provide day care without the need to register, if it is provided as an integral part of the estab- lishment's activities. The requirement to register is triggered, however, if such an organization permits day care services to be provided by another in its premises. The requirement to register is contained in s 79D, with the requirements in respect of any application being contained in s 79E and the regulations. Knowingly making a false or misleading statement which is material in any application is an offence contrary to s 79E(5). On summary conviction a defendant is liable to a fine not exceeding level 5.

5.3.2 Day care registration

An applicant for day care registration with Her Majesty's Chief Inspector of Schools must demonstrate compliance with the 14 National Standards and good practice guidelines. In Wales an application is submitted to the Assembly in accordance with regulations issued under s 79C(2). The registered person must be the individual or body with overall responsibility for the provision. A person in charge may be appointed by the registered person to take day-to-day responsibility for the service, provided that that person has the necessary aptitude, skill and experience.

The definition of day care in Pt X of the Children Act 1989 is wide. It is immater- ial at what time of the day or night provision is provided. The four aspects of regula- tion are common to the other areas of national standards, being registration, inspection, investigation and enforcement, as are the aims, bringing child protection and the promotion of consistency and high quality into service provision. Applications fall into four subcategories: full day care (four hours or more in any day), sessional day care (less than four hours in any day, for example morning and afternoon playgroups), crèches (occasional care which is open for a continuous period of over two hours), and out of school care (before and/or after school and/or during holidays for over two hours in any day, for which see Pt XA). Babysitting is excluded here if it takes place between 6 pm and 2 am (s 79A(8)). The standards for day care are understandably less stringent than those for children's homes, and provide a much more general framework for considering the suitability of staff (s 79B(3)(a)–(b)), premises (s 79B(3)(c)), equipment, activities and compliance with any regulations issued under ss 79B(3)(d) and 79C.

The Chief Inspector (s 79N(1)) has a duty to keep the Secretary of State informed about general provision of childminding and day care and can give advice to the Secretary of State on any matter connected with it. In Wales the Assembly has wide powers covering training, inspection and other matters under ss 79S and 79T.

5.3.3 Day care standards

- Adults providing day care must be suitable.
- The registered person must comply with adult to child ratios, training, provision of space and resources to meet children's needs. These are expected to be relaxed to take into account that there is a deficit of provision.
- There must be planning opportunities for care, learning and play, in order to develop the full range of each child's capabilities.
- The premises must be safe, secure and suitable to the purpose.
- All equipment must be appropriate and provide an accessible and stimulating environment.
- The registered person must ensure safety and precautions to prevent accidents.
- Positive steps must be taken to promote good health and prevent the spread of infection.
- Regular food and drink must be provided, appropriate to need and taking account of dietary and religious requirements.
- The registered person must actively promote equality of opportunity and anti-discriminatory practice for all children.
- Special needs in children require appropriate action and proactive steps to promote welfare and development in partnership with parents and others involved with the child.
- Adults must be capable of managing appropriately with a wide range of children's behaviour.
- The registered person and staff must work in partnership with other carers, and share information.
- The registered person must comply with child protection procedures, and ensure that such procedures are put into practice.
- Records, policies and procedures must be kept as are required for the efficient and safe management of the service.

5.3.4 Other requirements

Section 79 of the 2000 Act introduces a requirement for certificates of suitability for those persons working with children over the age of seven. Regulations will cover the provision of care to children over seven for more than five hours per week, who are not caught by Pt XA of the Children Act 1989. Those providing care will have to hold a valid certificate (s 79W) which will cover all children under the age of 15, or 17 in the case of disabled children. Section 79W(6) and the regulations make it an offence not to do so.

5.3.5 Appeals

The mechanism for appeals is now provided by the Protection of Children and Vulnerable Adults and Care Standards Tribunal (Amendment) Regulations 2003 SI 2003 No. 626. The regulations are produced at Appendix 3.

5.4 RESIDENTIAL FAMILY CENTRE

A residential family centre is an establishment where monitoring and assessment of a carer or carers' capacity to respond to children's needs and to safeguard their welfare is carried out, together with such advice, guidance and counselling as may be necessary, with the provision of accommodation for the family (s 4(2)(a)–(c) of the 2000 Act). Such centres are most commonly used to carry out Children Act 1989, s 37 inquiries in care proceedings or, where the threshold criteria for the making of a care or supervision order are clearly made out on other evidence or conceded, to investigate the appropriateness of a care plan, particularly one involving rehabilitation of the child to the parent or parents.

Residential family centres now provide for a wide range of needs. In the years since the 1989 Act came into force residential family centres have developed from primarily psychiatric mother and baby facilities to include services targeted at parents with multiple disabilities and learning disabilities, families with a history of domestic violence or sexual abuse, and smaller units supporting observation of and intervention in generally inadequate parenting. The definition appears to catch mother and baby 'foster placements' in the foster carer's home; such placements are often used where very young or significantly disabled mothers with untested parenting abilities might otherwise have a child removed at birth or in early infancy until their parenting skills can be assessed. The mechanism for placement is most commonly under an interim care order, with a local authority requirement that the mother can retain day-to-day care only while she resides in the supervised setting. Regulation of small facilities of this kind might reasonably be avoided if the 'foster mother' does not participate in any way in monitoring or assessment, but merely provides advice and guidance to the mother.

There are wide powers governing rights of entry (s 79U of the Children Act 1989), inspection (s 79U(3)), seizure (s 79U(3)(c)) and rights to interview (under caution where necessary) granted to authorized inspectors. It is an offence wilfully to obstruct an inspector (s 79U(7)). The definition of authorized inspector is relevant to the exercise of the power. It is envisaged that an unauthorized inspector may become authorized when s 79U(5) is enacted, but it is suggested that this power may not be exercised retrospectively.

Protection of children and vulnerable adults under Pt VII is dealt with in chapter 7 below.

5.5 NURSERY EDUCATION/EARLY YEARS CHILD CARE INSPECTORS

The Protection of Children and Vulnerable Adults and Care Standards Tribunal (Amendment No. 2) Regulations 2003 SI 2003 No. 1060 provides the mechanism for appeals against the decision of the Chief Inspector of Schools in England either not to renew the registration of nursery education inspectors or early years child care inspectors, to impose or vary any conditions upon registration or to remove from the Register. The regulations are at Appendix 4. See also the Child Minding and Day Care (Suspension of Registration) (England) Regulation 2003 SI 2003/332 and in particular Regulation 8(1).

6

SOCIAL CARE WORKERS

6.1 OVERVIEW

Part IV of the 2000 Act introduces for the first time principles governing the regulation and training of care staff, now called social care workers. Section 54 establishes from 1 October 2000 the General Social Care Council and the Care Council for Wales ('the Councils'); both organizations are executive non-departmental public bodies.

The duties of both Councils are stated in s 54(2) and (3) to be:

- to promote high standards of conduct, practice and training, weeding out unfit and unsuitable social care workers;
- to regulate and oversee training and measure its success by reference to fitness and practice;
- to set requirements for training and qualifications and to encourage ongoing professional development; and
- to register and maintain a register of qualified social care workers, registered in separate categories under s 56(1)(b).

Social care workers will be expected to have and maintain high standards of conduct and practice when providing care. Qualified social workers are expected to be the first group of social care workers on the register in the latter part of 2003. The Councils' mission statement is to 'improve public protection, raising professional standards with a view to creating a well trained, effective and accountable social care workforce' in both the public and private sectors. On 14 April 2003 the General Social Care Council issued a consultation document setting out its outline proposals for post-qualification training and future training, inviting discussion and comment. In May it announced the setting of bursaries and the payment of tuition fees. These proposals have been generally welcomed and it is hoped they will lead to a proper career structure for this traditionally hardworking but undervalued workforce.

The Councils will maintain a register of social care workers under s 56. The Councils will have the power to remove any social care worker who is unfit to practise on grounds of misconduct, abuse, poor care practice, that they suffer from ill-health or have been negligent. The English Council has indicated that it expects to exercise that power sparingly. At present, no scheme exists to offer legal advice and support to social care workers who face sanction, in stark contrast to the legal advice available to the Councils. Reference is made to representation by lawyer or trade union representative but how that will work in practice remains a moot point. Many social care workers will not be members of a union and certainly will not be able to afford representation.

In England the Council envisages registering approximately 1.2 million social care workers. The system will be policed by the Councils, the National Care Standards Commission and the Social Services Inspectorate, the latter two bodies being responsible for enforcing the Code of Practice against employers. Section 62 places a duty on the Councils to develop codes of practice. At the time of writing this chapter it is understood that from 2004 the Commission for Social Care Inspection may have a policing role with the Councils if the Health and Social Care (Community Health and Standards) Bill is enacted in its current form.

Social care workers will be required to apply for registration under s 57. Any person who has such a position, whether in the public or private sector, and who is not registered commits a criminal offence under s 61(1)(b) and is liable to a fine in the magistrates' court at level 5.

A social care worker is defined in s 55(2). The definition contained in this section is explored in more detail below but, in essence, extends to any person who provides services at any of the establishments or agencies covered by the 2000 Act. In addition to that broad description, the definition encompasses any person who provides social work in connection with health, education or social services. The problems that the authors identify in respect of this will be dealt with below.

6.1.1 Definition of social care worker

There are four categories of persons who are currently included within the term 'social care worker' under the provisions of s 55(2). This generic category of worker will cover nearly all those employed providing care. In addition, it is likely that regulations will provide for another seven categories of persons to be caught by this definition, including: those inspecting children's homes; independent schools and colleges; those providing personal care; and persons employed in day centres. In due course trainee social workers may also be covered by regulation. At the date of writing formal regulations have not been produced but readers are referred to the General Social Care Council's website at www.gscc.org.uk and in Wales to www.ccwales.org.uk.

6.1.2 Relevant social work

The first category of persons caught by s 55(2) is anyone 'who engages in relevant social work'. Relevant social work is defined in s 55(4) as 'social work which is required in connection with any health, education or social services provided by any person...'.

The 2000 Act does not define 'social work'. Nor does there appear to be any statutory definition of 'social work' in England and Wales. It is, however, referred to in the Health and Social Services and Social Security Adjudications Act 1983, Sch 3. In Scotland it appears in the Social Work (Scotland) Act 1968.

The White Paper *Modernizing Social Services* sets out the areas of involvement in social services, such as services providing 'a wide range of care and support for' inter alia: elderly people; people with physical disabilities or learning disabilities; people with mental health problems; people with drug or alcohol abuse problems; families, particularly where children have special needs; child protection; children in care; and young offenders. Despite there being extensive references to 'social services' in, for example, the Local Authority Social Services Act 1970, it is impossible to provide any neat definition of 'social work'. The authors speculate, but can give no answer, as to whether the definition extends to a person who is employed, for example, as an accountant in a care home. Does the definition extend to a teacher? The authors are disposed to take the view that 'relevant social work' encompasses only those providing direct 'social services'. However, this point is certainly arguable.

6.1.3 Employment at a children's home, care home or residential family centre, or for the purpose of a domiciliary care agency, fostering or voluntary adoption agency

The second category of persons caught by s 55(2) will cover the vast majority of the 1.2 million social care workers the Council expects to register from 2002 and regulate from April 2003.

The definition of residential family centre is the same as that in s 4(2) and (6), for domiciliary care in s 4(3) and (6), for fostering agencies in s 4(4) and (6) and voluntary adoption agencies in the Adoption Act 1976 and s 4(7) of the 2000 Act. The Adoption Act 1976 has been amended by the 2000 Act, the terms of which appear in Sch 4.

6.1.4 Manager of an establishment or agency

The third category of person caught by the Act and the forthcoming regulations covers all those who manage an establishment (the definition of which appears in s 3) or agency (s 4(9)), for which see the categories mentioned in s 55(2)(b) covering children's homes, care homes, residential family centres, domiciliary care agencies, fostering agencies or voluntary adoption agencies.

6.1.5 Domiciliary care agencies

The fourth category of persons caught by s 55(2) will be workers supplied by domiciliary care agencies who provide personal care to any person in their home, where that person, because of ill-health or disability, cannot maintain themselves without assistance.

6.1.6 Others

Regulation may also provide in due course that those persons referred to in s 55(3) should also be registered. Subsection (3) says that the following shall be treated as social care workers:

- a person undertaking social service type functions or similar services provided by a local authority;
- a person engaged in the provision of personal care to any person;
- a person who manages or is employed in an undertaking, which is not an establishment or agency, supplying or providing services for the purposes of supplying or providing personal care;
- a person employed in connection with the discharge of functions concerning the protection of children and vulnerable adults, pursuant to s 80;
- those employed by the Commission or the Assembly who undertake inspections of children accommodated in independent schools and colleges and those inspectors exercising inspection powers under s 31 (establishments or agencies) and those inspecting adoption and fostering services under s 45;
- those who are responsible for persons who carry out inspections;
- those who inspect childminding and day care facilities in Wales;
- those employed in a day centre; and
- persons who wish to become social care workers and who have enrolled on an approved course pursuant to s 63.

At the date of writing no such regulations have yet been made, though draft regulations are well advanced and expected to reinforce the contents of the Council's mission statement and encompass some of the concerns expressed in Phase II of the Climbié inquiry. The Councils recognize that there has been considerable public disquiet about the lack of regulation in the past and appear determined to regulate properly the provision of services to those who are most vulnerable. This laudable aim is to be welcomed. Readers are referred to both Councils' websites and the General Social Care Council (Registration of Social Workers) Rules 2003 (available at www.gscc.org.uk/care_rules.htm.

6.2 REGISTRATION

A social worker or person who wishes to become a social care worker or any other person specified by the Minister as covered by the rules, will need to apply for registration. An applicant will be granted registration by the Council (the Admissions Committee) if he satisfies the criteria set out in s 58. The Codes of Conduct and Practice for social workers and employers are available from the Councils. These provisions are being phased in and those required to apply will not need to do so until a register has been 'opened'. It appears likely that registration will be for a specified period, probably three years, with a fee being payable.

The Council will register an applicant where he or she satisfies the following criteria:

- He or she is of good character. An applicant will be required to obtain an 'enhanced level' check from the Criminal Records Bureau.
- He or she is physically and mentally fit to perform the whole or part of the work for which he or she is to be registered. The Councils say they have power to request medical information and may ask for an applicant to consent to disclose medical details or provide a confidential doctor's reference. The power to require this is not clear, though it is assumed that if it is not forthcoming an applicant will be refused registration. In an appropriate case this may be the subject of challenge, unless the Councils specify the basis upon which it is sought. The authors fail to see why a general request for medical information is appropriate. If it is to be requested it ought to be limited to physical and mental fitness covering a finite period. A general trawl through someone's medical history would arguably constitute a breach of statutory duty.
- He or she has successfully completed an approved (s 63) course for persons wishing to become social care workers. A social worker will be required to have completed a relevant social work course, as set out in the Schedule to the draft Registration Rules for Social Care Workers.
- He or she has obtained social care or equivalent qualifications elsewhere and can satisfy the Councils that those qualifications are comparable (see s 64).
- He or she satisfies or agrees to abide by any other requirements as to training which the Council may by rules impose.
- He or she has satisfied the requirements as to conduct and competence.

Concern has been expressed by trade unions and other bodies about the requirements under s 58(1)(b) to satisfy the 'physically and mentally fit' criteria. Councils and employers will need to be careful how they interpret this provision to ensure that they do not offend the Disability Discrimination Act 1995. The draft rules envisage that 'contentious' applications (see r 10) will be formally considered by the Admission Committee. That Committee has significant power which, it is suggested, must be carefully exercised, having regard to principles of fairness and other relevant administrative law provisions. Whether the provisions of r 10(3) prohibiting the right to be heard will stand the test of time remains to be seen. It is suggested that the legal adviser may advise the Committee that the applicant should be able to make representations and be present to hear the case against him or her. Stating, as the rules do, that an applicant has a right of appeal to the Care Standards Tribunal under s 9 of the 2000 Act where an applicant has not had the right to be heard may not satisfy the requirement for a fair hearing.

As touched upon above, those wishing to register will have to abide by the Councils' Codes of Practice and Conduct Rules which aim to promote high standards of conduct in accordance with the general duty placed upon the English and Welsh Councils as set out in s 54(2) and (3) and s 62. It is envisaged that the Code will cover both prospective social care workers and, importantly, their employers. Whether such Codes will extend to employers who have not submitted an application for registration is likely to be the subject of argument. The laudable aims of the Code are to be welcomed, although some of the draft terminology is wide and vague, requiring social care workers for example to 'balance the rights of service users and carers with the interests of society' and 'justify public trust and confidence in social care services'. It is the view of the authors that such concepts are unlikely to be understood by the vast majority of those applying.

6.2.1 Conditions

The Councils have power to attach conditions to the grant of registration to a social care worker. Section 58(1)(c) entitles the Council to grant the application 'either unconditionally or subject to such conditions as it thinks fit'. It is the view of the authors that the Council would, in an appropriate case, be entitled to impose wide conditions going beyond those set out in s 58(2) and (3). The rules envisage that those applying to become social care workers should sign an undertaking agreeing to abide by the terms of the Code. Such conditions could be in addition to conditions such as requiring an applicant to complete an approved course (s 63), or any other requirements governing conduct and competence (s 58(3)). Where concern has been expressed about a particular or proposed social care worker, the Councils, it is argued, will have power to specify that registration should be granted for a (limited) specified period under s 60(c) or be subject to more frequent renewal than the three years currently contemplated.

6.2.2 Refusal/cancellation

An applicant or social care worker will have their application refused or their registration removed by reference to the criteria in s 58 and the Code of Practice. In summary, such reasons will cover the following circumstances:

- not being of good character or loss of good character;
- being physically or mentally unfit subject to the requirements of the Disability Discrimination Act 1995 (a self-declaration will be required);
- failure to satisfy or abide by conditions;
- the non-recognition of qualifications gained elsewhere; and
- failure to satisfy requirements as to conduct and competence.

The above list is not meant to be exhaustive but gives an outline of the potential grounds for refusal or cancellation.

The authors suggest that the current Code of Conduct is not helpful on the issue of loss of character. Rules should be clear so far as is possible. Is, for example, a conviction two years ago for personal possession of cannabis (now declassified in certain parts of England as being a Class C drug) relevant? Or, say, a conviction for assault committed nine years ago when the applicant was young and in a state of intoxication? The Councils should be giving clear guidance as to what is acceptable and what is not. Those interested in this area could usefully review the guidance given by the Chartered Institute of Personnel and Development in their paper, *Employing people with a conviction*, available at www.cipd.co.uk.

The General Social Care Council has a highly experienced Chair and Chief Executive and has 15 lay members advised by a leading firm of City solicitors. The Council suggests that it will only become involved where a case has been referred by the Investigatory Committee to the Conduct Committee. If a matter proceeds beyond the investigation stage then any hearing will be in public, unless there is good reason to hold a private hearing. The proposed rules of evidence are set out in r 32. A written decision will have to be given (r 36). The Committee has a power to suspend a social care worker once an allegation comes to light pursuant to r 45.

Care staff are amongst the hardest working and most poorly paid public and private sector workers. This new regime will quite properly set new requirements for training, qualifications and ongoing professional development which are welcomed. Against that, it must be remembered that there are serious staff shortages and a high turnover of care staff. If potential applicants are refused registration except in clear and valid circumstances, the pool of available staff will be that much smaller, leading to an ever greater burden on existing care staff.

6.2.3 Removal from the Register

The Councils have been given wide powers under s 59 to determine their own criteria for the removal of a person from the Register or part of the Register. See the Conduct Rules for Social Care Workers 2002 for how these powers are likely to be interpreted in practice. The Council has the power to:

- remove a person from part of the Register for a specified or unspecified period;
- restore a person to the Register;
- suspend a person from part of the Register for a specified period;
- terminate a period of suspension;
- remove, alter or restore an entry in part of the Register; and
- make a caution order where facts are admitted.

It is envisaged that the rules will provide for any disciplinary proceedings to take place in public (s 59(3)) except where the rules (rr 12–15) specify otherwise. Decisions will be published on the website, which is to be welcomed.

6.2.4 Appeal

Any appeal against refusal of registration or removal from part of the Register lies to the Tribunal under s 68. It is not clear where the burden of proof will lie though it is suggested that in a child case it may be on the appellant (see the decisions in *Hett v Gwynedd CC*, decision number 214 and *Bryn Alyn Community Ltd v Clywd CC*, decision number 231). The General Social Care Council indicate in their draft rules (r 14(4)) that any appeal lies to the Protection of Children Act Tribunal though it will now be the Care Standards Tribunal. In a case involving an adult home, an appeal will also lie to the Care Standards Tribunal.

In addition to the old powers on appeal the Tribunal now has power to vary any conditions (s 68(3)(a)), to direct that any conditions shall cease to have effect (s 68(3)(b)), or impose new conditions under s 68(3)(c).

Regulations relating to appeals under s 68 are now made under The Protection of Children and Vulnerable Adults and Care Standards Tribunal (Amendment) Regulations 2003 SI No. 626. The regulations are to be found at Appendix 3.

7

CARE STANDARDS ACT 2000 AND THE PROTECTION OF VULNERABLE ADULTS

7.1 OVERVIEW

Part VII of the 2000 Act deals with the protection of children and vulnerable adults.

The essential mechanism of protection of both children and vulnerable adults requires that those individuals who are deemed unsuitable to work with either vulnerable adults or children are to be included in a list held by the Secretary of State and any person on that list is not to be offered employment in such a position.

The analysis below will concentrate on the protection of vulnerable adults, which is largely dealt with by the 2000 Act. The Protection of Children Act 1999, which performs a similar function in relation to children, is considered in outline only.

7.2 PROTECTION OF VULNERABLE ADULTS

7.2.1 Care worker

Section 80(2) of the 2000 Act defines a 'care worker' as an individual who is or has been employed in a position which either enables him or her to have regular contact in the course of his or her duties with adults who reside at a care home or such an individual employed by (which includes has been employed) an independent hospital, an independent clinic, an independent medical agency or a National Health Service body or an individual who provides care to a vulnerable adult, defined for the purpose of the section as someone in need of assistance because of illness, infirmity or disability, in that person's home.

Thus, in essence, the statutory provision is designed to encompass all those employed in care homes, hospitals (including clinics and agencies), and providing domiciliary assistance.

The definition includes both present and previous employment. Thus, a person who has been dismissed from, say, a care home and is no longer an employee, is nonetheless caught by the 2000 Act.

7.2.2 Employment

'Employment' is defined as having the same meaning as set out in the Protection of Children Act 1999 (s 80(4) of the 2000 Act). The term 'employment' is defined by s 12(1) of the Protection of Children Act 1999 as:

(a)   … any employment, whether paid or unpaid and whether under a contract of service or apprenticeship, under a contract for services or otherwise than under a contract; and
(b)   includes an office established by or by virtue of a prescribed enactment …

The statutory provision in the Protection of Children Act 1999 is wide-reaching. It includes employment under the usual type of employment contract; apprenticeship, which includes any formal probationary service; and those who provide services as an independent contractor. The term 'otherwise than under a contract' is capable of application to temporary employment which is unpaid, or the use of a family member.

The prescribed enactments referred to are set out in the Protection of Children (Child Care Organisations) Regulations 2000, SI 2000/2432.

7.2.3 Supply worker

This refers to an individual supplied by an employment agency or an employment business 'in a care position'. 'Care position' refers to the work of a care home, hospital or domiciliary care, as referred to above (s 80(5) of the 2000 Act).

7.2.4 Vulnerable adults

This term includes an adult to whom accommodation and nursing or personal care is provided in a care home or an adult to whom personal care is provided in their own home under arrangements made by a domiciliary care agency or an adult to whom prescribed services are provided by a hospital (as defined above).

'Nursing care' is essentially a matter of fact. The concept of 'personal care' has been litigated in the case of *Harrison v Cornwall CC* (The Times, 1 August 1991, CA). The Court of Appeal referred to s 20 of the Registered Homes Act 1984, which defined 'personal care' as 'care which includes assistance with bodily functions, where such assistance is required'. The Court of Appeal held that the statutory definition was not exhaustive and, for example, included emotional and psychiatric as well as physical care. According to the court one also has to look at whether the establishment provided care, even if not provided to the resident in question.

'Prescribed services' means prescribed by regulation. Regulations are yet to be made under this section.

7.2.5 Care providers

Persons who provide care for vulnerable adults include anyone who carries on a care home, a domiciliary care agency or an independent hospital (including clinics and agencies providing prescribed services), and a National Health Service body which provides prescribed services. As above, there is as yet no definition of prescribed services.

The Secretary of State has a duty to keep a list of individuals who are considered unsuitable to work with vulnerable adults (s 81(1) of the 2000 Act). The Secretary of State has power to remove an individual from the list if he is satisfied that that person should not have been included in it (s 81(3)).

7.2.6 Duty to refer

A person who provides care for vulnerable adults (see 7.2.4 above) has a duty to refer a care worker (see 7.2.1 above) to the Secretary of State if the care worker is either dismissed or would have been dismissed, or is transferred to a position which is not a care position, or has been suspended, on the grounds of misconduct (whether or not in the course of his or her employment) which harmed or placed at risk of harm a vulnerable adult (s 82 of the 2000 Act).

Section 82(3) expands on the above by adding that if there has been dismissal, resignation, retirement or transfer on different grounds but information subsequently shows that misconduct as referred to above has occurred, then the duty to refer arises.

Pending a determination by the Secretary of State the care worker (which of course includes an ex-care worker) should be provisionally included in the list.

However, before the care worker's place on the list is confirmed, he or she is to be invited to submit observations on the information supplied by his or her employer and the employer is to be invited to comment on those observations.

Once the Secretary of State has considered all that information, together with any other information which is considered relevant, and where the worker has been dismissed or transferred, then the Secretary of State is entitled to confirm the care worker's inclusion on the list if he is satisfied (s 82(6) and (7)):

(a) that the provider reasonably considered the worker to be guilty of misconduct ... which harmed or placed at risk of harm a vulnerable adult; and

(b) that the worker is unsuitable to work with vulnerable adults.

The reference in s 82(6) to the worker's dismissal includes the care worker's resignation, retirement, being made redundant or being transferred to a position which is not a care position (s 82(8)).

The provision does not apply where the care worker is a supply worker to a domiciliary care agency or independent medical agency, which includes an employment agency or an employment business (s 82(1)).

Finally, the Act does not apply retrospectively (s 82(10)).

7.2.7 Employment agencies and businesses

The duty to refer also applies to any person who carries on either an employment agency or an employment business in relation to supply workers.

In relation to the former, the person carrying on the agency must refer where he has decided not to do any further business with a worker on the grounds of misconduct, as defined above, or where he has decided on similar grounds not to find the worker employment or supply him for further employment in a care position. In relation to the latter (where the worker is in fact an employee of the business), dismissal (or where there would have been a dismissal but for resignation or retirement) or a decision not to supply the worker for further employment in the care position on the grounds of misconduct (as defined above), crystallizes a duty to refer.

The Secretary of State's duties in relation to the list are similar to those in relation to care workers (s 83).

7.2.8 Registration authorities

If there has been no reference of the care worker by either the provider of the care home, hospital or domiciliary agency or by an employment agency or business, then either the Commission or the National Assembly may refer in similar circumstances (see s 84).

7.2.9 Inquiries

A care worker or supply worker whose conduct is referred to in an inquiry carried out under the 2000 Act or under certain other Acts, such as the Children Act 1989, the National Health Service Act 1977 or the Local Authority Social Services Act 1970 may be considered and then included in the list kept by the Secretary of State.

There are similar provisions for the triggering of liability for inclusion in the list and the procedures to be adopted by the Secretary of State for inclusion in the list (s 85). However, there is an additional requirement that prior to making an order the Secretary of State must consult the Assembly (s 85(8)).

7.2.10 Appeals

Section 86 of the 2000 Act entitles an individual included in the list (but not provisionally) to appeal to the Tribunal.

There is also a right of appeal against provisional inclusion in the list, where that has occurred for a period of in excess of nine months. However, such an appeal can only be launched with the leave of the Tribunal. If leave is granted, then the issue of inclusion in the list is determined by the Tribunal and not by the Secretary of State.

The Tribunal is empowered to allow the appeal if it is not satisfied of either of the following:

(a)   that the individual is guilty of misconduct (whether or not in the course of his duties) which harmed or placed at risk of harm a vulnerable adult; and
(b)   that the individual is unsuitable to work with vulnerable adults.

Where the individual has been convicted of an offence, involving misconduct, as defined above, a finding of fact on which the conviction 'must be taken' to have been based cannot be challenged.

Where provisional inclusion on the list is based upon civil or criminal proceedings, no application for leave to appeal can be made before the end of the period of six months following the final determination of the proceedings.

7.2.11 Applications for removal from the list

There is a reserve power to apply for removal from the list in the case of an individual who was a child when he was included in the list or who has been on the list for five years and made no previous application during the course of that time for removal from the list. In the case of an adult, the period is ten years.

The Tribunal is directed not to grant any application unless:

(a)   ... the individual's circumstances have changed ...
(b)   ... the change is such that leave should be granted.

Leave to apply to the Tribunal must be obtained and will only be granted if the conditions referred to above are fulfilled (ss 87 and 88).

7.2.12 Effect of inclusion in the list

The effect of inclusion in the list is to bar a prospective employee from working in a care position whilst on the list.

If a person who provides care to vulnerable adults discovers that an individual employed by him is included on the list, that person shall be dismissed forthwith.

Where it is proposed to offer employment to a supply worker, the duty cast on the owner of the care home, hospital or domiciliary agency is to satisfy himself that the supplying agency or business has carried out a check within the last 12 months and provides written confirmation of that fact (s 89).

7.3 PROTECTION OF CHILDREN ACT 1999

It is outside the scope of this book to deal with the Protection of Children Act 1999. It contains provisions in relation to children that are similar to those provisions relating to vulnerable adults in Pt VII of the 2000 Act, as described above.

It should also be noted that the 1999 Act includes the list held by the Department for Education and Employment, which lists teachers barred from teaching. The reader is referred to the Protection of Children and Vulnerable Adults and Care Standards Tribunal Regulations 2002, SI 2002/816 (see appendix 2).

8

AGENCIES

8.1 OVERVIEW

Five types of agency are identified in the 2000 Act (s 4(9)):

- independent medical agency;
- nurses agency;
- domiciliary care agency;
- fostering agency;
- voluntary adoption agency.

8.1.1 Independent medical agency

Section 2(5) defines an 'independent medical agency' as 'an undertaking (not being an independent clinic) which consists of or includes the provision of services by medical practitioners'.

However, if any of the services are provided for the purposes of an independent clinic, or by medical practitioners in pursuance of the National Health Service Act 1997, then it is not an independent medical agency (s 2(5)).

On 24 July 2001 the Department of Health and the National Care Standards Commission (NCSC) issued a consultation document on the regulations and national minimum standards for independent health care. In February 2002 the Independent Health Care National Minimum Standards and Regulations were published by the Secretary of State for Health under s 23(1).

An independent medical agency is to be distinguished from the following entities (a neutral term is used for the moment):

- a Health Service hospital (s 2(2));
- an independent hospital (s 2(3));
- an independent clinic (s 2(4)).

A Health Service hospital is a National Health Service hospital and is exempt from the 2000 Act. Independent hospitals and independent clinics are both establishments and are dealt with in chapter 9. However, because of the definition of an independent medical agency it will be necessary to consider what is an independent clinic and what is a National Health Service hospital for the purposes of the 2000 Act.

8.1.2 Nurses agency

The definition of a 'nurses agency' means, subject to any regulations made, 'an employment agency or employment business, being (in either case) a business which consists of or includes supplying, or providing services for the purposes of supplying, registered nurses, registered midwives or registered health visitors (s 4 (5)).

'Registered' means registered by the UK Central Council for Nursing, Midwifery and Health Visiting (now Nursing and Midwifery Council) (see the Nurses, Midwives and Health Visitors Act 1997).

The Nurses Agencies Regulations 2002, SI 2002/3212, made under s 4(6) came into force on 1 April 2003.

8.1.3 Domiciliary care agency

A domiciliary care agency means an undertaking which consists of or includes arranging the provision of personal care in their own homes for persons who by reason of illness, infirmity or disability are unable to provide it for themselves without assistance (s 4(3)).

The Domiciliary Care Agencies Regulations 2002, SI 2002/3214, made under s 4(6) came into force on 1 April 2003.

8.1.4 Fostering agency

A fostering agency means, subject to any exception provided by regulations:

(a) an undertaking, which consists of or includes discharging functions of local authorities in connection with the placing of children with foster parents; or
(b) a voluntary organisation which places children with foster parents under section 59(1) of the 1989 Act.

The Fostering Services Regulations 2002, SI 2002/57, have been made under s 4(6).

8.1.5 Voluntary adoption agency

'Voluntary adoption agency' means an adoption society within the meaning of the Adoption Act 1976, which is a voluntary organization within the meaning of that Act. Where a local authority discharges relevant adoption functions, this service is also described as an adoption agency.

There is no exception by way of regulations in relation to such organizations. Two sets of regulations were brought into force on 30 April 2003, the Voluntary Adoption Agencies and the Adoption Agencies (Miscellaneous Amendments) Regulations 2003, SI 2003/367, and the Local Authority Adoption Service (England) Regulations 2003, SI 2003/370.

8.2 INDEPENDENT MEDICAL AGENCIES

As noted above, in February 2002 the Secretary of State for Health issued the Independent Health Care National Minimum Standards and Regulations.

That document sets out the regulations and national minimum standards for the regulation of independent health care providers from April 2002. It applies to a range of service providers, which include independent health care establishments, registration for which is currently required under the Registered Homes Act 1984 and independent health care providers, which were newly regulated from April 2002, namely exclusively private doctors, hyperbaric oxygen chambers and establishments where treatment is provided using intense light sources.

For convenience, hospitals and similar institutions which constitute establishments are dealt with in chapter 9. This section deals with independent medical agencies. In essence (see p 177 of the Independent Health Care National Minimum Standards and Regulations) it deals with private doctors who provide treatment to private patients, but not from establishments that could be registered.

At p 116 of the Independent Health Care National Minimum Standards and Regulations it is observed that the NCSC do not consider that regulations should extend to private medical practitioners to whom the general public does not have access. An example is given of doctors whose work solely comprises the provision of occupational health services for the employees of an organization, or doctors who provide services to insurance companies or government departments.

8.2.1 Specific issues

The statutory definition of an independent medical agency as contained in s 2(5) of the 2000 Act is set out at 8.1.1 above.

The first issue is the definition of the word 'undertaking'. Section 121(1) of the 2000 Act provides the definition as follows:

'Undertaking' includes any business or profession and –
(a) in relation to a public or local authority, includes the exercise of any functions of that authority; and
(b) in relation to any other body of persons, whether corporate or unincorporate, includes any of the activities of that body ...

The scope of 'undertaking' is wide, but limited by the concept of business or profession. Given that the statutory definition is directed at doctors (albeit there is no statutory definition of 'medical practitioners' in the Act, other than to exclude those acting under the National Health Service Act 1977), it is plain that it captures private call-out medical practitioners.

'Medical practitioner' is not defined by the 2000 Act. The Medical Act 1983 refers (s 2) to a 'medical practitioner', but the definition section of that Act does not refer to this term further. Section 2 of that Act specifically refers to 'the register of medical practitioners'. The jurisdiction conferred by the Medical Act 1983 is only over registered medical practitioners.

The Medical Act 1983, s 56, Sch 6, para 11(1) provides that in any enactment passed before 1 January 1979 'a legally qualified medical practitioner' or 'duly qualified medical practitioner' or any expression in legislation describing a person recognized by law as a member of the medical profession must be construed to mean a fully registered person, unless the contrary intention appears. In any enactment passed after that date the expression 'registered medical practitioner' means a fully registered person, unless contrary intention appears. See also the Interpretation Act 1978, Sch 1.

8.2.2 National Minimum Standards

The Independent Health Care National Minimum Standards focus on ensuring that patients who receive treatment and services in independent healthcare establishments, or those provided by independent medical agencies, are safe and of an assured quality.

Page vii of the Independent Health Care National Minimum Standards and Regulations sets out the relationship between the standards and the regulations:

The CSA sets out a broad range of regulations-making powers covering, amongst other matters, the management, staff, premises and conduct of social and health care establishments and agencies. Section 23 gives powers to the Secretary of State to publish statements of national minimum standards that the NCSC must take into account when making its decisions. These standards will form the basis for judgments made by the NCSC about registration and the imposition of conditions for registration, variation of any conditions and enforcement of compliance with the CSA and associated regulations, including proceedings for cancellation of registration or prosecution. The NCSC will therefore consider the degree to which a regulated service complies with the standards when determining whether or not a service should be registered or have its registration cancelled, or whether to take any action for breach of regulations.

The document further observes:

The regulations and national minimum standards for independent health care focus on ensuring that patients receive treatment and services in independent health care establishments, or provided by independent medical agencies, that are safe and quality-assured.

The national minimum standards consists of core standards that apply to all independent health care providers regulated by the NCSC, supplemented by service-specific standards that apply to the relevant individual areas of health care services to be regulated. The Private and Voluntary Health Care Regulations follow this core and service-specific format.

Each standard is preceded by a statement of the intended outcome for patients.

Whilst the standards are qualitative—they provide a tool for judging if patients are receiving safe and quality-assured treatment and services—they are also measurable. Regulators will look for evidence that the requirements are being met through:

- discussions with patients, staff, managers and others;
- observation of arrangements in the establishment;
- scrutiny of written policies, procedures and records.

The regulators will look for evidence that the policies and day-to-day operation of both independent health care establishments and agencies reflect the following:

- patient-centred services—ensuring that providers put patients' safety and quality assurance at the centre of what they do;
- patient information—providers must ensure that patients and prospective patients have clear and accurate information about independent health care providers and that providers listen to and publish feedback from patients;
- accountability—patients must receive treatment and services that are safe and quality assured;
- safety and quality assurance—the procedures must address how safety and quality assurance can be best achieved;
- consistency—the standards are based on the key principle that they need to be compatible with standards in the National Health Service.

The core standards are not set out here, but are contained in the Independent Health Care National Minimum Standards and Regulations, pp 3 and 37. They include, for example, information; provision; quality of treatment; care complaints; premises, facilities and equipment standards; risk management procedures; and record and information management.

8.2.3 Standards (applicable to independent medical agencies)

The specific standards that apply to independent medical agencies are, in general terms, as follows:

- patients are to be assured that appropriate arrangements for all aspects of their treatment are in place;

- medication is to be prescribed safely and effectively;
- patients must be assured that effective pathology services are in place;
- patients must be offered the opportunity to give or refuse consent for information on their treatment to be passed to their normal GP.

For more specific details of the applicable standards, reference should be made to the Independent Health Care National Minimum Standards and Regulations pp 171-174.

8.2.4 Regulations

The primary regulations are the Private and Voluntary Health Care (England) Regulations 2001, SI 2001/3968, which came into force on 1 April 2002. There are a number of regulations of general application. The reader is referred to the regulations under Pts I–III. A more detailed reference should be made to chapter 9 on hospital and clinics.

The only additional requirement that applies to an independent medical agency is the obligation to include the name of the medical practitioner by whom each patient is treated (reg 49).

It should be noted that there are extensive requirements that apply to independent medical agencies.

8.3 NURSES AGENCIES

8.3.1 General

'Nurses agency' means, subject to any regulations, an employment agency or employment business, being (in either case) a business which consists of or includes supplying, or providing services for the purpose of supplying registered nurses, registered midwives or registered health visitors.

A consultation document was issued by the Department of Health relating to the national minimum standards and regulations which are to be applied to nursing agencies. These National Minimum Standards are now published by the Secretary of State for Health in accordance with s 23 of the 2000 Act. They apply as from 1 April 2003.

The relationship between the regulations and standards is as follows: regulations are mandatory and must be complied with. If they are breached, this constitutes an offence and providers will be given a notice setting out:

- the regulation breached;
- how the service is considered deficient;
- what must be done to remedy the deficiency;
- a timescale within which the deficiency must be remedied.

If the deficiency is not remedied, proceedings for prosecution may follow.

When the Commission makes a decision about a breach of regulation (or any decision to do with registration, cancellation, variation or imposition of conditions) it must take the national minimum standards into account. It may also take into account any other factors that it considers reasonable or relevant.

Thus, if standards were breached only occasionally or minimally this would not necessarily lead to enforcement action. It is therefore likely that the NCSC's approach to the interrelationship between standards and regulations will be as set out in the Independent Health Care National Minimum Standards and Regulations.

There are approximately 800 licensed nurses agency offices operating in England and Wales. About 40 per cent of the agencies are operated by five providers operating on a national basis and many agencies supplying nurses also operate as employment agencies or businesses supplying other types of staff.

8.3.2 National minimum standards

The published standards fall into five subject areas and the most important elements within each topic are mentioned below. The full set of numbered paragraphs must be met in order to comply with the standard.

- Section 1: Information (Standard 1)
  —Prospective service users should have the information they need about the agency in order to make an informed decision on whether to engage its services.
- Section 2: Registered Persons (Standard 2)
  —Service users are to be assured of the integrity of the agency and have confidence that it is run by a fit person or organization.
- Section 3: Recruitment and supply of nurses (Standards 3–6)
  —The process for recruitment and selection of nurses must meet all the requirements of legislation and employment law, including those relating to equal opportunities and anti-discriminatory practice.
  —Nurses supplied by the agency must be competent and trained to undertake the activities for which they are employed and responsible.
  —The agency must regularly appraise the standard practice of nurses supplied, where the agency is an employment business (see 8.3.3 below).
- Section 4: Complaints and Protection (Standards 7–11)
  —Service users are to be confident that their complaints will be listened to, taken seriously and acted upon.
  —Service users who are also patients are to be protected from abuse, where the agency is an employment business (see 8.3.3 below).
  —Service users who are patients are to be protected by the agency's procedures for assistance with medication, where the agency is an employment business (see 8.3.3 below).
  —Action must be taken to protect confidentiality of information relating to service users who are also patients, their carers or advocates.

—The health, safety and welfare of service users who are also patients, and of nurses, must be promoted and protected, where the agency is an employment business (see 8.3.3 below).

- Section 5: Management and Administration (Standards 12–18)

—Approved accounting and financial procedures are to be adopted to ensure the effective and efficient running of the business and its continued financial viability.

—There must be designated premises suitably equipped for the purpose of the day-to-day operation and management of the service.

—There must be an appropriate management structure and clear lines of accountability in place.

—Nurses supplied by the agency must know the standards of conduct expected of them and be aware of the agency's organizational policies, where the agency is an employment business (see 8.3.3 below).

—There must be a written agreement between the agency and nurses.

—Service users' and nurses' interests must be safeguarded by the agency's record-keeping policies and procedures.

—The agency must operate in the best interests of service users and of nurses supplied by it.

8.3.3 Employment business

The 2000 Act requires nurses agencies to comply with the requirements of the Employment Agencies Act 1973 and the regulations made under that Act. That Act and the regulations are enforced by the Employment Agency Standards Inspectorate. The regulations are concerned mainly with issues relating to the way an agency conducts its business. However, the 2000 Act requires certain standards to be adhered to where the agency is an employment business. The 2000 Act repeals the Nurses Agencies Act 1957 and requires nurses agencies to be registered by the NCSC. Until recently nurses agencies have been exempt from the requirements of the Employment Agencies Act 1973 and its regulations. However by the 2000 Act nurses agencies are now required to comply with the requirements of that Act and the regulations. It is not within the scope of this text to examine either the Employment Agencies Act 1973 or the regulations made under that Act. However, where it has been indicated above that certain standards apply where the agency is an employment business, those particular standards will have to be adhered to.

8.3.4 Nurses Agencies Regulations 2002

The Nurses Agencies Regulations 2002, SI 2002/3212, which came into force on 1 April 2003, apply in relation to nurses agencies in England only.

Part 1 of the Regulations provides that the registered person shall compile a written statement (referred to in the Regulations as 'the statement of purpose') and that must consist of a statement as to the matters listed in Sch 1. A copy of this statement has to be provided to the Commission and a copy made available for inspection by every service user.

The statement of purpose must be kept under review and revised where appropriate, and any revisions must be notified to the Commission within 28 days of that revision.

The registered provider has a duty to appoint an individual to manage the agency if the registered provider (reg 8):

(a)   is an organisation; or
(b)   is not a fit person to manage an agency; or
(c)   it is not or does not intend to be in full-time day to day charge of the agency.

The manager must be fit. The concept of fitness is dealt with below (reg 7).

Both the registered provider and the registered manager shall carry on or manage the agency with sufficient care, competence and skill. They are duty bound to take such training as is appropriate (reg 10).

The registered person or 'responsible individual' (where the registration is with an organization) has a duty to notify the Commission of his or her conviction of any criminal offence, either in England or Wales or elsewhere, and give details of the same (reg 11).

The registered person has a duty to ensure that staff are fit and that selection of a nurse for supply to a service user is made by or under the supervision of a nurse and that 'full and satisfactory information is available in relation to her in respect of each of the matters specified in Schedule 3' (reg 12(1)).

The registered person has a duty to ensure that a nurse supplied by the agency, when working for a service user, is instructed that she must at all times wear identification showing her name, the name of the agency and a recent photograph (reg 12(3)).

Where nurses are supplied directly to patients by an agency in its capacity as an employment business, it has a duty to prepare and implement various written policies and have a procedure for the provision and the keeping of records. Any allegations and reviews of neglect or other harm and action taken in respect of the allegations must be reported. There is also a duty to keep information about the patient confidential (reg 13).

Where the agency is an employment business, the registered person has a duty to ensure that there is an appropriate number of staff employed by the agency. Staff employed for the purposes of the agency must receive supervision. She must be aware of her own responsibilities and those of other employees. There is also a duty to undertake an annual appraisal performance and take all the steps necessary to address any aspect of the nurses' clinical practice. A written statement of terms and conditions should be provided to employees (reg 14).

Where the agency is an employment business the registered person has a duty to prepare a handbook and provide a copy to each member of staff (reg 15).

The registered person has a duty to ensure that a service user is given the name of the member of staff who is responsible for the supply of the nurse and, where the agency is an employment business, details of how they may contact the registered person or somebody nominated on their behalf. Where the service user is a patient, that information should be provided to the patient's relatives or carers (reg 16).

There is a duty on the registered person to keep the records required by Sch 4 to the Regulations up to date and to retain such records for a period of not less than three years beginning on the date of the last entry (reg 17).

There is a duty on the registered person to establish a complaints procedure and to ensure that every complaint is fully investigated (reg 18).

There is a duty on the registered person to review the quality of service provision and provide a report to the Commission in respect of any review and to make that report available to service users and persons acting on behalf of service users or patients (reg 19).

The registered person has a duty to ensure that the premises are 'suitable for the purposes of achieving the aims and objectives of the agency set out in the statement of purpose' (reg 20).

The registered person should ensure that the Commission is provided with all relevant accounts (reg 21).

Where the registered provider or manager proposes to be absent for a period of 28 days or more, the registered person has a duty to give notice of that in writing to the Commission. Where the absence arises from an emergency, the registered person must give notice of the absence within one week of its occurrence, and must inform the Commission (reg 22) of:

- the length or expected length of the absence;
- the reason for the absence; and
- the arrangements which have been made for running the agency during that absence.

The registered person has a duty to notify the Commission of various changes to the agency (reg 23) and a liquidator or similar has a duty to notify the Commission of his appointment (reg 24).

Any failure to comply with regs 4–6 or 11–23 is an offence, but notice of a breach and an opportunity to rectify the same should be given before there can be a prosecution (reg 27).

Under the provisions of Sch 2, various information must be supplied in respect of the registered provider and manager of an agency and nurses responsible for selecting nurses to be supplied to service users. Under Sch 3, information must be supplied in respect of nurses supplied by the agency. The Schedule identifies 12 pieces of information to be provided (the information required under Sch 2 by comparison requires only nine pieces of information), which includes proof of identity, details of any criminal offences, two written references from nurses or other health professionals, and details of health records. Schedule 4 details records to be maintained for inspection. The records relate to supply of nurses, all information provided to the Commission for the purposes of registration in relation to the agency, and details of every allegation of abuse against a nurse or by a nurse.

8.3.5 General matters relating to the Regulations

There are four types of entities who may owe duties.

- 'Registered person'. This means anyone who is the registered provider or the registered manager.
- 'Registered provider'. That is the person who is registered as the person carrying on the agency.
- 'Registered manager'. That is the person registered as manager of the agency in the circumstances where the provider is either an organization or not fit to manage the agency or does not intend to be in full-time, day-to-day charge of the agency (see reg 5).
- 'Responsible individual'. Where the registered provider is an organization, then an individual who is a director, manager, secretary or other officer of the organization must be nominated by the organization as the responsible individual acting on its behalf.

The definition of 'organization' appears in reg 5 and means 'a body corporate or any unincorporated association other than a partnership'.

The concept of fitness in relation to a registered provider and manager requires the provider and the manager to be (reg 7(3)):

(a) ... of integrity and good character;
(b) ... physically and mentally fit to carry on the agency ...
(c) full and satisfactory information in respect of each of the matters listed in Schedule 2 [must be available].

The registered provider or individual acting on its behalf must also demonstrate that he has not been adjudged bankrupt or entered into a composition with his creditors (see reg 7(4)).

The fitness of a nurse supplied by an agency requires that:

- she is of integrity and good character;
- she has all the qualifications, skill and experience which are necessary for the work which she is to perform;
- she is physically and mentally fit for that work; and
- full and satisfactory information in respect of each of the matters listed in Sch 3 have been obtained in relation to her.

All nurses to be supplied by the agency must be selected by a nurse themselves: that nurse must comply with the provisions of Sch 2 to the Act (reg 12).

8.3.6 Frequency of inspection

The proposed frequency of inspection for nurses agencies is one per year.

8.3.7 Employment Agencies Act 1973

Those nursing agencies which are within the remit of the Employment Agencies Act 1973 and the regulations are subject to the enforcement powers available to the Employment Agency Standards Inspectorate. Those enforcement powers entitle a prosecution to be brought in the magistrates' court and may result in a penalty of up to £5,000. Proceedings can also be brought before an employment tribunal for the purpose of prohibiting those running agencies for a maximum of ten years.

8.4 DOMICILIARY CARE AGENCIES

8.4.1 Introduction

A domiciliary care agency means, subject to any regulations that may be made, 'an undertaking which consists of or includes arranging the provision of personal care in their own homes to persons who by reason of illness, infirmity or disability are unable to provide it for themselves without assistance'.

The number of domiciliary care agencies operating in England is not known. The UK Home Care Association has around 1,200 members but the total number of agencies could be higher. According to the partial regulatory impact assessment issued by the Department of Health, their estimates place the number of people working in this sector at 150,000 individuals.

The object of the scheme of regulation is to control the activities of all domiciliary care providers delivering personal care services. However, the scheme does not extend to a sole individual working alone.

8.4.2 Cost

It is proposed that the cost of registration will be £2,600. The annual continuation will be £730. It is anticipated in the partial regulatory impact assessment paper that the cost of registration will be passed on to those paying for, or from entities funding, the services.

8.4.3 Size of the market

There are no accurate figures on the size of the sector. A recent 2000 survey suggested that 51 per cent of the likely market was in the independent sector. Overall it is thought there may be 3,000 registrable providers.

8.4.4 National minimum standards

Following consultation, a document which sets out National Minimum Standards has now been published by the Secretary of State for Health in accordance with s 23 of the 2000 Act. They apply as from 1 April 2003.

The standards apply to agencies providing personal care to 'a wide range of people who need care and support whilst living in their own home', including:

- older people;
- people with physical disabilities;
- people with sensory loss, including dual sensory impairment;
- people with mental health problems;
- people with learning disabilities;
- children and their families;
- 'personal or primary carers'.

The consultation document goes on to observe that regulations will apply to all agencies which provide personal care in their own homes to persons who by reason of illness, infirmity or disability, are unable to provide it for themselves without assistance.

The regulations and standards will apply to all providers of personal domiciliary care services in private, voluntary and public sectors and will include local authorities and NHS trusts.

Where an agency operates from more than one branch, each branch will have to register and be inspected and will be required to have a responsible and registered 'fit manager' in charge of day-to-day provision. Where a national voluntary organization has a number of affiliated branches or franchises, each will be required to be registered and is treated as a separate business or agency for the purposes of registration and regulation.

All agencies will be required to have a 'fit' person, with overall responsibility for the service. Where that person ('the registered person') is not responsible for the day-to-day management of the service or where they lack the required qualifications and experience or where the service is provided from more than one location, they will be required to appoint a manager, who must be registered with the Commission as 'fit' (see 8.3.5 above).

The National Minimum Standards offer a definition of 'personal care' (and observe that there is no definition in the 2000 Act) as being the undertaking of any activity which requires a degree of close personal and physical contact with persons, who for reasons of disability, frailty, illness or personal physical incapacity, are unable to provide it themselves without assistance. The activities given as examples include:

- assistance in getting up and dressed or undressed and going to bed;
- helping the person have a wash, shower or bath, including washing of hair, shaving and oral hygiene;

- assisting the person with toilet requirements;
- helping the person to eat their food;
- helping with their medication or other health-related tasks;
- assistance getting in or out of a chair;
- personal support of a sensitive or specialist nature.

In summary, personal care covers assistance with bodily functions, and other care involving physical and intimate touching. It is the view of the Department of Health that non-physical care (such as emotional and physiological support) does not give rise to registration, but it observes that reference should be made to the NCSC if in doubt.

The published standards are grouped under five subject areas and the most important elements within each topic are mentioned below.

8.4.4.1 *User focused services (Standards 1–6)*

- The registered person must produce a statement of purpose and a service user's guide. Current and potential service users and their carers should be provided with comprehensive information, so that they can make informed decisions on whether the agency is able to meet their specific care needs.
- The needs of service users and their carers are to be individually assessed before a domiciliary care service is offered.
- Service users and their representatives should know the service they receive will meet their assessed care needs.
- Each service user should have a written contract or statement of terms and conditions under which the care is provided. The contract shall be provided within seven days.
- Service users and their carers/representatives should be satisfied that their personal information is handled appropriately and kept confidential.
- Service users should receive flexible assistance and reliable personal care service.

8.4.4.2 *Personal care (Standards 7–10)*

- Care needs, wishes, preferences and personal goals for each individual service user are to be recorded in their personal service user plan.
- Service users should be treated with respect and as a valued person and their right for privacy should be upheld.
- Service users are to be helped to exercise control over their lives and to be supported in maintaining their independence.
- Service users are to be assisted to maintain responsibility for their own medication and to remain in their own home and, when unable to administer their own medicines, protected by the agency's policies and procedures dealing with medicine. The agency must have a clear written policy.

8.4.4.3 *Protection (Standards 11–16)*

- The health, safety and welfare of service users and staff should be promoted and protected.
- The risks of accidents and harm to service users and staff must be minimized.
- Money and property of service users must be protected at all times whilst providing the care service.
- Service users are to be protected from abuse, neglect and self-harm.
- Service users are to be protected and their safety and security in their own home should be provided for.
- The health, best interests and rights of service users are to be safeguarded when maintaining records of key events and activities in the home. Records kept include administration of medication.

8.4.4.4 *Managers and staff (Standards 17–21)*

- The well-being, health and security of service users must be protected by the agency's policies and procedures on recruitment and selection of staff.
- The selection of staff must include a policy which complies with the requirements of legislation, equal opportunities and anti-discriminatory practice.
- The selection shall include various checks including a criminal record check and a check of the Protection of Vulnerable Adults and Protection of Children registers.
- All staff are to comply with the Code of Conduct.
- Service users are to benefit.
- There should be written job descriptions, person and work specifications, and a staff handbook for all jobs.
- Service users are to know that staff are appropriately trained to meet their personal care needs.
- There must be an induction process, lasting a minimum of three days which covers topics in Appendix C of the Standards.
- There must be specialist advice, training and information when necessary.
- The agency must have financial resources allocated, and plans and operational procedures to achieve and monitor the requirements for training.
- The personal care of service users is to be provided by qualified and competent staff.
- 50 per cent of all personal care by the provider is to be delivered by workers who are NVQ qualified (or equivalent or better) by April 2008.
- Managers must obtain NVQ 4 or equivalent within five years of the application of the standards, or afterwards, within three years of employment.
- Service users are to know and benefit from having staff who are supervised and whose performance is appraised regularly.
- All care and support staff are to receive regular supervision and must have their standard of practice appraised annually.

8.4.4.5 *Organization and running of the business (Standards 22–27)*

- Service users are to receive a consistent and well-managed and planned service.
- The service is to be managed and provided from sound and permanent premises.
- Those premises are to be located appropriately.
- Those premises are to be properly equipped and resourced.
- There must be a sufficient number of staff for the business.
- There must be a business and financial plan.
- The continuity of the service provided to service users must be safeguarded by the accounting and financial procedures of the agency.
- There must be systems in place to bill accurately.
- Where there are no audited accounts, certified annual accounts must be available.
- There must be insurance cover.
- The rights and best interests of service users are to be safeguarded by the agency keeping accurate and up-to-date records.
- The service user's rights, health and best interests are to be safeguarded by robust policies and procedures, implemented consistently by the agency.
- Service users and their carers must be confident that their complaints will be listened to, taken seriously and acted upon.
- There must be a publicized complaints procedure.
- Complaints must be dealt with expeditiously.
- The service must be run in the best interests of the service users.
- There must be a Quality Assurance system.
- There must be a method of measuring quality and performance.
- The outcome from the Quality Assurance process is to be published annually and circulated to service users, carers, stakeholders in the agency and made available to the Commission.

8.4.4.6 *Other matters*

The appendices to the National Minimum Standards include a glossary of terms; detailed matters that must be covered by the code of practice of the agency; the content of the induction programme; the content of health and safety training; the topics requiring specialist training and advice; data to be kept on all service users; and the ambit of the policies and procedures of the agency.

8.4.5 Domiciliary Care Agencies Regulations 2002

8.4.5.1 *Excepted undertakings, statement of purpose, service users guide and agency documents*

These Regulations, SI 2002/3214 came into force on 1 April 2003.

The Regulations except from the definition of 'domiciliary care agency' an individual who does not employ any other person and who is not involved with any other individual or employed by any organization to carry on the business of the agency.

The registered person is obliged to ensure the compilation of a statement of purpose, which consists of a statement of the aims and objectives of the agency, the personal care services which the agency will provide and a statement of the matters listed in Sch 1 to the Regulations. Those matters require the identity of the registered person to be specified, the nature of the services which the agency provides, and the geographical area in which the services are to be provided. For details reference should be made to Sch 1. The statement of purpose should be made available at the agency's premises for inspection.

The registered person also has an obligation to produce the service users guide, which should contain a summary of the statement of purpose, the geographical area in which the services are provided, terms and conditions and a description of the staff structure. A copy should be supplied to the service user and to the Commission. If arrangements have been made with a local authority, a copy of those arrangements should be supplied to the service user. There is a duty on the registered person to review and revise the statement of purpose and service users guide and to give notice to the Commission and any service user of any changes in either.

There is a duty to ensure that all correspondence from the agency contains details of its registration.

8.4.5.2 *Registered persons*
The definitions and fitness requirements of the registered provider, responsible individual and manager are largely as the requirements referred to in other regulations set out above.

There is a duty upon the registered person or responsible individual to notify the Commission of any criminal offence.

8.4.5.3 *Service provision*
The registered person must make suitable arrangements to ensure that the agency is conducted and the care provided by it is such as to protect the safety of service users. They should be made safe against abuse or neglect. Their independence should be promoted. The safety and security of the service users' property in their homes should be preserved. Privacy, dignity and confidential information is to be promoted with due regard to sex, religious persuasion, racial origin, cultural and linguistic background, disability and 'the way in which they conduct their lives'.

The registered person has a duty, after consultation with the service user, to prepare a care plan and to ensure that that care plan is made available to the service user, kept under review, revised and that any revision is notified to the service user. There is also an obligation to ensure that the needs specified in the care plan are met. There is also a duty to ensure that it takes into account the wishes and feelings of the service user. They should be provided with information and encouraged to make their own decisions about the personal care provided to them.

There are duties in relation to the provision of services which require the registered person to, inter alia, set out (reg 14(6)):

- the procedures to be followed after an allegation of abuse;
- the procedures to be adopted in relation to the administration of medication;
- the arrangements for assisting the service user with mobility;
- the procedure to be followed where money is to be held by a domiciliary care worker.

The registered person also has a duty to make arrangements in relation to (reg 14(7)–(11)):

- the administration and disposal of medicines;
- the training of staff;
- the operating of a safe system of work;
- the prevention of harm to the service users;
- the recording of any physical restraint used and the avoidance of physical restraints unless that is the only practical means of securing the welfare of that or any other service user where there are exceptional circumstances.

A registered person also has a duty to ensure that any worker employed is fit in accordance with reg 12. Fitness is defined as it is in every other regulation (see 8.3.5 above). There is also a duty to ensure the provision of an adequate number of staff and to show that those staff are suitably qualified, trained and appraised and supervised (reg 15).

A staff handbook must be provided (reg 16). The member of staff to be supplied to a service user should be identified (reg 17) and carry suitable identification (reg 18).

8.4.5.4 *Records*
Regulation 19 specifies that there is a duty on the registered person to hold the records set out in Sch 4 to the Regulations. Specific reference should be made to Sch 4. The records must contain details of all financial records, information provided to the Commission for the purposes of registration, details of allegations of abuse or neglect or other harm, their investigation and outcome of those investigations, physical restraint and the care plans.

8.4.5.5 *Complaints*
There is an obligation on the registered person to ensure that a complaints procedure is in place. He must ensure the complaints are investigated and that the outcome of the complaint is notified to the complainant. Records of the complaint, the investigations and the outcome must be kept. A summary must be provided to the Commission if requested (reg 20).

8.4.5.6 *Comment and review*

A system must be introduced and maintained to review quality of service provision, and must provide for consultation (reg 21). No frequency for these reviews is specified in the Regulations, however the relevant standard (27) suggests that standards and the Quality Assurance process are reviewed and revised on an annual basis.

8.4.5.7 *Premises*

The registered person has a duty to ensure that the agency premises are suitable for its objectives and that they are sound and safe (reg 22).

8.4.5.8 *Notices*

The Commission is to be notified of various matters. There is an obligation to report any absence in excess of 28 days of either the registered provider or the registered manager (reg 24). There is a duty to notify changes in the running of the agency to the Commission (reg 25). Finally, there is a duty to notify the appointment of a liquidator or similar person to the Commission. That duty falls upon the liquidator (reg 26).

8.4.5.9 *Further offences*

Regulation 28 imposes a duty on a registered person to comply with the Regulations. Where there is more than one registered person the duty is satisfied if compliance is achieved by the other.

Finally, reg 29 makes it an offence to fail to comply with regulations 4–6 and 11–25, providing notice of the breach is given and the registered person has an opportunity to comply with the Regulations.

8.5 FOSTERING AGENCIES

8.5.1 Introduction

The definition of a 'fostering agency' is set out in s 4(4) of the 2000 Act:

(4) 'Fostering agency' means, subject to subsection (6)

(a) an undertaking which consists of or includes discharging functions of local authorities in connection with the placing of children with foster parents; or

(b) a voluntary organisation which places children with foster parents under section 59(1) of the 1989 Act.

The regulations and standards replace the Foster Placement (Children) Regulations 1991, SI 1991/910. They are applicable to local authority fostering services, independent fostering agencies and voluntary organizations providing fostering services under s 59 of the Children Act 1989.

The National Minimum Standards for Fostering Services were issued in March 2002. The Fostering Services Regulations 2002, SI 2002/57, came into force on 1 April 2002.

8.5.2 The standards

8.5.2.1 *Standard 1*

- There should be a clear statement of the aims and objectives of the fostering service and the fostering service is to ensure that those aims and objectives are met.
- Where the agency is not a local authority the statement should be approved by the registered provider. In the case of a local authority it should be approved by the elected members.
- The statement is to include matters contained in standard 1.4, including the status and constitution of the agency, the management structure, the service provided, the aims, objective principles and standards of care, the staff, the foster carers, number of children placed, complaints, financial position and procedure.

8.5.2.2 *Standards 2–3*

- The fostering service is to be carried on and managed by those with appropriate skills and experience to do so efficiently and effectively and by those who are suitable to work with children.
- The manager must have either NVQ level 4 or the DipSW or equivalent and qualification in NVQ management or equivalent by 2005, and at least two years' experience of working with children in the last five years and in addition at least one year's experience of working at a senior level.
- The checks on managers set out in the regulations should be made and repeated every three years and a record kept of their taking and the outcome.

8.5.2.3 *Standards 4 and 5*

- The fostering service is to be managed ethically and efficiently, delivering a good quality foster care service within the resources available and avoiding confusion and conflicts of role.
- There should be clear procedures for monitoring and controlling the activities of the service and ensuring quality of performance.
- The financial processes and systems should be properly operated and maintained.
- Information should be provided to the purchasers of services and others to include charges, statements of amounts paid to foster carers and itemized amounts for wider services, including health and education.

8.5.2.4 *Standards 6–13*

- The fostering service should promote and safeguard the child/young person's physical, mental and emotional welfare.
- The foster carer's home and transport should be secure.

- If the child is being abused by or abuses another child, the child should have his own room.
- Written guidelines or health and safety responsibilities should be provided by the agency.
- Foster carers should be told they may be interviewed or visited as part of the Commission's inspection process.
- The fostering service is to ensure that children and young people and their families are provided with foster care services which value diversity and promote equality.
- Children with a disability can receive services and support to help maximize potential.
- Each child should be given encouragement and access to opportunities to develop and pursue the child's interests and hobbies.
- The fostering service should ensure that each child or young person placed in foster care is provided with a carer capable of meeting that child's needs.
- Where a trans-racial or trans-community placement is made the fostering service should provide the foster family with training, support and information so as to enable the child to be provided with the best possible care to develop a positive understanding of his heritage.
- The fostering service should protect each child or young person from abuse, neglect, exploitation or deprivation.
- Corporal punishment is not acceptable and this should be made plain to foster carers.
- The fostering service should make sure that each child/young person in foster care is encouraged to maintain and develop family contacts and friendships.
- The fostering service should ensure that provision of health care to the child is made.
- The fostering service should give a high priority to meeting the educational needs of each child.
- The fostering service should ensure that foster care services help to develop the skills, confidence and knowledge of the child necessary for adult living.

8.5.2.5 *Standards 14–22*

- The people who work in or for the fostering service must be suitable to work with children and young people and must be managed, trained and supported appropriately.
- The number of staff and carers and their range of qualifications and experience must be sufficient to achieve the purposes and functions of the organization.
- Staff are to be organized and managed in a way which delivers the best possible foster care service within the resources available.
- Local authority fostering services that use agencies must check that agency arrangements for assessment and approval are satisfactory.

- Where local authority fostering services use an agency they must have a system to ensure quality control.
- The fostering service should have an adequate number of sufficiently experienced and qualified staff and recruit a range of carers to meet the needs of children and young people for whom it aims to provide a service.
- There should be an assessment process for carers, which should take into account those matters identified in reg 16.7.
- The fostering services are to be fair and competent employers with sound employment practices and good support for staff and carers.
- There is to be training and appraisal of all staff.
- All staff employed by the fostering services must be properly accountable and supported.
- The fostering service is to provide effective management and supervision for its staff and have a clear strategy for working with and supporting carers.
- There should be supervision of and support for foster carers.
- Foster carers who move from local registers following investigations for abuse are to be referred to the Department of Health POCA list.
- The fostering service should ensure that foster carers are trained in the necessary skills.

8.5.2.6 *Standards 23 and 24*

- All appropriate records must be kept and must be accessible in relation to the fostering services and the individual foster carers and foster children.
- The foster carer must be trained and provided with the necessary equipment to report significant life events of the child and to encourage the child in that process.
- The fostering service's administrative records must contain all significant information relevant to the running of the foster care service as is required by the Regulations.

8.5.2.7 *Standard 25*

- Premises used as offices by the fostering services must be appropriate.
- Those premises should have proper facilities for the secure retention of records, appropriate measures to safeguard IT systems and a security alarm system.

8.5.2.8 *Standards 26 and 27*

- The fostering services are financially viable and appropriate payments are made to the foster carers.
- The financial processes/systems of the agency should be properly operated and maintained in accordance with appropriate standards and practices.

8.5.3 Fostering Services Regulations 2002

8.5.3.1 *General*

Two sets of fostering agency are covered by the Regulations (SI 2002/57). First, a non-local authority fostering agency, which includes a voluntary organization within s 59(1) of the Children Act 1989, and secondly, a local authority fostering service. Where the former type of fostering agency is referred to there has to be a registered person. There is no such requirement in relation to the local authority fostering service.

The former, but not the latter, have to be registered under the 2000 Act.

However, both local authorities and fostering agencies must provide a statement of purpose within reg 3. This statement must be kept under review and the commission must be notified of any change. It must be made available to any employee, foster parent and prospective foster parent of the fostering service, the child placed with the foster parent by the fostering service and any parent of such a child. The fostering service provider has a duty to ensure that a fostering service is provided in a manner consistent with the statement of purpose.

8.5.3.2 *Registered persons and management of local authority fostering services*

In the case of a fostering agency there is an obligation to register the person carrying on the agency. In the case of a company a responsible individual has to be nominated. The registered provider must appoint an individual to manage the fostering agency. Both the registered person (or responsible individual) and the manager must establish their fitness, as discussed at 8.3.5 above.

A local authority is obliged to appoint one of its officers to manage the fostering service and notify the Commission of that appointment. Requirements as to fitness in respect of a manager are equally applicable to a local authority.

The registered person or responsible individual, or manager in the case of a local authority, has a duty to notify the Commission of any criminal events.

8.5.3.3 *Conduct of fostering services*

Regulation 11 imposes a duty on the registered person (which term, of course, includes the registered provider in the case of an independent agency and the manager in the case of a local authority service), to ensure that the welfare of children placed or to be placed with foster parents is safeguarded and promoted at all times. Consideration is to be given to the child's 'wishes and feelings in the light of his age and understanding' and the child's religious, racial, cultural and linguistic background.

The fostering service provider (again this term includes local authorities) should draft a written child protection policy for the purpose of safeguarding children placed with foster parents from abuse and neglect, setting out the procedure to be followed in the case of any allegation of such a matter. There are detailed requirements for the procedure which applies in relation to a private provider (reference should be made to reg 12(2)).

There is also a duty to draw up a written policy on acceptable measures of control, restraint and discipline of children placed with foster parents (reg 13). This duty is placed upon the fostering service provider. That policy must preclude any form of corporal punishment and only allow physical restraint for the prevention of injury to the child or other persons or serious damage to property. There should also be a written policy about children absconding from the foster parents' home.

There are also duties upon the fostering service provider to permit contact between children and their natural parents (reg 14), to promote the health and development of children (reg 15) and to promote high standards of educational attainment of children (reg 16).

The fostering service provider is obliged to provide foster parents with 'suitable and sufficient' training, advice, information and support, including out of hours support (reg 17). That duty entails a requirement to ensure that foster parents are familiar with and act in accordance with the written policies in relation to child protection and discipline. The provider should also ensure that appropriate information is given in respect of any child placed or to be placed with a foster parent (reg 17).

The registered person of an independent fostering agency has a duty to ensure that there is a proper complaints procedure, but that it is not intended to displace any provision of the Representations Procedure (Children) Regulation 1991 (SI 1991/894 as amended by SI 1991/2033 and SI 1993/3069).

8.5.3.4 *Staffing (regs 19–21)*
The fostering service provider has a duty to ensure that there is adequate staffing and that the staff employed by it are fit, as discussed at 8.3.5 above. There must also be a period of probation in relation to permanent appointments, a job description and person specification and a staff disciplinary procedure. It must be provided that the disciplinary procedure includes a failure to report an incident of abuse to an appropriate person, ie manager of fostering services, child's social worker, an officer of the Commission, a police officer or an officer of the National Society for the Prevention of Cruelty to Children. The provider must make arrangements for training, supervision and appraisal and also make arrangements so as to ensure that unlawful discrimination is prevented and a policy of opportunity is promoted.

8.5.3.5 *Records (regs 22–25)*
The fostering service provider has a duty to maintain case records for each foster parent and to keep a register of foster carers and details of approval and review of approval. On that register there should also be entered the name and address of every person with whom a child has been placed for emergency provision. There is also a duty to retain and keep confidential the records held.

8.5.3.6 *Premises (reg 26)*
A fostering service must operate from suitable office premises. Those premises have to be adequately secured, as do the records contained within them.

8.5.3.7 *Approval of foster parents (regs 27–32)*

This task is remitted to a combination of a fostering panel and an assessment carried out by the fostering service provider.

All fostering service providers are required to establish fostering panels. The task of the fostering panel is to consider applications for approval and to make recommendations and to carry out reviews.

The fostering panel should comprise no more than ten members. It is to be chaired by a senior member of staff of the fostering service provider or by someone, who is not an employee, member or director of the fostering service, who has the skills and experience necessary to chair the panel. The remaining members should comprise two social workers, in the case of a fostering agency at least one of the directors or responsible individual, and in the case of a local authority one elected member of the authority, a foster parent from another fostering service provider, and either someone with experience and expertise in child health, a representative of the community in which the fostering service is situated or which it serves or a person above the age of 18 who has been placed with foster parents or whose child has been placed with foster parents. Further details of the membership of the foster panel are set out in reg 27.

In addition, as noted above, the fostering service provider is obliged to assess the suitability of any person applying to be a foster parent. The detailed requirements of that assessment are set out in reg 30. There are provisions relating to notice to be given to a potential foster parent who is deemed to be unsuitable and an opportunity for them to make representations (reg 30). There is a duty upon the fostering service provider to review the approval of each foster parent every year.

8.5.3.8 *Placements (regs 33–41)*

The duty falls on all responsible authorities, that is the local authority or voluntary organisation responsible for the child's placement, to approve that placement and to enter into a written foster placement agreement with the foster parent, which must contain matters set out in Sch 6. Thereafter, the responsible authority must supervise the placement and not allow it to continue if it no longer is the most suitable way of performing its duty. Many of these duties can be delegated to independent fostering agencies (reg 41).

There are provisions for both short term and immediate placements by local authorities.

8.5.3.9 *Local authority visits (reg 42)*

A duty is placed upon local authorities to visit every child who is placed with a foster parent within their area by a voluntary organization within 28 days of placement and every six months thereafter. The precise details as to visiting are set out in reg 42(1). If the local authority has any concerns it has a duty to report them to the Commission.

8.5.3.10 *Miscellaneous (regs 43–49)*

Regulation 43 imposes a duty to monitor various aspects of placement upon the registered person.

There is a duty to notify various authorities of serious events, such as the death of a child or a complaint relating to child abuse (see Sch 9 and reg 44).

The registered provider has a duty to ensure the financial viability of the organization, to supply a copy of the accounts certified by the accountant to the Commission and to provide certain other information as to the agency's financial position (reg 45).

There is a duty to notify the absence of the registered manager for more than 28 days; to give notice of changes as to the management of the agency (reg 47) and a duty upon a liquidator or similar person to notify their appointment to the Commission.

8.5.3.11 *Offences (reg 50)*

Breach of the Regulations, provided that notice has been duly given and the time has expired for complying with that notice, is an offence (reg 50).

8.6 VOLUNTARY ADOPTION AGENCIES

8.6.1 General

A voluntary adoption agency means an adoption society within the meaning of the Adoption Act 1976 and which is a voluntary organization within the meaning of that Act (s 4(7) of the 2000 Act).

A voluntary adoption agency is a non-profit making organization approved by the Secretary of State for Health to provide an adoption service. That service may include the recruitment and assessment of prospective adopters, the approval of prospective adopters and the provision of a counselling service.

Additional services may also be provided, such as training, supervision and guardian ad litem work.

8.6.2 Standards

A statement of National Minimum Standards was published jointly by the Department of Health and the Welsh Assembly Government under ss 23(1) and 49(1) of the 2000 Act. These standards apply from 30 April 2003. The statement is applicable to voluntary adoption agencies (as defined by s 4(7) of the 2000 Act) and local authority adoption services (as defined by s 43(3)(a)) and both are referred to as 'adoption agencies' in the statement.

Many of the requirements of managers and staff (such as fitness and training), as well as requirements as to a statement of purpose, information, reviews and records are similar to those specified in the standards and regulations above.

8.6.2.1 *Standard 1*

- There should be a clear statement of the aims and objectives of the adoption agency (statement of purpose) and the agency is to ensure that those aims and objectives are met.

8.6.2.2 *Standard 2. Securing and Promoting Children's Welfare*

- Children are to be matched with adopters who best meet their assessed needs.
- The adoptive placement should reflect the child's ethnic and cultural background, religion and language. It should also allow the child to live with brothers and sisters if appropriate

8.6.2.3 *Standards 3–6. Prospective and Approved Adopters*

- The adoptive agency is to recruit and support adopters from diverse backgrounds. Copies of written eligibility criteria, information on becoming adoptive parents, and what is expected of adopters should be provided
- Prospective adopters are to be assessed and checked, and are to include status, health, and enhanced Criminal Record Bureau (CRB) checks.
- Personal references and other inquiries are needed.
- Prospective adopters are to receive written information about matching, introductions, and the placement process. They are to provide information for the child about themselves, eg, their home and pets.
- The adoptive agency will provide information advice and support to prospective adopters.

8.6.2.4 *Standards 7–9. Birth Parents and Birth Families*

- Birth parents are to be involved in adoption plans, and their views sought.
- To maintain the child's heritage, work will be done with the birth parents to obtain clear and appropriate information.
- The adoption agency must have a clear strategy for working with and supporting birth parents and families both before and after adoption.

8.6.2.5 *Standards 10–13. Adoption Panels and Agency Decisions*

- Functions of the adoption panels are outlined.
- The constitution and membership of the panel, and training and appropriateness of panel members, are outlined.
- Panels will meet regularly and their decisions should be made and conveyed without delay.

8.6.2.6 *Standards 14–15 . Fitness to provide or manage an adoption agency*

- Those involved in carrying on and managing the adoption agency must possess knowledge and experience of child care law and practice. They must have management skills and financial expertise.

- The manager must have a professional qualification, either NVQ level 4, DipSW or equivalent.
- The person carrying on or managing the adoption agency must be a suitable person, and must have a satisfactory enhanced disclosure from the CRB.
- CRB checks are repeated every three years.

8.6.2.7 *Standards 16–18. Provision and Management of the adoption agency*

- The agency is to be run effectively and efficiently, and in accordance with the statement of purpose.
- There are to be clear written procedures for monitoring and controlling the activities of the adoption agency.
- Information to be provided to purchasers of services includes charges for its services and statements of any amounts paid to adopters.
- The adoption agency should have specialist advisers, eg, medical and legal.

8.6.2.8 *Standards 19–21. Employment and Management of Staff*

- All people working in or for the agency are interviewed as part of the selection process and have written references checked to assess suitability before taking up duties.
- CRB checks are to be made on all staff, including temporary workers.
- No one shall start work until satisfactory references and CRB checks are complete.
- All social workers shall have a DipSW or equivalent and a good understanding of adoption, including up-to-date knowledge of relevant statutes.
- Staff policies are to encourage retention of salaried staff by providing support, training and services.
- There is a written whistleblowing policy made known to all staff.
- There is to be a clear and good quality training programme.
- All new staff are to be given induction programmes within seven days of their start.
- The agency is to keep staff abreast of changes in law and guidance relevant to their job.
- The standard relating to the making of complaints (standard 24) applies to voluntary adoption agencies only.

8.6.2.9 *Standards 25–28. Records*

- Appropriate records are to be maintained securely and are accessible as required.
- Comprehensive and accurate case records are to be maintained for each child, and for prospective and approved adopters with whom the agency has worked.

- Records are to be kept of status, health and CRB checks, and written references and inquiries.
- The adoption agency is to provide records as requested and promptly to other adoption agencies and local authorities.
- Personnel files are to be maintained for each member of staff and member of the adoption panel.

8.6.2.10 *Standard 29. Fitness of Premises*

- There must be identifiable office premises.
- There are to be efficient and robust administrative systems.

8.6.2.11 *Standards 30–31. Financial Viability*

- The agency is to ensure it is financially viable and has sufficient financial resources (voluntary adoption agencies only).
- Financial systems must be maintained in accordance with sound and appropriate accounting standards and practice (voluntary adoption agencies only).

8.6.3 Regulations

As mentioned at 8.1.5 above, two sets of regulations were brought into force on 30 April 2003, the Voluntary Adoption Agencies and the Adoption Agencies (Miscellaneous Amendments) Regulations 2003, and the Local Authority Adoption Service (England) Regulations 2003.

9

HOSPITALS AND CLINICS

9.1 HOSPITALS—GENERAL

An independent hospital to which the 2000 Act applies, excludes NHS hospitals (s 2(2)). An independent hospital is defined in s 2(3) as:

(a) an establishment –
    (i) the main purpose of which is to provide medical or psychiatric treatment for illness or mental disorder or palliative care; or
    (ii) in which (whether or not other services are also provided) any of the listed services are provided;
(b) any other establishment in which treatment or nursing (or both) are provided for persons liable to be detained under the Mental Health Act 1983.

'Listed services' means (s 2(7)):

(a) medical treatment under anaesthesia or sedation;
(b) dental treatment under general anaesthesia;
(c) obstetric services and, in connection with childbirth, medical services;
(d) termination of pregnancy;
(e) cosmetic surgery;
(f) treatment using prescribed techniques or prescribed technology.

Regulations may be made excepting any description of establishment from the definition of hospital and modifying the extent of 'listed services' within subs (7) (s 2(8)).

Independent hospitals do not include nursing homes.

It is intended that the Commission will co-operate with the Commission for

Health Improvement (CHI). Thus, according to the Independent Health Care National Minimum Standards and Regulations, where the CHI has concerns about the quality of care provided at a private hospital which has a contract with an NHS trust, it will be able to pass on that information to the Commission. In addition, s 9 of the 2000 Act will empower the Secretary of State to make regulations to set out functions which either the Commission or CHI may exercise on behalf of the other. However, it is anticipated that this will not happen for the next two years.

9.2 HOSPITALS—STANDARDS

The standards provide for core standards which will apply to all independent health care providers. There is then provision for specific standards which apply to the various entities within the independent health care service. These core standards are addressed below, and the specific standards mentioned in summary form only.

9.2.1 Standard C1 Information Provision

Patients are to receive clear and accurate information about their treatment. Advertisements must meet the requirements of the Advertising Standards Authority. Information given to the media must respect the confidentiality of the patients, their families, carers and staff.

9.2.2 Standards C2–C7 Quality of Treatment and Care

The registered person (as to which see Standard C8) is to have policies and procedures to ensure that the care provided is patient-centred. Those policies and procedures should include:

- timely, appropriate and accurate assessment and diagnosis of health needs;
- consent by a patient to all intimate examinations and the offer of a chaperone if undergoing such examinations;
- consultation with patients and relatives about the planning and delivery of services;
- access to health records;
- patients' rights should be central to the resuscitation policy;
- facilitation of access by people of different cultural, ethnic and mobility backgrounds;
- clinical procedures should be explained and written consent should be obtained before the administration of treatment which involves significant risk or side effects.

Treatment should be provided in line with relevant clinical guidelines.

Patients should be assured that monitoring of the quality of treatment and care takes place and appropriate written policies and procedures are set out, which should include such matters as clinical audits, assessment of the outcomes of clinical and nursing audits and a complaints procedure.

Dying and the death of patients should be handled in an appropriate and sensitive manner.

A patient's view should be obtained by the establishment and used to inform the provision of treatment and care to prospective patients. This observation includes the requirement that there are regular patient surveys.

All policies and procedures should be in place and available to all members of staff. This includes a duty to evaluate practice against policy and procedures at least every three years.

9.2.3 Standards C8–C13 Management and Personnel

Patients are to be assured that the establishment is run by a fit person and that there is a clear line of accountability for the delivery of services. The person 'carrying on' the establishment is the registered provider, and must be registered with the NCSC. If that person does not run the business on a day to day basis (for example where the registered provider is a company or a charity), then a manager (registered manager) is appointed and also must be registered with the NCSC.

The obligation on the manager of the establishment is to demonstrate that he or she has had training and there must be a job description setting out the responsibilities of the manager. There must be clear lines of accountability and the manager must ensure that all relevant certificates and licences which are required are obtained and kept up-to-date and displayed.

Patients are to receive care from appropriately recruited, trained and qualified staff. This entails the provision of a human resource policy and procedures which, inter alia, govern advertising, recruitment, induction and employment of staff. There should also be an application pack which requires potential staff to declare their status in relation to fitness to practise and whether or not they have been the subject of any police investigation or conviction. There is to be provision for interview, proof of registration by a relevant professional body, confirmation of identity, continuing training, effective induction and review. There should also be a policy on equality of opportunity.

Patients are to receive treatment from appropriately recruited, trained, and qualified clinicians and practitioners. In addition to the keeping of information about registration, training and fitness to practise in relation to practitioners, there is also a duty to ensure that there is a written agreement setting out the details of practising privileges and compliance with the complaints procedure between the establishment and the practitioner.

There is an obligation on all clinical staff to abide by published codes of professional practice. Clinical staff and practitioners are obliged to take part in the ongoing continual professional development organized by their various specialist colleges. Their accreditation status should be checked annually.

There is a duty to ensure that personnel are not infected by viruses such as Hepatitis B, Hepatitis C and HIV. If they are, they are not to be permitted to undertake any exposure-prone procedure. They are to provide documentary evidence of their vaccination status with regard to Hepatitis B. There are to be written instructions requiring them to inform the registered manager as soon as they become aware of the carrying of any blood-borne viruses.

Where children are treated there are to be child protection procedures in place.

9.2.4 Standards C14–C16 Complaints Management

Patients should have access to an effective complaints process. That process should provide for acknowledgement within two working days of receipt of the complaint and a full response within 20 working days of the complaint. If there is any delay, that should be notified to the complainant.

Patients should receive appropriate information about how to make a complaint.

Staff should be able to express their concerns about questionable or poor practice and raise concerns within the Public Interest Disclosure Act 1998.

9.2.5 Standards C17–C19 Premises, Facilities and Equipment

Patients are to receive treatment in premises that are safe and appropriate for that treatment.

Within this obligation there is a duty to comply with all matters relating to maintenance, fail-safe emergency advice, requirements of the fire authority and the environmental health department, disabled access, lighting, changing room facilities, access to single sex toilets and washing facilities, safe temperatures in relation to hot water supplies and heating appliances, cleanliness, hygiene, waste and records of passenger lifts and all pressure vessels.

There is a similar duty in relation to equipment and food, so that patients receive treatment using equipment that is safe, and appropriate catering services.

9.2.6 Standards C20–C28 Risk Management Procedures

There is an obligation to ensure that patients, staff and visitors to the premises are assured that all risks connected with the establishment, treatment and services are identified, assessed and managed appropriately.

To this end there must be a comprehensive written risk management policy and supporting procedures. These include having arrangements in place for dealing with 'alert letters'. There must be a procedure in place for informing the Commission about the suspension of staff or practitioners' practising privileges. There must be named members of staff to receive information from the Medical Devices Agency and from the Medicines Control Agency.

Appropriate health and safety measures are to be in place. These include written procedures for the classification, storage, collection, transport and disposal of waste, with a written procedure for the interruption of the medical gas line. There is an obligation to comply with various protective legislation. Staff should be provided with protective equipment and clothing. There should be a policy on the moving and handling of patients. Needle-stick injuries should be recorded.

There should be appropriate measures to ensure the safe management and handling of medicines.

Medicines, dressings and medical gases are to be handled in a safe and secure fashion.

Patients are not to be treated with contaminated medical devices.

There is to be a written policy on resuscitation. Interestingly, patients who do not wish to be resuscitated should have their wishes observed.

There must be written, dated and signed contracts in place which relate to the supply and provision of goods and services to the establishment and a policy audit of those services and goods must be provided.

9.2.7 Standards C29–C31 Records and Information Management

Records are to be created, maintained and stored in accordance with the Data Protection Act 1998. There should be a nominated post-holder for the updating and safekeeping of specific sets of records.

There should be appropriately completed health records for patients, which should be dated, timed and signed. The signature should be accompanied by the name and designation of the signatory. Those records should be legible.

There should be a written information management policy.

9.2.8 Standard 32 Research

There must be a written policy which states whether or not research is carried out in the establishment. If research is being carried out, there must be written procedures governing it. Research projects must be conducted within the relevant Department of Health research governance framework.

There must be documented agreements in place with the delegation of responsibilities in relation to such projects. A lead professional must be nominated for each project who is responsible for the management and monitoring of the project.

There must be a written agreement for the ownership, exploitation and income from any intellectual property that arises from the research. Records must be kept of all research projects, including information about patients involved, for 15 years after the conclusion of the project.

Finally, the consent or authorization must be obtained for the participation of any patient in any research project.

9.2.9 Standard service—specific standards

In the scope of this book it is not possible to set out the specific standards relating to the five specific types of establishment which constitute hospitals, namely acute hospitals, mental health establishments, hospices, maternity hospitals, termination of pregnancy establishments, and prescribed techniques and technologies. However, it is proper to consider each area, albeit with only a very broad brush. The reader is referred to the standards contained in the Independent Health Care National Minimum Standards and Regulations for specific matters. See appendix 3 for a convenient reference.

9.2.9.1 *Acute hospitals (Standards A1–A45)*

The standards specify that they apply to:

- establishments where one or more overnight beds are provided and the main purpose of which is to provide medical treatment for illness (subject to certain exceptions (reg 3(2) of SI 2001/3968);
- other establishments the main purpose of which is to provide medical treatment under anaesthesia and sedation.

The common theme that runs through the standards is:

There must be assurance about the quality of the treatment and services the patients receive and appropriate safeguards must be in place. To this end, the key elements throughout the standards are that all those who work within acute hospitals must be suitably qualified, trained and competent, that the right mix of workers for the particular clinical services is in place, and safe and appropriate equipment is used.

There are a total of 45 standards relating to acute hospitals. They cover information provision, staffing, risk management, infection control, decontamination, resuscitation, resuscitation equipment, child services, surgery, critical care, radiology, pharmacy, storage and supply of medical gases, pathology services and cancer services.

9.2.9.2 *Mental health establishments (Standards M1–M47)*

The standards apply to a range of premises where mental health treatment is provided.

With the exception of Standard 1 (Working with the Mental Health National Service Framework), the standards for mental health establishments apply to those establishments providing mental health services for children and adolescents.

The standards fall into two categories. First, those that apply to all mental health establishments, including those for children and adolescents, covered in the definition of 'independent hospitals'; secondly, those that in addition apply to mental health establishments that can take people liable to be detained (including children and adolescents).

The standards do not apply to care homes, but to establishments that mainly provide counselling or psychiatrists' consulting rooms.

There are 47 standards in all relating to mental health establishments. They cover the following areas: the overall management of mental health services; staffing; risk management; patient treatment and care; additional standards for child and adolescent mental health services; and those applicable to establishments for those detained under the Mental Health Act 1983.

9.2.9.3 *Hospices (Standards H1–H15)*
The standards apply to establishments the main purpose of which is to provide palliative care. Such establishments are for convenience referred to as 'hospices'.

The standards address two issues. First, 'the need to respond to issues with a sense of urgency as time is limited for the patient nearing the end of their life. Second, the often complex and diverse needs of both the patient and their carers need to be met by access to a multi-professional specialist palliative care team ...'

The standards are divided into two sections. The first covers standards that apply to both adults and childrens' hospices. The second contains additional standards applicable to childrens' hospices only.

There are 15 standards in all. They cover hospices generally, palliative care expertise and training for multi-professional teams, assessments of patients' and carers' needs, delivery of palliative care, records, infection control, resuscitation, responsibility of pharmaceutical services, medicines and medical gases. The additional standards for childrens' hospices cover the assessment and care of children, staff and environment.

9.2.9.4 *Maternity hospitals (Standards MC1–MC8)*
The standards apply to establishments which provide obstetric services and/or services provided in connection with childbirth. For convenience these establishments are referred to as maternity hospitals.

The standards reflect the important factors in ensuring patients receive safe and effective maternity services. They are:

- recognition of the special nature of the clinical care involved;
- ensuring that those involved in providing the services are appropriately qualified and trained;
- recognition of the role of GPs, midwives and obstetricians;
- ensuring that urgent and emergency procedures can take place quickly and safely;
- ensuring that the routine and special needs of the mother and newborn baby are met.

There are a total of eight standards. They relate to staffing, record management, antenatal care, additional standards for midwife-led units, childbirth, maternal death or stillbirth and care of the newborn baby.

9.2.9.5 *Termination of pregnancy establishments (Standards TP1–TP5)*

These standards apply to what are known as abortion clinics. Currently, proprietors will have had to ensure compliance with the Abortion Act 1968, as amended, and the Department's Required Standard Operating Principles.

The new standards are to ensure that:

- services comply with the requirements of the Abortion Act;
- appropriate information is provided to those seeking or obtaining an abortion; and
- information is provided to help facilitate the inspection of services.

The Independent Health Care National Minimum Standards and Regulations observe that women need objective sources of information about abortion and the possible alternatives and they should not feel pressurized. Additionally, because abortions are generally day care procedures, complications might develop or women who have undergone abortions might suffer pain or be anxious as to how much bleeding might be expected. It is important that they are given contact telephone numbers to ring for advice.

There are five applicable standards. They relate to quality of treatment and care, information for patients, privacy and confidentiality for patients, respect for foetal tissue and emergency procedures.

9.2.9.6 *Prescribed techniques and technologies (Standards P1–P16)*

Establishments which provide the treatments set out below will be caught by the standards. They are as follows:

- class 3B and 4 lasers and/or intensive pulsed light sources (P1–P3);
- dialysis (P4–P6);
- endoscopy;
- hyperbaric oxygen treatment/therapy (P7–P11);
- in vitro fertilization (P12–P16).

Standards P1–P3 will regulate the delivery of laser or intensive light source treatment. They are used, for example, in acute hospitals; in dental treatment; beauty salons; for the removal of hair, tattoos, birthmarks and other skin blemishes. The standards are to ensure, inter alia, that there are clear lines of responsibility on the use of lasers and intense lights, and clear policies and procedures on the maintenance of the relevant equipment. Users are to undergo specialized training and learning. They must maintain an effective core of knowledge, effective record-keeping, safe working areas, protective eye-wear and other risk avoidance measures.

Standards P4–P6 relate to the provision of dialysis. Haemodialysis and peritoneal dialysis are carried out in such diverse places as acute hospitals, holiday sites and private satellite units under contract to the NHS. The standards do not apply to dialysis that takes place in private homes.

The standards are designed to address the need for safety and appropriate procedures, to ensure that the environment is safe and appropriate, staff have relevant expertise and that there are procedures for the control of infection.

Endoscopy includes the use of both flexible and rigid endoscopes. These are medical devices inserted into the body for diagnostic or surgical purposes. Flexible endoscopy uses the body's natural orifices, and involves general procedures for investigation of the internal organs. Rigid endoscopy is more commonly known as keyhole surgery and includes arthroscopy, laproscopy, hysteroscopy and cystoscopy. The relevant standards are those relating to medical devices and decontamination, which will be found in these four standards and those for acute hospitals.

Hyperbaric oxygen treatment (P7–P11) is the inhalation of pure oxygen through a mask while in a sealed chamber which is gradually pressurized with compressed air until the pressure inside the chamber reaches the desired level. This is usually one atmosphere, which equates to being ten metres under the sea.

The best known use of this treatment is for divers with decompression sickness. However, it has a number of medical uses as well, such as air or gas embolism. It is also used in the treatment for the sufferers of multiple sclerosis, although such treatment is yet to gain approval from orthodox medicine. The treatment poses a safety risk if chambers are incorrectly operated. There is an obvious risk of fire and strict control is needed to minimize the presence of flammable matters and materials.

The standards, which will apply to all multi-place and mono-place chambers (save for very limited exemptions), relate to the arrangements for treatment in accordance with appropriate procedures, staff qualifications and training for multi-place chambers with facilities for treatment or therapy. It should be noted that only the arrangements (standard 8) apply to both multi-place and mono-place chambers.

In vitro fertilization is licensed by the Human Fertilization and Embryology Authority. Establishments providing fertility treatment will be regulated by the 2000 Act. The standards relate to appropriate staffing, treatment, patient information and decision-making, counselling for patients and the provision of facilities for assisted conception services (P12–P16).

9.3 INDEPENDENT CLINICS—GENERAL

Section 2(4) of the 2000 Act defines an 'independent clinic' as:

… an establishment of the prescribed kind (not being a hospital) in which services are provided by medical practitioners (whether or not any services are also provided for the purposes of the establishment elsewhere).

But an establishment in which, or for the purposes of which, services are provided by medical practitioners in pursuance of the National Health Service Act 1977 is not an independent clinic.

'Medical practitioner' means a registered medical practitioner who is registered by the Private and Voluntary Health Care (England) Regulations 2001, SI 2001/3968, reg 2(1). See also the Interpretation Act 1978.

Regulation 4 defines independent clinics as including establishments of the following kinds:

(a) a walk-in centre, in which one or more medical practitioners provide services of a kind which, if provided in pursuance of the NHS Act, would be provided as general medical services under Part II of that Act; and

(b) a surgery or consulting room in which a medical practitioner who provides no services in pursuance of the NHS Act provides medical services of any kind (including psychiatric treatment), otherwise than under arrangements made on behalf of the patients by their employer or another person.

9.4 INDEPENDENT CLINICS—STANDARDS

There are eight standards which apply to independent clinics. They cover the arrangements for provision of treatment, the management of patients, minor surgery, midwifery and antenatal care, prescribing, pathology services, contacting practitioners and out-of-hours services and information to GPs.

The specific standards applicable to independent medical agencies are dealt with in chapter 8 above.

9.4.1 Private and Voluntary Health Care (England) Regulations 2001

These Regulations, which came into force on 1 April 2002, apply to both independent medical agencies and establishments. The specific requirements relating to an independent medical agency are dealt with in chapter 8.

This section covers the more general requirements that apply to both agencies and establishments.

9.4.1.1 *Definitions (regs 1–5)*

The term 'establishment' includes both independent hospitals and independent clinics.

A general practitioner is someone who either provides general medical services under Pt II of the NHS Act 1977, or performs personal medical services in connection with a pilot scheme under the NHS (Primary Care) Act 1997 or provides services 'which correspond' to services provided under Pt II of the NHS Act. A medical practitioner means a medical practitioner registered with the General Medical Council (GMC), so it is, therefore, clear that the practitioner who provides services 'corresponding' to Pt II services means only a doctor registered with the GMC.

A 'health care professional' is a person who is registered as a member of any profession covered by s 60(2) of the Health Act 1999. This includes, amongst others, a pharmacist, dentist, optician, osteopath, chiropractor and midwife. It also covers professions regulated by the Professions Supplementary to Medicine Act 1960 and other professions regulated by Order in Council under the provisions of s 60(2) of the Health Act 1999. A clinical psychologist or child psychotherapist is also included within the definition. See reg 2(1)(c).

In relation to the definition of 'independent hospital' it should be noted that the list of prescribed techniques or technologies includes 'broad band non-coherent light .... such filtered radiation being delivered to the body with the aim of causing thermal, mechanical or chemical damage...'. Plainly, cosmetic alteration is being targeted.

The decompression of divers or decompression chambers used for the treatment of workers in connection with their work is excepted from hyperbaric oxygen therapy (reg 3(3)(e)).

The list of 'listed services' includes haemodialysis, peritoneal dialysis, endoscopy and in vitro fertilization techniques.

The definition of independent hospitals excludes:

- an establishment which is a hospital solely because its main purpose is to provide medical or psychiatric treatment for illness and mental disorder and which provides no overnight beds;
- an establishment which is a service hospital;
- an establishment which is or forms part of a prison, remand centre, young offender institution or secure training centre;
- an independent clinic;
- establishments which have as their sole or main purpose the provision by a GP of general medical services under Pt II of the NHS Act 1977;
- the private residence of a patient or patients;
- sports grounds;
- gymnasia where health professionals provide treatment to persons taking part in sporting activities and events;
- a surgery or consulting room where medical services are provided at the behest of an employer or similar person (reg 3(3)).

Section 2(7) of the 2000 Act excludes cosmetic surgery which involves ear and body piercing, tattooing, subcutaneous injection into the skin for cosmetic purposes and the removal of hair roots or small blemishes on the skin by the use of an electric current.

In relation to independent clinics, reg 4(2) makes plain that where there are two or more medical practitioners using different parts of the same premises as a surgery or consulting room, each of them shall be regarded as carrying on separate independent clinics unless they are in practice together.

9.4.1.2 *Statement of purpose, patient's guide, and policies and procedures (regs 6–9)*

In relation to either an establishment or agency the registered person is to compile and update both a statement of purpose and a patient's guide.

The statement of purpose should contain (reg 6 and Sch 1):

- the aims and objectives;
- the name and address of the registered provider and registered manager (if any);
- the qualifications and experience of the provider or manager;
- the numbers, qualifications and experience of staff;
- the organization and structure;
- the kinds of treatment and services provided;
- the arrangements made for consultation with patients;
- the arrangements made for contact between patients and relatives;
- the arrangements for dealing with complaints; and
- arrangements for respecting the privacy and dignity of patients.

The patient's guide is to include (reg 7):

- a summary of the statement of purpose;
- terms and conditions of service;
- standard form of contract;
- summary of the complaints procedure;
- summary of the result of consultation;
- the contact address and telephone number of the Commission; and
- the most recent inspection report or information as to where that report can be obtained.

In relation to an establishment only, there should be a written statement of policies and procedures relating to the arrangements for the admission of patients, the arrangements for assessment, diagnosis and treatment of patients, the fitness of the premises, the fitness of equipment and facilities, risk assessment procedure, recording procedure, provision of information to patients and the recruitment, induction and retention of employees and their employment conditions. It should also include the relevant policy on the consent of patients where research is carried out. In the cases of both an agency and an establishment the policies should also include provisions relating to the competence of each patient to consent to treatment, the nature of consent, consultation with those patients not competent and a disclosure policy. The written statement of policy and procedure must be reviewed within a space of not more than three years. The policy must be available for inspection by the Commission.

9.4.1.3 *Registered persons (regs 10–14)*

The fitness of registered providers and (where necessary) managers is the same as set out in chapter 8 above in relation to the relevant nurses agency regulations. The duties of the registered person are as referred to in chapter 8 above. The duty to notify the Commission of events is again in similar terms. There is a general obligation on the registered person (whether registered provider or registered manager) to manage with confidence. There is a specific duty on the registered provider to undertake appropriate training or to ensure that training is undertaken where there is an organization or partnership.

9.4.1.4 *Quality of service provision (regs 15–24)*
The registered person is responsible for:

- the quality of treatment;
- the quality of equipment;
- the appropriate procedures for reusable medical devices;
- the administration of drugs;
- the making of arrangements to minimize the risk of infection; and
- if food is provided, to ensure its quality.

There is also a duty to provide for the care and welfare of patients, to review the quality of their treatment and other services provided to them, to ensure that there are an appropriate number of suitably qualified, skilled and experienced persons employed with the corresponding duty to ensure training, supervision and appraisal. This also encompasses an obligation to appraise and address clinical practice and the performance of any other member of staff.

The duty extends to ensuring that no one is employed unless they are fit. Fitness, as is common, is a combination of the necessary experience, physical and mental qualities and the information required by Sch 2 (proof of identity, a police check where necessary, written references, documentary evidence of every qualification, full employment history, evidence of registration and, where work with children is involved, verification of the reason why that work ceased). There is also a duty to ensure that any code of ethics or professional practice issued by a professional body is available (reg 20). Records of patients, required by Pt 2 of Sch 3, are to be kept secure. In addition, there are duties in respect of complaints and in respect of research (regs 23 and 24).

9.4.1.5 *Premises (reg 25)*
Regulation 25 provides that the registered person has a duty in respect of the fitness of premises. That duty extends to the premises themselves, facilities and accommodation for employees and fire precautions.

9.4.1.6 *Management (regs 26–27)*
There is a duty to visit the premises at least once every six months in order to be satisfied as to the standards of treatment. The visits shall be unannounced. There has to be an inspection of records, interviews of patients, their representatives and such employees as seems necessary to form a view of the standard of treatment, and a report prepared on the conduct of the establishment or agency. That report should be supplied, inter alia, to the Commission, registered manager and, where the provider is a company, to each of the directors and other persons responsible for management of the organization (reg 24).

The Commission must be provided with details of the financial position of the establishment or agency (reg 27).

9.4.1.7 *Notices (regs 28–32)*

The Commission should be given a notice of relevant events such as the death of a patient, the outbreak of any infection or disease, or an allegation of misconduct resulting in actual or potential harm to a patient whether by a registered person or employee or any medical practitioner with practising privileges. Notice must be given within 24 hours (reg 28).

There is a provision for giving notice of absence on the part of the registered provider or manager where that absence is going to last for a period of 28 days or more (reg 29). There is also an obligation to give notice to the Commission of various changes in the organizational structure (reg 30) as well as a duty on liquidators to notify the Commission of their appointment (reg 31). That duty extends to the trustee in bankruptcy.

9.4.1.8 *Additional requirements applying to independent hospitals (regs 33–47)*

There are various specific duties applying to independent hospitals where (a) there are overnight beds and the main purpose is to provide medical treatment for illness, and (b) where medical treatment is provided under anaesthesia or sedation.

In essence, the duties relate to the provision of pathology services (reg 34), resuscitation policy (reg 35), and the treatment of children (reg 36).

Where surgical procedures are to be carried out under anaesthesia or sedation, there are obligations relating to the design, equipment and maintenance of operating theatres, staffing, treatment and consent (reg 37).

Where dental treatment is provided under general anaesthesia the regulations require that there are appropriately qualified dentists and employees and adequate facilities, drugs and equipment (reg 38).

Where obstetric services are provided then a Head of Midwifery Services must be appointed. If the hospital is not staffed primarily by midwives a Head of Obstetric Services must be appointed. There must be adequate and expert staff (reg 39). There must also be provision for emergency intervention, intensive care and the treatment of sick patients or newborn children. Any death of a patient or stillborn/neonatal death must be recorded (reg 40).

Where the independent hospital provides a termination of pregnancy service, there is an obligation to comply with the requirements of the Abortion Act 1967. There are various duties as to recording. There are also duties in relation to the giving of notice of a death of a patient (reg 41).

Where the independent hospital provides laser or equivalent treatment, there must be a professional protocol drawn up by a trained and experienced medical practitioner or dentist; the treatment has to be administered by a person who has taken the appropriate training (reg 42).

Where the independent hospital provides medical or psychiatric treatment for mental disorder and where treatment or nursing are provided for persons liable to be detained under the Mental Health Act 1983, various duties have to be observed, including policies and procedures relating to the safety of patients (which include a suicide protocol). The policy should also set out how disturbed behaviour is to be dealt with, including permitted measures of restraint, reporting and the taking of action in relation to such incidents (regs 44–45). There must also be a written procedure in respect of patients receiving visitors (reg 46). There is a duty to ensure that statutory records are kept for a period of not less than five years (reg 47).

9.4.1.9 *Additional requirement applying to independent clinics*
Where independent clinics provide antenatal care to patients, the registered person shall ensure that the health care professional who is primarily responsible for providing that care is a midwife or an appropriately qualified general practitioner or a medical practitioner with a specialist qualification in obstetrics (reg 48).

9.4.1.10 *Miscellaneous*
The provisions of reg 51 provide that the breach of certain regulations constitutes an offence. However, proceedings are not to be brought unless notice has been given and the period specified in the notice has expired. The notice which may be given by the Commission must specify:

(a) in what respect in its opinion the registered person has contravened or is contravening any of the regulations, or his failure to comply with the requirements of any of the regulations;

(b) what action, in the opinion of the Commission, the registered person should take so as to comply with any of those regulations; and

(c) the period, not exceeding three months, beginning on the date on which the notice is given, within which the registered person should take action.

There are specific provisions dealing with who may be prosecuted and enabling a prosecution to be brought against a person who was once a registered person in respect of a failure to comply with reg 21 (records).

10

PROCEDURE

10.1 PROTECTION OF CHILDREN AND VULNERABLE ADULTS AND CARE STANDARDS TRIBUNAL REGULATIONS 2002

The Protection of Children and Vulnerable Adults and Care Standards Tribunal Regulations 2002, SI 2002/816, came into force on 1 April 2002, save for vulnerable adult list appeals, as to which see 10.6 below.

The Regulations throughout refer to 'the Tribunal': this term will be used below. The Tribunal was established by s 9 of the Protection of Children Act 1999 and its jurisdiction was extended by the 2000 Act.

The constitution of the Tribunal is to be found in the Schedule to the Protection of Children Act 1999. The Schedule prescribes (para 1) that the Tribunal shall consist of a legally qualified Chairman nominated by the President of the Tribunal from the Chairman's Panel and two persons nominated by the President of the Tribunal from the Lay Panel. The Chairman's Panel members must be legally qualified. This means a seven-year general qualification within the meaning of s 71 of the Courts and Legal Services Act 1990. The members of the Lay Panel are to be appointed by the Lord Chancellor after consultation with the Secretary of State (para 2). The tenure of members of the Chairman's or Lay Panels is to be specified under the terms of instruments of appointment. Specific provision is made for resignation and the termination of appointment upon cessation of the holding of office (para 3).

Regulation 3 of the 2002 Regulations sets out the requirements for membership of the Lay Panel.

The Tribunal is added to the list of tribunals which are subject to the Tribunals and Inquiries Act 1992 and are thus amenable to appeal on point of law to the High Court (see Protection of Children Act 1999, Sch, para 8: Tribunals and Inquiries Act 1992, Sch 1, para 36B).

Parliament has now approved two sets of amendment regulations: the Protection of Children and Vulnerable Adults and Care Standards Tribunal (Amendment) Regulations 2003 SI no. 626 and the Protection of Children and Vulnerable Adults and Care Standards Tribunal (Amendment No. 2) Regulations SI No. 1060. These are set out as appendices 3 and 4 of this book.

10.1.1 The functions of the Tribunal

The Protection of Children Act 1999 provides for an independent judicial tribunal to hear appeals against decisions of the Secretary of State for Health to include the names of persons on the list of those considered unsuitable to work with children.

The 1999 Act also provides for the Tribunal to hear appeals from those barred from employment by the Secretary of State for Education and Skills under the relevant provisions of the Education Reform Act 1998.

The Care Standards Act 2000 provides for appeals brought under the terms of that Act to lie to the Tribunal.

The detailed provisions relating to specific areas of appeal under the 2000 Act will be considered below.

10.1.2 The Regulations

The Protection of Children and Vulnerable Adults and Care Standards Tribunal Regulations 2002 govern procedure in the Tribunal and are reproduced in appendix 2.

The 2002 Regulations set out the provisions that apply to all Tribunal hearings and then, by schedule, those provisions that apply to specific provisions of the Care Standards Act 2000, the Children Act 1989 and the Protection of Children Act 1999. The Protection of Children and Vulnerable Adults and Care Standards Tribunal (Amendment) Regulations 2003 SI 2003 No. 626 and the Protection of Children and Vulnerable Adults and Care Standards Tribunal (Amendment No. 2) Regulations 2003 SI 2003 No. 1060 (the Amendment Regulations and Amendment (No. 2) Regulations) set out the procedure for appeals in respect of social care workers, childminders/day care and nursery education inspectors or early years child care inspectors. The two sets of Amendment Regulations appear at Appendices 3 and 4.

The overall governance of the Tribunal is vested in the President (currently HH Judge Pearl). The powers of the President conferred by the 2002 Regulations may be exercised by a member of the Chairman's Panel authorized by the President, save for powers of nomination of a specific panel under reg 5 and those contained under reg 25(4) which relate to a review hearing.

10.1.2.1 *Appointment*
The Tribunal is to be comprised of one legally qualified member as Chairman (see 10.1 above) and two members of the Lay Panel (reg 5(1)). The Chairman of the Tribunal may determine any application which includes an application made in the case for leave (reg 5(3)).

10.1.2.2 *Directions*
There are detailed provisions for directions hearings, which may be fixed, either through a request by a party to a hearing or upon the motion of the chairman (or by the President: matters relating to any application can be dealt with by the President: this will not be referred to further below) if he so decides (reg 6(1)). The directions hearing is to be heard as soon as possible after the expiry of the five working days referred to in the detailed provisions that govern the various sorts of appeals. If neither party asks for a directions hearing (referred to in the Regulations as a 'preliminary hearing') and none is fixed by the Chairman, then the various directory powers referred to below are to be exercised by the Chairman within ten working days after the expiry of the five working days referred to in the detailed provisions governing each of the appeals.

At the directions hearing (whether sought by the parties, fixed by the Chairman or mandatory) the Chairman (reg 6(2)):

- is to give directions as to the dates by which any documents, witness statements or other material upon which either party is intending to rely should be sent to the Tribunal and, if appropriate, to the other party;
- make any other direction in the exercise of his powers under the case management powers which is appropriate or which is requested by either party;
- where the applicant has requested that the case be determined without an oral hearing, give a direction as to the date (which should not be less than ten working days after the date of the direction for service of evidence) by which the parties should send any written representations regarding their appeal to the Tribunal.

The directions given to exchange witness statements or other material should specify whether they should be exchanged simultaneously or sequentially (reg 6(3)). In relation to childminder or day care appeals the detailed provisions for directions hearings as set out above do not apply. The President or the nominated Chairman may make less complex directions (reg 6A).

The Secretary is bound to notify the parties in writing of any directions given by the Chairman and also of the hearing date of any directions hearing (reg 6(4) and (5)).

Any person can represent either of the parties at any directions hearing.

When there is to be an oral hearing (that is where the applicant has not asked for a written hearing) it must be fixed by the Secretary no sooner than 15 working days after the latest date on which the Chairman has directed that the evidence of the parties should be filed and exchanged (reg 7(2)). The parties must be given no less than 20 working days' notice of the date fixed for the hearing, which can be adjourned either by consent or on the Tribunal's own motion. However, an adjournment is not to be granted unless refusing the adjournment would prevent the just disposal of the case. Parties are to be notified of the new date. Appeals relating to childminders or those providing day care shorter time periods for the fixing and notification of hearings are laid down (Reg 6 Amendment Regulations).

There are also powers to give directions in relation to two or more cases which relate to the same person, establishment or agency (reg 8).

There is provision for the Chairman to vary any directions given, either on his own motion or upon application of either party. Before doing so he is bound to give the parties an opportunity to address matters in writing.

The Chairman may decide that a directions hearing should be held or one may have been requested by either of the parties in any event (reg 9).

The Chairman is given new powers to enforce any order which is made in the directions hearing by the provision of a discretion to determine the appeal or application in favour of the non-defaulting party (reg 10). There is an obligation on the part of the Secretary to give notice of an order which proposes that an 'unless order' is going to be made unless a step specified in the extant order is taken within a determined period. If there is non-compliance with that notice, an unless order can be made.

The rules in directions hearings form a radical step in relation to Tribunal procedure. Previously, for example, the Registered Homes Tribunal would routinely hold directions hearings and make various orders, but there was no method of enforcement of any order that it chose to make. The position now is that if, for example, an order is made as to exchange of witness statements which is not complied with by one or other party, then the Chairman has a discretion to make an unless order dismissing the application or appeal or, as the case may be, upholding the same.

There is, as yet, no case law as to how the unless order power is to be exercised. Undoubtedly, advocates will point to the jurisprudence of the High Court on this issue, but it is not known how the discretion will be exercised by the Tribunal. Practitioners are referred to CPR 3.4(2)(a) and para D1-015 of the White Book.

The authors are of the view that the extent of default will be an important matter. However, it must be pointed out that if a proposed respondent to an appeal, such as the National Care Standards Commission, does not comply with a directions order then, presumably, an appeal against the decision must be allowed. The effect of this revolutionary step has yet to be worked out.

Those advising appellants are reminded of the power to appeal on a point of law under the Tribunal and Inquiries Act 1992. It is likely that such an appeal is limited to final decisions only. Equally, there is power to apply for judicial review of a Tribunal's decision, but the standard judicial review grounds would have to be shown.

10.1.2.3 *Disclosure*

Under the provisions of the Regulations (reg 12) the Chairman can either direct the disclosure of any 'documents or other material' which he considers will assist the Tribunal and provide that copies are made for the other party; or he can grant the other party the right to inspect and take copies of such documents or material 'which ... is in the power of the other party to disclose'. It is anticipated that the usual rules as to materiality and what is and is not in the power of the other party to disclose will apply. For a detailed analysis of these issues see the Civil Procedure Rules Pt 31 and the commentary in the White Book.

There is also a power for the Chairman to order disclosure against a person not a party to the proceedings, provided that the document is likely to be material, and that it is 'likely to support the Applicant's case or adversely affect the case of the other party; it is within that third party's power and disclosure is necessary for the fair determination of the case'. If disclosure against a third party is ordered it will be a condition (see reg 12(3)) that the document or material should only be used for the purpose of the proceedings.

Whether disclosure is ordered against a party or a non-party, both are dependent upon disclosure being obtainable in legal proceedings in the county court. Once again, for a detailed analysis of the compellability of production of documents and the circumstances in which production is not compellable, see the Civil Procedure Rules and various specialist texts on the laws of evidence.

The Tribunal is specifically directed to take into account, in relation to any of its disclosure powers, the need to protect any matter 'which relates to intimate personal or financial circumstances, is commercially sensitive or was communicated or obtained in confidence' (reg 12(5)).

The powers in relation to disclosure are novel in this area of the law. It is expected that tribunals will exercise their powers in accordance with the jurisprudence of the Civil Procedure Rules. However, it should be noted that the provisions of reg 12(5), namely the need to take into account personal or financial circumstances, commercial sensitivity or confidence, are not reflected in the Civil Procedure Rules. It remains to be seen how these powers are to be exercised, in particular the last mentioned limitations. However, it is noted that in relation to the much disputed issue of obtaining disclosure of social services files, that is within the discretion of the Tribunal.

10.1.2.4 *Expert evidence*

The Chairman is given power where he thinks it desirable to have an expert appointed to assist the Tribunal. A copy of that report is to be supplied to the parties who will have an opportunity to make representations on that report before the hearing. There is power in the Chairman of the Tribunal to direct the expert's attendance (reg 13).

This too is a novel provision. It should be noted that the power to call for expert assistance on the part of the Tribunal does not preclude any party before the Tribunal from calling their own expert evidence. The parties' experts will undoubtedly wish to comment upon the Tribunal's expertise.

It is the experience of the authors that the Tribunal, when fully constituted, has a wealth of experience and accordingly it is envisaged that this power will be exercised sparingly. Where the power is to be exercised, many issues are raised including the terms of instruction of the expert, and whether these should be discussed with the legal representatives of the parties. It seems almost inevitable that the appellant will view the instruction of an expert by the Tribunal as evidence of it entering the adversarial process.

10.1.2.5 *Evidence of witnesses*
Regulation 14 provides for the exchange of witness statements and a requirement that there be a statement of truth in each witness statement, which must be signed by the person making it.

There is a power in the Chairman to direct that a document, or the evidence of any witness (other than the applicant), be excluded from consideration because it would be unfair to consider the evidence or document or because there has been a failure by a party to submit the evidence or document in accordance with the terms of a directions order. There is the 'catch-all' of relevance.

The Chairman is also given the power to allow the evidence or the document to be heard or read subject to the exercise of his powers in relation to the making of a costs order under reg 24 (see 10.1.2.13 below).

The Chairman may also direct that a witness, other than the applicant, shall not give oral evidence.

10.1.2.6 *Withholding medical evidence*
The Chairman is given the power by reg 15 to order that a medical report obtained by the respondent ought not to be disclosed if he is satisfied:

(a) that disclosure to the applicant of all or any part of the contents of the report would be so harmful to his health or welfare that it would be wrong to disclose it to him; and
(b) that in all the circumstances it would not be unfair if the report or that part of it is considered by the Tribunal ...

There is provision for assessment of the likely harm to an applicant by a 'person having appropriate skills of experience'.

It is not clear whether, if the Chairman decides that the report should be considered by the Tribunal, but not disclosed to the applicant, there should be disclosure to the applicant's representative. Regulation 15 is silent upon this point. Many situations can be envisaged where non-disclosure of such material to an appellant's representative would make the handling of the applicant's case very difficult.

10.1.2.7 *Summoning of witnesses*

The Chairman is given the power (reg 16) to direct the attendance of any witness who may also be required to produce any document or other material in his possession or under his control. If such a direction is to be made then a witness summons should be issued. The person summoned may apply to set aside the summons. In any event, there is no obligation to attend pursuant to a summons unless five working days' notice of a hearing has been given to the witness (unless the witness has consented to a shorter period of notice) and his or her expenses of attendance are paid or tendered, either by the party summoning the witness or by the Tribunal. A witness summons does not require the person summoned to give an answer or produce a document or other material which he could not be required to produce before a county court.

The principles of privilege and the privilege against self-incrimination are preserved.

10.1.2.8 *Children and vulnerable adults*

Regulation 17 places restrictions on the giving of evidence by both children and vulnerable adults. In the case of a child (it is assumed that no difference is made between the giving of oral evidence by a vulnerable adult and the giving of evidence 'in person' by a child: ie the two words are to be equated) where a person proposes to call such a witness, either side should have the opportunity of making written representations. The Chairman must consider that the welfare of the child or vulnerable adult would not be prejudiced by giving oral evidence.

A distinction is drawn between the position of a child and that of a vulnerable adult. In relation to the former, if the Chairman decides that a child is to give evidence he must make any arrangements considered appropriate to safeguard the welfare of the child and appoint a person 'with appropriate skills or experience' to assist the child to give evidence. The parties may find it useful to consider how the criminal courts approach this issue. While the protection put in place is mostly statutory (Youth and Criminal Evidence Act 1999, ss 16–18) the guidance and Special Measures Directions ratified may be a helpful guide to those having to grapple with a difficult child procedural issue. In relation to a vulnerable adult the presumption is in favour of oral evidence unless the Chairman takes the view that it would not be in the best interests of the vulnerable adult: in those circumstances the written representations process is engaged. The duty to have regard to the available evidence and representations is qualified by the consideration of whether the vulnerable adult could give evidence if appropriate arrangements were made and a person appointed to facilitate the giving of that evidence.

The fee for the appointment of such a person shall be paid by the Tribunal.

This regulation is directed at the giving of oral evidence. By definition, it does not apply where it is proposed that the child or vulnerable adult should given written evidence only. There is the reserve power in the Chairman to direct that a witness should not give oral evidence (reg 14(5)).

10.1.2.9 *Restricted reporting orders*

The Chairman is empowered to make a restricted reporting order prohibiting the publication 'of any matter likely to lead members of the public to identify the applicant, any child, any vulnerable adult or any other person who the President or nominated Chairman ... considers should not be identified'.

The power to make a restricted reporting order in relation to applicants is unique. Under the existing legislation (see the Children and Young Persons Act 1933) there is power to conceal the identity of any child involved in any proceedings. There is no equivalent power in relation to vulnerable adults. Thus, for example, a care home need not necessarily fear the publicity of a hearing and the likely damage caused by it if a restricted reporting order is made.

That order can be made for a limited period of time and may be varied or revoked before or at the hearing. However, such an order is unlikely to be made merely to save embarrassment or adverse publicity about alleged poor care practice in the care home or other facility. Presumably there is no power in the Tribunal to consider variation or revocation of a restricted reporting order after the termination of the hearing. This may be a matter for an application for judicial review.

Note also that:

- a restricted reporting order relates to a 'written publication' or a programme for reception in England and Wales;
- there is no attempt to change the general principles of law that apply to reporting orders made, for example, in the criminal jurisdiction;
- reference should be made to specialist texts on the ambit of restricted reporting orders in other cases.

10.1.2.10 *Exclusion of press and public*

There is power (reg 19) to direct that members of the press and public be excluded from all or part of the hearing. That power can be exercised either because the applicant has requested it or on the Chairman's own initiative. The grounds for exercising this discretion are that:

... it is necessary in order to –
(a)   safeguard the welfare of any child or vulnerable adult;
(b)   protect a person's private life; or
(c)   avoid the risk of injustice in any legal proceedings.

It is trite law that justice must be seen to be done and thus, with the exception of children and vulnerable adults, the overriding principle is that a hearing should take place in public and not private. See also reg 21, which requires hearings to be in public. This will, undoubtedly, be a fruitful source of jurisprudence.

The concept of the 'risk of injustice in any legal proceedings' presumably means legal proceedings other than the appeal before the Tribunal. If, for example, charges have been made against an applicant or senior member of staff in criminal proceedings, it has often been argued that the proceedings before the Registered Homes Tribunal should be postponed until the criminal proceedings are heard. Such an argument is often attractive to a court. However, it should be borne in mind that unless clear prejudice to those proceedings can be shown, such an application should be refused. It is the authors' view that where an application is made by an appellant to postpone his appeal because criminal proceedings are contemplated by the police or Crown Prosecution Service, such an application will only be granted in exceptional circumstances. It is important that any appeal is heard quickly. The Tribunal has power to control its own procedure and can ameliorate the possible prejudicial effect of proceeding where criminal charges are contemplated or where the appellant is charged.

10.1.2.11 *The hearing*

The procedure at the hearing is governed by the provision of regs 20–22. This gives the Tribunal power to regulate its own procedure. It is also provided that the Chairman should explain the order of proceedings at the outset. A party may be represented or assisted by any person. The Tribunal can hear the matter in the absence of either party and make a determination.

All hearings are to be held in public unless a direction has been made under reg 20. Where the hearing is held in private, certain people who are neither members of the Tribunal nor parties are entitled to be present, for example a member of the Council on Tribunals, the President, the Clerk and any person nominated by the Chairman who is there to assist the Tribunal.

Only members of the Tribunal are entitled to participate in the Tribunal's deliberations, although such deliberations can be attended by a member of the Council on Tribunals and the President.

The Tribunal is empowered to consider any evidence, whether or not it would be admissible in a court of law. The applicant has the right to give evidence at the hearing in person and any other witness may do so unless directed to the contrary by the Chairman. The provisions in relation to the giving of evidence by a child or vulnerable adult are dealt with at 10.1.2.8 above. In respect of a child there can be no cross-examination, save by the Tribunal or the relevant person appointed under reg 17(2). In the case of a vulnerable adult, an equivalent provision applies where an order to that effect has been made. Evidence may be given on oath or affirmation as directed by the Tribunal.

10.1.2.12 *The decision*

The Tribunal's decision, if not unanimous, can be given by a majority and the decision shall so record. The decision may be announced at the end of the hearing or reserved, but in any event it should be contained in a document signed and dated by the Chairman. The document should give the reasons for the decision and the order made by the Tribunal. The Tribunal's decision should contain an outline of 'the story', a summary of the Tribunal's basic factual conclusions, and a statement of the reasons which led to the conclusions on the basic facts (see *Meek v Birmingham District Council* [1987] IRLR 250 and Wade & Forsyth, *Administrative Law* (8th edn) 916–9). The decision should then be sent to all parties, explaining any right of appeal to which they are entitled and the right to apply for a review (see 10.1.2.14 below). Except where the decision is announced at the end of the hearing, the decision shall be treated as having been made on the day on which a copy of the decision letter is sent to the applicant.

10.1.2.13 *Costs*
There is now power in the Tribunal to make a costs order if 'a party has acted unreasonably in bringing or conducting the proceedings'.

Before the making of a costs order the Tribunal is required to invite the party in whose favour a costs order has been made to provide a schedule of costs and to invite representations from the party against whom a costs order has been made and to consider those representations.

The Tribunal's powers on making a costs order include the power to order a payment of a sum which has been agreed between the parties or to decide what sum is appropriate or whether whole or part of the costs incurred in connection with the proceedings are to be assessed. Any assessment may be carried out in a county court and a costs order can be enforced in the same manner as a judgment or order of the county court with leave of that court.

No detailed analysis of the preliminary requirement of unreasonable behaviour is made in this text. It can be observed that in a comparable jurisdiction, namely that of the Employment Tribunal, where a similar power exists, cost orders are infrequently made. See, for example, *Davidson v John Calder (Publishers) Ltd & Calder Educational Trust Ltd* [1985] IRLR 97.

The relevant regulation is 24.

10.1.2.14 *Review*
A party may apply to the President for the Tribunal decision to be reviewed on the grounds that (reg 25(1)):

- it was wrongly made as a result of an error on the part of the Tribunal's staff;
- a party, who was entitled to be heard at the hearing, but failed to appear or to be represented, has given sufficient reason for failing to appear;
- there was an obvious error in the decision.

Where such an application is made it must be made not later than ten working days after the date on which the decision was sent to the party applying for a review and that application must be in writing and set out the grounds for the application in full.

If the application is to be heard, which it must be unless the Chairman decides that it has no reasonable prospects of success, then both parties have a right to present their cases orally.

A review can be proposed by the Tribunal on its own initiative, and in those circumstances must be done not later than ten working days after the date on which the decision was sent and both parties have a right to be heard in relation to it.

If the Tribunal is satisfied that grounds exist for a review, it should order a review and it may order that further particulars, evidence or statements are provided by any party in order to assist it.

If the Tribunal grants a review then it has the power to either set aside or vary the decision it has previously made or substitute such other decision as it thinks fit or order a rehearing before the same or a differently constituted Tribunal.

10.1.2.15 *Publication*

Decisions of the Tribunal must be published, but they can be published in edited form or subject to deletions at the discretion of the Chairman. The discretion requires the Chairman to bear in mind:

- the need to safeguard the welfare of any child or vulnerable adult;
- the need to protect the privacy of any person;
- any representations on the matter which either party has provided in writing;
- the effect of any subsisting restricted reporting order; and
- the effect of any direction under reg 15.

It should be observed that the discretion conferred upon the Chairman is wide. On occasions it would be sufficient to refer to a child or a vulnerable adult or other person whose privacy should be protected by an initial. However, it may be that wider restrictions are called for if such measures are insufficient.

10.1.2.16 *Supplementary*

Various regulations (regs 28–35) are made to deal with:

- the method of sending documents;
- curing of irregularities;
- the making of an application on behalf of a person under a disability;
- the striking out of a case where an applicant dies;
- amendment of a case or application for leave;
- withdrawal of proceedings or opposition to proceedings;
- proof of documents and certification of decisions;
- the extension of any time limit specified in the Regulations.

Power to extend time is in the discretion of the Chairman. It is exercisable if he or she takes the view that (a) it would be unreasonable to expect the time limit to have been complied with, and (b) it would be unfair not to extend it. However, the power to extend time does not apply to the time limits provided for initiating an appeal under para 1 of Sch 1 and para 1 of Sch 2 (see 10.2 and 10.3 below), or to the initiation of appeals under Schedules 6, 7 or 8.

10.2 APPEALS UNDER S 21 OF THE 2000 ACT AGAINST A DECISION OF THE REGISTRATION AUTHORITY OR AN ORDER OF A DISTRICT JUDGE OR JUSTICES OF THE PEACE

10.2.1 General

Section 21 of the Care Standards Act 2000 is concerned with appeals against a decision of the registration authority under Pt II of the Act, or an order made by a district judge or justices of the peace under s 20 of the Act.

The provisions of Sch 1 govern appeals from the National Care Standards Commission ('the Commission') and the National Assembly for Wales ('the Assembly') in respect of appeals relating to the registration of establishments or agencies specified in Pt I of the 2000 Act. It also deals with emergency cancellation orders.

As has been said previously, all establishments (namely children's homes, independent hospitals, independent hospitals providing for the treatment or nursing of those detained under the Mental Health Act 1983, independent clinics, care homes or residential family centres) and all agencies (namely independent medical agencies, domiciliary care agencies, nurses agencies, fostering agencies and voluntary adoption agencies) are required to be registered by the Commission or the Assembly.

Thus, the refusal of registration, the grant of registration upon conditions, the cancellation of registration and emergency cancellation by a district judge or justices of the peace are all susceptible to an appeal to the Tribunal.

10.2.2 Initiating an appeal

An appeal must be brought within 28 days after service upon the proposed appellant of notice of the decision or order (s 21(2)). Within that time an appeal can be initiated by application in writing to the Secretary of the Tribunal, which may be made upon the application form available from the Secretary.

In any event the notice of appeal must:

- give the applicant's name and full postal address, if the applicant is an individual his date of birth and, if the applicant is a company, the address of its registered office;
- give the name, address and profession of the person (if any) representing the applicant;
- give the address within the United Kingdom to which the Secretary should send documents concerning the appeal;
- give, where these are available, the applicant's telephone number, fax number and email address and those of the applicant's representative;
- identify the decision or order against which the appeal is brought and give particulars of:
  —whether the appeal is against a refusal of registration, an imposition or variation of conditions of registration, a refusal to remove or vary any conditions, or a cancellation of registration;

—whether the appeal is against a decision of the registration authority or an order made by a justice of the peace;

—where the appeal is in respect of a cancellation of registration, whether the establishment or agency in respect of which the appeal is made remains open and, in the case of an establishment, the number of residents in that establishment;

- give a short statement of the grounds of appeal; and
- be signed and dated by the applicant.

Once the application for appeal is launched it must be acknowledged by the Secretary to the Tribunal, who enters particulars of it and the date of its receipt in the records and must send a copy of it, together with any supporting documentation supplied by the applicant, to the respondent.

The Secretary is empowered to correct an obvious error in the application, but must notify the applicant that he has done so. The Secretary's application stands unless the applicant notifies him of any objection within five days of receipt of the notification.

10.2.3 Response to application

The Secretary of the Tribunal must send the notice of appeal to the respondent, together with a request that a response is made to the application within 20 working days of receipt.

If the respondent fails to make any response, he will not be entitled to take any further part in the proceedings.

If a response is made, it must:

- acknowledge that the respondent has received a copy of the application;
- indicate whether or not the respondent opposes it and, if he does, give the reasons why he opposes the application;
- provide the following information and documents:
  —the name, address and profession of the person (if any) representing the respondent and whether the Secretary should send documents concerning the appeal to the representatives rather than to the respondent;
  —in the case of an appeal under s 21(1)(a) of the 2000 Act, a copy of the written notice of the decision and the reasons for the decision; or
  —in the case of an appeal under s 21(1)(b) of the 2000 Act, a copy of the order of the justice of the peace.

Once the Secretary to the Tribunal has received a copy of the response, together with any supporting documentation, he must send a copy of the same to the applicant.

10.2.4 Misconceived appeals

The Chairman has the power to strike out any appeal on the grounds that it has not been made in accordance with the requirements for initiating an appeal, or that it is outside the jurisdiction of the Tribunal or is otherwise misconceived, or that it is scandalous, frivolous or vexatious.

Before making an order for striking out the parties should be invited to make representations and, if the applicant so requests, make oral representations.

The question of whether an appeal is within or without the jurisdiction or is otherwise misconceived will be one of law. The issue of whether an appeal is 'scandalous, frivolous or vexatious' is primarily a question of fact. There are many reported cases on this issue. See, for example, the cases referred to in para 18/19/15 of the *Supreme Court Practice 1999*.

10.2.5 Further information to be sent by the applicant and respondent

When the respondent has provided his response to the application, the Secretary must write to each party requesting that the party send, within 15 working days, the following information:

- the name of any witnesses whose evidence the party wishes the Tribunal to consider and the nature of that evidence;
- whether either party wishes the Chairman to give directions or exercise any of the powers of case management;
- whether a party wishes there to be a directions hearing;
- a provisional time estimate;
- the earliest date on which a party considers he would be able to prepare his case for hearing;
- in the case of the applicant, whether he wishes his appeal to be determined without a hearing.

Once the information has been received from both parties, copies of the same must be supplied to the other side by the Secretary.

Within five working days of receiving the further information in respect of the other party, a party can ask the Secretary to amend or to add to any of the information given.

Note that under the provisions of reg 35, time can be extended in the circumstances indicated above.

10.3 APPEALS UNDER S 79M OF THE CHILDREN ACT 1989 AGAINST A DECISION OF THE REGISTRATION AUTHORITY OR AN ORDER OF A DISTRICT JUDGE OR JUSTICES OF THE PEACE

10.3.1 General

Section 79, which inserts Pt XA into the Children Act 1989, governs childminding and day care for young persons. By s 79D of the 1989 Act anybody providing services as a childminder or providing day care on a premises is required to be registered: in England by the Chief Inspector of Schools and in Wales by the Assembly. Any refusal of registration, grant of registrations subject to conditions, suspension of registration or emergency action (under s 79K of the Children Act 1989) is subject to an appeal to the Tribunal under s 79M.

10.3.2 Procedure for appeal

Schedule 2 to the Regulations specifies the formula set out at 10.2 above for (a) initiating an appeal, (b) acknowledgement and notification of application, (c) response to application, (d) misconceived appeals, and (e) further information. Thus, the procedure specified for Sch 1 appeals applies to Sch 2.

10.4 APPEALS UNDER S 65A OF THE CHILDREN ACT 1989 AGAINST A DECISION OF THE APPROPRIATE AUTHORITY REFUSING TO GIVE CONSENT UNDER S 65 OF THAT ACT

10.4.1 General

Section 65 of the Children Act 1989 provides that anyone who is disqualified under s 68 of that Act from fostering a child privately shall not carry on or be otherwise concerned in the management of or have any financial interest in a children's home unless he has:

• disclosed to the responsible authority the fact that he is so disqualified; and
• obtained their written consent.

There is a prohibition on the employment of such a person in a children's home unless there has been disclosure as above and the obtaining of written consent from the relevant authority.

The appeal was formerly made to the Registered Homes Tribunal (s 65(3)). That appeal now lies to the Tribunal.

10.4.2 Procedure

The procedure for the appeal is the same as that set out under Sch 1 to the 2000 Act. It is governed by the provisions of Sch 3 to the 2000 Act. However, it should be noted that the period of time for initiating an appeal is no later than the first working day after the expiry of three months from the date of the letter informing the applicant of the decision.

10.5 APPEALS AND APPLICATION FOR LEAVE TO APPEAL UNDER S 4 OF THE PROTECTION OF CHILDREN ACT 1999 AND APPEALS UNDER REG 13 OF THE EDUCATION REGULATIONS

10.5.1 General

These relate to applications for leave to appeal against a decision to include any person in the Department of Health list and appeals by teachers under the Education Regulations (the Education (Restriction of Employment) Regulations 2000, SI 2000/2419, as amended by the Education (Restriction of Employment) (Amendment) Regulations 2001, SI 2001/1269) against inclusion in the Secretary of State for Education and Skills' list of those barred from teaching.

10.5.2 Procedure

The procedure is as set out in relation to appeals under Sch 1. The relevant procedure is contained in Sch 4 to the 2002 Regulations. The procedure in relation to appeals under s 4(1)(a) of the Protection of Children Act 1999 and under reg 13 of the Education Regulations 2000 is largely the same as those in relation to a decision of a registration authority or an order of a district judge or justices of the peace under Sch 1, save that the period for lodging an appeal is no later than the first working day after the expiry of three months from the date of the letter informing the applicant of the decision and the period of supplying further information is 20 working days (see Sch 4, para 8).

Where there is an appeal to the Tribunal under s 4(1)(b) of the 1999 Act against a decision not to remove the applicant from the POCA list or an application to have the issue of the applicant's inclusion in the POCA list determined under s 4(2) of the 1999 Act then there has to be application for leave to appeal.

The time limits for making an application for leave are the same as those for an appeal as indicated above, namely no later than the first working day after the expiry of three months from the date of the letter informing the applicant of the decision.

In addition, the applicant must give the dates of any previous appeal under the 1999 Act and the application for leave the applicant has made will also give details of any new evidence of material change of circumstances since the last appeal or application for leave. Where there is an application to have the issue of inclusion in the POCA list determined by the Tribunal there is an obligation to give details of any civil or criminal proceedings relating to the misconduct of which the applicant is alleged to have been guilty. See generally Sch 4, para 2(4) of the 2002 Regulations.

The Chairman can grant or refuse leave on the papers without a hearing if he sees fit. If leave is refused then a mechanism is provided whereby the applicant can renew the application orally. See 2002 Regulations, Sch 5, paras 6 and 7.

10.6 APPEALS AND APPLICATIONS FOR LEAVE UNDER S 86 OF THE 2000 ACT

10.6.1 General

By virtue of s 81 of the 2000 Act, the Secretary of State is obliged to keep a list of individuals who are considered unsuitable to work with vulnerable adults. This relates to anyone who has regular contact in the course of his duties with adults to whom accommodation is provided at care homes or contact with an adult at an independent hospital, an independent clinic, an independent medical agency or a National Health Service body or anyone who provides personal care to persons who, by reason of illness, infirmity or disability, are unable to provide it for themselves without assistance, provided such care takes place in their own homes (see s 80 of the 2000 Act). The Domiciliary Care National Minimum Standards contain a definition of 'personal care'. Practitioners where appropriate should refer to this and to s4(3)–(6) of the 2000 Act.

Thus, the potential for those within the scope of s 81 is substantial. Section 86 of the 2000 Act provides a right of appeal against inclusion in the list to the Tribunal.

The appeal right is both against a decision by the Secretary of State to include a person on the list and, with leave of the Tribunal, against any decision of the Secretary of State not to remove a person from the list.

An individual who has been provisionally included in the list for a period of more than nine months may, with the leave of the Tribunal, have the issue of his inclusion in the list determined by the Tribunal instead of by the Secretary of State. This is subject to circumstances where the misconduct which is alleged against the individual is the subject of civil or criminal proceedings. An application for leave may not be made before the end of the period of six months immediately following the final determination of those proceedings.

'Final determination' means that the proceedings are terminated with no decision being made or a decision is made against which no appeal lies or, where an appeal lies, the relevant time limits for such an appeal (or leave to appeal) have been exhausted.

The power of the Tribunal is to allow the appeal or determine the issue in the individual's favour and (in either case) direct their removal from the list where (s 86(3)):

... the Tribunal is not satisfied of either of the following, namely –
(a) that the individual was guilty of misconduct (whether or not in the course of his duties) which harmed or placed at risk of harm a vulnerable adult; and
(b) that the individual is unsuitable to work with vulnerable adults ...

Thus, where an individual who has been named within the list kept by the Secretary of State can satisfy the evidential burden that either they did not carry out the alleged misconduct or that they are suitable to work with vulnerable adults then the appeal will be allowed and their name removed from the list. The legal burden of proving the reverse lies on the Secretary of State.

Where an individual has been convicted of an offence involving misconduct, then no finding of fact on which the conviction must be taken to have been based shall be challenged in the appeal.

Where an individual has been on the list for ten years, or in the case of a child for five years, then they are entitled to apply to the Tribunal for leave to apply for removal of their name from the list.

In either case the Tribunal must be satisfied that the individual is no longer unsuitable to work with vulnerable adults.

In the case of an individual who was a child when he was included on the list, an application for leave to the Tribunal cannot be made unless that individual has been on the list for a continuous period of five years and in the period of five years ending with the time when he makes the application he has made no other application to the Tribunal.

In the case of any other individual the conditions are that that individual has been on the list for a period of ten years and in the period of ten years concluding with the time when he makes the application no other application to the Tribunal has been made.

In respect of either, the Tribunal is not empowered to grant the application unless the Tribunal considers that the individual's circumstances have changed and that the change is such that leave should be granted.

The conditions for the grant of an application contained in s 88(5) and those contained in s 86(2) do not sit easily with each other unless the word 'application' in relation to applications for removal from the list is construed as an application for leave rather than an appeal, as indicated by Sch 5. Despite the use of rather confusing terminology, in relation to an individual who has been on the list for ten years (or in the case of a child, five years) there should be no grant of an application for leave unless there has been a change of circumstances which is material.

The effect of inclusion on the s 81 list is to preclude individuals from taking employment in a position where they provide care to vulnerable adults or knowingly apply for, offer to do, accept or do any work in a care position (s 89). If employment has been offered to such a person, the employer is bound to cease the employment forthwith, on discovering that the individual is on the s 81 list.

10.6.2 Procedure

The procedure is the same as set out in Sch 1, save that the period for serving a letter of appeal is the same as that for Schs 3 and 4, ie the first working day after the expiry of three months from the date of the letter informing the applicant of the decision. In addition, in common with appeals under Schs 3 and 4, the period for further information under para 8 is 20 days.

Where there is an application for leave to appeal, the applicant must in addition give:

- sufficient information to make it clear whether the appeal falls within subparas (1)(a) or (b) of Sch 5;
- the reasons why the applicant believes the decision was wrong or, as the case may be, why he believes he should not be included in the POCA list;
- the dates of any previous appeal under s 86 of the 2000 Act and (where applicable) application for leave;
- details of any new evidence or material change of circumstances since that appeal or (where applicable) application for leave was determined which might lead the Tribunal to a different decision;
- in the case of an application to have the issue of inclusion in the POCA list determined by the Tribunal, details of any civil or criminal proceedings relating to the misconduct of which the applicant is alleged to have been guilty.

There are also provisions relating to the grant or refusal of leave and the reconsideration of a decision to refuse leave. In the first instance a decision as to the grant or refusal of leave is conducted on paper by the Chairman of the Tribunal. A decision to refuse leave can be the subject of a review at the applicant's request and can be done so orally (see Sch 5, paras 6 and 7).

10.7 GENERAL

The reader is advised to refer to the specific provisions of the Schedules to the 2002 Regulations for the precise mechanics of each sort of appeal and application for leave.

The same applies to the appeals dealt with by the Amendment Regulations and the Amendment No. 2 Regulations. The two sets of Amendment Regulations have been added at Appendices 3 and 4.

11

JUDICIAL REVIEW AND STATUTORY APPEALS

11.1 THE USE OF JUDICIAL REVIEW

The Care Standards Act 2000 is in essence a regulatory device for controlling a number of related activities. Like its statutory predecessor, the Registered Homes Act 1984, decisions of the Care Standards Tribunal are subject to appeal on point of law to the Administrative Court by virtue of the Tribunal and Inquiries Act 1992. However, the Act does not preclude the use of the judicial review procedure, which may be particularly apposite for challenges to decisions which are made prior to the engagement of the mechanism provided by the Act and where classic judicial review grounds are made out within proceedings commenced under the Act, for example:

- a decision by the National Commission to bring regulatory proceedings;
- a plain defect within those proceedings, such as procedural impropriety and unfairness;
- a decision by the Tribunal relating to procedure which is interlocutory;
- a decision made by another body, such as a decision made by a local authority as to the closure of a care home.

Thus, one needs to understand the procedures which underpin the judicial review process.

The objective of this part of this chapter is to explain the judicial review process in outline. For a more detailed review of the process readers are referred to specialist texts.

11.2 AN OVERVIEW OF THE JUDICIAL REVIEW PROCESS

Judicial review, since 2 October 2000, is governed by Pt 54 of the Civil Procedure Rules. References below will be to those Rules (for example, 54.1) and to the accompanying practice direction (for example, PD 54, para 00).

The judicial review process, which has its roots in medieval times, is designed to deal with administrative and minor judicial decisions. This chapter does not analyse the numerous cases which deal with the question of when judicial review may or may not be appropriate. Suffice to say that every decision made by the National Commission or National Assembly (or any other registration body or equivalent in the Act), whether under or by reference to the Act, is amenable to judicial review. The National Commission or National Assembly is undoubtedly a public body, operating under an Act of Parliament, and its decisions are therefore plainly amenable to challenge by way of judicial review.

All challenges are launched by way of a claim form. Although it is possible to get a claim for judicial review listed urgently, recent experience shows that this is more difficult to obtain now than under the old Rules. However, a new direction has been issued by the Administrative Court to deal with this problem. Under the new procedure the claim form must be served upon the National Commission or National Assembly (these two bodies will be used as the examples, but, as noted above, every decision-making body under the Act is susceptible to judicial review), which must file an acknowledgement of service in reply. The claim form, which is dealt with in more detail at 11.4 below, sets out the claimant's challenge. The claimant must serve evidence with his claim form. The acknowledgement of service sets out in brief the defendant's response. The defendant does not need to serve evidence at this stage, but should set out its case in response in detail. The matter then comes before a judge of the Administrative Court, who deals with the case on paper, either granting permission to bring judicial review proceedings or refusing the same. If permission is refused, there is a right on the claimant's part to renew the application orally before the judge, provided that notice is given to the proposed defendant. If permission is refused by the court there is a further right of renewal of the application to the Court of Appeal.

If permission is granted then the defendant has 35 days to serve detailed grounds for contesting the claim and any written evidence.

If the court concludes in the claimant's favour, there are a number of remedies available to it, the principle of which is to make a quashing order requiring the decision-maker to reconsider.

11.3 THE GROUNDS ON WHICH JUDICIAL REVIEW LIES

The trilogy of grounds in respect of judicial review claims are (a) illegality, (b) procedural impropriety, and (c) irrationality. Within these grounds there are subcategories. For example, within procedural impropriety are included the general principle of fairness and the duty on a public body not to abuse its powers. Within illegality there is included the requirement of acting for a proper and not an improper purpose. There is also the requirement that a public body should not fetter its discretion by following its own policy with undue rigidity (*British Oxygen Co v Minister of Technology* [1971] AC 610). There should be no error of 'jurisdictional fact' (*R v Secretary of State for the Home Department, ex p Khawaja* [1984] 1 AC 874). New grounds may develop. For example, on the same day that Pt 54 CPR came into effect the Human Rights Act 1998 was enacted into domestic law. That Act, which is considered in chapter 12, confers upon individuals (which also includes corporations) a number of rights which may well be the subject of judicial review proceedings.

11.3.1 Illegality

The Administrative Court's approach is that any error made by a public body, in its interpretation of either an Act, or secondary legislation made under an Act, or of non-statutory material, such as the standards, is an error of law which is subject to judicial review. Thus, to give an example, under the Registered Homes Act 1984 there was some dispute as to whether the local authority could take into account an applicant's financial status. The local authority took the view that it could. A Registered Homes Tribunal took the opposite view. This was a question about the interpretation of s 9 of the Registered Homes Act 1984. The local authority's view prevailed (*R v Registered Homes Tribunal, ex p Hertfordshire CC* 95 LGR 76).

Also comprised within this head of challenge is error as to a 'jurisdictional fact'. Suppose that there is an issue of fact as to whether a company is carrying on a care home. Under the old law this would arise frequently in respect of the provision by a body of accommodation under a lease which had available to it both a kitchen and care staff. Both were chargeable under the lease. The question of whether the old Registered Homes Act 1984 applies to such a situation may be one of law. It is also likely to be one of 'jurisdictional fact'. If the facts are not such as to give jurisdiction to a local authority under the old Act, and they purport, for example, to require registration, then it is likely that a challenge can be made on the basis of illegality.

11.3.2 Procedural impropriety

Much ink has been spilt by the courts and various writers as to the extent of procedural impropriety. There is no doubt that it applies where there has been a breach of the rules of natural justice or a failure to comply with procedural fairness. However, it also applies where a claimant can show that he has a 'legitimate expectation', such as an expectation of being consulted before action is taken. It also applies where a public body acts in a way which is generally unfair or abusive of their powers. Let us take an example of the simplest kind. If there is a hearing of a deregistration issue before the Tribunal and it takes into account a piece of evidence upon which the applicant has had no opportunity to comment, then that is probably a matter which falls outside the rules that govern the Tribunal (as to which see chapter 10) and it can be remedied by way of a judicial review application based upon breach of the rules of natural justice.

Another example could be where a local authority operates a care home. It proposes to close that care home because it is too expensive. A circular is sent to the residents of the care home, suggesting that they have been treated unfairly and it will take into account the views of the residents and their families. However, the local authority does not in fact consult with anyone before making the decision to close the home. The decision to close the home, which falls outside the ambit of the Act, is nonetheless subject to judicial review on the grounds that the local authority had given the residents and their families a 'legitimate expectation' that they would be consulted and then denied that expectation (*R v Durham CC, ex p Baker* [1995] 1 All ER 73).

It should be kept in mind that any type of abuse of power or act of unfairness on the part of anyone engaged in the care home business or social work business (to give examples) may well be amenable to judicial review on the grounds of procedural impropriety.

11.3.3 Irrationality

The classic formulation of the principle which underlies a challenge based on irrationality is to be found in *Associated Picture Houses Limited v Wednesbury Corporation* [1948] 1 KB 223. This principle is often referred to as a *Wednesbury* challenge, which is, in essence, based either upon frank unreasonableness ('the National Commission has made a decision which is stark staring mad') or there has been a failure to have regard to relevant considerations or regard has been paid to irrelevant considerations.

It is rare to succeed upon a challenge based upon frank unreasonableness. This has been described by Professor Craig in *Administrative Law* (4th edn, Sweet & Maxwell) as the 'first carriage' type of *Wednesbury* challenge. One has to show that no reasonable decision-maker could possibly have reached that conclusion.

A challenge based on the 'second carriage' of the *Wednesbury* formulation, ie a failure to take into account a relevant consideration or the taking into account of an irrelevant consideration, is more common. To take an example, the 2000 Act lays down specific criteria for the grant or refusal of registration of care homes. The National Commission purports to apply the Act and, acting within its discretion refuses registration to a respectable but possibly financially shaky company. The National Commission overlooks the fact that the company accounts show that the company is underpinned by a substantial guarantee from either another company or a private individual, which will finance the company in the future. To ignore such a consideration is a failure to take into account a relevant consideration.

11.4 THE CLAIM FORM

The claim form is divided into eight sections. Section 1 requires the details of the claimant and defendant. Section 2 requires the insertion of the details of other interested parties. Thus, for example, in the case of the closure of a care home run by a local authority by the National Commission or the National Assembly, the name of the local authority should be inserted here. Section 3 requires details of the decision to be judicially reviewed and the date of that decision. In the case of the review of a decision of the Tribunal this should give the date on which the written reasons are handed down. Section 4 requires details of the permission application to be inserted. This is self-explanatory, save for whether or not the claim raises issues under the Human Rights Act 1998. For example, a judicial review of the decision of the Tribunal closing a care home may involve questions relating to the application of Art 8 of the European Convention on Human Rights (see chapter 12). Section 5 requires a detailed statement of the grounds of challenge. Section 6 requires details of the remedy, including any interim remedy, being sought. The traditional forms of relief are (a) quashing of the decision, (b) a mandatory order requiring compliance with the decision of the court, and (c) a declaratory decision. Section 7 allows other applications to be made. This is to be used where interim relief or expedition is sought. Thus, an order for an interim injunction or stay is appropriate here. Examples of interim relief include the grant of an interim stay or injunction which may be relevant to the keeping open of a care home or the exclusion of the name of an individual from the relevant lists. Section 8 requires the facts in the case to be set out.

The claim form should be supported by a witness statement, to which there should be exhibited the documents relied upon. Section 10 sets out the documents which should be lodged in support of the claim. One should note in particular the requirement that a copy of the relevant statutory material be lodged and a list of essential documents. The bundle as lodged should be indexed and paginated.

11.4.1 Time limits

CPR 54.5 requires that the claim form must be filed '(a) promptly; and (b) in any event not later than three months after the grounds to make the claim first arose'.

Parties cannot extend the time limits by agreement (CPR 54.5(2)). The court has a discretion to extend the time limit for bringing a claim. Generally speaking, that discretion will not be exercised in allowing a claim to be brought after the three-month time limit (and in some cases a shorter time span is deemed appropriate) unless good reasons for extending the time limit can be shown.

Readers are referred to more specialist texts, which include examples of cases in which the time limits will and will not be extended.

11.4.2 Service

CPR 54.7 requires the claim form to be served upon the defendant and any person the claimant considers to be an interested party within seven days after the date of issue in the Administrative Court.

11.4.3 Acknowledgement of service

The acknowledgement of service is divided into five sections. Section A requires the defendant to specify whether it is intended to defend all or part of the claim. Section B sets out the type of remedy being sought by the defendant if different from the claimant. That section may be appropriately completed if some but not all of the relief is being contested or a different form is suggested by defendants, such as declaratory relief only. Section C requires the defendant to set out in summary terms the basis for contesting the claim. Section D requires the defendant to specify any application that may be made by it, such as an application for expedition. Section D requires a signature and details of where further communication should be made.

The acknowledgement of service must be filed within 21 days after the service of the claim form. It should be served on the claimant and, subject to any direction by the court, any other person named in the claim form.

Where no acknowledgement of service is filed then the defendant may not be allowed to participate in the permission application. However, the defendant may be allowed to participate in the main hearing, provided it complies with the court's direction as to a filing and service of detailed grounds for contesting the claim (see 11.4.5 below) and written evidence. However, the failure to file an acknowledgement of service may be taken into account when deciding what order to make as to costs (CPR 54.9).

11.4.4 Permission given

Once the claim form has been lodged and the time has expired for the filing of an acknowledgement of service, the court will decide whether it ought to give or refuse permission and, in the event of giving permission, issue any directions that it should make (CPR 54.11).

If permission is refused or given subject to conditions or on limited grounds then a renewed application for permission to bring judicial review proceedings or permission to bring them without condition or on wider grounds may be made. A request for another hearing should be made within seven days after the service of the court's reason for giving or refusing permission. Any person who has filed an acknowledgement of service will be given two days' notice of the hearing date (CPR 54.12). Once permission is granted, a defendant or interested person may not apply to set aside (CPR 54.13).

The practice direction provides that case management directions can be given on the grant of permission. Generally speaking the question of permission is decided without a hearing. If it is conducted orally (in the circumstances described above) then a defendant or any other interested party may appear. If they do so the court will not generally make an order for costs against the claimant (see PD 54, para 8.6). However, recent case law suggests that such an order can be made (see the note in the White Book to CPR 54.12.6).

11.4.5 Response

Once permission is given a defendant or any other person served with the claim form who wishes to contest the claim or support the decision on additional grounds must file and serve detailed grounds for contesting the claim or supporting the decision on any additional grounds and any written evidence within 35 days after service of the order giving permission. PD 54, para 10.1 provides that where a defendant or other party filing the response intends to rely on documents not already filed, a bundle of those documents must be lodged when the detailed grounds are filed.

11.4.6 Additional grounds

Where the claimant wishes to rely on additional grounds other than those upon which he has been given permission to proceed he must apply to court (CPR 54.15).

11.4.7 Evidence, disclosure and cross-examination

The only evidence (generally) admissible in judicial review proceedings is written evidence. Unless such evidence has been lodged in accordance with the above rules, then permission is required from the court to file further evidence.

Generally speaking oral evidence or cross-examination of written evidence is not permitted. However, in exceptional cases this will be allowed.

Again, generally speaking, there is no disclosure of documents. However, the claimant, when he lodges the claim form, is expected to produce all relevant documents, consistent with the general duty to make full and frank disclosure. A similar duty does not apply to a defendant or other interested party. However, the courts have said that such a party should 'play with their cards face up'.

PD 54, para 12.1 specifies that disclosure is not required unless the court otherwise orders.

11.4.8 The hearing

As noted above, the hearing is conducted on written evidence, save in exceptional circumstances. The procedure is for oral submissions to be made. However, there is a power for the court to decide a matter without a hearing 'where all parties agree' (CPR 54.18). This is rarely used.

On the hearing of an application for judicial review any person may apply for permission, either to file evidence or make representations at that hearing (CPR 54.17).

11.4.9 Practice Direction

Specific provision is made for skeleton arguments to be lodged on the part of the claimant not less than 21 working days before the date of the hearing or the warned date, or on the part of the defendant not less than 14 days before those dates.

15.3 Skeleton arguments must contain
   (1) a time estimate for the complete hearing, including delivery of judgment;
   (2) a list of issues;
   (3) a list of the legal points to be taken (together with any relevant authorities with page references to the passages relied on);
   (4) a chronology of events (with page references to the bundle of documents (see paragraph 16.1));
   (5) a list of essential documents for the advance reading of the court (with page references to the passages relied on) (if different from that filed with the claim form) and a time estimate for that reading; and
   (6) a list of persons referred to.

The claimant has a duty to file a paginated and indexed bundle of all documents required for the hearing of the judicial review, including those relied upon by the defendants and any other party (PD 54, paras 16.1 and 16.2).

11.4.10 Disposal by consent

PD 54, para 17.1, specifies that the parties may agree as to the order to be made in a claim for judicial review and should lodge an order at court setting out the matters agreed on 'with a short statement of the matters relied on as justifying the proposed agreed order and copies of any authorities or statutory provisions relied on'. If the court is satisfied it will grant the order made. If not, it will direct an oral hearing.

Where the hearing relates to costs only then there is no need for an attendance, but a document can be filed setting out the terms of agreement (PD 54, para 17.4).

At any stage of the proceedings the court can order a claim to continue as if it had not been started under Pt 54.

11.4.11 Pre-action protocol

A pre-action protocol has now been published which governs judicial review proceedings. The protocol specifically states that it does not affect the time limits for bringing judicial review proceedings and the footnotes to the document state that 'compliance with the protocol alone is unlikely to be sufficient to persuade the Court to allow a late claim'.

The protocol goes on to specify that it is a 'code of good practice and contains the steps which parties should generally follow before making a claim for judicial review'. However, it is not appropriate where the defendant does not have the legal power to change the decision being challenged. Thus, a challenge to any decision of the Tribunal does not attract the provisions of the protocol, because the Tribunal has no legal power to alter its decision. However, the text makes clear that it is good practice even in emergency cases to use the protocol.

The protocol, in essence, requires the claimant to send a standard letter before action, which sets out, inter alia, the matter being challenged, why it is contended to be wrong and the action sought. The public body is required to send a letter in response setting out why it proposes to contest the claim if it does so. The draft letters before claim and the response are annexed to the protocol.

The protocol notes that where a public body should have provided relevant documents or information the court may impose sanctions for the failure so to do. A public body (in this case the National Commission or National Assembly or the Tribunal) is best advised to disclose such documents in its response.

11.5 STATUTORY APPEALS

Section 121(1) of the 2000 Act defines the Tribunal as the Tribunal established by s 9 of the Protection of Children Act 1999. Schedule 4, para 21 of the 2000 Act provides that the Tribunal is to be governed by the Tribunals and Inquiries Act 1992.

Under the terms of the 1992 Act an appeal lies on a point of law from a decision of the Tribunal to the High Court.

There has been much judicial consideration and academic discussion over the meaning of a point of law. There is little point in trying to define what a point of law is. However, when one is challenging evidential matters, unless one can show that there was simply no evidence of a particular fact, such a challenge will not constitute a point of law. In those circumstances judicial review may be the better route of appeal.

One should also bear in mind that the right of statutory appeal lies only against decisions of the Tribunal. Where one is challenging a decision of the Commission or Assembly or, for example, a decision of a public body such as a local authority to close down a care home, then judicial review is the appropriate remedy.

11.5.1 Procedure

An appeal under the 1992 Act is governed by CPR 52. It is outside the scope of this book to consider the detailed procedure governing a Pt 52 appeal. Readers are referred to specialist texts on civil procedure such as the White Book.

Section 11 of the 1992 Act allows an appeal on a point of law, or the Tribunal can be required to sign and state a case. However, the latter is unnecessary because of the requirement to deliver a reasoned decision.

PD 52, para 17 governs statutory appeals in this case. It provides that an appellant's notice (which should be in form 161) is to be filed within 28 days after the date of the decision of the lower court. Time runs from the date of the written decision, not notice of the decision. PD 52, para 17.5 specifies that the appellant's notice should be served on the Chairman of the Tribunal.

The most important part of the appellant's notice is Section 7 which sets out the grounds for appeal.

Part 52 provides for the service of a respondent's notice.

11.5.2 Examples of appellate cases

The Rules of Procedure for the Tribunal permit it a wide discretion as to the evidence that it is prepared to admit. However this wide discretion entails concomitant care as to the weight to be applied to such evidence. In a case where the evidence is adduced in relation to events some of which are momentary, some of which are hearsay, and some of which are stale, this is particularly important. Great care should be exercised by the Tribunal when dealing with allegations which may be the result of personal animosity. Where the evidence before the Tribunal is of a poor quality, then for that reason alone the utmost care must be exercised before it is relied upon. It has invariably been the practice in the past that the Tribunal has admitted allegations against a homeowner which have been very stale and/or have formed no part of the statement of reasons. The Tribunal has said that it can weigh the evidence and determine its quality at a later stage. Such allegations are highly prejudicial and it is becoming increasingly the practice to disallow such allegations of past unresolved complaints. The President of the Tribunal reached such a conclusion in a transfer case called *Jugessur* which was abandoned before all the evidence could be called. It is thought that if a similar approach is not adopted, this will give grounds for appeal.

Once the Tribunal has handed down its written decision, unless there are special circumstances it has no power to reconsider its decision (*Spring Grove Services Group plc v Hickinbottom* [1990] ICR 111 and *Akewushola v Secretary of State for the Home Department* [2000] 1 WLR 2295). The power to reopen a decision will be very rare indeed (*Hanks v Ace High Productions Ltd* [1978] ICR 1155). Such a power may be available to the Tribunal where there has been a mistake of fact or law and prejudice is established. This might be a ground for review rather than appeal.

11.5.3 Appeals to the Court of Appeal

The reader is referred to specialist text books such as the White Book on the procedure governing an appeal to the Court of Appeal.

It is, however, relevant to point out that permission will be required from the Court of Appeal (CPR 52.13(1)). The Court of Appeal will not give permission (CPR 52.13(2)) unless:

It considers that –
(a)   the appeal would raise an important point of principle or practice; or
(b)   there is some other compelling reason for the Court of Appeal to hear it.

12

EUROPEAN CONVENTION ON HUMAN RIGHTS

12.1 INTRODUCTION

On 2 October 2000 the Human Rights Act 1998 ('the 1998 Act') came into force. It introduced into UK domestic law the key provisions of the European Convention on Human Rights.

12.1.1 Areas of impact

The following four areas of potential impact of the European Convention on Human Rights ('the Convention') will be considered in this chapter:

- the impact of Art 6 ('the right to a fair trial') on a without notice application for an emergency closure order (under s 20 of the 2000 Act);
- the impact of Art 6 on either a fast or slow closure, where the registered person no longer has the establishment or agency, but where that person for any other reason (ss 14 and 20 of the 2000 Act) wishes to dispute any allegation of 'unfitness';
- the impact of Art 8 ('the right to respect for private and family life') on a closure of an establishment (or possibly, but less likely, an agency) from a client's point of view;

- the impact of Art 1 of the First Protocol ('protection of property') on the fast or slow closure of an establishment or agency from an owner's perspective.

However, before embarking upon the consideration of the above topics, it is necessary to have an overview of the 1998 Act.

12.1.2 Section 6 of the 1998 Act

The provisions of s 6 of the 1998 Act are key so far as, inter alia, the National Commission/National Assembly and Tribunal are concerned:

- it is unlawful for a public authority (for definition see below) 'to act in a way which is incompatible with a Convention Right';
- however, a public authority can act in a way which is incompatible with a Convention right where it does so in accordance with the provisions of primary legislation, which cannot be given effect to in a way compatible with Convention rights;
- the term 'public authority' includes:
  —a court or tribunal, and
  —any person certain of whose functions are functions of a public nature, 'but does not include either House of Parliament or a person exercising functions in connection with proceedings in parliament ...';
  —in relation to a 'public authority' which is only such because certain functions are those of a public nature, its acts are not necessarily within s 6 'if the nature of the act is private'.

12.2 HUMAN RIGHTS ACT 1998

The essential objective of the 1998 Act is to incorporate the rights and fundamental freedoms set out in Arts 2–12 and 14, Arts 1–3 of the First Protocol and Arts 1 and 2 of the Sixth Protocol of the Convention. All relevant Articles are set out in Sch 1 to the 1998 Act.

Any court or tribunal (and thus, in particular, the Care Standards Tribunal) must take into account, when determining any question which has arisen in connection with a 'Convention right', any of the authority of the European Court of Human Rights, together with the opinions and decisions of the Commission and Committee of Ministers.

All primary and secondary legislation must be read and given effect to in a way which is compatible with the Convention rights whenever enacted.

If a provision of primary legislation cannot be read so as to be compatible with a Convention right, then the senior courts (namely the House of Lords, the Privy Council, the Court of Appeal (both divisions) and the High Court) can make a declaration of incompatibility of the primary legislation with the 1998 Act.

12.2.1 Proceedings under the 1998 Act

Where a public authority has acted (or proposes to act) in a way which is unlawful, ie not compatible with a Convention right and not capable of being justified under primary legislation which cannot be read in a 'Convention' way, then proceedings can be brought against that authority or Convention rights can be relied on as a defence to proceedings by that authority by any person who is (or would be) a victim of the unlawful act.

It should be noted that proceedings can only be brought against a public authority within a one-year limitation period, subject to 'any rule imposing restricted time limits in relation to the procedure in question', unless time is extended by the relevant court or tribunal. In relation to an application of the 1998 Act by way of a defence to a claim, there is no statutory limitation period.

12.2.2 Relief

Where the victim establishes that an action of a public authority is unlawful, the court can award 'such relief or remedy or make such Order' as are within its powers. This power includes an award of damages, the quantum of which is to be calculated in accordance with case law in the European Court.

12.2.3 Amending legislation

A Minister of the Crown or Her Majesty in Council may amend any provision of either primary or secondary legislation which is found to be unlawful or which is incompatible with the Convention in the light of any decision of the European Court.

12.2.4 Freedom of expression/thought

There are specific provisions in relation to the grant of relief in respect of persons seeking to rely on the right to freedom of expression and the right to freedom of thought, conscience and religion.

12.2.5 Derogation

The 1998 Act preserves the entitlement on the part of the Government to derogate and make reservations to the Convention.

12.3 EMERGENCY CLOSURE AND THE RIGHT TO A FAIR TRIAL

12.3.1 Article 6

Article 6 of the Convention provides a right to a fair trial:

1. In the determination of his civil rights and obligations or of any criminal charge against him, everyone is entitled to a fair and public hearing within a reasonable time by an independent and impartial tribunal established by law ...

12.3.2 Section 20 of the 2000 Act

Section 20 of the 2000 Act provides that the National Commission/National Assembly may seek the emergency closure of an establishment or agency before a justice of the peace without notice to the registered person, where there is a serious risk to the life, health or well-being of a person.

It is clear from the existing domestic case law in relation to the Registered Homes Act 1984 that such a without notice application can properly be made. However, if the application is improperly made, ie on the basis of insufficient evidence, then judicial review may go to restrain the order of the magistrates' court (see *R v Ealing, Hammersmith and Hounslow HA, ex p Wilson* (1996) 30 BMLR 92).

12.3.3 Article 6 compliant?

The question, following the incorporation of the Convention into English law, is whether the use of the without notice procedure complies with the requirements of Art 6. Furthermore, is the existence of a right of appeal to the Tribunal a satisfaction of this particular Convention right?

A preliminary issue is whether the National Care Standards Commission or National Assembly is a 'public authority' for the purposes of the Human Rights Act 1998.

The next question is whether the 'licence' held by a registered person to operate a home, including a nursing home, is a 'civil right ... and obligation ...'. The answer to this question must be in the affirmative if the protection of Art 6 is to be triggered. Traditionally, the European Court has drawn a distinction between public law and private law. In relation to the former it has been unwilling to hold that the licence can constitute 'a civil right'. In relation to the latter it has been prepared to hold that it is.

However, the European Court has proved ready to find a civil right, either alongside or within a public law right (*Gaygusuz v Austria* (1996) 23 EHRR 364 and *Jordebo Foundation of Christian Schools v Sweden* (1987) 61 DR 92 (especially para 87)). The court held in *Jordebo* that the right or the grant of permission to run a private school held by a local School Board was a 'civil right and obligation' because the 'private character of a right to run a school does not change because of the administrative supervision to which the school is subject'.

In the authors' opinion it is likely that the right to operate an establishment or agency will be equated with a 'civil right[s] and obligation[s]' and thus will fall within Art 6 of the Convention.

The final question is whether it can be said that the existence of an appeal to the Tribunal at some date in the future discharges Art 6. In the authors' view the point is arguable. Section 20(2) states that an application 'may' be made without notice. Parliament intended that the district judge or justices should have a discretion as to whether the registered person should be put on notice of the application. The authors' opinion is that the Commission/National Assembly should not shy away from giving notice of the intended application. If the evidence of 'serious risk' to life, health or well-being is compelling, the application will be granted regardless of whether it is opposed. It is contended that those who will lose their livelihood and face the prospect of their names being put on the list of cancelled persons if the s 20 application is granted are entitled to be heard, especially if they are given several hours' notice. During that time officials can safeguard the vulnerable at the home if it is felt that they may be at further risk as a result of the registered person being put on notice. Even if it is found that the without notice entitlement under the 2000 Act is Convention-proof, the inevitable delay between a magistrates' court order and a Tribunal hearing may or may not be said to be 'reasonable'.

12.4 CLOSURE

12.4.1 Possession of an establishment/agency as a prerequisite to the right to appeal

The issue is whether a registered person who is the owner of an establishment (or the premises in which an agency operates) who is the subject of a closure order either under s 14 or s 20 of the 2000 Act has the right to bring an appeal under s 21 of the 2000 Act where the premises have been lost.

12.4.1.1 *The issue*
The relevant decisions under the Registered Homes Act 1984 hold that as a matter of domestic law the loss of a residential care or nursing home will preclude any appeal or continuation of an appeal from proceeding. See most recently *Sanjivi v East Kent HA* (2001) 59 BMLR 115). The court in *Sanjivi* relied on the cases of *Woodward v North Somerset DC* (1998) 1 FLR 950 and *Jenkins v Essex CC* (1999) 1 FLR 420.

12.4.1.2 *The 2000 Act*
Under the terms of s 1(1) of the Registered Homes Act 1984 registration was required in respect of any 'establishment':

Subject to the following provisions of this section, registration under this part of this Act is required in respect of any establishment which provides or is intended to provide … residential accommodation …

Under the provisions of s 11 of the 2000 Act it is the person and not the establishment or agency that requires registration. See in particular s 12 of the 2000 Act:

(1) A person seeking to be registered under this Part shall make an application to the registration authority …

If the reasoning in *Sanjivi* is applied to the construction of ss 4 and 12 of the 2000 Act, then the High Court and the Court of Appeal (only on the issue of permission) have held that there is no incompatibility with the Convention. This view has not been tested in the European Court.

The Court of Appeal found that there was no disharmony between the provisions of the Registered Homes Act 1984 and those contained in Art 6, Art 8 or Art 1 of the First Protocol relating to deprivation of possession (see 12.3.1, 12.5.1 and 12.6.1 respectively).

The authors' view remains that the deprivation of a right of appeal, if the reasoning in *Sanjivi* is applied to the 2000 Act (as it might be), runs contrary to all of the above provisions. In other words, it is wrong in principle for the owner of premises which constitute an establishment or from which an agency operates to be deprived of a licence to use those premises without a right of appeal.

12.5 CLOSURE AND THE RIGHT TO RESPECT FOR PRIVATE AND FAMILY LIFE

12.5.1 Article 8

Article 8 of the Convention provides as follows:

1. Everyone has the right to respect for his private and family life, his home and his correspondence.
2. There shall be no interference by a public authority with the exercise of this right except such as is in accordance with the law and is necessary in a democratic society in the interests of national security, public safety or the economic well-being of the country, for the prevention of disorder or crime, for the protection of health or morals, or for the protection of the rights and freedoms of others.

The first question is whether an establishment, particularly a care home, can properly be said to be the 'home' of a resident or patient within it.

12.5.2 Domestic law

In *R v North East Devon HA, ex p Coughlan* [2001] QB 213, the Court of Appeal held, inter alia, that if a public body exercising a statutory function made a promise as to how it would behave in the future, which induced a legitimate expectation of benefit which was substantive, rather than procedural, to frustrate that expectation would be so unfair that it would amount to an abuse of power (see para 93 of the judgment of Lord Woolf MR).

There is no extant case law of the European Court on this topic. However, the decision in *Coughlan* suggests that a care home might be protected by Art 8 of the Convention. The issue that nonetheless remains is what is the position in relation to closure of a residential or nursing care establishment.

On the assumption that a care home equates to a home within the meaning of Art 8.1 (and that seems to be the case: see *Coughlan*) and on the further assumption that the closure of a nursing home necessarily interferes with the right to respect for that home, then the question is whether that interference can be justified under Art 8.

There would be no question but that the closure could be justified as being 'in accordance with the law': the National Commission or National Assembly would undoubtedly point to their rights under the Act to police care homes. However, that is not in itself sufficient; it must also be for a 'reason' within Art 8(2). One could undoubtedly point to 'the protection of health'. This question is likely to be answered in favour of the registration authority.

12.6 CLOSURE AND THE PROTECTION OF PROPERTY

12.6.1 Article 1 of the First Protocol

Article 1 of the First Protocol provides:

Every natural or legal person is entitled to the peaceful enjoyment of his possessions. No one shall be deprived of his possessions except in the public interest and subject to the conditions provided for by law and by the general principles of international law.

The preceding provisions shall not, however, in any way impair the right of a State to enforce such laws as it deems necessary to control the use of property in accordance with the general interest or to secure the payment of taxes or other contributions or penalties.

12.6.2 Possession

'Possession' plainly includes 'property' and also includes the right to use property. See, for example, *Chassagnou v France* (2000) 29 EHRR 615. The case related to hunting rights over property. It specifically held that the compulsory assignment of the right to hunt under the relevant French law was:

[a] restriction on the free exercise of the right of use [which] undoubtedly constitutes an interference with the Applicant's enjoyment of their rights as the owners of property. Accordingly, the second paragraph of Article 1 is applicable in the case ...

12.6.3 Property

According to *Halsbury's Laws of England, Constitutional Law and Human Rights*, para 165, the first paragraph in Art 1 of the First Protocol guarantees the right to property, which includes the entitlement to use property (*Herrick v UK* (1985) 8 EHRR 66); the right to continue to hold a licence to carry on an economic activity where the licensee has a reasonable and legitimate expectation as to the lasting nature of the licence and to the continuation and benefit from it (*Pudas v Sweden* (1984) 40 DR 234); the economic interest connected with the running of a business

(*Tre Traktorer AB v Sweden* Series A No 159 (1989) 13 EHRR 309); and the right to exercise a profession (*Van Marle v Netherlands* Series A No 101 (1986) 8 EHRR 483). See most recently in relation to solicitors' practices: *Holder v Law Society*, Peter Smith J (The Times, 9 September 2002). This view was not dissented from by the Court of Appeal (The Times, 29 January 2003).

12.6.4 Removal of rights

That right can be removed 'if in the public interest and subject to conditions provided by law'. According to the footnote in *Halsbury's Laws*:

Whether an expropriation or other deprivation of possessions is in the public interest will be subjected to a very marginal review, as the margin of appreciation available to the national legislature in implementing social and economic policies is a wide one; the legislature's judgement as to what is in the public interest would be respected unless that judgement is manifestly without reasonable foundation: see *Handyside v United Kingdom* A 24 (1976), 1 EHRR 737; *James v United Kingdom* A 98 (1986), 8 EHRR 123.

If this is right then a decision to close, for example, a care home, is likely to be deemed not to be in breach of the provisions of Art 1 of the First Protocol. However, this issue is moot.

12.6.5 Proportionate

The measures adopted will have to be proportionate: 'a fair balance must be struck between the demands of the general interest of the community and the requirement of the protection of the individual's fundamental rights, the search for such a fair balance being inherent in the whole of the Convention': see, inter alia, *James v UK* and *Tre Traktorer AB v Sweden*; see also *Lithgow v UK* Series A No 1020 (1986) 8 EHRR 329.

The same approach applies to the second paragraph of Art 1 of the First Protocol, namely the right of a state to enforce such laws as it deems necessary to control the use of property. The key question is proportionality.

12.6.6 Conclusion

In the authors' view it is very likely that the extant provisions of the 2000 Act and the regulations made under that Act will be held to be proportionate.

13

CRIMINAL OFFENCES AND LIABILITIES

13.1 GENERAL

The 2000 Act, with amendments to related legislation including the Children Act 1989 and the Adoption Act 1976, creates an array of new statutory criminal offences. This chapter considers the new criminal provisions in some detail.

13.1.1 The decision to prosecute

Any decision to prosecute an individual or corporate entity is a serious step with wide-ranging implications for all involved. Before commencing a prosecution the Commission, Assembly or Ofsted should satisfy itself that there is sufficient evidence to provide a realistic prospect of conviction against a defendant on each charge. Those considering prosecuting ought to consider and take into account what the defence case may be and how that may affect any prosecution before any decision is taken.

13.1.2 The test

What is the test to be applied? An objective test ought to be applied when determining whether there is a realistic prospect of a conviction in any case. What that test requires is whether a properly directed district judge or bench of lay magistrates are more likely than not to convict the individual or corporate defendant of the charge or charges alleged. This is not the same test as the court applies when determining whether the prosecution has satisfied the court of the defendant's guilt.

Those prosecuting ought also to determine whether a prosecution is in the public interest. In 1951, Lord Shawcross (then the Attorney-General) made his well-known statement on the public interest in the House of Commons (*Hansard,* HC vol 483, col 681 (29 January 1951)) when he said that:

It has never been the rule in this country, I hope it never will be, that suspected criminal offences must automatically be the subject of prosecution ...

Public interest factors that affect the decision to prosecute usually depend on the seriousness of the offence and the circumstances of it. An obvious example of this will be the running of an unregistered children's service where, unless there are compelling reasons not to prosecute, there ought to be a prosecution in all cases.

13.1.3 Actus reus and mens rea

It is a general principle of UK common and statute criminal law that there must be someone who is blameworthy before an offence can be committed. Offences can be committed in all manners of ways, but those prosecuting must in most cases demonstrate that the act was committed by negligence, guilty knowledge or fault; in other words what is called mens rea.

The concepts of actus reus and mens rea for the most part underpin UK criminal law. A number of statutes do, however, create offences of strict liability where no fault needs to be established by those prosecuting. A full commentary on these criminal concepts is beyond the scope of this book and those who wish to undertake further research are directed to a standard text such as *Halsbury's Laws*, vol 11(1); *The Digest (Annotated British Commonwealth and European Cases)*, vol 14(1), second re-issue; *Archbold* and *Blackstone's Criminal Practice*, the latter two both published annually.

13.1.4 The burden of proof

In nearly all cases the burden of proof is upon those who prosecute to establish the defendant's guilt, throughout the course of proceedings (*Woolmington v DPP* (1935) AC 462, 481; *R v Hunt* (1987) AC 352; and *R v Lambert* (2001) 3 WLR 206, which considered the applicability of Art 6 of the European Convention on Human Rights).

13.1.5 The standard of proof

Before convicting a defendant, the district judge who sits alone, or lay magistrates of which there must be at least two justices, must be satisfied beyond a reasonable doubt or be sure of the defendant's guilt. Thus if, at the end of all the evidence, there is a reasonable doubt created by the evidence, whether that be the prosecution's or the defendant's evidence, the prosecution will not have made out its case and the defendant is entitled to be acquitted (*Woolmington v DPP* (1935) AC 462, 481–2 and *R v Bentley (Deceased)* (2001) Cr App R 21).

13.1.6 The commencement of proceedings

Proceedings are commenced in the county in which the alleged offence was committed by virtue of s 2(1) of the Magistrates' Courts Act 1980. A prosecution is commenced by the laying of an information before a magistrates' clerk or district judge or lay bench by the prosecutor. Under r 4(1) of the Magistrates' Courts Rules 1981, SI 1981/552, the prosecutor is the person who signs or authorizes the written information to be laid. In the case of an oral information, the prosecutor is the person who goes before the magistrate or magistrates' clerk to make the allegation against the defendant. Whilst the prosecutor is an individual, for all practical purposes the prosecution will be commenced by the Commission, the Assembly or Ofsted. In the magistrates' court neither the prosecutor nor the accused need to be legally represented, but it is usual that they are represented by either counsel or a solicitor, both of whom have rights of audience. Magistrates have an inherent power to regulate their own procedure in their own courts where it is in the interests of justice to do so and that power includes a discretion to allow someone other than a legal representative to present a case. The general rule is that proceedings are in open court, because the public at large are concerned to see that justice is properly administered, though that general rule can be departed from in exceptional circumstances. (See *Att-Gen v Leveller Magazine Ltd* (1979) AC 440, 449–50 and Magistrates' Courts Act 1980, ss 121 and 122.)

13.2 OVERVIEW OF OFFENCES UNDER THE 2000 ACT

The 2000 Act puts on a statutory footing various offences permitting criminal proceedings under ss 24–31 of the Act. Under the Registered Homes Act 1984 it was principally a breach of specified regulations that gave rise to criminal liability. The 2000 Act creates a number of specific offences outside the regulations. The Act is silent on the notice provisions, ie whether notice of an intended prosecution must be given, and it will be interesting to see how the Commission and Assembly approach this, in particular the burden of proof to be applied at that stage. A detailed analysis of the notice provisions is outside the scope of this book, but those interested are referred to *Stone's Justices' Manual*, and other textbooks.

Under the 2000 Act inspectors, or any other person authorized by the registration authority, have wide powers under ss 31 and 32 to enter and inspect premises, interview various persons, examine, seize and remove documents. Where the registration authority is obstructed or finds evidence of breaches of the regulations it will need to determine what enforcement action, if any, it ought to take, ie cancellation of registration under s 14, possibly urgent cancellation under s 20 where there appears to be a serious risk to a person's life, health or well-being, or prosecution for obstruction under ss 31(9) or 32.

13.2.1 Offences created under the 2000 Act

13.2.1.1 *Failure to register*

Section 11(1) makes it an offence for any person to carry on or manage an establishment or agency without being registered. (A voluntary adoption agency falls outside the scope of the registration requirements.) Section 11(2) requires an agency that is carried on from two or more branches to be separately registered. Those contemplating the laying of an information or the issuing of a summons are directed to the wording of s 11(5) and (6). The definition of 'managers' is contained in s 12(3). In *Varcoe v Devon CC* (RHT decision number 48) HH Judge Gerrard considered the interpretation of the word 'manager' in s 3 of the Registered Homes Act 1984. He refused to give general guidance, saying that each case ought to be determined on its own facts, but then went on to look at the level of day-to-day management in that case. On summary conviction a person guilty of an offence is liable to a fine not exceeding level 5 of the standard scale, currently £5,000.

13.2.1.2 *Failure to comply with conditions*

Section 24 makes it an offence for a registered person who is involved in running an establishment (s 4(8)) or agency (s 4(9)) to, without reasonable excuse, fail to comply with any condition imposed. The corporate offence is committed under s 30. On summary conviction the person or establishment is liable to a fine not exceeding level 5 of the standard scale, currently £5,000.

13.2.1.3 *Contravention of regulations*

Section 25 makes it an offence to contravene any regulation promulgated under Pt II of the Act. The definition of regulation is that set out in s 121(1) of the Act and the regulations themselves. On summary conviction a person found guilty of such breach is liable to a fine not exceeding level 4 of the standard scale, currently £2,500.

13.2.1.4 *False description*

Section 26 makes it an offence for any person knowingly to make a false or misleading statement which purports to indicate that the establishment or agency has been registered by the Commission or the Assembly. Thus, a homeowner who purports to represent that his establishment is suitable to accommodate a resident who has nursing needs when it is not, will be guilty of an offence. The prosecuting authority must prove intent to deceive. See the well-known definition of intent to defraud ('deceive') given by Lord Radcliffe in *Welham v DPP* [1961] AC 103, 122–128 and applied in *R v Withers* [1974] 2 WLR 26. On summary conviction the defendant is liable to a fine not exceeding level 5 of the standard scale.

13.2.1.5 *False statement*

For the first time, s 27 makes it a specific offence for an applicant knowingly to make a material false or misleading statement in his application for registration or in any application for a variation of any condition covering the establishment or agency. An offence of making a false statement is committed at the place where it is received and at the time when it is received by the person or authority to whom it is addressed (*Lawrence v Ministry of Agriculture, Fisheries and Foods* [1992] Crim LR 874). The authors have reservations as to recklessness in the context of making a false statement as recent decisions of the Court of Appeal seem to be moving away from the decision of the House of Lords in *R v Caldwell and Lawrence* (1982) AC 510 despite being bound by it. It is likely that the prosecuting authority's task of establishing its case has been made easier with the warning contained in the application forms that criminal offences will be committed in such circumstances. It has to be hoped that the Commission and the Assembly in Wales will take obvious and wilful breaches of these provisions seriously. There is a clear public interest in ensuring that those who knowingly make false or misleading statements will be prosecuted, thereby sending a clear message to providers that such conduct will not be tolerated.

13.2.1.6 *Failure to display certificate of registration*
Section 28 makes it an offence for an establishment to fail to place the issued certificate of registration in a conspicuous place. Breach of s 28 renders the establishment or agency liable to summary proceedings with a maximum fine of £500. The authors presume that proceedings will only be instituted where earlier requests to display or move to a more prominent place have been ignored or where a provider is being prosecuted for a number of offences.

13.2.1.7 *Proceedings for offences*
Section 29 states that only the Commission, the Secretary of State under s 113 or the Assembly may bring proceedings under Pt II. Others (it does not specify who) may bring proceedings so long as they have been granted permission or a fiat by the Attorney-General. Section 29(2) requires these proceedings to be brought within six months of sufficient evidence being available to support a prosecution. The subsection uses the words 'in the opinion of the prosecutor ...' and it is the view of the authors that that would cover evidence within the knowledge of an inspector or other official. There is an absolute bar on the bringing of proceedings more than three years after the commission of an offence. Importantly, s 29(2) confirms that proceedings may be brought at any time up to three years after the date of knowledge of commission of an offence. The wording of the section is, in the view of the authors, clear. Proceedings must be brought within six months of the date of knowledge of any summary offence, reflecting the well-known provisions of s 127 of the Magistrates' Courts Act 1980. Where evidence comes to light after that period then criminal prosecution may be initiated up to but not beyond three years.

13.2.1.8 *Offences by bodies corporate*

Section 30 deals with corporate offences and offences committed by local or health authorities. Thus, where regulations are breached or the above offences are committed with the consent or connivance of, or are attributable to any neglect on the part of, a director, manager or company secretary, or any person who purports to act in such capacity, then either that individual or the body corporate will be guilty of an offence and liable on summary conviction to be sentenced to a financial penalty on the scales set out above.

13.2.1.9 *Obstructing an inspection*

Section 31(9) makes it an offence intentionally to obstruct an inspection, without reasonable excuse. This definition has caused problems of interpretation in several areas of the criminal law and, in particular, in deciding on the mens rea of the offence. Practitioners are referred to s 89 of the Police Act 1996 and cases such as *Rice v Connolly* [1966] 2 QB 414. Section 31 will require the prosecuting authority to establish wilful obstruction, ie a positive act and not a mere refusal to act. In the vast majority of cases this will clearly be established by the simple facts given in evidence by the inspector in the magistrates' court. Section 31(3) is wide-ranging and authorizes an inspector or other duly authorized person to examine the premises and treatment of patients or persons accommodated or cared for, to take copies of any relevant documents, to interview in private the manager or any other person carrying on the establishment or agency, any person employed there, any patient or person accommodated and to remove records, and documents whether stored in writing or on computer. Section 31(3)(c)–(e) entitles the Commission or Assembly to interview the persons mentioned therein via its inspectors. Section 67(9) of the Police and Criminal Evidence Act 1984 requires persons who are not police officers and who are charged with a duty of investigating offences or charging offenders to have regard to the provisions of the Codes of Practice issued under ss 60 and 66 of the 1984 Act. There are very detailed provisions in Code B dealing with the searching of premises and in Code C covering the interviewing of suspects. Where an offence is committed and a suspect is interviewed without a caution being administered (see Code C, para 10(4)), any evidence obtained during the course of the interview may be excluded by virtue of s 78 of the 1984 Act. Section 78 provides that in any criminal proceedings the court may refuse to allow evidence on which the prosecution proposes to rely if it appears to the court, having regard to all the circumstances, including the circumstances in which the evidence was obtained, that the admissibility of the evidence would have an adverse effect on the fairness of the proceedings so that the court ought not to admit it (*R v Jelen* (1989) 90 Cr App R 456, 464–5). In *Dudley Metropolitan BC v Debenhams plc*, The Times, 16 August 1994, the Divisional Court held that a routine inspection by a trading standards officer was a search within the ordinary meaning of the word and the provisions of Code B of the Police and Criminal Evidence Act 1984 could apply.

13.2.1.10 *Wales*

The Children's Commissioner for Wales will have wide powers under s 75 (when it comes into effect) to deal with obstruction and other acts and omissions. The Commissioner may certify that an offence has been committed and refer an individual or company to the High Court which has all the powers at its disposal under the Civil Procedure Rules; see for example the offence of wilfully obstructing a person (inspector or other) lawfully exercising inspection powers under s 79U(7) and (8). Again, the time limits for the initiation of criminal proceedings in Wales (s 79X) are the same as those in England. Given the long-standing and widespread concerns about the protection of children, the authors understand that a swift and robust prosecution action will be taken where a breach is shown.

13.2.1.11 *Effect of inclusion in the list*

Section 89 requires those who provide care to vulnerable adults to ascertain whether any prospective employee has been included on the list kept by the Secretary of State, through the Criminal Records Bureau (see 7.2.5 above). Thus there is a requirement on an employer immediately to cease employing a person if information comes to light that they are included on the list. It is an offence under s 89(5) for an individual to apply for work caring for the vulnerable where he knows his name is on the list. The only defence is that set out in s 89(6). An individual found guilty of such serious conduct is liable on summary conviction to a term of imprisonment not exceeding six months or to a fine or both and on trial on indictment to a term of imprisonment not exceeding five years, or to a fine or both. The Tribunal has power to review the circumstances of those included on the list under Pt VII. Where a breach of s 89(5) is established, it is the view of the authors that there should always be a prosecution and, in the most serious cases, proceedings should be on indictment. At the time of writing, the Criminal Records Bureau, an executive agency, has extended the deadline for CRB checks for existing care home staff (but not registered providers or managers) ie those staff already in posts before 1 April 2002, so that the deadline for those staff checks to be carried out is now 31 October 2004. However, staff appointed after 1 April 2002 do require CRB checks. Those wishing to review the position can do so at the CRB website at www.crb.gov.uk/media_news.htm.

13.2.1.12 *Other statutory offences*

Amendments have been made to the Children Act 1989 creating a number of offences and there have been consequential amendments to ss 1(3) and 9(2) of the Adoption Act 1976 by Sch 4 to the 2000 Act.

13.2.2 Offences created by regulation

Breach of a fairly large number of the regulations issued by the Secretary of State in the exercise of powers conferred on him under ss 4(6), 22(1), (2)(a)–(d) and (f)–(j),

(5)(a), (7)(a)–(h), 25, 34(1) and 118(5)–(7) of the 2000 Act create criminal offences. It is beyond the scope of this book to deal with all of the offences created and readers are directed to the respective regulations. However, to demonstrate the wide ambit of the potential criminal offences created, two sets of regulations are examined below.

Regulation 29 of the Domiciliary Care Agencies Regulations 2002, SI 2002/3214, which came into force on 1 April 2003, makes it an offence to fail to comply with regs 4–6 and 11–25. Regulation 29(2) acts to prevent the Commission from bringing criminal proceedings following a contravention or failure to comply with the Regulations before it has complied with the various procedural require-ments. Subject to reg 29(4) the person concerned must be registered. The Commission may, however, bring criminal proceedings against a person who was once, but is no longer registered, in respect of a failure to comply with reg 19, which requires records to be kept up-to-date, in good order, properly secured and retained for a period of not less than three years beginning on the date of the last entry. Such records include a copy of the service user's plan and a detailed record of the personal care provided to the service user.

There are important and mandatory notice requirements which, if not complied with, will render any criminal proceedings a nullity. Regulation 29(2)(b) requires the notice to be served on the registered person specifying the following:

- in what respect, in the opinion of the Commission, the registered person has contravened any of the Regulations, or failed or is failing to comply with the requirements of the Regulations;
- where it is practical to do so, what action the registered person ought to take to comply with any of the Regulations;
- giving the registered person up to three months to take action in accordance with reg 29(3)(b).

The notice must state that the registered person is entitled to make representations in a period not exceeding one month about the contents of and service of the notice.

There are similar provisions in the Care Homes Regulations 2001, SI 2001/3965 which by reg 36 make contravention or failure to comply with regs 4, 5, 11, 12(1)–(4), 13(1)–(4) and (6)–(8), 14, 15, 16(1)(2)(a)–(j), (l)–(n) and (3), 17–26 and 37–40 an offence. Practitioners considering whether an offence has been committed will need to look at reg 3 of the Care Standards Act 2000 (Establishments and Agencies) (Miscellaneous Amendments) Regulations 2002, SI 2002/865 which makes a number of consequential amendments to the list of offences specified in the Care Homes Regulations 2001. As before the Commission should not bring proceed-ings against a person in respect of any contravention or failure to comply with the Regulations unless he is a registered person (but see reg 43(4)) and he has been served with a notice and has contravened or failed to comply with the notice.

There has been some discussion within the Commission about what test ought to be adopted in considering whether there has been a breach of regulation and a crimi-nal offence committed. The authors are not entirely clear why this information is disclosable to the defendant in any event, but it is suggested that the test at this stage is lower, ie 'I suspect but cannot prove on the balance of probabilities'. If it is otherwise, it is an exceptionally high test that has to be met and it ought to be recalled that it will be for the criminal courts to decide at a later stage, if proceedings are brought, whether the prosecution has proved its case so that the magistrates are sure of guilt.

13.2.3 Costs

Where there has been a successful prosecution by the Commission, the National Assembly or Ofsted, they will be able to apply for a costs order under s 18 of the Prosecution of Offences Act 1985. The court has power to make a costs order against an accused as it considers just and reasonable. Some guidance is given as to how the discretion should be exercised in *Practice Direction (Costs in Criminal Proceedings)* [1991] 1 WLR 498. The amount of costs, if any, to be paid must be specified in an order.

If a person pleads guilty there is no rule that a costs order cannot be made against him. It is clear from s 17(6) of the 1985 Act that 'prosecution costs' includes those of a public body.

A person who successfully defends proceedings may apply for an award from central funds in respect of his own costs. This is known as a defendant's costs order. Practitioners are referred to s 16 of the 1985 Act and the *Practice Direction* (above). There are a number of cases governing the exercise of the court's discretion and practitioners are referred to the specialist criminal practice texts, such as *Archbold*.

Appendix 1

CARE STANDARDS ACT 2000

ARRANGEMENT OF SECTIONS

PART I
INTRODUCTORY

Preliminary

Registration authorities

PART II
ESTABLISHMENTS AND AGENCIES

Registration

PART III
LOCAL AUTHORITY SERVICES

CHAPTER II
SUPPLEMENTAL

CARE STANDARDS ACT 2000

An Act to establish a National Care Standards Commission; to make provision for the registration and regulation of children's homes, independent hospitals, independent clinics, care homes, residential family centres, independent medical agencies, domiciliary care agencies, fostering agencies, nurses agencies and voluntary adoption agencies; to make provision for the regulation and inspection of local authority fostering and adoption services; to establish a General Social Care Council and a Care Council for Wales and make provision for the registration, regulation and training of social care workers; to establish a Children's Commissioner for Wales; to make provision for the registration, regulation and training of those providing child minding or day care; to make provision for the protection of children and vulnerable adults; to amend the law about children looked after in schools and colleges; to repeal the Nurses Agencies Act 1957; to amend Schedule 1 to the Local Authority Social Services Act 1970; and for connected purposes.

[20th July 2000]

BE IT ENACTED by the Queen's most Excellent Majesty, by and with the advice and consent of the Lords Spiritual and Temporal, and Commons, in this present Parliament assembled, and by the authority of the same, as follows:–

PART I
INTRODUCTORY

Preliminary

1. Children's homes

(1) Subsections (2) to (6) have effect for the purposes of this Act.

(2) An establishment is a children's home (subject to the following provisions of this section) if it provides care and accommodation wholly or mainly for children.

(3) An establishment is not a children's home merely because a child is cared for and accommodated there by a parent or relative of his or by a foster parent.

(4) An establishment is not a children's home if it is–

    (a) a health service hospital;

    (b) an independent hospital or an independent clinic; or

    (c) a residential family centre,

or if it is of a description excepted by regulations.

(5) Subject to subsection (6), an establishment is not a children's home if it is a school.

(6) A school is a children's home at any time if at that time accommodation is provided for children at the school and either–

    (a) in each year that fell within the period of two years ending at that time, accommodation was provided for children, either at the school or under arrangements made by the proprietor of the school, for more than 295 days; or

    (b) it is intended to provide accommodation for children, either at the school or under arrangements made by the proprietor of the school, for more than 295 days in any year;

and in this subsection 'year' means a period of twelve months.

But accommodation shall not for the purposes of paragraph (a) be regarded as provided to children for a number of days unless there is at least one child to whom it is provided for that number of days; and paragraph (b) shall be construed accordingly.

(7) For the purposes of this section a person is a foster parent in relation to a child if–

    (a) he is a local authority foster parent in relation to the child;

    (b) he is a foster parent with whom a child has been placed by a voluntary organisation under section 59(1)(a) of the 1989 Act; or

    (c) he fosters the child privately.

2. Independent hospitals etc.

(1) Subsections (2) to (6) apply for the purposes of this Act.

(2) A hospital which is not a health service hospital is an independent hospital.

(3) 'Hospital' (except in the expression health service hospital) means–

    (a) an establishment–

        (i) the main purpose of which is to provide medical or psychiatric treatment for illness or mental disorder or palliative care; or

        (ii) in which (whether or not other services are also provided) any of the listed services are provided;

    (b) any other establishment in which treatment or nursing (or both) are provided for persons liable to be detained under the Mental Health Act 1983.

(4) 'Independent clinic' means an establishment of a prescribed kind (not being a hospital) in which services are provided by medical practitioners (whether or not any services are also provided for the purposes of the establishment elsewhere).

But an establishment in which, or for the purposes of which, services are provided by medical practitioners in pursuance of the National Health Service Act 1977 is not an independent clinic.

(5) 'Independent medical agency' means an undertaking (not being an independent clinic) which consists of or includes the provision of services by medical practitioners.

But if any of the services are provided for the purposes of an independent clinic, or by medical practitioners in pursuance of the National Health Service Act 1977, it is not an independent medical agency.

(6) References to a person liable to be detained under the Mental Health Act 1983 do not include a person absent in pursuance of leave granted under section 17 of that Act.

(7) In this section 'listed services' means–

    (a) medical treatment under anaesthesia or sedation;

    (b) dental treatment under general anaesthesia;

    (c) obstetric services and, in connection with childbirth, medical services;

    (d) termination of pregnancies;

   (e) cosmetic surgery;

   (f) treatment using prescribed techniques or prescribed technology.

(8) Regulations may–

   (a) except any description of establishment from the definitions in subsections (2) to (4);

   (b) except any description of undertaking from the definition in subsection (5);

   (c) modify the definition in subsection (7).

3. Care homes

(1) For the purposes of this Act, an establishment is a care home if it provides accommodation, together with nursing or personal care, for any of the following persons.

(2) They are–

   (a) persons who are or have been ill;

   (b) persons who have or have had a mental disorder;

   (c) persons who are disabled or infirm;

   (d) persons who are or have been dependent on alcohol or drugs.

(3) But an establishment is not a care home if it is–

   (a) a hospital;

   (b) an independent clinic; or

   (c) a children's home,

or if it is of a description excepted by regulations.

4. Other basic definitions

(1) This section has effect for the purposes of this Act.

(2) 'Residential family centre' means, subject to subsection (6), any establishment at which–

   (a) accommodation is provided for children and their parents;

   (b) the parents' capacity to respond to the children's needs and to safeguard their welfare is monitored or assessed; and

   (c) the parents are given such advice, guidance or counselling as is considered necessary.

In this subsection 'parent', in relation to a child, includes any person who is looking after him.

(3) 'Domiciliary care agency' means, subject to subsection (6), an undertaking which consists of or includes arranging the provision of personal care in their own homes for persons who by reason of illness, infirmity or disability are unable to provide it for themselves without assistance.

(4) 'Fostering agency' means, subject to subsection (6)–

   (a) an undertaking which consists of or includes discharging functions of local authorities in connection with the placing of children with foster parents; or

   (b) a voluntary organisation which places children with foster parents under section 59(1) of the 1989 Act.

(5) 'Nurses agency' means, subject to subsection (6), an employment agency or employment business, being (in either case) a business which consists of or includes supplying, or providing services for the purpose of supplying, registered nurses, registered midwives or registered health visitors.

(6) The definitions in subsections (2) to (5) do not include any description of establishment, undertaking or organisation excepted from those definitions by regulations.

(7) 'Voluntary adoption agency' means an adoption society within the meaning of the Adoption Act 1976 which is a voluntary organisation within the meaning of that Act.

(8) Below in this Act–

(a) any reference to a description of establishment is a reference to a children's home, an independent hospital, an independent hospital in which treatment or nursing (or both) are provided for persons liable to be detained under the Mental Health Act 1983, an independent clinic, a care home or a residential family centre;

(b) a reference to any establishment is a reference to an establishment of any of those descriptions.

(9) Below in this Act–

(a) any reference to a description of agency is a reference to an independent medical agency, a domiciliary care agency, a nurses agency, a fostering agency or a voluntary adoption agency;

(b) a reference to any agency is a reference to an agency of any of those descriptions.

Registration authorities

5. Registration authorities

For the purposes of this Act–

(a) the registration authority in relation to England is the National Care Standards Commission;

(b) the registration authority in relation to Wales is the National Assembly for Wales (referred to in this Act as 'the Assembly').

6. National Care Standards Commission

(1) There shall be a body corporate, to be known as the National Care Standards Commission (referred to in this Act as 'the Commission'), which shall exercise in relation to England the functions conferred on it by or under this Act or any other enactment.

(2) The Commission shall, in the exercise of its functions, act–

(a) in accordance with any directions in writing given to it by the Secretary of State; and

(b) under the general guidance of the Secretary of State.

(3) Schedule 1 shall have effect with respect to the Commission.

(4) The powers of the Secretary of State under this Part to give directions include power to give directions as to matters connected with the structure and organisation of the Commission, for example–

(a) directions about the establishment of offices for specified areas or regions;

(b) directions as to the organisation of staff into divisions.

7. General duties of the Commission

(1) The Commission shall have the general duty of keeping the Secretary of State informed about the provision in England of Part II services and, in particular, about–

(a) the availability of the provision; and

(b) the quality of the services.

(2) The Commission shall have the general duty of encouraging improvement in the quality of Part II services provided in England.

(3) The Commission shall make information about Part II services provided in England available to the public.

(4) When asked to do so by the Secretary of State, the Commission shall give the Secretary of State advice or information on such matters relating to the provision in England of Part II services as may be specified in the Secretary of State's request.

(5) The Commission may at any time give advice to the Secretary of State on–

(a) any changes which the Commission thinks should be made, for the purpose of securing improvement in the quality of Part II services provided in England, in the standards set out in statements under section 23; and

(b) any other matter connected with the provision in England of Part II services.

(6) The Secretary of State may by regulations confer additional functions on the Commission in relation to Part II services provided in England.

(7) In this section and section 8, 'Part II services' means services of the kind provided by persons registered under Part II, other than the provision of–

(a) medical or psychiatric treatment, or

(b) listed services (as defined in section 2).

8. General functions of the Assembly

(1) The Assembly shall have the general duty of encouraging improvement in the quality of Part II services provided in Wales.

(2) The Assembly shall make information about Part II services provided in Wales available to the public.

(3) In relation to Part II services provided in Wales, the Assembly shall have any additional function specified in regulations made by the Assembly; but the regulations may only specify a function corresponding to a function which, by virtue of section 7, is exercisable by the Commission in relation to Part II services provided in England.

(4) The Assembly may charge a reasonable fee determined by it in connection with the exercise of any power conferred on it by or under this Act.

(5) The Assembly may provide training for the purpose of assisting persons to attain standards set out in any statements published by it under section 23.

9. Co-operative working

(1) The Commission for Health Improvement ('CHI') and the National Care Standards Commission ('NCSC') may, if authorised to do so by regulations, arrange–

(a) for prescribed functions of the NCSC to be exercised by CHI on behalf of the NCSC;

(b) for prescribed functions of CHI, so far as exercisable in relation to England, to be exercised by the NCSC on behalf of CHI,

and accordingly CHI and the NCSC each have power to exercise functions of the other in accordance with arrangements under this subsection.

(2) The Assembly and CHI may arrange for any functions of the Assembly mentioned in section 10(6) to be exercised by CHI on behalf of the Assembly; and accordingly CHI has power to exercise functions of the Assembly in accordance with arrangements under this subsection.

(3) The Assembly and CHI may, if authorised to do so by regulations, arrange for prescribed functions of CHI, so far as exercisable in relation to Wales, to be exercised by the Assembly on behalf of CHI; and accordingly the Assembly has power to exercise functions of CHI in accordance with arrangements under this subsection.

(4) References in this section to exercising functions include a reference to assisting with their exercise.

(5) Regulations under this section shall be made by the Secretary of State; but the Secretary of State may not make regulations under subsection (3) without the agreement of the Assembly.

10. Inquiries

(1) The Secretary of State may cause an inquiry to be held into any matter connected with the exercise by the Commission of its functions.

(2) The appropriate Minister may cause an inquiry to be held into any matter connected with a service provided in or by an establishment or agency.

(3) Before an inquiry is begun, the person causing the inquiry to be held may direct that it shall be held in private.

(4) Where no direction has been given, the person holding the inquiry may if he thinks fit hold it, or any part of it, in private.

(5) Subsections (2) to (5) of section 250 of the Local Government Act 1972 (powers in relation to local inquiries) shall apply in relation to an inquiry under this section as they apply in relation to a local inquiry under that section; and references in those provisions as so applied to a Minister shall be taken to include references to the Assembly.

(6) Subsections (3) and (4) apply in relation to an inquiry under section 35 of the Government of Wales Act 1998 into any matter relevant to the exercise of–
    (a) any functions exercisable by the Assembly by virtue of section 5(b) or 8(3); or
    (b) any other functions exercisable by the Assembly corresponding to functions exercisable by the Commission in relation to England,
as they apply in relation to an inquiry under this section.

(7) The report of the person who held the inquiry shall, unless the Minister who caused the inquiry to be held considers that there are exceptional circumstances which make it inappropriate to publish it, be published in a manner which that Minister considers appropriate.

PART II
ESTABLISHMENTS AND AGENCIES

Registration

11. Requirement to register

(1) Any person who carries on or manages an establishment or agency of any description without being registered under this Part in respect of it (as an establishment or, as the case may be, agency of that description) shall be guilty of an offence.

(2) Where the activities of an agency are carried on from two or more branches, each of those branches shall be treated as a separate agency for the purposes of this Part.

(3) The reference in subsection (1) to an agency does not include a reference to a voluntary adoption agency.

(4) The Secretary of State may by regulations make provision about the keeping of registers by the Commission for the purposes of this Part.

(5) A person guilty of an offence under this section shall be liable on summary conviction–
    (a) if subsection (6) does not apply, to a fine not exceeding level 5 on the standard scale;
    (b) if subsection (6) applies, to imprisonment for a term not exceeding six months, or to a fine not exceeding level 5 on the standard scale, or to both.

(6) This subsection applies if–

(a) the person was registered in respect of the establishment or agency at a time before the commission of the offence but the registration was cancelled before the offence was committed; or

(b) the conviction is a second or subsequent conviction of the offence and the earlier conviction, or one of the earlier convictions, was of an offence in relation to an establishment or agency of the same description.

12. Applications for registration

(1) A person seeking to be registered under this Part shall make an application to the registration authority.

(2) The application–

(a) must give the prescribed information about prescribed matters;

(b) must give any other information which the registration authority reasonably requires the applicant to give,

and must be accompanied by a fee of the prescribed amount.

(3) A person who applies for registration as the manager of an establishment or agency must be an individual.

(4) A person who carries on or manages, or wishes to carry on or manage, more than one establishment or agency must make a separate application in respect of each of them.

13. Grant or refusal of registration

(1) Subsections (2) to (4) apply where an application under section 12 has been made with respect to an establishment or agency in accordance with the provisions of this Part.

(2) If the registration authority is satisfied that–

(a) the requirements of regulations under section 22; and

(b) the requirements of any other enactment which appears to the registration authority to be relevant,

are being and will continue to be complied with (so far as applicable) in relation to the establishment or agency, it shall grant the application; otherwise it shall refuse it.

(3) The application may be granted either unconditionally or subject to such conditions as the registration authority thinks fit.

(4) On granting the application, the registration authority shall issue a certificate of registration to the applicant.

(5) The registration authority may at any time–

(a) vary or remove any condition for the time being in force in relation to a person's registration; or

(b) impose an additional condition.

14. Cancellation of registration

(1) The registration authority may at any time cancel the registration of a person in respect of an establishment or agency–

(a) on the ground that that person has been convicted of a relevant offence;

(b) on the ground that any other person has been convicted of such an offence in relation to the establishment or agency;

(c) on the ground that the establishment or agency is being, or has at any time been, carried on otherwise than in accordance with the relevant requirements;

(d) on any ground specified by regulations.

(2) For the purposes of this section the following are relevant offences–

    (a) an offence under this Part or regulations made under it;

    (b) an offence under the Registered Homes Act 1984 or regulations made under it;

    (c) an offence under the 1989 Act or regulations made under it;

    (d) in relation to a voluntary adoption agency, an offence under regulations under section 9(2) of the Adoption Act 1976 or section 1(3) of the Adoption (Intercountry Aspects) Act 1999.

(3) In this section 'relevant requirements' means–

    (a) any requirements or conditions imposed by or under this Part; and

    (b) the requirements of any other enactment which appear to the registration authority to be relevant.

15. Applications by registered persons

(1) A person registered under this Part may apply to the registration authority–

    (a) for the variation or removal of any condition for the time being in force in relation to the registration; or

    (b) for the cancellation of the registration.

(2) But a person may not make an application under subsection (1)(b)–

    (a) if the registration authority has given him notice under section 17(4)(a) of a proposal to cancel the registration, unless the registration authority has decided not to take that step; or

    (b) if the registration authority has given him notice under section 19(3) of its decision to cancel the registration and the time within which an appeal may be brought has not expired or, if an appeal has been brought, it has not been determined.

(3) An application under subsection (1) shall be made in such manner and state such particulars as may be prescribed and, if made under paragraph (a) of that subsection, shall be accompanied by a fee of such amount as may be prescribed.

(4) If the registration authority decides to grant an application under subsection (1)(a) it shall serve notice in writing of its decision on the applicant (stating, where applicable, the condition as varied) and issue a new certificate of registration.

(5) If different amounts are prescribed under subsection (3), the regulations may provide for the registration authority to determine which amount is payable in a particular case.

16. Regulations about registration

(1) Regulations may make provision about the registration of persons under this Part in respect of establishments or agencies, and in particular about–

    (a) the making of applications for registration;

    (b) the contents of certificates of registration.

(2) Regulations may provide that no application for registration under this Part may be made in respect of a fostering agency, or a voluntary adoption agency, which is an unincorporated body.

(3) Regulations may also require persons registered under this Part to pay to the registration authority an annual fee of such amount, and at such a time, as may be prescribed.

(4) A fee payable by virtue of this section may, without prejudice to any other method of recovery, be recovered summarily as a civil debt.

Registration procedure

17. Notice of proposals

(1) Subsections (2) and (3) apply where a person applies for registration in respect of an establishment or agency.

(2) If the registration authority proposes to grant the application subject to any conditions which have not been agreed in writing between it and the applicant, it shall give the applicant written notice of its proposal and of the conditions subject to which it proposes to grant his application.

(3) The registration authority shall give the applicant notice of a proposal to refuse the application.

(4) Except where it makes an application under section 20, the registration authority shall give any person registered in respect of an establishment or agency notice of a proposal–

    (a) to cancel the registration (otherwise than in accordance with an application under section 15(1)(b));

    (b) to vary or remove (otherwise than in accordance with an application under section 15(1)(a)) any condition for the time being in force in relation to the registration; or

    (c) to impose any additional condition in relation to the registration.

(5) The registration authority shall give the applicant notice of a proposal to refuse an application under section 15(1)(a).

(6) A notice under this section shall give the registration authority's reasons for its proposal.

18. Right to make representations

(1) A notice under section 17 shall state that within 28 days of service of the notice any person on whom it is served may make written representations to the registration authority concerning any matter which that person wishes to dispute.

(2) Where a notice has been served under section 17, the registration authority shall not determine any matter to which the notice relates until either–

    (a) any person on whom the notice was served has made written representations to it concerning the matter;

    (b) any such person has notified the registration authority in writing that he does not intend to make representations; or

    (c) the period during which any such person could have made representations has elapsed.

19. Notice of decisions

(1) If the registration authority decides to grant an application for registration in respect of an establishment or agency unconditionally, or subject only to conditions which have been agreed in writing between it and the applicant, it shall give the applicant written notice of its decision.

(2) A notice under subsection (1) shall state the agreed conditions.

(3) If the registration authority decides to adopt a proposal under section 17, it shall serve notice in writing of its decision on any person on whom it was required to serve notice of the proposal.

(4) A notice under subsection (3) shall–

    (a) explain the right of appeal conferred by section 21;

(b) in the case of a decision to adopt a proposal under section 17(2), state the conditions subject to which the application is granted; and

(c) in the case of a decision to adopt a proposal under section 17(4)(b) or (c), state the condition as varied, the condition which is removed or (as the case may be) the additional condition imposed.

(5) Subject to subsection (6), a decision of the registration authority to adopt a proposal under section 17(2) or (4) shall not take effect–

(a) if no appeal is brought, until the expiration of the period of 28 days referred to in section 21(2); and

(b) if an appeal is brought, until it is determined or abandoned.

(6) Where, in the case of a decision to adopt a proposal under section 17(2), the applicant notifies the registration authority in writing before the expiration of the period mentioned in subsection (5)(a) that he does not intend to appeal, the decision shall take effect when the notice is served.

20. Urgent procedure for cancellation etc.

(1) If–

(a) the registration authority applies to a justice of the peace for an order–

    (i) cancelling the registration of a person in respect of an establishment or agency;

    (ii) varying or removing any condition for the time being in force by virtue of this Part; or

    (iii) imposing an additional condition; and

(b) it appears to the justice that, unless the order is made, there will be a serious risk to a person's life, health or well-being,

the justice may make the order, and the cancellation, variation, removal or imposition shall have effect from the time when the order is made.

(2) An application under subsection (1) may, if the justice thinks fit, be made without notice.

(3) As soon as practicable after the making of an application under this section, the registration authority shall notify the appropriate authorities of the making of the application.

(4) An order under subsection (1) shall be in writing.

(5) Where such an order is made, the registration authority shall, as soon as practicable after the making of the order, serve on the person registered in respect of the establishment or agency–

(a) a copy of the order; and

(b) notice of the right of appeal conferred by section 21.

(6) For the purposes of this section the appropriate authorities are–

(a) the local authority in whose area the establishment or agency is situated;

(b) the Health Authority in whose area the establishment or agency is situated; and

(c) any statutory authority not falling within paragraph (a) or (b) whom the registration authority thinks it appropriate to notify.

(7) In this section 'statutory authority' means a body established by or under an Act of Parliament.

21. Appeals to the Tribunal

(1) An appeal against–

(a) a decision of the registration authority under this Part; or

(b) an order made by a justice of the peace under section 20,

shall lie to the Tribunal.

(2) No appeal against a decision or order may be brought by a person more than 28 days after service on him of notice of the decision or order.

(3) On an appeal against a decision of the registration authority the Tribunal may confirm the decision or direct that it shall not have effect.

(4) On an appeal against an order made by a justice of the peace the Tribunal may confirm the order or direct that it shall cease to have effect.

(5) The Tribunal shall also have power on an appeal against a decision or order–

(a) to vary any condition for the time being in force in respect of the establishment or agency to which the appeal relates;

(b) to direct that any such condition shall cease to have effect; or

(c) to direct that any such condition as it thinks fit shall have effect in respect of the establishment or agency.

Regulations and standards

22. Regulation of establishments and agencies

(1) Regulations may impose in relation to establishments and agencies any requirements which the appropriate Minister thinks fit for the purposes of this Part and may in particular make any provision such as is mentioned in subsection (2), (7) or (8).

(2) Regulations may–

(a) make provision as to the persons who are fit to carry on or manage an establishment or agency;

(b) make provision as to the persons who are fit to work at an establishment or for the purposes of an agency;

(c) make provision as to the fitness of premises to be used as an establishment or for the purposes of an agency;

(d) make provision for securing the welfare of persons accommodated in an establishment or provided with services by an establishment, an independent medical agency or a domiciliary care agency;

(e) make provision for securing the welfare of children placed, under section 23(2)(a) of the 1989 Act, by a fostering agency;

(f) make provision as to the management and control of the operations of an establishment or agency;

(g) make provision as to the numbers of persons, or persons of any particular type, working at an establishment or for the purposes of an agency;

(h) make provision as to the management and training of such persons;

(i) impose requirements as to the financial position of an establishment or agency;

(j) make provision requiring the person carrying on an establishment or agency to appoint a manager in prescribed circumstances.

(3) Regulations under subsection (2)(a) may, in particular, make provision for prohibiting persons from managing an establishment or agency unless they are registered in, or in a particular part of, one of the registers maintained under section 56(1).

(4) Regulations under subsection (2)(b) may, in particular, make provision for prohibiting persons from working in such positions as may be prescribed at an establishment, or for the

purposes of an agency, unless they are registered in, or in a particular part of, one of the registers maintained under section 56(1).

(5) Regulations under paragraph (d) of subsection (2) may, in particular, make provision–

(a) as to the promotion and protection of the health of persons such as are mentioned in that paragraph;

(b) as to the control and restraint of adults accommodated in, or provided with services by, an establishment;

(c) as to the control, restraint and discipline of children accommodated in, or provided with services by, an establishment.

(6) Regulations under paragraph (e) of subsection (2) may, in particular, make provision–

(a) as to the promotion and protection of the health of children such as are mentioned in that paragraph;

(b) as to the control, restraint and discipline of such children.

(7) Regulations may make provision as to the conduct of establishments and agencies, and such regulations may in particular–

(a) make provision as to the facilities and services to be provided in establishments and by agencies;

(b) make provision as to the keeping of accounts;

(c) make provision as to the keeping of documents and records;

(d) make provision as to the notification of events occurring in establishments or in premises used for the purposes of agencies;

(e) make provision as to the giving of notice by the person carrying on an establishment or agency of periods during which he or (if he does not manage it himself) the manager proposes to be absent from the establishment or agency, and specify the information to be supplied in such a notice;

(f) provide for the making of adequate arrangements for the running of an establishment or agency during a period when the manager is absent from it;

(g) make provision as to the giving of notice by a person registered in respect of an establishment or agency of any intended change in the identity of the manager or the person carrying it on;

(h) make provision as to the giving of notice by a person registered in respect of an establishment or agency which is carried on by a body corporate of changes in the ownership of the body or the identity of its officers;

(i) make provision requiring the payment of a fee of such amount as may be prescribed in respect of any notification required to be made by virtue of paragraph (h);

(j) make provision requiring arrangements to be made by the person who carries on, or manages, an establishment or agency for dealing with complaints made by or on behalf of those seeking, or receiving, any of the services provided in the establishment or by the agency and requiring that person to take steps for publicising the arrangements;

(k) make provision requiring arrangements to be made by the person who carries on, or manages, an independent hospital, independent clinic or independent medical agency for securing that any medical or psychiatric treatment, or listed services, provided in or for the purposes of the establishment or (as the case may be) for the purposes of the agency are of appropriate quality and meet appropriate standards;

(l) make provision requiring arrangements to be made by the person who carries on, or manages, a care home for securing that any nursing provided by the home is of appropriate quality and meets appropriate standards.

(8) Regulations may make provision–

(a) requiring the approval of the appropriate Minister for the provision and use of accommodation for the purpose of restricting the liberty of children in children's homes;

(b) imposing other requirements (in addition to those imposed by section 25 of the 1989 Act (use of accommodation for restricting liberty)) as to the placing of a child in accommodation provided for the purpose mentioned in paragraph (a), including a requirement to obtain the permission of any local authority who are looking after the child;

(c) as to the facilities which are to be provided for giving religious instruction to children in children's homes.

(9) Before making regulations under this section, except regulations which amend other regulations made under this section and do not, in the opinion of the appropriate Minister, effect any substantial change in the provision made by those regulations, the appropriate Minister shall consult any persons he considers appropriate.

(10) References in this section to agencies do not include references to voluntary adoption agencies.

(11) In subsection (7)(k), 'listed services' has the same meaning as in section 2.

23. National minimum standards

(1) The appropriate Minister may prepare and publish statements of national minimum standards applicable to establishments or agencies.

(2) The appropriate Minister shall keep the standards set out in the statements under review and may publish amended statements whenever he considers it appropriate to do so.

(3) Before issuing a statement, or an amended statement which in the opinion of the appropriate Minister effects a substantial change in the standards, the appropriate Minister shall consult any persons he considers appropriate.

(4) The standards shall be taken into account–

(a) in the making of any decision by the registration authority under this Part;

(b) in any proceedings for the making of an order under section 20;

(c) in any proceedings on an appeal against such a decision or order; and

(d) in any proceedings for an offence under regulations under this Part.

Offences

24. Failure to comply with conditions

If a person registered in respect of an establishment or agency fails, without reasonable excuse, to comply with any condition for the time being in force by virtue of this Part in respect of the establishment or agency, he shall be guilty of an offence and liable on summary conviction to a fine not exceeding level 5 on the standard scale.

25. Contravention of regulations

(1) Regulations under this Part may provide that a contravention of or failure to comply with any specified provision of the regulations shall be an offence.

(2) A person guilty of an offence under the regulations shall be liable on summary conviction to a fine not exceeding level 4 on the standard scale.

26. False descriptions of establishments and agencies

(1) A person who, with intent to deceive any person–

(a) applies any name to premises in England or Wales; or

(b) in any way describes such premises or holds such premises out,

so as to indicate, or reasonably be understood to indicate, that the premises are an establishment, or an agency, of a particular description shall be liable on summary conviction to a fine not exceeding level 5 on the standard scale unless registration has been effected under this Part in respect of the premises as an establishment or agency of that description.

(2) References to premises in subsection (1) shall be taken to include references to an undertaking or organisation.

(3) No person shall, with intent to deceive any person, in any way describe or hold out an establishment or agency as able to provide any service or do any thing the provision or doing of which would contravene a condition for the time being in force by virtue of this Part in respect of the establishment or agency.

(4) A person who contravenes subsection (3) shall be liable on summary conviction to a fine not exceeding level 5 on the standard scale.

27. False statements in applications

(1) Any person who, in an application for registration under this Part or for the variation of any condition in force in relation to his registration, knowingly makes a statement which is false or misleading in a material respect shall be guilty of an offence.

(2) A person guilty of an offence under this section shall be liable on summary conviction to a fine not exceeding level 4 on the standard scale.

28. Failure to display certificate of registration

(1) A certificate of registration issued under this Part in respect of any establishment or agency shall be kept affixed in a conspicuous place in the establishment or at the agency.

(2) If default is made in complying with subsection (1), any person registered in respect of the establishment or agency shall be guilty of an offence and liable on summary conviction to a fine not exceeding level 2 on the standard scale.

29. Proceedings for offences

(1) Proceedings in respect of an offence under this Part or regulations made under it shall not, without the written consent of the Attorney General, be taken by any person other than–

(a) the Commission or, in relation to any functions of the Commission which the Secretary of State is by virtue of section 113 for the time being discharging, the Secretary of State; or

(b) the Assembly.

(2) Proceedings for an offence under this Part or regulations made under it may be brought within a period of six months from the date on which evidence sufficient in the opinion of the prosecutor to warrant the proceedings came to his knowledge; but no such proceedings shall be brought by virtue of this subsection more than three years after the commission of the offence.

30. Offences by bodies corporate

(1) This section applies where any offence under this Part or regulations made under it is committed by a body corporate.

(2) If the offence is proved to have been committed with the consent or connivance of, or to be attributable to any neglect on the part of–

(a) any director, manager, or secretary of the body corporate; or

(b) any person who was purporting to act in any such capacity,

he (as well as the body corporate) shall be guilty of the offence and shall be liable to be proceeded against and punished accordingly.

(3) The reference in subsection (2) to a director, manager or secretary of a body corporate includes a reference–

(a) to any other similar officer of the body; and

(b) where the body is a local authority, to any officer or member of the authority.

Miscellaneous and supplemental

31. Inspections by persons authorised by registration authority

(1) The registration authority may at any time require a person who carries on or manages an establishment or agency to provide it with any information relating to the establishment or agency which the registration authority considers it necessary or expedient to have for the purposes of its functions under this Part.

(2) A person authorised by the registration authority may at any time enter and inspect premises which are used, or which he has reasonable cause to believe to be used, as an establishment or for the purposes of an agency.

(3) A person authorised by virtue of this section to enter and inspect premises may–

(a) make any examination into the state and management of the premises and treatment of patients or persons accommodated or cared for there which he thinks appropriate;

(b) inspect and take copies of any documents or records (other than medical records) required to be kept in accordance with regulations under this Part, section 9(2) of the Adoption Act 1976, section 23(2)(a) or 59(2) of the 1989 Act or section 1(3) of the Adoption (Intercountry Aspects) Act 1999;

(c) interview in private the manager or the person carrying on the establishment or agency;

(d) interview in private any person employed there;

(e) interview in private any patient or person accommodated or cared for there who consents to be interviewed.

(4) The powers under subsection (3)(b) include–

(a) power to require the manager or the person carrying on the establishment or agency to produce any documents or records, wherever kept, for inspection on the premises; and

(b) in relation to records which are kept by means of a computer, power to require the records to be produced in a form in which they are legible and can be taken away.

(5) Subsection (6) applies where the premises in question are used as an establishment and the person so authorised–

(a) is a medical practitioner or registered nurse; and

(b) has reasonable cause to believe that a patient or person accommodated or cared for there is not receiving proper care.

(6) The person so authorised may, with the consent of the person mentioned in subsection (5)(b), examine him in private and inspect any medical records relating to his treatment in the establishment.

The powers conferred by this subsection may be exercised in relation to a person who is incapable of giving consent without that person's consent.

(7) The Secretary of State may by regulations require the Commission to arrange for premises which are used as an establishment or for the purposes of an agency to be inspected on such occasions or at such intervals as may be prescribed.

(8) A person who proposes to exercise any power of entry or inspection conferred by this section shall if so required produce some duly authenticated document showing his authority to exercise the power.

(9) Any person who–
- (a) intentionally obstructs the exercise of any power conferred by this section or section 32; or
- (b) fails without a reasonable excuse to comply with any requirement under this section or that section,

shall be guilty of an offence and liable on summary conviction to a fine not exceeding level 4 on the standard scale.

32. Inspections: supplementary

(1) A person authorised by virtue of section 31 to enter and inspect any premises may seize and remove any document or other material or thing found there which he has reasonable grounds to believe may be evidence of a failure to comply with any condition or requirement imposed by or under this Part.

(2) A person so authorised–
- (a) may require any person to afford him such facilities and assistance with respect to matters within the person's control as are necessary to enable him to exercise his powers under section 31 or this section;
- (b) may take such measurements and photographs and make such recordings as he considers necessary to enable him to exercise those powers.

(3) A person authorised by virtue of section 31 to inspect any records shall be entitled to have access to, and to check the operation of, any computer and any associated apparatus which is or has been in use in connection with the records in question.

(4) The references in section 31 to the person carrying on the establishment or agency include, in the case of an establishment or agency which is carried on by a company, a reference to any director, manager, secretary or other similar officer of the company.

(5) Where any premises which are used as an establishment or for the purposes of an agency have been inspected under section 31, the registration authority–
- (a) shall prepare a report on the matters inspected; and
- (b) shall without delay send a copy of the report to each person who is registered in respect of the establishment or agency.

(6) The registration authority shall make copies of any report prepared under subsection (5) available for inspection at its offices by any person at any reasonable time; and may take any other steps for publicising a report which it considers appropriate.

(7) Any person who asks the registration authority for a copy of a report prepared under subsection (5) shall be entitled to have one on payment of a reasonable fee determined by the registration authority; but nothing in this subsection prevents the registration authority from providing a copy free of charge when it considers it appropriate to do so.

(8) Where the Secretary of State has specified regions in a direction made under paragraph 9 of Schedule 1, the reference in subsection (6) to offices is, in relation to premises in England

which are used as an establishment or for the purposes of an agency, a reference to the Commission's offices for the region in which the premises are situated.

33. Annual returns

(1) Regulations may require the person carrying on an establishment or agency to make an annual return to the registration authority.

(2) Provision may be made by the regulations as to the contents of the return and the period in respect of which and date by which it is to be made.

34. Liquidators etc.

(1) Regulations may—
  (a) require any person to whom this section applies to give notice of his appointment to the registration authority;
  (b) require any person to whom this section applies to appoint a person to manage the establishment or agency in question.

(2) This section applies to any person appointed as—
  (a) a receiver or manager of the property of a relevant company;
  (b) the liquidator or provisional liquidator of a relevant company; or
  (c) the trustee in bankruptcy of a relevant individual.

(3) In this section—
'company' includes a partnership;
'relevant company' means a company which is registered under this Part in respect of an establishment or agency; and
'relevant individual' means an individual who is registered under this Part in respect of an establishment or agency.

35. Death of registered person

(1) Regulations may—
  (a) provide for the provisions of this Part to apply with prescribed modifications in cases where a person who was the only person registered under this Part in respect of an establishment or agency has died;
  (b) require the personal representatives of a deceased person who was registered in respect of an establishment or agency to notify the registration authority of his death.

(2) Regulations under subsection (1)(a) may in particular—
  (a) provide for the establishment or agency to be carried on for a prescribed period by a person who is not registered in respect of it; and
  (b) include provision for the prescribed period to be extended by such further period as the registration authority may allow.

36. Provision of copies of registers

(1) Subject to subsection (3), the registration authority shall secure that copies of any register kept for the purposes of this Part are available at its offices for inspection at all reasonable times by any person.

(2) Subject to subsections (3) and (4), any person who asks the registration authority for a copy of, or of an extract from, a register kept for the purposes of this Part shall be entitled to have one.

(3) Regulations may provide that subsections (1) and (2) shall not apply–
- (a) in such circumstances as may be prescribed; or
- (b) to such parts of a register as may be prescribed.

(4) A fee determined by the registration authority shall be payable for the copy except–
- (a) in prescribed circumstances;
- (b) in any other case where the registration authority considers it appropriate to provide the copy free of charge.

37. Service of documents

(1) Any notice or other document required under this Part to be served on a person carrying on or managing, or intending to carry on or manage, an establishment or agency may be served on him–
- (a) by being delivered personally to him; or
- (b) by being sent by post to him in a registered letter or by the recorded delivery service at his proper address.

(2) For the purposes of section 7 of the Interpretation Act 1978 (which defines 'service by post') a letter addressed to a person carrying on or managing an establishment or agency enclosing a notice or other document under this Act shall be deemed to be properly addressed if it is addressed to him at the establishment or agency.

(3) Where a notice or other document is served as mentioned in subsection (1)(b), the service shall, unless the contrary is proved, be deemed to have been effected on the third day after the day on which it is sent.

(4) Any notice or other document required to be served on a body corporate or a firm shall be duly served if it is served on the secretary or clerk of that body or a partner of that firm.

(5) For the purposes of this section, and of section 7 of the Interpretation Act 1978 in its application to this section, without prejudice to subsection (2) above, the proper address of a person shall be–
- (a) in the case of a secretary or clerk of a body corporate, that of the registered or principal office of that body;
- (b) in the case of a partner of a firm, that of the principal office of the firm; and
- (c) in any other case, the last known address of the person.

38. Transfers of staff under Part II

(1) The appropriate Minister may by order make a scheme for the transfer to the new employer of any eligible employee.

(2) In this section–
> 'eligible employee' means a person who is employed under a contract of employment with an old employer on work which would have continued but for the provisions of this Part;
> 'new employer' means the registration authority;
> 'old employer' means a local authority or a Health Authority.

39. Temporary extension of meaning of 'nursing home'

In section 21 of the Registered Homes Act 1984 (meaning of nursing home)–
- (a) in subsection (1), after '(3)' there is inserted 'and (3A)';
- (b) in subsection (2), for 'subsection (1) above' there is substituted 'this section';
- (c) in subsection (3)(e)(ii), 'dental practitioner or' is omitted; and
- (d) after subsection (3) there is inserted–

'(3A) The definition in subsection (1) above does not include any premises used, or intended to be used, wholly or mainly by a dental practitioner for the purpose of treating his patients unless subsection (3B) or (3C) below applies.

(3B) This subsection applies if–

(a)   the premises are also used, or intended to be used, by that or another dental practitioner for the purpose of treating his patients under general anaesthesia; and

(b)   the premises are not used, or intended to be used, by any dental practitioner for the purpose of treating his patients under general anaesthesia-

(i)   in pursuance of the National Health Service Act 1977; or

(ii) under an agreement made in accordance with Part I of the National Health Service (Primary Care) Act 1997.

(3C) This subsection applies if the premises are used, or intended to be used, for the provision of treatment by specially controlled techniques and are not excepted by regulations under subsection (3)(g) above.'

40. Temporary extension of meaning of 'children's home'

In section 63(3)(a) of the 1989 Act (meaning of 'children's home'), for 'more than three children at any one time' there shall be substituted 'children'.

41. Children's homes: temporary provision about cancellation of registration

(1) In paragraph 1(4) of Schedule 5 to the 1989 Act (voluntary homes and voluntary organisations)–

(a)   in paragraph (a), after 'is not' there shall be inserted ', or has not been,';

(b)   after 'is' there shall be inserted ', or has been,'.

(2) In paragraph 2 of that Schedule, after sub-paragraph (5) there shall be inserted–

'(6) In relation to a home which has ceased to exist, the reference in sub-paragraph (4) to any person carrying on the home shall be taken to be a reference to each of the persons who carried it on.'

(3) In paragraph 3(3) of Schedule 6 to the 1989 Act (registered children's homes), after 'is being' there shall be inserted 'and has been'.

(4) In paragraph 4 of that Schedule–

(a)   in sub-paragraph (3) after 'is being' there shall be inserted ', or has been,';

(b)   after sub-paragraph (4) there shall be inserted–

'(5) In relation to a home which has ceased to exist, references in this paragraph and paragraph 5(4) to the person, or any person, carrying on the home include references to each of the persons who carried it on.'

42. Power to extend the application of Part II

(1) Regulations may provide for the provisions of this Part to apply, with such modifications as may be specified in the regulations, to prescribed persons to whom subsection (2) or (3) applies.

(2) This subsection applies to–

(a) local authorities providing services in the exercise of their social services functions; and

(b) persons who provide services which are similar to services which–
    (i) may or must be so provided by local authorities; or
    (ii) may or must be provided by Health Authorities, Special Health Authorities, NHS trusts or Primary Care Trusts.

(3) This subsection applies to persons who carry on or manage an undertaking (other than an establishment or agency) which consists of or includes supplying, or providing services for the purpose of supplying, individuals mentioned in subsection (4).

(4) The individuals referred to in subsection (3) are those who provide services for the purpose of any of the services mentioned in subsection (2).

PART III
LOCAL AUTHORITY SERVICES

43. Introductory
(1) This section has effect for the purposes of this Part.

(2) 'Relevant functions', in relation to a local authority, means relevant adoption functions and relevant fostering functions.

(3) In relation to a local authority–
    (a) 'relevant adoption functions' means functions under the Adoption Act 1976 of making or participating in arrangements for the adoption of children; and
    (b) 'relevant fostering functions' means functions under section 23(2)(a) of the 1989 Act or regulations under any of paragraphs (a), (b) or (d) to (f) of paragraph 12 of Schedule 2 to that Act.

44. General powers of the Commission
The Commission may at any time give advice to the Secretary of State on–
    (a) any changes which the Commission thinks should be made, for the purpose of securing improvement in the quality of services provided by local authorities in England in the exercise of relevant functions, in the standards set out in statements under section 49; and
    (b) any other matter connected with the exercise by local authorities in England of relevant functions.

45. Inspection by registration authority of adoption and fostering services
(1) Subject to section 47(6)–
    (a) the registration authority may at any time require a local authority to provide it with any information relating to the discharge by the local authority of relevant functions which the registration authority considers it necessary or expedient to have for the purposes of its functions under this Part;
    (b) a person authorised to do so by the registration authority may at any time enter and inspect premises which are used, or which he has reasonable cause to believe to be used, by a local authority in its discharge of relevant functions.

(2) A person authorised by virtue of this section to enter and inspect premises may–

(a) inspect and take copies of any documents or records relating to the discharge by the local authority of relevant functions;

(b) interview in private any employee of the local authority.

(3) The powers under subsection (2)(a) include–

(a) power to require the local authority to produce any documents or records, wherever kept, for inspection on the premises; and

(b) in relation to records which are kept by means of a computer, power to require the records to be produced in a form in which they are legible and can be taken away.

(4) Subject to section 47(6), the Secretary of State may by regulations require the Commission to arrange for premises which are used by a local authority in its discharge of relevant functions to be inspected on such occasions or at such intervals as may be prescribed.

(5) Subsections (8) and (9) of section 31 shall have effect as if any reference in them to section 31 included a reference to this section and section 46.

46. Inspections: supplementary

(1) A person authorised by virtue of section 45 to enter and inspect any premises may seize and remove any document or other material or thing found there which he has reasonable grounds to believe may be evidence of a failure to comply with the regulatory requirements.

(2) A person so authorised–

(a) may require any person to afford him such facilities and assistance with respect to matters within the person's control as are necessary to enable him to exercise his powers under section 45 or this section;

(b) may take such measurements and photographs and make such recordings as he considers necessary to enable him to exercise those powers.

(3) A person authorised by virtue of section 45 to inspect any records shall be entitled to have access to, and to check the operation of, any computer and any associated apparatus or material which is or has been in use in connection with the records in question.

(4) Where any premises which are used by a local authority in its discharge of relevant functions have been inspected under section 45, the registration authority–

(a) shall prepare a report on the discharge by the local authority of relevant functions; and

(b) shall without delay send a copy of the report to the local authority.

(5) The registration authority shall make copies of any report prepared under subsection (4) available for inspection at its offices by any person at any reasonable time; and may take any other steps for publicising a report which it considers appropriate.

(6) Any person who asks the registration authority for a copy of the report shall be entitled to have one on payment of a reasonable fee determined by the registration authority; but nothing in this subsection prevents the registration authority from providing a copy free of charge when it considers it appropriate to do so.

(7) In this section and section 47 'the regulatory requirements' means the requirements of regulations under–

(a) section 48;

(b) section 23(2)(a) of the 1989 Act (regulations about the placing of children with foster parents);

(c) section 9(3) of the Adoption Act 1976 (regulation of adoption agencies); and

(d) section 1(1) of the Adoption (Intercountry Aspects) Act 1999 (regulations giving effect to the Convention on Protection of Children and Co-operation in respect of Intercountry Adoption).

(8) Where the Secretary of State has specified regions in a direction made under paragraph 9 of Schedule 1, the reference in subsection (5) to offices is, in relation to premises in England which are used by a local authority in its discharge of relevant functions, a reference to the Commission's offices for the region in which the premises are situated.

47. Action following inspection

(1) If the Commission considers at any time–

(a) that the discharge by a local authority of relevant functions fails to satisfy the regulatory requirements; and

(b) that the failure is substantial,

it shall report that fact to the Secretary of State.

(2) Subsections (3) and (4) apply in relation to a local authority where–

(a) a person authorised by the Commission has exercised in relation to the authority any power conferred by section 45(1)(b); or

(b) the Commission has given the authority a notice under subsection (5) and the time specified (in accordance with paragraph (b) of that subsection) in the notice has expired.

(3) If the Commission considers that the discharge by the authority of relevant functions satisfies the regulatory requirements, it shall report that fact to the Secretary of State.

(4) If the Commission considers that the discharge by the authority of relevant functions fails to satisfy the regulatory requirements, but that the failure is not substantial, the Commission shall–

(a) report that fact to the Secretary of State; or

(b) if it considers that it is not appropriate to make a report under paragraph (a), give the authority a notice under subsection (5) and inform the Secretary of State that it has done so.

(5) A notice under this subsection is a notice which–

(a) specifies the respects in which the Commission considers that the discharge by the authority of relevant functions fails to satisfy the regulatory requirements and any action which the Commission considers the authority should take to remedy the failure; and

(b) specifies the time by which the failure should be remedied.

(6) Where the Commission has made a report to the Secretary of State under subsection (1) or (4)(a), the powers conferred by section 45(1) shall not be exercisable in relation to the authority concerned at any time unless the Secretary of State has notified the Commission that this subsection has ceased to apply.

48. Regulation of the exercise of relevant fostering functions

(1) Regulations may make provision about the exercise by local authorities of relevant fostering functions, and may in particular make provision–

(a) as to the persons who are fit to work for local authorities in connection with the exercise of such functions;

(b) as to the fitness of premises to be used by local authorities in their exercise of such functions;

(c) as to the management and control of the operations of local authorities in their exercise of such functions;

(d) as to the numbers of persons, or persons of any particular type, working for local authorities in connection with the exercise of such functions;

(e) as to the management and training of such persons.

(2) Regulations under subsection (1)(a) may, in particular, make provision for prohibiting persons from working for local authorities in such positions as may be prescribed unless they are registered in, or in a particular part of, one of the registers maintained under section 56(1).

49. National minimum standards

(1) Subsections (1), (2) and (3) of section 23 shall apply to local authorities in their exercise of relevant functions as they apply to establishments and agencies.

(2) The standards shall be taken into account in the making of any decision under section 47.

50. Annual returns

(1) Regulations may require a local authority to make to the registration authority an annual return containing such information with respect to the exercise by the local authority of relevant functions as may be prescribed.

(2) Provision may be made by the regulations as to the period in respect of which and date by which the return is to be made.

51. Annual fee

(1) Regulations may require any local authority in relation to which powers conferred by section 45(1) may be exercised to pay to the registration authority an annual fee of such amount, and at such a time, as may be prescribed.

(2) A fee payable by virtue of this section may, without prejudice to any other method of recovery, be recovered summarily as a civil debt.

52. Contravention of regulations

(1) Regulations under this Part may provide that a contravention of or failure to comply with any specified provision of the regulations shall be an offence.

(2) A person guilty of an offence under the regulations shall be liable on summary conviction to a fine not exceeding level 4 on the standard scale.

53. Offences: general provisions

Sections 29 and 30 apply in relation to this Part as they apply in relation to Part II.

PART IV

SOCIAL CARE WORKERS

Preliminary

54. Care Councils

(1) There shall be–

(a) a body corporate to be known as the General Social Care Council (referred to in this Act as 'the English Council'); and

(b) a body corporate to be known as the Care Council for Wales or Cyngor Gofal Cymru (referred to in this Act as 'the Welsh Council'),

which shall have the functions conferred on them by or under this Act or any other enactment.

(2) It shall be the duty of the English Council to promote in relation to England–
    (a) high standards of conduct and practice among social care workers; and
    (b) high standards in their training.

(3) It shall be the duty of the Welsh Council to promote in relation to Wales–
    (a) high standards of conduct and practice among social care workers; and
    (b) high standards in their training.

(4) Each Council shall, in the exercise of its functions, act–
    (a) in accordance with any directions given to it by the appropriate Minister; and
    (b) under the general guidance of the appropriate Minister.

(5) Directions under subsection (4) shall be given in writing.

(6) Schedule 1 shall have effect with respect to a Council.

(7) In this Act, references to a Council are–
    (a) in relation to England, a reference to the General Social Care Council,
    (b) in relation to Wales, a reference to the Care Council for Wales.

55. Interpretation

(1) This section has effect for the purposes of this Part.

(2) 'Social care worker' means a person (other than a person excepted by regulations) who–
    (a) engages in relevant social work (referred to in this Part as a 'social worker');
    (b) is employed at a children's home, care home or residential family centre or for the purposes of a domiciliary care agency, a fostering agency or a voluntary adoption agency;
    (c) manages an establishment, or an agency, of a description mentioned in paragraph (b); or
    (d) is supplied by a domiciliary care agency to provide personal care in their own homes for persons who by reason of illness, infirmity or disability are unable to provide it for themselves without assistance.

(3) Regulations may provide that persons of any of the following descriptions shall be treated as social care workers–
    (a) a person engaged in work for the purposes of a local authority's social services functions, or in the provision of services similar to services which may or must be provided by local authorities in the exercise of those functions;
    (b) a person engaged in the provision of personal care for any person;
    (c) a person who manages, or is employed in, an undertaking (other than an establishment or agency) which consists of or includes supplying, or providing services for the purpose of supplying, persons to provide personal care;
    (d) a person employed in connection with the discharge of functions of the appropriate Minister under section 80 of the 1989 Act (inspection of children's homes etc.);
    (e) staff of the Commission or the Assembly who–
        (i) inspect premises under section 87 of the 1989 Act (welfare of children accommodated in independent schools and colleges) or section 31 or 45 of this Act; or
        (ii) are responsible for persons who do so;

and staff of the Assembly who inspect premises under section 79T of that Act (inspection of child minding and day care in Wales) or are responsible for persons who do so;

(f) a person employed in a day centre;

(g) a person participating in a course approved by a Council under section 63 for persons wishing to become social workers.

(4) 'Relevant social work' means social work which is required in connection with any health, education or social services provided by any person.

(5) 'Day centre' means a place where nursing or personal care (but not accommodation) is provided wholly or mainly for persons mentioned in section 3(2).

Registration

56. The register

(1) Each Council shall maintain a register of–

(a) social workers; and

(b) social care workers of any other description specified by the appropriate Minister by order.

(2) There shall be a separate part of the register for social workers and for each description of social care workers so specified.

(3) The appropriate Minister may by order provide for a specified part of the register to be closed, as from a date specified by the order, so that on or after that date no further persons can become registered in that part.

(4) The appropriate Minister shall consult the Council before making, varying or revoking any order under this section.

57. Applications for registration

(1) An application for registration under this Part shall be made to the Council in accordance with rules made by it.

(2) An application under subsection (1) shall specify each part of the register in which registration is sought and such other matters as may be required by the rules.

58. Grant or refusal of registration

(1) If the Council is satisfied that the applicant–

(a) is of good character;

(b) is physically and mentally fit to perform the whole or part of the work of persons registered in any part of the register to which his application relates; and

(c) satisfies the following conditions,

it shall grant the application, either unconditionally or subject to such conditions as it thinks fit; and in any other case it shall refuse it.

(2) The first condition is that–

(a) in the case of an applicant for registration as a social worker–

(i)   he has successfully completed a course approved by the Council under section 63 for persons wishing to become social workers;

(ii) he satisfies the requirements of section 64; or

(iii) he satisfies any requirements as to training which the Council may by rules impose in relation to social workers;

(b) in the case of an applicant for registration as a social care worker of any other description, he satisfies any requirements as to training which the Council may by rules impose in relation to social care workers of that description.

(3) The second condition is that the applicant satisfies any requirements as to conduct and competence which the Council may by rules impose.

59. Removal etc. from register

(1) Each Council shall by rules determine circumstances in which, and the means by which–

(a) a person may be removed from a part of the register, whether or not for a specified period;

(b) a person who has been removed from a part of the register may be restored to that part;

(c) a person's registration in a part of the register may be suspended for a specified period;

(d) the suspension of a person's registration in a part of the register may be terminated;

(e) an entry in a part of the register may be removed, altered or restored.

(2) The rules shall make provision as to the procedure to be followed, and the rules of evidence to be observed, in proceedings brought for the purposes of the rules, whether before the Council or any committee of the Council.

(3) The rules shall provide for such proceedings to be in public except in such cases (if any) as the rules may specify.

(4) Where a person's registration in a part of the register is suspended under subsection (1)(c), he shall be treated as not being registered in that part notwithstanding that his name still appears in it.

60. Rules about registration

A Council may by rules make provision about the registration of persons under this Part and, in particular–

(a) as to the keeping of the register;

(b) as to the documentary and other evidence to be produced by those applying for registration or for additional qualifications to be recorded, or for any entry in the register to be altered or restored;

(c) for a person's registration to remain effective without limitation of time (subject to removal from the register in accordance with rules made by virtue of section 59) or to lapse after a specified period or in specified cases, or to be subject to renewal as and when provided by the rules.

61. Use of title 'social worker' etc.

(1) If a person who is not registered as a social worker in any relevant register with intent to deceive another–

(a) takes or uses the title of social worker;

(b) takes or uses any title or description implying that he is so registered, or in any way holds himself out as so registered,

he is guilty of an offence.

(2) For the purposes of subsection (1), a register is a relevant register if it is–

(a) maintained by a Council; or

(b) a prescribed register maintained under a provision of the law of Scotland or Northern Ireland which appears to the appropriate Minister to correspond to the provisions of this Part.

(3) A person guilty of an offence under this section shall be liable on summary conviction to a fine not exceeding level 5 on the standard scale.

Codes of practice

62. Codes of practice

(1) Each Council shall prepare and from time to time publish codes of practice laying down–

(a) standards of conduct and practice expected of social care workers; and

(b) standards of conduct and practice in relation to social care workers, being standards expected of persons employing or seeking to employ them.

(2) The Council shall–

(a) keep the codes under review; and

(b) vary their provisions whenever it considers it appropriate to do so.

(3) Before issuing or varying a code, a Council shall consult any persons it considers appropriate to consult.

(4) A code published by a Council shall be taken into account–

(a) by the Council in making a decision under this Part; and

(b) in any proceedings on an appeal against such a decision.

(5) Local authorities making any decision about the conduct of any social care workers employed by them shall, if directed to do so by the appropriate Minister, take into account any code published by the Council.

(6) Any person who asks a Council for a copy of a code shall be entitled to have one.

Training

63. Approval of courses etc.

(1) Each Council may, in accordance with rules made by it, approve courses in relevant social work for persons who are or wish to become social workers.

(2) An approval given under this section may be either unconditional or subject to such conditions as the Council thinks fit.

(3) Rules made by virtue of this section may in particular make provision–

(a) about the content of, and methods of completing, courses;

(b) as to the provision to the Council of information about courses;

(c) as to the persons who may participate in courses, or in parts of courses specified in the rules;

(d) as to the numbers of persons who may participate in courses;

(e) for the award by the Council of certificates of the successful completion of courses;

(f) about the lapse and renewal of approvals; and

(g) about the withdrawal of approvals.

(4) A Council may–

(a) conduct, or make arrangements for the conduct of, examinations in connection with such courses as are mentioned in this section or section 67; and

(b) carry out, or assist other persons in carrying out, research into matters relevant to training for relevant social work.

(5) A course for persons who wish to become social workers shall not be approved under this section unless the Council considers that it is such as to enable persons completing it to attain the required standard of proficiency in relevant social work.

(6) In subsection (5) 'the required standard of proficiency in relevant social work' means the standard described in rules made by the Council.

(7) The Council shall from time to time publish a list of the courses which are approved under this section.

64. Qualifications gained outside a Council's area

(1) An applicant for registration as a social worker in the register maintained by the English Council satisfies the requirements of this section if–

  (a) being a national of any EEA State–

    (i) he has professional qualifications, obtained in an EEA State other than the United Kingdom, which the Secretary of State has by order designated as having Community equivalence for the purposes of such registration; and

    (ii) he satisfies any other requirements which the Council may by rules impose; or

  (b) he has, elsewhere than in England, undergone training in relevant social work and either–

    (i) that training is recognised by the Council as being to a standard sufficient for such registration; or

    (ii) it is not so recognised, but the applicant has undergone in England or elsewhere such additional training as the Council may require.

(2) An applicant for registration as a social worker in the register maintained by the Welsh Council satisfies the requirements of this section if–

  (a) being a national of any EEA State–

    (i) he has professional qualifications, obtained in an EEA State other than the United Kingdom, which the Assembly has by order designated as having Community equivalence for the purposes of such registration; and

    (ii) he satisfies any other requirements which the Council may by rules impose; or

  (b) he has, elsewhere than in Wales, undergone training in relevant social work and either–

    (i) that training is recognised by the Council as being to a standard sufficient for such registration; or

    (ii) it is not so recognised, but the applicant has undergone in Wales or elsewhere such additional training as the Council may require.

(3) An order under subsection (1)(a) or (2)(a) may provide that a professional qualification designated by the order is to be regarded as having Community equivalence for the purposes of registration as a social worker in the register maintained by the English or, as the case may be, Welsh Council only if prescribed conditions required by a directive issued by the Council of the European Communities are fulfilled; and different conditions may be prescribed with respect to the same qualification for different circumstances.

(4) Any person who–

  (a) is not a national of an EEA State; but

  (b) is, by virtue of a right conferred by Article 11 of Council Regulation (EEC) No. 1612/68 (on freedom of movement for workers within the Community) or any other enforceable Community right, entitled to be treated, as regards the right to engage in relevant social work, no less favourably than a national of such a State, shall be treated for the purposes of subsection (1)(a) or (2)(a) as if he were such a national.

(5) In this section–

'EEA State' means a Contracting Party to the EEA Agreement;

'EEA Agreement' means the Agreement on the European Economic Area signed at Oporto on 2nd May 1992 as adjusted by the Protocol signed at Brussels on 17th March 1993;

'national', in relation to an EEA State, means the same as it does for the purposes of the Community Treaties.

65. Post registration training

(1) A Council may make rules requiring persons registered under this Part in any part of the register to undertake further training.

(2) The rules may, in particular, make provision with respect to persons who fail to comply with any requirements of rules made by the Council, including provision for their registration to cease to have effect.

(3) Before making, or varying, any rules by virtue of this section the Council shall take such steps as are reasonably practicable to consult the persons who are registered in the relevant part of the register and such other persons as the Council considers appropriate.

66. Visitors for certain social work courses

(1) A Council may by rules make provision for the visiting of places at which or institutions by which or under whose direction–

(a) any relevant course (or part of such a course) is, or is proposed to be, given; or

(b) any examination is, or is proposed to be, held in connection with any relevant course.

(2) The rules may make provision–

(a) for the appointment of visitors;

(b) for reports to be made by visitors on–

(i) the nature and quality of the instruction given, or to be given, and the facilities provided or to be provided, at the place or by the institution visited; and

(ii) such other matters as may be specified in the rules;

(c) for the payment by the Council of fees, allowances and expenses to persons appointed as visitors;

(d) for such persons to be treated, for the purposes of Schedule 1, as members of the Council's staff.

(3) In subsection (1) 'relevant course', in relation to a Council, means–

(a) any course for which approval by the Council has been given, or is being sought, under section 63; or

(b) any training which a person admitted to the part for social workers of the register maintained by the Council may be required to undergo after registration.

67. Functions of the appropriate Minister

(1) The appropriate Minister has the function of–

(a) ascertaining what training is required by persons who are or wish to become social care workers;

(b) ascertaining what financial and other assistance is required for promoting such training;

(c) encouraging the provision of such assistance;

(d) drawing up occupational standards for social care workers.

(2) The appropriate Minister shall encourage persons to take part in courses approved by a Council under section 63 and other courses relevant to the training of persons who are or wish to become social care workers.

(3) If it appears to the appropriate Minister that adequate provision is not being made for training persons who are or wish to become social care workers, the appropriate Minister may provide, or secure the provision of, courses for that purpose.

(4) The appropriate Minister may, upon such terms and subject to such conditions as the Minister considers appropriate—

(a) make grants, and pay travelling and other allowances, to persons resident in England and Wales, in order to secure their training in the work of social care workers;

(b) make grants to organisations providing training in the work of social care workers.

(5) Any functions of the Secretary of State under this section—

(a) may be delegated by him to the English Council; or

(b) may be exercised by any person, or by employees of any person, authorised to do so by the Secretary of State.

(6) Any functions of the Assembly under this section—

(a) may be delegated by the Assembly to the Welsh Council; or

(b) may be exercised by any person, or by employees of any person, authorised to do so by the Assembly.

(7) For the purpose of determining—

(a) the terms and effect of an authorisation under subsection (5)(b) or (6)(b); and

(b) the effect of so much of any contract made between the appropriate Minister and the authorised person as relates to the exercise of the function,

Part II of the Deregulation and Contracting Out Act 1994 shall have effect as if the authorisation were given by virtue of an order under section 69 of that Act and, in respect of an authorisation given by the Assembly, references to a Minister included the Assembly; and in subsection (5)(b) and (6)(b) 'employee' has the same meaning as in that Part.

Miscellaneous and supplemental

68. Appeals to the Tribunal

(1) An appeal against a decision of a Council under this Part in respect of registration shall lie to the Tribunal.

(2) On an appeal against a decision, the Tribunal may confirm the decision or direct that it shall not have effect.

(3) The Tribunal shall also have power on an appeal against a decision—

(a) to vary any condition for the time being in force in respect of the person to whom the appeal relates;

(b) to direct that any such condition shall cease to have effect; or

(c) to direct that any such condition as it thinks fit shall have effect in respect of that person.

69. Publication etc. of register

(1) A Council shall publish the register maintained by it in such manner, and at such times, as it considers appropriate.

(2) Any person who asks the Council for a copy of, or of an extract from, the register shall be entitled to have one.

70. Abolition of Central Council for Education and Training in Social Work

(1) The Central Council for Education and Training in Social Work (referred to in this Act as 'CCETSW') shall cease to exercise in relation to England and Wales the functions conferred on it by or under section 10 of the Health and Social Services and Social Security Adjudications Act 1983.

(2) Her Majesty may by Order in Council make a scheme under subsection (3), or make any provision under subsection (4), which She considers necessary or expedient in consequence of the functions of CCETSW referred to in subsection (1) ceasing, by virtue of that subsection, an Act of the Scottish Parliament or an Act of the Northern Ireland Assembly, to be exercisable in relation to any part of the United Kingdom.

(3) A scheme may provide–

   (a) for the transfer to the new employer of any eligible employee;

   (b) for the transfer to any person of any property belonging to CCETSW;

   (c) for any person to have such rights and interests in relation to any property belonging to CCETSW as Her Majesty considers appropriate (whether in connection with a transfer or otherwise);

   (d) for the transfer to any person of any liabilities of CCETSW.

(4) The Order in Council may make–

   (a) any supplementary, incidental or consequential provision;

   (b) any transitory, transitional or saving provision,

including provision amending Schedule 3 to that Act or repealing that Schedule, section 10 of that Act and any reference in any enactment to CCETSW.

(5) In this section–

   'eligible employee' means a person who is employed under a contract of employment with the old employer;

   'new employer' means–

   (a) in relation to England or Wales, the Council;

   (b) in relation to Scotland or Northern Ireland, any body established under a provision of the law of Scotland or (as the case may be) Northern Ireland which appears to Her Majesty to perform functions corresponding to those of a Council;

   'old employer' means CCETSW;

   'property' includes rights and interests of any description.

71. Rules

(1) Any power of a Council to make rules under this Part may be exercised–

   (a) either in relation to all cases to which the power extends, or in relation to all those cases subject to specified exceptions, or in relation to any specified cases or classes of case; and

   (b) so as to make, as respects the cases in relation to which it is exercised, the same provision for all cases in relation to which the power is exercised, or different provision for different cases or different classes of case, or different provision as respects the same case or class of case for different purposes.

(2) Rules made by a Council under this Part may make provision for the payment of reasonable fees to the Council in connection with the discharge of the Council's functions.

(3) In particular, the rules may make provision for the payment of such fees in connection with–

(a) registration (including applications for registration or for amendment of the register);

(b) the approval of courses under section 63;

(c) the provision of training;

(d) the provision of copies of codes of practice or copies of, or extracts from, the register, including provision requiring persons registered under this Part to pay a periodic fee to the Council of such amount, and at such time, as the rules may specify.

(4) No rules shall be made by a Council under this Part without the consent of the appropriate Minister.

PART V
THE CHILDREN'S COMMISSIONER FOR WALES

72. Children's Commissioner for Wales

(1) There shall be an office of the Children's Commissioner for Wales or Comisiynydd Plant Cymru.

(2) Schedule 2 shall have effect with respect to the Children's Commissioner for Wales (referred to in this Act as 'the Commissioner').

73. Review and monitoring of arrangements

(1) The Commissioner may review, and monitor the operation of, arrangements falling within subsection (2), (3) or (4) for the purpose of ascertaining whether, and to what extent, the arrangements are effective in safeguarding and promoting the rights and welfare of children to whom this Part applies.

(2) The arrangements falling within this subsection are the arrangements made by the providers of regulated children's services in Wales, or by the Assembly, for dealing with complaints or representations in respect of such services made by or on behalf of children to whom this Part applies.

(3) The arrangements falling within this subsection are arrangements made by the providers of regulated children's services in Wales, or by the Assembly, for ensuring that proper action is taken in response to any disclosure of information which may tend to show–

(a) that a criminal offence has been committed;

(b) that a person has failed to comply with any legal obligation to which he is subject;

(c) that the health and safety of any person has been endangered; or

(d) that information tending to show that any matter falling within one of the preceding paragraphs has been deliberately concealed,

in the course of or in connection with the provision of such services.

(4) The arrangements falling within this subsection are arrangements made (whether by providers of regulated children's services in Wales, by the Assembly or by any other person) for making persons available–

(a) to represent the views and wishes of children to whom this Part applies; or

(b) to provide such children with advice and support of any prescribed kind.

(5) Regulations may confer power on the Commissioner to require prescribed persons to provide any information which the Commissioner considers it necessary or expedient to have for the purposes of his functions under this section.

74. Examination of cases

(1) Regulations may make provision for the examination by the Commissioner of the cases of particular children to whom this Part applies.

(2) The regulations may include provision about–

(a) the types of case which may be examined;

(b) the circumstances in which an examination may be made;

(c) the procedure for conducting an examination, including provision about the representation of parties;

(d) the publication of reports following an examination.

(3) The regulations may make provision for–

(a) requiring persons to provide the Commissioner with information; or

(b) requiring persons who hold or are accountable for information to provide the Commissioner with explanations or other assistance,

for the purposes of an examination or for the purposes of determining whether any recommendation made in a report following an examination has been complied with.

(4) For the purposes mentioned in subsection (3), the Commissioner shall have the same powers as the High Court in respect of–

(a) the attendance and examination of witnesses (including the administration of oaths and affirmations and the examination of witnesses abroad); and

(b) the provision of information.

(5) No person shall be compelled for the purposes mentioned in subsection (3) to give any evidence or provide any information which he could not be compelled to give or provide in civil proceedings before the High Court.

(6) The regulations may make provision for the payment by the Commissioner of sums in respect of expenses or allowances to persons who attend or provide information for the purposes mentioned in subsection (3).

75. Obstruction etc.

(1) The Commissioner may certify an offence to the High Court where–

(a) a person, without lawful excuse, obstructs him or any member of his staff in the exercise of any of his functions under regulations made by virtue of section 73(5) or 74; or

(b) a person is guilty of any act or omission in relation to an examination under regulations made by virtue of section 74 which, if that examination were proceedings in the High Court, would constitute contempt of court.

(2) Where an offence is so certified the High Court may inquire into the matter; and after hearing–

(a) any witnesses who may be produced against or on behalf of the person charged with the offence; and

(b) any statement that may be offered in defence,

the High Court may deal with the person charged with the offence in any manner in which it could deal with him if he had committed the same offence in relation to the High Court.

76. Further functions

(1) Regulations may confer power on the Commissioner to assist a child to whom this Part applies–

    (a) in making a complaint or representation to or in respect of a provider of regulated children's services in Wales; or

    (b) in any prescribed proceedings,

and in this subsection 'proceedings' includes a procedure of any kind and any prospective proceedings.

(2) For the purposes of subsection (1), assistance includes–

    (a) financial assistance; and

    (b) arranging for representation, or the giving of advice or assistance, by any person,

and the regulations may provide for assistance to be given on conditions, including (in the case of financial assistance) conditions requiring repayment in circumstances specified in the regulations.

(3) The Commissioner may, in connection with his functions under this Part, give advice and information to any person.

(4) Regulations may, in connection with the Commissioner's functions under this Part, confer further functions on him.

(5) The regulations may, in particular, include provision about the making of reports on any matter connected with any of his functions.

(6) Apart from identifying any person investigated, a report by the Commissioner shall not–

    (a) mention the name of any person; or

    (b) include any particulars which, in the opinion of the Commissioner, are likely to identify any person and can be omitted without impairing the effectiveness of the report,

unless, after taking account of the public interest (as well as the interests of any person who made a complaint and other persons), the Commissioner considers it necessary for the report to mention his name or include such particulars.

(7) For the purposes of the law of defamation, the publication of any matter by the Commissioner in a report is absolutely privileged.

77. Restrictions

(1) This Part does not authorise the Commissioner to enquire into or report on any matter so far as it is the subject of legal proceedings before, or has been determined by, a court or tribunal.

(2) This Part does not authorise the Commissioner to exercise any function which by virtue of an enactment is also exercisable by a prescribed person.

78. Interpretation

(1) This Part applies to a child to or in respect of whom regulated children's services in Wales are provided.

(2) In this Part, 'regulated children's services in Wales' means any of the following services for the time being provided in respect of children–

    (a) services of a description provided by or in Part II undertakings, so far as provided in Wales;

    (b) services provided by local authorities in Wales in the exercise of relevant adoption functions or relevant fostering functions;

    (c) services of a description provided by persons registered under Part XA of the 1989 Act, so far as provided in Wales;

    (d) accommodation provided by schools or by an institution within the further education sector (as defined in section 91 of the Further and Higher Education Act 1992), so far as provided in Wales.

(3) For the purposes of this Part–

    (a) in the case of the services mentioned in subsection (2)(a), the person who carries on the Part II undertaking is to be treated as the provider of the services;

    (b) in the case of the services mentioned in subsection (2)(d), the relevant person (as defined in section 87 of the 1989 Act) is to be treated as the provider of the services.

(4) For the purposes of this section, an establishment or agency, and an undertaking of any other description, is a Part II undertaking if the provider of the services in question is for the time being required to be registered under that Part.

(5) Where the activities of an undertaking are carried on from two or more branches, each of those branches shall be treated as a separate undertaking for the purposes of this Part.

(6) Regulations may provide–

    (a) for this Part to be treated as having applied to a child at any time before the commencement of this Part if regulated children's services in Wales were at that time provided to or in respect of him;

    (b) for references in this Part to children to whom this Part applies to include references to persons who, at any prescribed time, were such children.

(7) In this Part–

'information' includes information recorded in any form;

'regulations' means regulations made by the Assembly.

(8) In this section, 'relevant adoption functions' and 'relevant fostering functions' have the same meanings as in Part III.

PART VI
CHILD MINDING AND DAY CARE

79. Amendment of Children Act 1989

(1) After Part X of the 1989 Act (child minding and day care for young children) there shall be inserted–

'PART XA
CHILD MINDING AND DAY CARE FOR CHILDREN IN ENGLAND AND WALES

Introductory

79A. Child minders and day care providers

(1) This section and section 79B apply for the purposes of this Part.

(2) 'Act as a child minder' means (subject to the following subsections) look after one or more children under the age of eight on domestic premises for reward; and 'child minding' shall be interpreted accordingly.

(3) A person who–
- (a) is the parent, or a relative, of a child;
- (b) has parental responsibility for a child;
- (c) is a local authority foster parent in relation to a child;
- (d) is a foster parent with whom a child has been placed by a voluntary organisation; or
- (e) fosters a child privately,

does not act as a child minder when looking after that child.

(4) Where a person–
- (a) looks after a child for the parents ('P1'), or
- (b) in addition to that work, looks after another child for different parents ('P2'),

and the work consists (in a case within paragraph (a)) of looking after the child wholly or mainly in P1's home or (in a case within paragraph (b)) of looking after the children wholly or mainly in P1's home or P2's home or both, the work is not to be treated as child minding.

(5) In subsection (4), 'parent', in relation to a child, includes–
- (a) a person who is not a parent of the child but who has parental responsibility for the child;
- (b) a person who is a relative of the child.

(6) 'Day care' means care provided at any time for children under the age of eight on premises other than domestic premises.

(7) This Part does not apply in relation to a person who acts as a child minder, or provides day care on any premises, unless the period, or the total of the periods, in any day which he spends looking after children or (as the case may be) during which the children are looked after on the premises exceeds two hours.

(8) In determining whether a person is required to register under this Part for child minding, any day on which he does not act as a child minder at any time between 2 am and 6 pm is to be disregarded.

79B. Other definitions, etc.

(1) The registration authority in relation to England is Her Majesty's Chief Inspector of Schools in England (referred to in this Part as the Chief Inspector) and references to the Chief Inspector's area are references to England.

(2) The registration authority in relation to Wales is the National Assembly for Wales (referred to in this Act as 'the Assembly').

(3) A person is qualified for registration for child minding if–
- (a) he, and every other person looking after children on any premises on which he is or is likely to be child minding, is suitable to look after children under the age of eight;
- (b) every person living or employed on the premises in question is suitable to be in regular contact with children under the age of eight;
- (c) the premises in question are suitable to be used for looking after children under the age of eight, having regard to their condition and the condition and appropriateness of any equipment on the premises and to any other factor connected with the situation, construction or size of the premises; and
- (d) he is complying with regulations under section 79C and with any conditions imposed by the registration authority.

(4) A person is qualified for registration for providing day care on particular premises if–

    (a) every person looking after children on the premises is suitable to look after children under the age of eight;

    (b) every person living or working on the premises is suitable to be in regular contact with children under the age of eight;

    (c) the premises are suitable to be used for looking after children under the age of eight, having regard to their condition and the condition and appropriateness of any equipment on the premises and to any other factor connected with the situation, construction or size of the premises; and

    (d) he is complying with regulations under section 79C and with any conditions imposed by the registration authority.

(5) For the purposes of subsection (4)(b) a person is not treated as working on the premises in question if–

    (a) none of his work is done in the part of the premises in which children are looked after; or

    (b) he does not work on the premises at times when children are looked after there.

(6) 'Domestic premises' means any premises which are wholly or mainly used as a private dwelling and 'premises' includes any area and any vehicle.

(7) 'Regulations' means–

    (a) in relation to England, regulations made by the Secretary of State;

    (b) in relation to Wales, regulations made by the Assembly.

(8) 'Tribunal' means the Tribunal established by section 9 of the Protection of Children Act 1999.

(9) Schedule 9A (which supplements the provisions of this Part) shall have effect.

Regulations

79C. Regulations etc. governing child minders and day care providers

(1) The Secretary of State may, after consulting the Chief Inspector and any other person he considers appropriate, make regulations governing the activities of registered persons who act as child minders, or provide day care, on premises in England.

(2) The Assembly may make regulations governing the activities of registered persons who act as child minders, or provide day care, on premises in Wales.

(3) The regulations under this section may deal with the following matters (among others)–

    (a) the welfare and development of the children concerned;

    (b) suitability to look after, or be in regular contact with, children under the age of eight;

    (c) qualifications and training;

    (d) the maximum number of children who may be looked after and the number of persons required to assist in looking after them;

    (e) the maintenance, safety and suitability of premises and equipment;

    (f) the keeping of records;

    (g) the provision of information.

(4) In relation to activities on premises in England, the power to make regulations

under this section may be exercised so as to confer powers or impose duties on the Chief Inspector in the exercise of his functions under this Part.

(5) In particular they may be exercised so as to require or authorise the Chief Inspector, in exercising those functions, to have regard to or meet factors, standards and other matters prescribed by or referred to in the regulations.

(6) If the regulations require any person (other than the registration authority) to have regard to or meet factors, standards and other matters prescribed by or referred to in the regulations, they may also provide for any allegation that the person has failed to do so to be taken into account–

(a) by the registration authority in the exercise of its functions under this Part, or

(b) in any proceedings under this Part.

(7) Regulations may provide–

(a) that a registered person who without reasonable excuse contravenes, or otherwise fails to comply with, any requirement of the regulations shall be guilty of an offence; and

(b) that a person guilty of the offence shall be liable on summary conviction to a fine not exceeding level 5 on the standard scale.

Registration

79D. Requirement to register

(1) No person shall–

(a) act as a child minder in England unless he is registered under this Part for child minding by the Chief Inspector; or

(b) act as a child minder in Wales unless he is registered under this Part for child minding by the Assembly.

(2) Where it appears to the registration authority that a person has contravened subsection (1), the authority may serve a notice ('an enforcement notice') on him.

(3) An enforcement notice shall have effect for a period of one year beginning with the date on which it is served.

(4) If a person in respect of whom an enforcement notice has effect contravenes subsection (1) without reasonable excuse (whether the contravention occurs in England or Wales), he shall be guilty of an offence.

(5) No person shall provide day care on any premises unless he is registered under this Part for providing day care on those premises by the registration authority.

(6) If any person contravenes subsection (5) without reasonable excuse, he shall be guilty of an offence.

(7) A person guilty of an offence under this section shall be liable on summary conviction to a fine not exceeding level 5 on the standard scale.

79E. Applications for registration

(1) A person who wishes to be registered under this Part shall make an application to the registration authority.

(2) The application shall–

(a) give prescribed information about prescribed matters;

(b) give any other information which the registration authority reasonably requires the applicant to give.

(3) Where a person provides, or proposes to provide, day care on different premises, he shall make a separate application in respect of each of them.

(4) Where the registration authority has sent the applicant notice under section 79L(1) of its intention to refuse an application under this section, the application may not be withdrawn without the consent of the authority.

(5) A person who, in an application under this section, knowingly makes a statement which is false or misleading in a material particular shall be guilty of an offence and liable, on summary conviction, to a fine not exceeding level 5 on the standard scale.

79F. Grant or refusal of registration

(1) If, on an application by a person for registration for child minding–

    (a) the registration authority is of the opinion that the applicant is, and will continue to be, qualified for registration for child minding (so far as the conditions of section 79B(3) are applicable); and

    (b) the applicant pays the prescribed fee,

the authority shall grant the application; otherwise, it shall refuse it.

(2) If, on an application by any person for registration for providing day care on any premises–

    (a) the registration authority is of the opinion that the applicant is, and will continue to be, qualified for registration for providing day care on those premises (so far as the conditions of section 79B(4) are applicable); and

    (b) the applicant pays the prescribed fee,

the authority shall grant the application; otherwise, it shall refuse it.

(3) An application may, as well as being granted subject to any conditions the authority thinks necessary or expedient for the purpose of giving effect to regulations under section 79C, be granted subject to any other conditions the authority thinks fit to impose.

(4) The registration authority may as it thinks fit vary or remove any condition to which the registration is subject or impose a new condition.

(5) Any register kept by a registration authority of persons who act as child minders or provide day care shall be open to inspection by any person at all reasonable times.

(6) A registered person who without reasonable excuse contravenes, or otherwise fails to comply with, any condition imposed on his registration shall be guilty of an offence.

(7) A person guilty of an offence under subsection (6) shall be liable on summary conviction to a fine not exceeding level 5 on the standard scale.

79G. Cancellation of registration

(1) The registration authority may cancel the registration of any person if–

    (a) in the case of a person registered for child minding, the authority is of the opinion that the person has ceased or will cease to be qualified for registration for child minding;

    (b) in the case of a person registered for providing day care on any premises, the authority is of the opinion that the person has ceased or will cease to be qualified for registration for providing day care on those premises,

or if an annual fee which is due from the person has not been paid.

(2) Where a requirement to make any changes or additions to any services, equipment or premises has been imposed on a registered person under section 79F(3), his registration shall not be cancelled on the ground of any defect or insufficiency in the services, equipment or premises if–

(a) the time set for complying with the requirements has not expired; and

(b) it is shown that the defect or insufficiency is due to the changes or additions not having been made.

(3) Any cancellation under this section must be in writing.

79H. Suspension of registration

(1) Regulations may provide for the registration of any person for acting as a child minder or providing day care to be suspended for a prescribed period by the registration authority in prescribed circumstances.

(2) Any regulations made under this section shall include provision conferring on the person concerned a right of appeal to the Tribunal against suspension.

79J. Resignation of registration

(1) A person who is registered for acting as a child minder or providing day care may by notice in writing to the registration authority resign his registration.

(2) But a person may not give a notice under subsection (1)–

(a) if the registration authority has sent him a notice under section 79L(1) of its intention to cancel the registration, unless the authority has decided not to take that step; or

(b) the registration authority has sent him a notice under section 79L(5) of its decision to cancel the registration and the time within which an appeal may be brought has not expired or, if an appeal has been brought, it has not been determined.

79K. Protection of children in an emergency

(1) If, in the case of any person registered for acting as a child minder or providing day care–

(a) the registration authority applies to a justice of the peace for an order–

(i) cancelling the registration;

(ii) varying or removing any condition to which the registration is subject; or

(iii) imposing a new condition; and

(b) it appears to the justice that a child who is being, or may be, looked after by that person, or (as the case may be) in accordance with the provision for day care made by that person, is suffering, or is likely to suffer, significant harm, the justice may make the order.

(2) The cancellation, variation, removal or imposition shall have effect from the time when the order is made.

(3) An application under subsection (1) may be made without notice.

(4) An order under subsection (1) shall be made in writing.

(5) Where an order is made under this section, the registration authority shall serve on the registered person, as soon as is reasonably practicable after the making of the order–

   (a) a copy of the order;

   (b) a copy of any written statement of the authority's reasons for making the application for the order which supported that application; and

   (c) notice of any right of appeal conferred by section 79M.

(6) Where an order has been so made, the registration authority shall, as soon as is reasonably practicable after the making of the order, notify the local authority in whose area the person concerned acts or acted as a child minder, or provides or provided day care, of the making of the order.

79L. Notice of intention to take steps

(1) Not less than 14 days before–

   (a) refusing an application for registration;

   (b) cancelling a registration;

   (c) removing or varying any condition to which a registration is subject or imposing a new condition; or

   (d) refusing to grant an application for the removal or variation of any condition to which a registration is subject,

the registration authority shall send to the applicant, or (as the case may be) registered person, notice in writing of its intention to take the step in question.

(2) Every such notice shall–

   (a) give the authority's reasons for proposing to take the step; and

   (b) inform the person concerned of his rights under this section.

(3) Where the recipient of such a notice informs the authority in writing of his desire to object to the step being taken, the authority shall afford him an opportunity to do so.

(4) Any objection made under subsection (3) may be made orally or in writing, by the recipient of the notice or a representative.

(5) If the authority, after giving the person concerned an opportunity to object to the step being taken, decides nevertheless to take it, it shall send him written notice of its decision.

(6) A step of a kind mentioned in subsection (1)(b) or (c) shall not take effect until the expiry of the time within which an appeal may be brought under section 79M or, where such an appeal is brought, before its determination.

(7) Subsection (6) does not prevent a step from taking effect before the expiry of the time within which an appeal may be brought under section 79M if the person concerned notifies the registration authority in writing that he does not intend to appeal.

79M. Appeals

(1) An appeal against–

   (a) the taking of any step mentioned in section 79L(1); or

   (b) an order under section 79K,

shall lie to the Tribunal.

(2) On an appeal, the Tribunal may–

   (a) confirm the taking of the step or the making of the order or direct that it shall not have, or shall cease to have, effect; and

   (b) impose, vary or cancel any condition.

Inspection: England

79N. General functions of the Chief Inspector

(1) The Chief Inspector has the general duty of keeping the Secretary of State informed about the quality and standards of child minding and day care provided by registered persons in England.

(2) When asked to do so by the Secretary of State, the Chief Inspector shall give advice or information to the Secretary of State about such matters relating to the provision of child minding or day care by registered persons in England as may be specified in the Secretary of State's request.

(3) The Chief Inspector may at any time give advice to the Secretary of State, either generally or in relation to provision by particular persons or on particular premises, on any matter connected with the provision of child minding or day care by registered persons in England.

(4) The Chief Inspector may secure the provision of training for persons who provide or assist in providing child minding or day care, or intend to do so.

(5) Regulations may confer further functions on the Chief Inspector relating to child minding and day care provided in England.

(6) The annual reports of the Chief Inspector required by subsection (7)(a) of section 2 of the School Inspections Act 1996 to be made to the Secretary of State shall include an account of the exercise of the Chief Inspector's functions under this Part, and the power conferred by subsection (7)(b) of that section to make other reports to the Secretary of State includes a power to make reports with respect to matters which fall within the scope of his functions by virtue of this Part.

79P. Early years child care inspectorate

(1) The Chief Inspector shall establish and maintain a register of early years child care inspectors for England.

(2) The register may be combined with the register maintained for England under paragraph 8(1) of Schedule 26 to the School Standards and Framework Act 1998 (register of nursery education inspectors).

(3) Paragraphs 8(2) to (9), 9(1) to (4), 10 and 11 of that Schedule shall apply in relation to the register of early years child care inspectors as they apply in relation to the register maintained for England under paragraph 8(1) of that Schedule, but with the modifications set out in subsection (4).

(4) In the provisions concerned–

    (a) references to registered nursery education inspectors shall be read as references to registered early years child care inspectors;

    (b) references to inspections under paragraph 6 of that Schedule shall be read as references to inspections under section 79Q (and references to the functions of a registered nursery education inspector under paragraph 6 shall be interpreted accordingly);

    (c) references to the registration of a person under paragraph 6 of that Schedule shall be read as references to the registration of a person under subsection (1) (and references to applications made under paragraph 6 shall be interpreted accordingly); and

    (d) in paragraph 10(2), for the words from 'to a tribunal' to the end there shall be substituted 'to the Tribunal established under section 9 of the Protection of Children Act 1999.'

(5) Registered early years child care inspectors are referred to below in this Part as registered inspectors.

79Q. Inspection of provision of child minding and day care in England

(1) The Chief Inspector may at any time require any registered person to provide him with any information connected with the person's activities as a child minder, or provision of day care, which the Chief Inspector considers it necessary to have for the purposes of his functions under this Part.

(2) The Chief Inspector shall secure that any child minding provided in England by a registered person is inspected by a registered inspector at prescribed intervals.

(3) The Chief Inspector shall secure that any day care provided by a registered person on any premises in England is inspected by a registered inspector at prescribed intervals.

(4) The Chief Inspector may comply with subsection (2) or (3) either by organising inspections or by making arrangements with others for them to organise inspections.

(5) In prescribing the intervals mentioned in subsection (2) or (3) the Secretary of State may make provision as to the period within which the first inspection of child minding or day care provided by any person or at any premises is to take place.

(6) A person conducting an inspection under this section shall report on the quality and standards of the child minding or day care provided.

(7) The Chief Inspector may arrange for an inspection conducted by a registered inspector under this section to be monitored by another registered inspector.

79R. Reports of inspections

(1) A person who has conducted an inspection under section 79Q shall report in writing on the matters inspected to the Chief Inspector within the prescribed period.

(2) The period mentioned in subsection (1) may, if the Chief Inspector considers it necessary, be extended by up to three months.

(3) Once the report of an inspection has been made to the Chief Inspector under subsection (1) he–

(a) may send a copy of it to the Secretary of State, and shall do so without delay if the Secretary of State requests a copy;

(b) shall send a copy of it, or of such parts of it as he considers appropriate, to any prescribed authorities or persons; and

(c) may arrange for the report (or parts of it) to be further published in any manner he considers appropriate.

(4) Subsections (2) to (4) of section 42A of the School Inspections Act 1996 shall apply in relation to the publication of any report under subsection (3) as they apply in relation to the publication of a report under any of the provisions mentioned in subsection (2) of section 42A.

Inspection: Wales

79S. General functions of the Assembly

(1) The Assembly may secure the provision of training for persons who provide or assist in providing child minding or day care, or intend to do so.

(2) In relation to child minding and day care provided in Wales, the Assembly shall have any additional function specified in regulations made by the Assembly; but the regulations may only specify a function corresponding to a function which, by virtue of section 79N(5), is exercisable by the Chief Inspector in relation to child minding and day care provided in England.

79T. Inspection: Wales

(1) The Assembly may at any time require any registered person to provide it with any information connected with the person's activities as a child minder or provision of day care which the Assembly considers it necessary to have for the purposes of its functions under this Part.

(2) The Assembly may by regulations make provision–

    (a) for the inspection of the quality and standards of child minding provided in Wales by registered persons and of day care provided by registered persons on premises in Wales;

    (b) for the publication of reports of the inspections in such manner as the Assembly considers appropriate.

(3) The regulations may provide for the inspections to be organised by–

    (a) the Assembly; or

    (b) Her Majesty's Chief Inspector of Education and Training in Wales, or any other person, under arrangements made with the Assembly.

(4) The regulations may provide for subsections (2) to (4) of section 42A of the School Inspections Act 1996 to apply with modifications in relation to the publication of reports under the regulations.

Supplementary

79U. Rights of entry etc.

(1) An authorised inspector may at any reasonable time enter any premises in England or Wales on which child minding or day care is at any time provided.

(2) Where an authorised inspector has reasonable cause to believe that a child is being looked after on any premises in contravention of this Part, he may enter those premises at any reasonable time.

(3) An inspector entering premises under this section may–

    (a) inspect the premises;

    (b) inspect, and take copies of–

        (i) any records kept by the person providing the child minding or day care; and

        (ii) any other documents containing information relating to its provision;

    (c) seize and remove any document or other material or thing found there which he has reasonable grounds to believe may be evidence of a failure to comply with any condition or requirement imposed by or under this Part;

    (d) require any person to afford him such facilities and assistance with respect to matters within the person's control as are necessary to enable him to exercise his powers under this section;

    (e) take measurements and photographs or make recordings;

    (f) inspect any children being looked after there, and the arrangements made for their welfare;

(g) interview in private the person providing the child minding or day care; and

(h) interview in private any person looking after children, or living or working, there who consents to be interviewed.

(4) Section 42 of the School Inspections Act 1996 (inspection of computer records for purposes of Part I of that Act) shall apply for the purposes of subsection (3) as it applies for the purposes of Part I of that Act.

(5) The registration authority may, in any case where it appears to the authority appropriate to do so, authorise a person who is not an authorised inspector to exercise any of the powers conferred by this section.

(6) A person exercising any power conferred by this section shall, if so required, produce some duly authenticated document showing his authority to do so.

(7) It shall be an offence wilfully to obstruct a person exercising any such power.

(8) Any person guilty of an offence under subsection (7) shall be liable on summary conviction to a fine not exceeding level 4 on the standard scale.

(9) In this section–

'authorised inspector' means a registered inspector or a person authorised by the Assembly or by any person with whom the Assembly has made arrangements under section 79T(3);

'documents' and 'records' each include information recorded in any form.

79V. Function of local authorities

Each local authority shall, in accordance with regulations, secure the provision–

(a) of information and advice about child minding and day care; and

(b) of training for persons who provide or assist in providing child minding or day care.

Checks on suitability of persons working with children over the age of seven

79W. Requirement for certificate of suitability

(1) This section applies to any person not required to register under this Part who looks after, or provides care for, children and meets the following conditions.
Requirement for certificate of suitability. References in this section to children are to those under the age of 15 or (in the case of disabled children) 17.

(2) The first condition is that the period, or the total of the periods, in any week which he spends looking after children or (as the case may be) during which the children are looked after exceeds five hours.

(3) The second condition is that he would be required to register under this Part (or, as the case may be, this Part if it were subject to prescribed modifications) if the children were under the age of eight.

(4) Regulations may require a person to whom this section applies to hold a certificate issued by the registration authority as to his suitability, and the suitability of each prescribed person, to look after children.

(5) The regulations may make provision about–

(a) applications for certificates;

(b) the matters to be taken into account by the registration authority in determining whether to issue certificates;

(c) the information to be contained in certificates;

(d) the period of their validity.

(6) The regulations may provide that a person to whom this section applies shall be guilty of an offence–

(a) if he does not hold a certificate as required by the regulations; or

(b) if, being a person who holds such a certificate, he fails to produce it when reasonably required to do so by a prescribed person.

(7) The regulations may provide that a person who, for the purpose of obtaining such a certificate, knowingly makes a statement which is false or misleading in a material particular shall be guilty of an offence.

(8) The regulations may provide that a person guilty of an offence under the regulations shall be liable on summary conviction to a fine not exceeding level 5 on the standard scale.

Time limit for proceedings

79X. Time limit for proceedings

(1) Proceedings for an offence under this Part or regulations made under it may be brought within a period of six months from the date on which evidence sufficient in the opinion of the prosecutor to warrant the proceedings came to his knowledge; but no such proceedings shall be brought by virtue of this section more than three years after the commission of the offence.

(2) Schedule 3 (which inserts a new Schedule 9A in the 1989 Act) shall have effect.

(3) The appropriate Minister may by order make a scheme for the transfer to the new employer of any eligible employee.

(4) In subsection (3)–

'eligible employee' means a person who is employed under a contract of employment with an old employer on work which would have continued but for the provisions of this section;

'new employer' means the registration authority (within the meaning of Part XA of the 1989 Act) and, in relation to Wales, includes Her Majesty's Chief Inspector of Education and Training in Wales;

'old employer' means a local authority.

(5) Part X of, and Schedule 9 to, the 1989 Act shall cease to extend to England and Wales.

PART VII
PROTECTION OF CHILDREN AND VULNERABLE ADULTS

Protection of vulnerable adults

80. Basic definitions

(1) Subsections (2) to (7) apply for the purposes of this Part.

(2) 'Care worker' means–

(a) an individual who is or has been employed in a position which is such as to enable him to have regular contact in the course of his duties with adults to whom accommodation is provided at a care home;

(b) an individual who is or has been employed in a position which is such as to enable him to have regular contact in the course of his duties with adults to whom prescribed services are provided by an independent hospital, an independent clinic, an independent medical agency or a National Health Service body;

(c) an individual who is or has been employed in a position which is concerned with the provision of personal care in their own homes for persons who by reason of illness, infirmity or disability are unable to provide it for themselves without assistance.

(3) 'Care position', in relation to an individual, means a position such as is mentioned in subsection (2)(a), (b) or (c).

(4) 'Employment' has the same meaning as in the Protection of Children Act 1999 (referred to in this Act as 'the 1999 Act'); and references to an individual being employed shall be construed accordingly.

(5) 'Supply worker'–

(a) in relation to an employment agency, means an individual supplied by the agency for employment in a care position or for whom the agency has found employment in a care position;

(b) in relation to an employment business, means an individual supplied by the business for employment in a care position.

(6) 'Vulnerable adult' means–

(a) an adult to whom accommodation and nursing or personal care are provided in a care home;

(b) an adult to whom personal care is provided in their own home under arrangements made by a domiciliary care agency; or

(c) an adult to whom prescribed services are provided by an independent hospital, independent clinic, independent medical agency or National Health Service body.

(7) The persons who provide care for vulnerable adults are–

(a) any person who carries on a care home;

(b) any person who carries on a domiciliary care agency;

(c) any person who carries on an independent hospital, an independent clinic or an independent medical agency, which provides prescribed services; and

(d) a National Health Service body which provides prescribed services.

(8) Regulations for the purposes of this section or section 91, 93 or 103 may only be made by the Secretary of State; and before making any regulations for the purposes of this section or section 93 or 103 the Secretary of State shall consult the Assembly.

81. Duty of Secretary of State to keep list

(1) The Secretary of State shall keep a list of individuals who are considered unsuitable to work with vulnerable adults.

(2) An individual shall not be included in the list except in accordance with this Part.

(3) The Secretary of State may at any time remove an individual from the list if he is satisfied that the individual should not have been included in it.

82. Persons who provide care for vulnerable adults: duty to refer

(1) A person who provides care for vulnerable adults ('the provider') shall refer a care worker to the Secretary of State if there is fulfilled–

(a) any of the conditions mentioned in subsection (2); or

(b) the condition mentioned in subsection (3).

(2) The conditions referred to in subsection (1)(a) are–

(a) that the provider has dismissed the worker on the grounds of misconduct (whether or not in the course of his employment) which harmed or placed at risk of harm a vulnerable adult;

(b) that the worker has resigned, retired or been made redundant in circumstances such that the provider would have dismissed him, or would have considered dismissing him, on such grounds if he had not resigned, retired or been made redundant;

(c) that the provider has, on such grounds, transferred the worker to a position which is not a care position;

(d) that the provider has, on such grounds, suspended the worker or provisionally transferred him to a position which is not a care position but has not yet decided whether to dismiss him or to confirm the transfer.

(3) The condition referred to in subsection (1)(b) is that–

(a) in circumstances not falling within subsection (2), the provider has dismissed the worker, he has resigned or retired or the provider has transferred him to a position which is not a care position;

(b) information not available to the provider at the time of the dismissal, resignation, retirement or transfer has since become available; and

(c) the provider has formed the opinion that, if that information had been available at that time and if (where applicable) the worker had not resigned or retired, the provider would have dismissed him, or would have considered dismissing him, on such grounds as are mentioned in subsection (2)(a).

(4) If it appears from the information submitted with a reference under subsection (1) that it may be appropriate for the worker to be included in the list kept under section 81, the Secretary of State shall–

(a) determine the reference in accordance with subsections (5) to (7); and

(b) pending that determination, provisionally include the worker in the list.

(5) The Secretary of State shall–

(a) invite observations from the worker on the information submitted with the reference and, if he thinks fit, on any observations submitted under paragraph (b); and

(b) invite observations from the provider on any observations on the information submitted with the reference and, if he thinks fit, on any other observations under paragraph (a).

(6) Where–

(a) the Secretary of State has considered the information submitted with the reference, any observations submitted to him and any other information which he considers relevant; and

(b) in the case of a reference under subsection (2)(d), the provider has dismissed the worker or, as the case may be, has confirmed his transfer on such grounds as are there mentioned,

the Secretary of State shall confirm the worker's inclusion in the list if subsection (7) applies; otherwise he shall remove him from the list.

(7) This subsection applies if the Secretary of State is of the opinion–

(a) that the provider reasonably considered the worker to be guilty of misconduct (whether or not in the course of his employment) which harmed or placed at risk of harm a vulnerable adult; and

(b) that the worker is unsuitable to work with vulnerable adults.

(8) The reference in subsection (6)(b) to the provider dismissing the worker on such grounds as are mentioned in subsection (2)(d) includes–

(a) a reference to his resigning, retiring or being made redundant in circumstances such that the provider would have dismissed him, or would have considered dismissing him, on such grounds if he had not resigned, retired or been made redundant; and

(b) a reference to the provider transferring him, on such grounds, to a position which is not a care position.

(9) This section does not apply where–

(a) the provider carries on a domiciliary care agency, or an independent medical agency, which is or includes an employment agency or an employment business; and

(b) the worker in question is a supply worker in relation to him.

(10) Nothing in this section shall require a person who provides care for vulnerable adults to refer a worker to the Secretary of State in any case where the dismissal, resignation, retirement, transfer or suspension took place or, as the case may be, the opinion was formed before the commencement of this section.

83. Employment agencies and businesses: duty to refer

(1) A person who carries on an employment agency or an employment business ('the provider') shall refer a supply worker to the Secretary of State if there is fulfilled–

(a) in the case of an employment agency, any of the conditions mentioned in subsection (2); or

(b) in the case of an employment business, any of the conditions mentioned in subsection (3).

(2) The conditions referred to in subsection (1)(a) are–

(a) that the provider has decided not to do any further business with the worker on grounds of misconduct (whether or not in the course of his employment) which harmed or placed at risk of harm a vulnerable adult;

(b) that the provider has decided on such grounds not to find the worker further employment, or supply him for further employment, in a care position.

(3) The conditions mentioned in subsection (1)(b) are–

(a) that the provider has dismissed the worker on the grounds of misconduct (whether or not in the course of his employment) which harmed or placed at risk of harm a vulnerable adult;

(b) that the worker has resigned or retired in circumstances such that the provider would have dismissed him, or would have considered dismissing him, on such grounds if he had not resigned or retired;

(c) that the provider has, on such grounds, decided not to supply the worker for further employment in a care position.

(4) If it appears from the information submitted with a reference under subsection (1) that it may be appropriate for the worker to be included in the list kept under section 81, the Secretary of State shall–

(a) determine the reference in accordance with subsections (5) to (7); and

(b) pending that determination, provisionally include the worker in the list.

(5) The Secretary of State shall–

    (a) invite observations from the worker on the information submitted with the reference and, if he thinks fit, on any observations submitted under paragraph (b); and

    (b) invite observations from the provider on any observations on the information submitted with the reference and, if he thinks fit, on any other observations under paragraph (a).

(6) Where the Secretary of State has considered the information submitted with the reference, any observations submitted to him and any other information which he considers relevant, the Secretary of State shall confirm the worker's inclusion in the list if subsection (7) applies; otherwise he shall remove him from the list.

(7) This subsection applies if the Secretary of State is of the opinion–

    (a) that the provider reasonably considered the worker to be guilty of misconduct (whether or not in the course of his employment) which harmed or placed at risk of harm a vulnerable adult; and

    (b) that the worker is unsuitable to work with vulnerable adults.

(8) Nothing in this section shall require a person who provides care for vulnerable adults to refer a worker to the Secretary of State in any case where the dismissal, resignation or retirement took place or, as the case may be, the decision was made before the commencement of this section.

84. Power of registration authority to refer

(1) The registration authority may refer a care worker to the Secretary of State if–

    (a) on the basis of evidence obtained by it in the exercise of its functions under Part II of this Act, the authority considers that the worker has been guilty of misconduct (whether or not in the course of his employment) which harmed or placed at risk of harm a vulnerable adult; and

    (b) the worker has not been referred to the Secretary of State under section 82 or 83 in respect of the misconduct.

(2) Section 82(4) to (7) shall apply in relation to a reference made by the registration authority under subsection (1) as it applies in relation to a reference made by a person under section 82(1).

(3) The reference in subsection (1) to misconduct is to misconduct which occurred after the commencement of this section.

85. Individuals named in the findings of certain inquiries

(1) Subsection (2) applies where–

    (a) a relevant inquiry has been held;

    (b) the report of the person who held the inquiry names an individual who is or has been employed in a care position; and

    (c) it appears to the Secretary of State from the report–

        (i) that the person who held the inquiry found that the individual was guilty of relevant misconduct; and

        (ii) that the individual is unsuitable to work with vulnerable adults.

(2) The Secretary of State–

    (a) may provisionally include the individual in the list kept under section 81; and

    (b) if he does so, shall determine in accordance with subsections (3) to (5) whether the individual's inclusion in the list should be confirmed.

(3) The Secretary of State shall–

(a) invite observations from the individual on the report, so far as relating to him, and, if the Secretary of State thinks fit, on any observations submitted under paragraph (b); and

(b) invite observations from the relevant employer on any observations on the report and, if the Secretary of State thinks fit, on any other observations under paragraph (a).

(4) Where the Secretary of State has considered the report, any observations submitted to him and any other information which he considers relevant, he shall confirm that individual's inclusion in the list if subsection (5) applies; otherwise he shall remove him from the list.

(5) This subsection applies if the Secretary of State is of the opinion–

(a) that the person who held the inquiry reasonably considered the individual to be guilty of relevant misconduct; and

(b) that the individual is unsuitable to work with vulnerable adults.

(6) In this section–

'relevant employer' means the person who, at the time mentioned in the definition of 'relevant misconduct' below, employed the individual in a care position;

'relevant misconduct' means misconduct which harmed or placed at risk of harm a vulnerable adult and was committed (whether or not in the course of his employment) at a time when the individual was employed in a care position.

(7) In this section 'relevant inquiry' means any of the following–

(a) an inquiry held under–

(i) section 10;

(ii) section 35 of the Government of Wales Act 1998;

(iii) section 81 of the 1989 Act;

(iv) section 84 of the National Health Service Act 1977;

(v) section 7C of the Local Authority Social Services Act 1970;

(b) an inquiry to which the Tribunals of Inquiry (Evidence) Act 1921 applies;

(c) any other inquiry or hearing designated for the purposes of this section by an order made by the Secretary of State.

(8) Before making an order under subsection (7) the Secretary of State shall consult the Assembly.

86. Appeals against inclusion in list

(1) An individual who is included (otherwise than provisionally) in the list kept by the Secretary of State under section 81 may appeal to the Tribunal against–

(a) the decision to include him in the list; or

(b) with the leave of the Tribunal, any decision of the Secretary of State not to remove him from the list under section 81(3).

(2) Subject to subsection (5), an individual who has been provisionally included for a period of more than nine months in the list kept by the Secretary of State under section 81 may, with the leave of the Tribunal, have the issue of his inclusion in the list determined by the Tribunal instead of by the Secretary of State.

(3) If on an appeal or determination under this section the Tribunal is not satisfied of either of the following, namely–

(a) that the individual was guilty of misconduct (whether or not in the course of his duties) which harmed or placed at risk of harm a vulnerable adult; and

(b) that the individual is unsuitable to work with vulnerable adults, the Tribunal shall allow the appeal or determine the issue in the individual's favour and (in either case) direct his removal from the list; otherwise it shall dismiss the appeal or direct the individual's inclusion in the list.

(4) Where an individual has been convicted of an offence involving misconduct (whether or not in the course of his employment) which harmed or placed at risk of harm a vulnerable adult, no finding of fact on which the conviction must be taken to have been based shall be challenged on an appeal or determination under this section.

(5) Where the misconduct of which the individual is alleged to have been guilty is the subject of any civil or criminal proceedings, an application for leave under subsection (2) may not be made before the end of the period of six months immediately following the final determination of the proceedings.

(6) For the purposes of subsection (5), proceedings are finally determined when–
  (a) the proceedings are terminated without a decision being made;
  (b) a decision is made against which no appeal lies;
  (c) in a case where an appeal lies with leave against a decision, the time limited for applications for leave expires without leave being granted; or
  (d) in a case where leave to appeal against a decision is granted or is not required, the time limited for appeal expires without an appeal being brought.

87. Applications for removal from list

(1) Subject to section 88, an individual who is included in the list kept by the Secretary of State under section 81 may make an application to the Tribunal under this section.

(2) On an application under this section the Tribunal shall determine whether or not the individual should continue to be included in the list.

(3) If the Tribunal is satisfied that the individual is no longer unsuitable to work with vulnerable adults it shall direct his removal from the list; otherwise it shall dismiss the application.

88. Conditions for application under section 87

(1) An individual may only make an application under section 87 with the leave of the Tribunal.

(2) An application for leave under this section may not be made unless the appropriate conditions are satisfied in the individual's case.

(3) In the case of an individual who was a child when he was included (otherwise than provisionally) in the list, the appropriate conditions are satisfied if–
  (a) he has been so included for a continuous period of at least five years; and
  (b) in the period of five years ending with the time when he makes the application under this section, he has made no other such application.

(4) In the case of any other individual, the appropriate conditions are satisfied if–
  (a) he has been included (otherwise than provisionally) in the list for a continuous period of at least ten years; and
  (b) in the period of ten years ending with the time when he makes the application under this section, he has made no other such application.

(5) The Tribunal shall not grant an application under this section unless it considers–
  (a) that the individual's circumstances have changed since he was included (otherwise than provisionally) in the list, or, as the case may be, since he last made an application under this section; and
  (b) that the change is such that leave should be granted.

89. Effect of inclusion in list

(1) Where a person who provides care to vulnerable adults proposes to offer an individual employment in a care position that person–

    (a) shall ascertain whether the individual is included in the list kept under section 81; and

    (b) if he is included in that list, shall not offer him employment in such a position.

(2) Where a person who provides care to vulnerable adults discovers that an individual employed by him in a care position is included in that list, he shall cease to employ him in a care position.

For the purposes of this subsection an individual is not employed in a care position if he has been suspended or provisionally transferred to a position which is not a care position.

(3) Where a person who provides care to vulnerable adults ('the provider') proposes to offer employment in a care position to an individual who has been supplied by a person who carries on an employment agency or employment business, there is a sufficient compliance with subsection (1) if the provider–

    (a) satisfies himself that, on a date within the last 12 months, the other person ascertained whether the individual was included in the list kept under section 81;

    (b) obtains written confirmation of the facts as ascertained by that person; and

    (c) if the individual was included in the list on that date, does not offer him employment in a care position.

(4) It is immaterial for the purposes of subsection (1) or (3) whether the individual is already employed by the provider.

(5) An individual who is included (otherwise than provisionally) in the list kept by the Secretary of State under section 81 shall be guilty of an offence if he knowingly applies for, offers to do, accepts or does any work in a care position.

(6) It shall be a defence for an individual charged with an offence under subsection (5) to prove that he did not know, and could not reasonably be expected to know, that he was so included in that list.

(7) An individual who is guilty of an offence under this section shall be liable–

    (a) on summary conviction, to imprisonment for a term not exceeding six months, or to a fine not exceeding the statutory maximum, or to both;

    (b) on conviction on indictment, to imprisonment for a term not exceeding five years, or to a fine, or to both.

90. Searches of list under Part V of Police Act 1997

(1) After subsection (3B) of section 113 of the Police Act 1997 (criminal record certificates) there shall be inserted–

'(3C) If an application under this section is accompanied by a statement by the registered person that the certificate is required for the purpose of considering the applicant's suitability to be employed, supplied to work, found work or given work in a position (whether paid or unpaid) within subsection (3D), the criminal record certificate shall also state–

    (a) whether the applicant is included in the list kept under section 81 of the Care Standards Act 2000; and

    (b) if he is included in that list, such details of his inclusion as may be prescribed.

    (3D) A position is within this subsection if it is–

(a) a care position within the meaning of Part VII of the Care Standards Act 2000; or

(b) a position of such other description as may be prescribed.'

(2) After subsection (6A) of section 115 of that Act (enhanced criminal record certificates) there shall be inserted–

'(6B) If an application under this section is accompanied by a statement by the registered person that the certificate is required for the purpose of considering the applicant's suitability to be employed, supplied to work, found work or given work in a position (whether paid or unpaid) falling within subsection (3D) of section 113, the enhanced criminal record certificate shall also state–

(a) whether the applicant is included in the list kept under section 81 of the Care Standards Act 2000; and

(b) if he is included in that list, such details of his inclusion as may be prescribed.'

91. Access to list before commencement of section 90

(1) In relation to any time before the commencement of section 90, any person seeking to ascertain whether a relevant individual is included in the list kept under section 81 shall be entitled to that information on making application for the purpose to the Secretary of State.

(2) For the purposes of subsection (1) a relevant individual is–

(a) an individual to whom the person proposes to offer employment in a care position;

(b) an individual for whom the person proposes to find employment, or whom he proposes to supply for employment, in a care position; or

(c) an individual of a prescribed description who does not fall within paragraph (a) or (b).

92. Persons referred for inclusion in list under Protection of Children Act 1999

(1) Section 2(4) to (7) of the 1999 Act (referrals for inclusion in list of individuals who are considered unsuitable to work with children) shall, in the case of any reference under section 2, 2A or 2D of that Act, apply in relation to the list kept under section 81 as they apply in relation to the list kept under section 1 of that Act, but as if the reference in subsection (7)(b) to children were a reference to vulnerable adults.

(2) Section 2B of the 1999 Act shall apply in relation to the list kept under section 81 as it applies in relation to the list kept under section 1 of that Act, but as if the references in subsections (1)(c)(ii) and (5)(b) to children were references to vulnerable adults.

(3) But the Secretary of State may not by virtue of subsection (1) or (2) provisionally include an individual in the list kept under section 81, or confirm his inclusion in that list, unless he provisionally includes him in the list kept under section 1 of the 1999 Act or, as the case requires, confirms his inclusion in that list.

(4) Where an individual has by virtue of subsection (1) or (2) been included in the list kept under section 81, section 86 shall apply to him as if the references in subsections (3)(a) and (4) to a vulnerable adult were references to a child.

93. Power to extend Part VII

(1) The Secretary of State may by regulations–

(a) add to the list in section 80(7) any prescribed persons to whom subsection (2) applies;

(b) amend the definitions of 'care worker', 'care position' and 'vulnerable adult' accordingly.

(2) This subsection applies to–
    (a) local authorities providing services to adults in the exercise of their social services functions;
    (b) persons who provide to adults services which are similar to services which–
        (i) may or must be so provided by local authorities; or
        (ii) may or must be provided by National Health Service bodies.

(3) In its application by virtue of subsection (1), this Part shall have effect–
    (a) if the regulations so provide, as if 'may' were substituted for 'shall' in sections 82(1) and 83(1), and section 89 were omitted;
    (b) with such other modifications as may be specified in the regulations.

The list kept under section 1 of the 1999 Act

94. Employment agencies and businesses

(1) In subsection (9) of section 2 of the 1999 Act (inclusion on reference to Secretary of State in list of individuals who are considered unsuitable to work with children)–
    (a) for 'This section' there shall be substituted 'Subsections (1) to (8) and (10) of this section'; and
    (b) for the words from '(a)' to 'harm' there shall be substituted–

'(a) in subsection (1), for the words from "there is" to the end there were substituted the following paragraphs–
    "(a) the organisation has decided not to do any further business with the individual on the grounds of misconduct (whether or not in the course of his employment) which harmed a child or placed a child at risk of harm; or
      (b) the organisation has decided on such grounds not to find the individual further employment, or supply him for further employment, in a child care position;"'

(2) After subsection (9) of that section there shall be inserted–

'(9A) Subsections (1) to (8) and (10) of this section shall have effect in relation to an organisation which carries on an employment business as if–
    (a) in subsection (1)-
        (i) for the words from 'who' to 'position' there were substituted the words 'who has been supplied by the organisation for employment in a child care position'; and
        (ii) paragraph (b) and the word 'or' preceding it were omitted;
    (b) for subsection (2)(c) and (d) there were substituted the following paragraph-
        '(c) that the organisation has, on such grounds, decided not to supply the individual for further employment in a child care position.'
        and
    (c) subsections (3), (6)(b) and (8) were omitted.'

95. Inclusion in 1999 Act list on reference by certain authorities
(1) After section 2 of the 1999 Act there is inserted–

'**2A. Power of certain authorities to refer individuals for inclusion in list**
(1) A person to whom this section applies may refer to the Secretary of State an individual who is or has been employed in a child care position if–
(a) on the basis of evidence obtained by him in the exercise of his functions under Part II of the Care Standards Act 2000 or Part XA of the Children Act 1989, the person considers that the individual has been guilty of misconduct (whether or not in the course of his employment) which harmed a child or placed a child at risk of harm; and
(b) the individual has not been referred to the Secretary of State under section 1 above in respect of the misconduct.
(2) The persons to whom this section applies are–
(a) the National Care Standards Commission;
(b) the National Assembly for Wales; and
(c) Her Majesty's Chief Inspector of Schools in England.
(3) Section 2(4) to (7) above shall apply in relation to a reference made by a person under subsection (1) above as it applies in relation to a reference made by an organisation under section 2(1) above.
(4) The reference in subsection (1) above to misconduct is to misconduct which occurred after the commencement of this section.'

(2) In section 1(2)(a) of that Act (duty of Secretary of State to keep list), after '2' there is inserted 'or 2A'.
(3) For the sidenote to section 2 of that Act there is substituted 'Inclusion in list on reference following disciplinary action etc.'.

96. Inclusion in 1999 Act list of individuals named in findings of certain inquiries
(1) After section 2A of the 1999 Act (inserted by section 95) there is inserted–

'**2B. Individuals named in the findings of certain inquiries**
(1) Subsection (2) applies where–
(a) a relevant inquiry has been held;
(b) the report of the person who held the inquiry names an individual who is or has been employed in a child care position; and
(c) it appears to the Secretary of State from the report-
(i) that the person who held the inquiry found that the individual was guilty of relevant misconduct; and
(ii) that the individual is unsuitable to work with children.
(2) The Secretary of State–
(a) may provisionally include the individual in the list kept under section 1 above; and
(b) if he does so, shall determine in accordance with subsections (3) to (5) below whether the individual's inclusion in the list should be confirmed.
(3) The Secretary of State shall–
(a) invite observations from the individual on the report, so far as relating to

him, and, if the Secretary of State thinks fit, on any observations submitted under paragraph (b) below; and

   (b) invite observations from the relevant employer on any observations on the report and, if the Secretary of State thinks fit, on any other observations under paragraph (a) above.

(4) Where the Secretary of State has considered the report, any observations submitted to him and any other information which he considers relevant, he shall confirm that individual's inclusion in the list if subsection (5) below applies; otherwise he shall remove him from the list.

(5) This subsection applies if the Secretary of State is of the opinion–

   (a) that the person who held the inquiry reasonably considered the individual to be guilty of relevant misconduct; and

   (b) that the individual is unsuitable to work with children.

(6) In this section–

   'relevant employer' means the person who, at the time referred to in the definition of 'relevant misconduct' below, employed the individual in a child care position;

   'relevant misconduct' means misconduct which harmed a child or placed a child at risk of harm and was committed (whether or not in the course of his employment) at a time when the individual was employed in a child care position.

(7) In this section 'relevant inquiry' means any of the following–

   (a) an inquiry held under-

      (i)   section 10 of the Care Standards Act 2000;

      (ii) section 35 of the Government of Wales Act 1998;

      (iii) section 81 of the Children Act 1989;

      (iv) section 84 of the National Health Service Act 1977;

      (v)   section 7C of the Local Authority Social Services Act 1970;

   (b) an inquiry to which the Tribunals of Inquiry (Evidence) Act 1921 applies;

   (c) any other inquiry or hearing designated for the purposes of this section by an order made by the Secretary of State.

(8) An order under subsection (7) above shall be made by statutory instrument which shall be subject to annulment in pursuance of a resolution of either House of Parliament.

(9) Before making an order under subsection (7) above the Secretary of State shall consult the National Assembly for Wales.'

(2) In section 1(2) of that Act (duty of Secretary of State to keep list), before the 'or' preceding paragraph (b) there shall be inserted–

'(aa) he has been included in the list under section 2B below;'.

97. Inclusion in 1999 Act list on reference under this Part

(1) After section 2B of the 1999 Act (inserted by section 95) there shall be inserted–

'2C. Inclusion in list on reference under Part VII of Care Standards Act 2000

(1) Section 82(4) to (7) of the Care Standards Act 2000 (persons who provide care for vulnerable adults: duty to refer) shall, in the case of any reference under subsection

(1) of that section or section 84 of that Act, apply in relation to the list kept under section 1 above as it applies in relation to the list kept under section 81 of that Act, but as if the reference in subsection (7)(b) to vulnerable adults were a reference to children.

(2) Section 83(4) to (7) of that Act (employment agencies and businesses: duty to refer) shall, in the case of any reference under subsection (1) of that section, apply in relation to the list kept under section 1 above as it applies in relation to the list kept under section 81 of that Act, but as if the reference in subsection (7)(b) to vulnerable adults were a reference to children.

(3) Section 85 of that Act (individuals named in the findings of certain inquiries) shall apply in relation to the list kept under section 1 above as it applies in relation to the list kept under section 81 of that Act, but as if the references in subsections (1)(c)(ii) and (5)(b) to vulnerable adults were references to children.

(4) But the Secretary of State may not by virtue of this section provisionally include an individual in the list kept under section 1 above, or confirm his inclusion in that list, unless he provisionally includes him in the list kept under section 81 of that Act or, as the case requires, confirms his inclusion in that list.

(5) Where an individual has by virtue of this section been included in the list kept under section 1 above, section 4 below shall apply to him as if the references in subsections (3)(a) and (4) to a child were references to a vulnerable adult.'

(2) In section 1(2)(a) of the 1999 Act (individuals who may be included on list), after 'below' there shall be inserted 'or Part VII of the Care Standards Act 2000'.

98. Individuals providing care funded by direct payments
(1) After section 2C of the 1999 Act (inserted by section 97) there is inserted–

'2D. Local authorities proposing to make direct payments in respect of services
(1) A local authority may refer a relevant individual to the Secretary of State where, as a result of enquiries made, or caused to be made, by it under section 47 of the Children Act 1989, the authority considers that the individual has been guilty of misconduct (whether or not in the course of his employment) which harmed a child or placed a child at risk of harm.

(2) Section 2(4) to (7) above shall apply in relation to a reference made by a local authority under subsection (1) above as it applies in relation to a reference made by an organisation under section 2(1) above.

(3) In this section–
    'funded care' means care in respect of a person's securing the provision of which the authority has made a payment under section 17A of the Children Act 1989 (direct payments);
    'relevant individual' means an individual who is or has been employed to provide funded care to a child.

(4) The reference in subsection (1) above to misconduct is to misconduct which occurred after the commencement of this section.'

(2) In section 7 of that Act (effect of inclusion in certain statutory lists), after subsection (1) there shall be inserted–

    '(1A) Where–

(a) a person ('the recipient') employs, or proposes to employ, an individual to provide care for a child; and

(b) a local authority proposes to make a payment to the recipient under section 17A of the Children Act 1989 (direct payments) in respect of his securing the provision of the care,

the authority shall, if the recipient asks it to do so, ascertain whether the individual is included in any of the lists mentioned in subsection (1) above.'

(3) After subsection (2) of that section there shall be inserted–

'(2A) Where a local authority is required under subsection (1A) above to ascertain whether an individual who has been supplied as mentioned in subsection (2) above is included in any of the lists there mentioned, there is sufficient compliance with subsection (1A) above if the authority–

(a) satisfies itself that, on a date within the last 12 months, the organisation which supplied the individual ascertained whether he was included in any of those lists; and

(b) obtains written confirmation of the facts as ascertained by the organisation.'

(4) In section 1(2)(a) of that Act (duty of Secretary of State to keep list), after 'or 2A' there is inserted 'or 2D'.

99. Transfer from Consultancy Service Index of individuals named in past inquiries

(1) Section 3 of the 1999 Act (inclusion in list on transfer from Consultancy Service Index) shall be amended as follows.

(2) In subsection (1), for 'This section' there shall be substituted 'Subsections (2) and (3) below' and in paragraph (a), for 'this section' there shall be substituted 'section 1 above'.

(3) After subsection (3) there shall be inserted–

'(4) Subsections (5) and (6) below apply where–

(a) a relevant inquiry has been held;

(b) the report of the person who held the inquiry names an individual who is or has been employed in a child care position;

(c) it appears to the Secretary of State from the report-

(i) that the person who held the inquiry found that the individual was guilty of relevant misconduct; and

(ii) that the individual is unsuitable to work with children; and

(d) the individual is included in the Consultancy Service Index (otherwise than provisionally) immediately before the commencement of section 1 above.

(5) The Secretary of State shall–

(a) invite observations from the individual on the report, so far as relating to him, and, if the Secretary of State thinks fit, on any observations submitted under paragraph (b) below; and

(b) invite observations from the relevant employer on any observations on the report and, if the Secretary of State thinks fit, on any other observations under paragraph (a) above.

(6) The Secretary of State shall include the individual in the list kept by him under

section 1 above if, after he has considered the report, any observations submitted to him and any other information which he considers relevant, he is of the opinion–

(a) that the person who held the inquiry reasonably considered the individual to be guilty of relevant misconduct; and

(b) that the individual is unsuitable to work with children.

(7) In this section–

'relevant employer', in relation to an individual named in the report of a relevant inquiry, means the person who, at the time referred to in the definition of 'relevant misconduct' below, employed the individual in a child care position;

'relevant inquiry' has the same meaning as in section 2B above;

'relevant misconduct' means misconduct which harmed a child or placed a child at risk of harm and was committed (whether or not in the course of his employment) at a time when the individual was employed in a child care position.'

Restrictions on working with children in independent schools

100. Additional ground of complaint

(1) In subsection (1) of section 469 (notice of complaint) of the Education Act 1996, for paragraph (d) there shall be substituted–

'(d)   the proprietor of the school or any teacher or other employee employed in the school–

(i) is unsuitable to work with children; or

(ii) is for any other reason not a proper person to be the proprietor of an independent school or (as the case may be) to be a teacher or other employee in any school;'.

(2) In subsection (2) of section 470 of that Act (determination of complaint by an Independent Schools Tribunal), for paragraph (f) there shall be substituted–

'(f)   if satisfied that any person alleged by the notice of complaint to be a person who–

(i) is unsuitable to work with children; or

(ii) is for any other reason not a proper person to be the proprietor of an independent school or to be a teacher or other employee in any school,

is in fact such a person, by order disqualify that person from being the proprietor of any independent school or (as the case may be) from being a teacher or other employee in any school.'

101. Effect of inclusion in 1996 Act list

(1) Section 7 of the 1999 Act (effect of inclusion in either list) shall be amended as follows.

(2) For subsection (1) there shall be substituted–

'(1) Where a child care organisation proposes to offer an individual employment in a child care position, the organisation–

(a)   shall ascertain whether the individual is included in–

(i) the list kept under section 1 above;

(ii) the list kept for the purposes of regulations made under section 218(6) of the 1988 Act ('the 1988 Act list'); or

(iii) any list kept by the Secretary of State or the National Assembly for Wales of persons disqualified under section 470 or 471 of the Education Act 1996 ('the 1996 Act list'); and

(b) if he is included in any of those lists, shall not offer him employment in such a position.'

(3) In subsection (2)–

(a) in paragraph (a), for the words from 'the list' to the end there shall be substituted 'any of the lists mentioned in subsection (1) above'; and

(b) in paragraph (c), for 'either list' there shall be substituted 'any of those lists'.

(4) For subsection (4) there shall be substituted–

'(4) In this section–

(a) any reference to inclusion in the 1988 Act list is a reference to inclusion in that list on the grounds mentioned in section 218(6ZA)(c) of the 1988 Act; and

(b) any reference to inclusion in the 1996 Act list is a reference to inclusion in that list as a person disqualified on the grounds mentioned in section 469(1)(d)(i) of the Education Act 1996.'

102. Searches of 1996 Act list

(1) In subsection (3A) of section 113 of the Police Act 1997 (criminal record certificates), for the words from 'in the list' to the end there shall be substituted 'in–

(i) the list kept under section 1 of the Protection of Children Act 1999;

(ii) the list kept for the purposes of regulations made under section 218(6) of the Education Reform Act 1988 ('the 1988 Act list'); or

(iii) any list kept by the Secretary of State or the National Assembly for Wales of persons disqualified under section 470 or 471 of the Education Act 1996 ('the 1996 Act list'); and

(b) if he is included in any of those lists, such details of his inclusion as may be prescribed, including-

(i) in the case of the 1988 Act list, the grounds on which he is so included; or

(ii) in the case of the 1996 Act list, the grounds on which he was disqualified under section 470 or 471.'

(2) In subsection (6A) of section 115 of that Act (enhanced criminal record certificates), for the words from 'in the list' to the end there shall be substituted 'in–

(i) the list kept under section 1 of the Protection of Children Act 1999;

(ii) the list kept for the purposes of regulations made under section 218(6) of the Education Reform Act 1988 ('the 1988 Act list'); or

(iii) any list kept by the Secretary of State or the National Assembly for Wales of persons disqualified under section 470 or 471 of the Education Act 1996 ('the 1996 Act list'); and

(b) if he is included in any of those lists, such details of his inclusion as may be prescribed, including-

(i) in the case of the 1988 Act list, the grounds on which he is so included; or

(ii) in the case of the 1996 Act list, the grounds on which he was disqualified under section 470 or 471.'

General

103. Temporary provision for access to lists

(1) Any person seeking to ascertain whether a relevant individual is included in–

(a) the list kept under section 1 of the 1999 Act;

(b) the list kept for the purposes of regulations made under section 218(6) of the Education Reform Act 1988; or

(c) any list kept by the Secretary of State or the Assembly of persons disqualified under section 470 or 471 of the Education Act 1996,

shall be entitled to that information on making, before the relevant commencement, an application for the purpose to the Secretary of State.

(2) In this section 'relevant individual' means–

(a) in relation to a person who carries on an employment agency, an individual with whom he proposes to do business or an individual of any other prescribed description;

(b) in relation to any other person, an individual to whom he proposes to offer, or whom he proposes to supply for employment in, a child care position or an individual of any other prescribed description.

(3) The relevant commencement is–

(a) for applications relating to the list mentioned in subsection (1)(a) or (b), the commencement of section 8 of the 1999 Act; and

(b) for applications relating to the list mentioned in subsection (1)(c), the commencement of section 102.

(4) Paragraphs (b) and (c) of subsection (1) are without prejudice to any right conferred otherwise than by virtue of those provisions.

104. Suitability to adopt a child: searches of lists

(1) The Police Act 1997 shall be amended as follows.

(2) In section 113 (criminal record certificates)–

(a) in subsection (3A), after '(3B),' there shall be inserted 'or his suitability to adopt a child,'; and

(b) after subsection (3D) (inserted by section 90) there shall be inserted–

'(3E) The references in subsections (3A) and (3C) to suitability to be employed, supplied to work, found work or given work in a position falling within subsection (3B) or (3D) include references to suitability to be registered–

(a) under Part II of the Care Standards Act 2000 (establishments and agencies);

(b) under Part IV of that Act (social care workers); or

(c) for child minding or providing day care under Part XA of the Children Act 1989, or under section 71 of that Act or Article 118 of the Children (Northern Ireland) Order 1995 (child minding and day care).'

(3) In section 115 (enhanced criminal record certificates)–
  (a) in subsection (5)–
    (i) after paragraph (e) there shall be inserted–

      '(ea) registration under Part II of the Care Standards Act 2000 (establishments
             and agencies);
      (eb)   registration under Part IV of that Act (social care workers);'; and

    (ii) after paragraph (g) there shall be inserted–

      '(h) a decision made by an adoption agency within the meaning of section 11 of
            the Adoption Act 1976 as to a person's suitability to adopt a child.'; and

  (b) in subsection (6A), after '113,' there shall be inserted 'or his suitability to adopt a
       child,'.

PART VIII

MISCELLANEOUS

Boarding schools and colleges

105. Welfare of children in boarding schools and colleges

(1) Section 87 of the 1989 Act (welfare of children accommodated in independent schools)
shall be amended in accordance with subsections (2) to (4).
(2) For subsections (1) to (5) there shall be substituted–

'(1) Where a school or college provides accommodation for any child, it shall be
the duty of the relevant person to safeguard and promote the child's welfare.

(2) Subsection (1) does not apply in relation to a school or college which is a children's home or care home.

(3) Where accommodation is provided for a child by any school or college the
appropriate authority shall take such steps as are reasonably practicable to enable them
to determine whether the child's welfare is adequately safeguarded and promoted while
he is accommodated by the school or college.

(4) Where the Commission are of the opinion that there has been a failure to
comply with subsection (1) in relation to a child provided with accommodation by a
school or college, they shall–
  (a) in the case of a school other than an independent school or a special school,
       notify the local education authority for the area in which the school is situ-
       ated;
  (b) in the case of a special school which is maintained by a local education
       authority, notify that authority;
  (c) in any other case, notify the Secretary of State.

(4A) Where the National Assembly for Wales are of the opinion that there has been
a failure to comply with subsection (1) in relation to a child provided with accommodation by a school or college, they shall–

    (a) in the case of a school other than an independent school or a special school, notify the local education authority for the area in which the school is situated;

    (b) in the case of a special school which is maintained by a local education authority, notify that authority.

(5) Where accommodation is, or is to be, provided for a child by any school or college, a person authorised by the appropriate authority may, for the purpose of enabling that authority to discharge its duty under this section, enter at any time premises which are, or are to be, premises of the school or college.'

(3) In subsection (6), for 'entering an independent school in exercise of' there shall be substituted 'exercising'.

(4) For subsection (10) there shall be substituted–

    '(10) In this section and sections 87A to 87D–

      "the 1992 Act" means the Further and Higher Education Act 1992;

      "appropriate authority" means-

      (a) in relation to England, the National Care Standards Commission;

      (b) in relation to Wales, the National Assembly for Wales;

        "college" means an institution within the further education sector as defined in section 91 of the 1992 Act;

        "the Commission" means the National Care Standards Commission;

        "further education corporation" has the same meaning as in the 1992 Act;

        "local education authority" and "proprietor" have the same meanings as in the Education Act 1996.

    (11) In this section and sections 87A and 87D "relevant person" means–

      (a) in relation to an independent school, the proprietor of the school;

      (b) in relation to any other school, or an institution designated under section 28 of the 1992 Act, the governing body of the school or institution;

      (c) in relation to an institution conducted by a further education corporation, the corporation.

    (12) Where a person other than the proprietor of an independent school is responsible for conducting the school, references in this section to the relevant person include references to the person so responsible.'

(5) In section 62 of the 1989 Act (duties of local authorities in relation to children provided with accommodation by voluntary organisations), at the end there shall be inserted–

    '(10) This section does not apply in relation to any voluntary organisation which is an institution within the further education sector, as defined in section 91 of the Further and Higher Education Act 1992, or a school.'

106. Suspension of duty under section 87(3) of the 1989 Act

(1) For section 87A of the 1989 Act (suspension of duty under section 87(3)) there shall be substituted–

'87A. Suspension of duty under section 87(3)

(1) The Secretary of State may appoint a person to be an inspector for the purposes of this section if–

(a) that person already acts as an inspector for other purposes in relation to schools or colleges to which section 87(1) applies, and

(b) the Secretary of State is satisfied that the person is an appropriate person to determine whether the welfare of children provided with accommodation by such schools or colleges is adequately safeguarded and promoted while they are accommodated by them.

(2) Where–

(a) the relevant person enters into an agreement in writing with a person appointed under subsection (1),

(b) the agreement provides for the person so appointed to have in relation to the school or college the function of determining whether section 87(1) is being complied with, and

(c) the appropriate authority receive from the person mentioned in paragraph (b) ("the inspector") notice in writing that the agreement has come into effect,

the appropriate authority's duty under section 87(3) in relation to the school or college shall be suspended.

(3) Where the appropriate authority's duty under section 87(3) in relation to any school or college is suspended under this section, it shall cease to be so suspended if the appropriate authority receive–

(a) a notice under subsection (4) relating to the inspector, or

(b) a notice under subsection (5) relating to the relevant agreement.

(4) The Secretary of State shall terminate a person's appointment under subsection (1) if–

(a) that person so requests, or

(b) the Secretary of State ceases, in relation to that person, to be satisfied that he is such a person as is mentioned in paragraph (b) of that subsection,

and shall give notice of the termination of that person's appointment to the appropriate authority.

(5) Where–

(a) the appropriate authority's duty under section 87(3) in relation to any school or college is suspended under this section, and

(b) the relevant agreement ceases to have effect,

the inspector shall give to the appropriate authority notice in writing of the fact that it has ceased to have effect.

(6) In this section references to the relevant agreement, in relation to the suspension of the appropriate authority's duty under section 87(3) as regards any school or college, are to the agreement by virtue of which the appropriate authority's duty under that provision as regards that school or college is suspended.'

(2) In section 87B of that Act (duties of inspectors under section 87A)–

(a) in subsections (2) and (3), after 'school', in each place where it occurs, there shall be inserted 'or college';

(b) in subsection (2), for 'to the Secretary of State' there shall be substituted–

'(a) in the case of a school other than an independent school or a special school, to the local education authority for the area in which the school is situated;

(b) in the case of a special school which is maintained by a local education authority, to that authority;

(c) in any other case, to the Secretary of State'; and

(c) for subsection (4) there shall be substituted the following subsection–

'(4) In this section "substitution agreement" means an agreement by virtue of which the duty of the appropriate authority under section 87(3) in relation to a school or college is suspended.'

107. Boarding schools: national minimum standards
After section 87B of the 1989 Act there shall be inserted–

'87C. Boarding schools: national minimum standards
(1) The Secretary of State may prepare and publish statements of national minimum standards for safeguarding and promoting the welfare of children for whom accommodation is provided in a school or college.

(2) The Secretary of State shall keep the standards set out in the statements under review and may publish amended statements whenever he considers it appropriate to do so.

(3) Before issuing a statement, or an amended statement which in the opinion of the Secretary of State effects a substantial change in the standards, the Secretary of State shall consult any persons he considers appropriate.

(4) The standards shall be taken into account–

(a) in the making by the appropriate authority of any determination under section 87(4) or (4A);

(b) in the making by a person appointed under section 87A(1) of any determination under section 87B(2); and

(c) in any proceedings under any other enactment in which it is alleged that the person has failed to comply with section 87(1).'

108. Annual fee for boarding school inspections
After section 87C of the 1989 Act (inserted by section 107) there shall be inserted–

'87D. Annual fee for boarding school inspections
(1) Regulations under subsection (2) may be made in relation to any school or college in respect of which the appropriate authority is required to take steps under section 87(3).

(2) The Secretary of State may by regulations require the relevant person to pay the appropriate authority an annual fee of such amount, and within such time, as the regulations may specify.

(3) A fee payable by virtue of this section may, without prejudice to any other method of recovery, be recovered summarily as a civil debt.'

109. Inspection of schools etc. by persons authorised by Secretary of State

(1) Section 80 of the 1989 Act (inspection of children's homes etc. by persons authorised by Secretary of State) shall be amended as follows.

(2) In subsection (1), in paragraph (l), for 'independent school' there shall be substituted 'school or college'.

(3) In subsection (5)–

    (a) in paragraph (d), at the end there shall be inserted 'or governing body of any other school';

    (b) after that paragraph there shall be inserted–

        '(da) governing body of an institution designated under section 28 of the Further and Higher Education Act 1992;

        (db) further education corporation;' and

    (c) after paragraph (i) there shall be inserted–

        '(j) person carrying on a fostering agency.'

(4) After subsection (12) there shall be inserted–

    '(13) In this section–

        "college" means an institution within the further education sector as defined in section 91 of the Further and Higher Education Act 1992;

        "fostering agency" has the same meaning as in the Care Standards Act 2000;

        "further education corporation" has the same meaning as in the Further and Higher Education Act 1992.'

Fostering

110. Extension of Part IX to school children during holidays

In paragraph 9(1) of Schedule 8 to the 1989 Act (extension of Part IX to certain school children during holidays), 'which is not maintained by a local education authority' shall be omitted.

Employment agencies

111. Nurses Agencies

(1) The Nurses Agencies Act 1957 shall cease to have effect.

(2) In section 13 of the Employment Agencies Act 1973 (interpretation), for subsection (8) there shall be substituted–

    '(8) This Act, in its application to Scotland, does not apply to–

        (a) any agency for the supply of nurses as defined in section 32 of the Nurses (Scotland) Act 1951 (but excluding any other business carried on in conjunction with such an agency);

        (b) the business carried on by any county or district nursing association or other similar organisation, being an association or organisation within paragraph (a) or (b) of that definition.',

and paragraphs (b) and (c) of, and the proviso to, subsection (7) shall be omitted.

Charges for local authority welfare services

112. Charges for local authority welfare services
In Schedule 1 to the Local Authority Social Services Act 1970 (enactments conferring functions assigned to social services committee), there shall be inserted at the appropriate place–

'Health and Social Services and Social   Charges for local authority welfare
   Security Adjudications Act 1983 (c. 41)   services'
Section 17, so far as relating to services
   provided under the enactments mentioned
   in subsection (2)(a) to (c)

PART IX
GENERAL AND SUPPLEMENTAL

CHAPTER I
GENERAL

113. Default powers of appropriate Minister
(1) The powers conferred by this section are exercisable by the Secretary of State if he is satisfied that the Commission or the English Council–
    (a) has without reasonable excuse failed to discharge any of its functions; or
    (b) in discharging any of its functions, has without reasonable excuse failed to comply with any directions or guidance given by him under section 6(2) or 54(4) in relation to those functions.
(2) The powers conferred by this section are exercisable by the Assembly if it is satisfied that the Welsh Council–
    (a) has without reasonable excuse failed to discharge any of its functions; or
    (b) in discharging any of its functions, has without reasonable excuse failed to comply with any directions or guidance given by the Assembly under section 54(4) in relation to those functions.
(3) The appropriate Minister may–
    (a) make an order declaring the authority in question to be in default; and
    (b) direct the authority to discharge such of its functions, and in such manner and within such period or periods, as may be specified in the direction.
(4) If the authority fails to comply with the appropriate Minister's direction under subsection (3), the appropriate Minister may–
    (a) discharge the functions to which the direction relates himself; or
    (b) make arrangements for any other person to discharge those functions on his behalf.

114. Schemes for the transfer of staff
(1) This section and the next apply to a scheme made under section 38, 70 or 79(3) for transferring eligible employees.
(2) Subject to those provisions, such a scheme may apply to all, or any description of, employees or to any individual employee.
(3) Such a scheme may be made by the appropriate Minister, and a recommendation may

be made to Her Majesty in Council to make an Order containing such a scheme, only if any prescribed requirements about consultation have been complied with in relation to each of the employees to be transferred under the scheme.

115. Effect of schemes

(1) The contract of employment of an employee transferred under the scheme–
  (a) is not terminated by the transfer; and
  (b) has effect from the date of transfer as if originally made between the employee and the transferee.

(2) Where an employee is transferred under the scheme–
  (a) all the rights, powers, duties and liabilities of the old employer under or in connection with the contract of employment are by virtue of this subsection transferred to the transferee on the date of transfer; and
  (b) anything done before that date by or in relation to the old employer in respect of that contract or the employee is to be treated from that date as having been done by or in relation to the transferee.
This subsection does not prejudice the generality of subsection (1).

(3) Subsections (1) and (2) do not transfer an employee's contract of employment, or the rights, powers, duties and liabilities under or in connection with it, if he informs the old employer or the transferee that he objects to the transfer.

(4) Where an employee objects as mentioned in subsection (3), his contract of employment with the old employer is terminated immediately before the date of transfer; but he is not to be treated, for any purpose, as having been dismissed by that employer.

(5) This section does not prejudice any right of an employee to terminate his contract of employment if a substantial change is made to his detriment in his working conditions.
But no such right arises by reason only that, by virtue of this section, the identity of his employer changes unless the employee shows that, in all the circumstances, the change is a significant change and is to his detriment.

(6) In this section–
  'date of transfer' means the date of transfer determined under the scheme in relation to the employee;
  'transferee' means the new employer to whom the employee is or would be transferred under the scheme;
and expressions used in this section and in the provision under which the scheme is made have the same meaning as in that provision.

116. Minor and consequential amendments

Schedule 4 (which makes minor amendments and amendments consequential on the provisions of this Act) shall have effect.

117. Transitional provisions, savings and repeals

(1) Schedule 5 (which makes transitional and saving provision) shall have effect; but nothing in that Schedule shall be taken to prejudice the operation of sections 16 and 17 of the Interpretation Act 1978 (which relate to the effect of repeals).

(2) The enactments mentioned in Schedule 6 to this Act are repealed to the extent specified in that Schedule.

CHAPTER II
SUPPLEMENTAL

118. Orders and regulations

(1) Any power conferred on the Secretary of State, the Assembly or the appropriate Minister to make regulations or an order under this Act except an order under section 38 or 79(3) shall be exercised by statutory instrument.

(2) An order making any provision by virtue of section 119(2) which adds to, replaces or omits any part of the text of an Act shall not be made by the Secretary of State unless a draft of the instrument has been laid before, and approved by resolution of, each House of Parliament.

(3) Subject to subsection (2), an instrument containing regulations or an order made by the Secretary of State, except an instrument containing an order under section 122, shall be subject to annulment in pursuance of a resolution of either House of Parliament.

In subsection (2) and this subsection, references to the Secretary of State include the Secretary of State and the Assembly acting jointly.

(4) Subsections (5) to (7) apply to any power of the Secretary of State, the Assembly or the appropriate Minister to make regulations or an order under this Act; and subsections (5) and (6) apply to any power of Her Majesty to make an Order in Council under section 70.

(5) The power may be exercised either in relation to all cases to which the power extends, or in relation to all those cases subject to specified exceptions, or in relation to any specified cases or classes of case.

(6) The power may be exercised so as to make, as respects the cases in relation to which it is exercised–

    (a) the same provision for all cases in relation to which the power is exercised, or different provision for different cases or different classes of case, or different provision as respects the same case or class of case for different purposes;

    (b) any such provision either unconditionally or subject to any specified condition.

(7) The power may be exercised so as to make–

    (a) any supplementary, incidental or consequential provision,

    (b) any transitory, transitional or saving provision,

which the person exercising the power considers necessary or expedient.

(8) The provision which, by virtue of subsection (7), may be made by regulations under the Part of this Act which relates to the Children's Commissioner for Wales includes provision amending or repealing any enactment or instrument.

119. Supplementary and consequential provision etc.

(1) The appropriate Minister may by order make–

    (a) any supplementary, incidental or consequential provision,

    (b) any transitory, transitional or saving provision,

which he considers necessary or expedient for the purposes of, in consequence of or for giving full effect to any provision of this Act.

(2) The provision which may be made under subsection (1) includes provision amending or repealing any enactment or instrument.

120. Wales

(1) Section 84(1) of the Government of Wales Act 1998 (payment of Assembly receipts

into the Consolidated Fund) does not apply to any sums received by the Assembly by virtue of any provision of this Act.

(2) The reference to the 1989 Act in Schedule 1 to the National Assembly for Wales (Transfer of Functions) Order 1999 is to be treated as referring to that Act as amended by or under this Act.

(3) Subsection (2) does not affect the power to make further Orders varying or omitting that reference.

121. General interpretation etc.

(1) In this Act–

'adult' means a person who is not a child;

'appropriate Minister' means–

(a) in relation to England, Scotland or Northern Ireland, the Secretary of State;

(b) in relation to Wales, the Assembly;

and in relation to England and Wales means the Secretary of State and the Assembly acting jointly;

'child' means a person under the age of 18;

'community home' has the same meaning as in the 1989 Act;

'employment agency' and 'employment business' have the same meanings as in the Employment Agencies Act 1973; but no business which is an employment business shall be taken to be an employment agency;

'enactment' includes an enactment comprised in subordinate legislation (within the meaning of the Interpretation Act 1978);

'to foster a child privately' has the same meaning as in the 1989 Act;

'harm'–

(a) in relation to an adult who is not mentally impaired, means ill-treatment or the impairment of health;

(b) in relation to an adult who is mentally impaired, or a child, means ill-treatment or the impairment of health or development;

'health service hospital' has the same meaning as in the National Health Service Act 1977;

'illness' includes any injury;

'independent school' has the same meaning as in the Education Act 1996;

'local authority' has the same meaning as in the 1989 Act;

'local authority foster parent' has the same meaning as in the 1989 Act;

'medical' includes surgical;

'mental disorder' means mental illness, arrested or incomplete development of mind, psychopathic disorder, and any other disorder or disability of mind;

'National Health Service body' means a National Health Service trust, a Health Authority, a Special Health Authority or a Primary Care Trust;

'parent', in relation to a child, includes any person who is not a parent of his but who has parental responsibility for him;

'parental responsibility' has the same meaning as in the 1989 Act;

'prescribed' means prescribed by regulations;

'proprietor', in relation to a school, has the same meaning as in the Education Act 1996;

'regulations' (except where provision is made for them to be made by the Secretary of State or the Assembly) means regulations made by the appropriate Minister;

'relative' has the same meaning as in the 1989 Act;

'school' has the same meaning as in the Education Act 1996;

'social services functions' means functions which are social services functions for the purposes of the Local Authority Social Services Act 1970;

'treatment' includes diagnosis;

'the Tribunal' means the tribunal established by section 9 of the 1999 Act;

'undertaking' includes any business or profession and–

    (a) in relation to a public or local authority, includes the exercise of any functions of that authority; and

    (b) in relation to any other body of persons, whether corporate or unincorporate, includes any of the activities of that body;

'voluntary organisation' has the same meaning as in the Adoption Act 1976.

(2) For the purposes of this Act–

    (a) a person is disabled if–

        (i) his sight, hearing or speech is substantially impaired;

        (ii) he has a mental disorder; or

        (iii) he is physically substantially disabled by any illness, any impairment present since birth, or otherwise;

    (b) an adult is mentally impaired if he is in a state of arrested or incomplete development of mind (including a significant impairment of intelligence and social functioning).

(3) In this Act, the expression 'personal care' does not include any prescribed activity.

(4) For the purposes of this Act, the person who carries on a fostering agency falling within section 4(4)(b), or a voluntary adoption agency, is the voluntary organisation itself.

(5) References in this Act to a person who carries on an establishment or agency include references to a person who carries it on otherwise than for profit.

(6) For the purposes of this Act, a community home which is provided by a voluntary organisation shall be taken to be carried on by–

    (a) the person who equips and maintains it; and

    (b) if the appropriate Minister determines that the body of managers for the home, or a specified member of that body, is also to be treated as carrying on the home, that body or member.

(7) Where a community home is provided by a voluntary organisation, the appropriate Minister may determine that for the purposes of this Act the home is to be taken to be managed solely by–

    (a) any specified member of the body of managers for the home; or

    (b) any other specified person on whom functions are conferred under the home's instrument of management.

(8) A determination under subsection (6) or (7) may be made either generally or in relation to a particular home or class of homes.

(9) An establishment is not a care home for the purposes of this Act unless the care which it provides includes assistance with bodily functions where such assistance is required.

(10) References in this Act to a child's being looked after by a local authority shall be construed in accordance with section 22 of the 1989 Act.

(11) For the purposes of this Act an individual is made redundant if–

    (a) he is dismissed; and

    (b) for the purposes of the Employment Rights Act 1996 the dismissal is by reason of redundancy.

(12) Any register kept for the purposes of this Act may be kept by means of a computer.

(13) In this Act, the expressions listed in the left-hand column have the meaning given by, or are to be interpreted in accordance with, the provisions listed in the right-hand column.

Expression	*Provision of this Act*
1989 Act	Children Act 1989
1999 Act	Protection of Children Act 1999
Assembly	Section 5
Care home	Section 3
CCETSW	Section 70
Children's home	Section 1
Commission	Section 6
Commissioner	Section 72
Council, the English Council, the Welsh Council	Section 54
Domiciliary care agency	Section 4
Fostering agency	Section 4
Hospital and independent hospital	Section 2
Independent clinic and independent medical agency	Section 2
Registration authority	Section 5
Residential family centre	Section 4
Voluntary adoption agency	Section 4

122. Commencement

This Act, except section 70(2) to (5) and this Chapter, shall come into force on such day as the appropriate Minister may by order appoint, and different days may be appointed for different purposes.

123. Short title and extent

(1) This Act may be cited as the Care Standards Act 2000.

(2) Subject to subsections (3) and (4), this Act extends to England and Wales only.

(3) Section 70 and, so far as relating to subsections (2) to (5) of that section, sections 114, 115 and 118 extend also to Scotland and Northern Ireland.

(4) The amendment or repeal by this Act of an enactment extending to Scotland or Northern Ireland extends also to Scotland or, as the case may be, Northern Ireland.

SCHEDULES

SCHEDULE 1

THE COMMISSION AND THE COUNCILS

Introductory

1.—(1) The authorities for the purposes of this Schedule are the Commission, the English Council and the Welsh Council.

(2) In this Schedule, in relation to the Welsh Council–
  (a) references to the Secretary of State or to Parliament are to be read as references to the Assembly;
  (b) references to the Comptroller and Auditor General are to be read as references to the Auditor General for Wales.

Status

2. An authority is not to be regarded as the servant or agent of the Crown or as enjoying any status, immunity or privilege of the Crown; and an authority's property is to not to be regarded as property of, or property held on behalf of, the Crown.

General powers

3.—(1) Subject to any directions given by the Secretary of State, an authority may do anything which appears to it to be necessary or expedient for the purpose of, or in connection with, the exercise of its functions.
  (2) That includes, in particular–
  (a) co-operating with other public authorities in the United Kingdom;
  (b) acquiring and disposing of land and other property; and
  (c) entering into contracts.

General duty

4. It is the duty of an authority to carry out its functions effectively, efficiently and economically.

Membership

5. Each authority is to consist of a chairman and other members appointed by the Secretary of State.

Appointment, procedure etc.

6. The Secretary of State may by regulations make provision as to–
  (a) the appointment of the chairman and other members of an authority (including the number, or limits on the number, of members who may be appointed and any conditions to be fulfilled for appointment);
  (b) the tenure of office of the chairman and other members of an authority (including the circumstances in which they cease to hold office or may be removed or suspended from office);
  (c) the appointment of, constitution of and exercise of functions by committees and sub-committees of an authority (including committees and sub-committees which consist of or include persons who are not members of the authority); and
  (d) the procedure of an authority and any committees or sub-committees of an authority (including the validation of proceedings in the event of vacancies or defects in appointment).

Remuneration and allowances

7.—(1) An authority may pay to its chairman, to any other member of the authority and to any member of a committee or sub-committee who is not a member of the authority, such remuneration and allowances as the Secretary of State may determine.

(2) If the Secretary of State so determines, an authority must pay or make provision for the payment of such pension, allowance or gratuities as the Secretary of State may determine to or in respect of a person who is or has been the chairman or any other member of an authority.

(3) If the Secretary of State determines that there are special circumstances that make it right for a person ceasing to hold office as chairman of an authority to receive compensation, the authority must pay to him or make provision for the payment to him of such compensation as the Secretary of State may determine.

Chief officer

8.—(1) There is to be a chief officer of each authority who is to be a member of the staff of the authority and is to be responsible to the authority for the general exercise of its functions.

(2) The first chief officer is to be appointed by the Secretary of State on such terms and conditions as the Secretary of State may determine.

(3) Any subsequent chief officer is to be appointed by the authority.

(4) An appointment under sub-paragraph (3) requires the approval of the Secretary of State.

Regional directors

9.—(1) The Secretary of State may direct the Commission to appoint directors for regions specified in the direction.

(2) Directors appointed under sub-paragraph (1) shall be members of the staff of the Commission and shall have such functions as may be prescribed.

Children's rights director

10.—(1) The Commission shall appoint a children's rights director who is to be a member of the staff of the Commission.

(2) The children's rights director shall have such functions as may be prescribed.

Director of private and voluntary health care

11.—(1) The Commission shall appoint a director of private and voluntary health care, who is to be a member of the staff of the Commission.

(2) The director shall have such functions as may be prescribed.

Staff

12.—(1) An authority may appoint such other staff as it considers appropriate.

(2) Subject to sub-paragraph (4), staff appointed by an authority are to be appointed on such terms and conditions as the authority may determine.

(3) Without prejudice to its powers apart from this paragraph, an authority may pay, or make provision for the payment of–

   (a) pensions, allowances or gratuities;

   (b) compensation for loss of employment or for reduction of remuneration,

to or in respect of staff appointed by them.

   (4) The Secretary of State may give directions as to–

     (a) the appointment of staff by an authority (including any conditions to be fulfilled for appointment);

     (b) their terms and conditions; and

     (c) ny other provision that may be made by the authority under sub-paragraph (3).

   (5) Sub-paragraphs (3) and (4)(c) apply to the first chief officer as they apply to other staff.

   (6) Different directions may be given under sub-paragraph (4) in relation to different categories of staff.

Delegation of functions

13.—(1) An authority may arrange for the discharge of any of its functions by a committee, sub-committee, member or member of staff of the authority.

   (2) An authority may make arrangements with persons under which they, or members of their staff, may perform functions of members of the staff of the authority.

Arrangements for the use of staff

14. The Secretary of State may by regulations provide for arrangements under which–

     (a) members of staff of an authority are placed at the disposal of a prescribed person for the purpose of discharging, or assisting in the discharge of, prescribed func tions of that person; or

     (b) members of staff of a prescribed person are placed at the disposal of an authority for the purpose of discharging, or assisting in the discharge of, any functions of the authority.

Training

15. The Commission may provide training for the purpose of assisting persons to attain standards set out in any statements published by the Secretary of State under section 23.

Payments to authorities

16. The Secretary of State may make payments to an authority of such amounts, at such times and on such conditions (if any) as he considers appropriate.

Fees

17.—(1) Subject to the provisions of this Act, the Commission may not, except with the consent of the Secretary of State, charge a fee in connection with the exercise of any power conferred on it by or under this Act.

   (2) Commission may charge a reasonable fee determined by it–

     (a) for any advice, forms or documents provided for the assistance of a person who proposes to apply, or is considering whether to apply, for registration under Part II; and

     (b) for any training provided by it under paragraph 15.

(3) The consent of the Secretary of State for the purposes of sub-paragraph (1) may be given in relation to the exercise of a power either generally or in a particular case.

Accounts

18.—(1) An authority must keep accounts in such form as the Secretary of State may determine.

(2) An authority must prepare annual accounts in respect of each financial year in such form as the Secretary of State may determine.

(3) An authority must send copies of the annual accounts to the Secretary of State and the Comptroller and Auditor General within such period after the end of the financial year to which the accounts relate as the Secretary of State may determine.

(4) The Comptroller and Auditor General must examine, certify and report on the annual accounts and must lay copies of the accounts and of his report before Parliament.

(5) In this paragraph and paragraph 19 'financial year', in relation to an authority, means–
- (a) the period beginning with the date on which the authority is established and ending with the next 31st March following that date; and
- (b) each successive period of twelve months ending with 31st March.

Reports and other information

19.—(1) As soon as possible after the end of each financial year, an authority must make a report to the Secretary of State on the exercise of its functions during the year.

(2) An authority must provide the Secretary of State with such reports and information relating to the exercise of its functions as he may from time to time require.

(3) A report made under sub-paragraph (1) must be published in a manner which the authority considers appropriate.

Application of seal and evidence

20. The application of the seal of an authority must be authenticated by the signature–
- (a) of any member of the authority; or
- (b) of any other person who has been authorised by the authority (whether generally or specifically) for that purpose.

21. A document purporting to be duly executed under the seal of an authority or to be signed on its behalf is to be received in evidence and, unless the contrary is proved, taken to be so executed or signed.

General

22. In Schedule 1 to the Public Records Act 1958 (definition of public records), the following entries shall be inserted at the appropriate places in Part II of the Table at the end of paragraph 3–

'Care Council for Wales.'
'General Social Care Council.'
'National Care Standards Commission.'

23. In the Schedule to the Public Bodies (Admission to Meetings) Act 1960 (bodies to which the Act applies), after paragraph (bc) of paragraph 1 there shall be inserted–

'(bd) the Care Council for Wales;
(be) the General Social Care Council;
(bf) the National Care Standards Commission;'.

24. In the Parliamentary Commissioner Act 1967, in Schedule 2 (departments and authorities subject to investigation), the following entries shall be inserted at the appropriate places–

'General Social Care Council.'
'National Care Standards Commission.'

25. In the House of Commons Disqualification Act 1975, in Part II of Schedule 1 (bodies of which all members are disqualified), the following entries shall be inserted at the appropriate places–

'The Care Council for Wales.'
'The General Social Care Council.'
'The National Care Standards Commission.'

26. In the Northern Ireland Assembly Disqualification Act 1975, the same entries as are set out in paragraph 25 are inserted at the appropriate places in Part II of Schedule 1.

27. In the Government of Wales Act 1998–
    (a) in section 118(2) (meaning of 'Welsh public records'), after 'referred to in subsection (1)(e) are–' there shall be inserted–

'(aa) the Care Council for Wales;'

    (b) in Schedule 4 (public bodies subject to reform by Assembly), after paragraph 3 there shall be inserted–

'3A. The Care Council for Wales.'

    (c) in paragraph 14(2) of Schedule 9 (bodies subject to investigation by the Welsh Administration Ombudsman), after paragraph (a) there shall be inserted–

'(ab) the Care Council for Wales;' and

    (d) in paragraph 1 of Schedule 17 (audit of Welsh public bodies), at the end there shall be inserted '(other than the Care Council for Wales)'.

SCHEDULE 2
THE CHILDREN'S COMMISSIONER FOR WALES

Status

1.—(1) The Commissioner is to be a corporation sole.

(2) The Commissioner is not to be regarded as the servant or agent or the Crown or as enjoying any status, immunity or privilege of the Crown; and the Commissioner's property is not to be regarded as property of, or property held on behalf of, the Crown.

Appointment and tenure of office

2. Regulations may make provision–
   (a) as to the appointment of the Commissioner (including any conditions to be fulfilled for appointment);
   (b) as to the filling of vacancies in the office of Commissioner;
   (c) as to the tenure of office of the Commissioner (including the circumstances in which he ceases to hold office or may be removed or suspended from office).

Remuneration

3. The Assembly shall–
   (a) pay the Commissioner such remuneration and allowances; and
   (b) pay, or make provision for the payment of, such pension or gratuities to or in respect of him,
as may be provided for under the terms of his appointment.

Staff

4.—(1) The Commissioner may appoint any staff he considers necessary for assisting him in the exercise of his functions, one of whom shall be appointed as deputy Commissioner.

(2) During any vacancy in the office of Commissioner or at any time when the Commissioner is for any reason unable to act, the deputy Commissioner shall exercise his functions (and any property or rights vested in the Commissioner may accordingly be dealt with by the deputy as if vested in him).

(3) Without prejudice to sub-paragraph (2), any member of the Commissioner's staff may, so far as authorised by him, exercise any of his functions.

General powers

5.—(1) Subject to any directions given by the Assembly, the Commissioner may do anything which appears to him to be necessary or expedient for the purpose of, or in connection with, the exercise of his functions.

(2) That includes, in particular–
   (a) co-operating with other public authorities in the United Kingdom;
   (b) acquiring and disposing of land and other property; and
   (c) entering into contracts.

Estimates

6.—(1) For each financial year after the first, the Commissioner shall prepare, and submit to the executive committee, an estimate of his income and expenses.

(2) Each such estimate shall be submitted to the executive committee at least five months before the beginning of the financial year to which it relates.

(3) The executive committee shall examine each such estimate submitted to it and, after having done so, shall lay the estimate before the Assembly with any such modifications as the committee thinks fit.

(4) Regulations shall specify the periods which are to be treated as the first and subsequent financial years of the Commissioner.

(5) In this paragraph and paragraph 10 'executive committee' has the same meaning as in the Government of Wales Act 1998.

Accounts

7.—(1) The Commissioner shall keep proper accounting records.

(2) The Commissioner shall prepare accounts for each financial year in such form as the Assembly may with the consent of the Treasury determine.

Reports

8. Regulations may provide for the Commissioner to make periodic or other reports to the Assembly relating to the exercise of his functions and may require the reports to be published in the manner required by the regulations.

Audit

9.—(1) The accounts prepared by the Commissioner for any financial year shall be submitted by him to the Auditor General for Wales not more than five months after the end of that year.

(2) The Auditor General for Wales shall–
  (a) examine and certify any accounts submitted to him under this paragraph; and
  (b) no later than four months after the accounts are submitted to him, lay before the Assembly a copy of them as certified by him together with his report on them.

(3) In examining any accounts submitted to him under this paragraph, the Auditor General for Wales shall, in particular, satisfy himself that the expenditure to which the accounts relate has been incurred lawfully and in accordance with the authority which governs it.

Accounting officer

10.—(1) The accounting officer for the Commissioner's Office shall be the Commissioner.

(2) The accounting officer for the Commissioner shall have, in relation to the accounts of the Commissioner and the finances of the Commissioner's Office, the responsibilities which are from time to time specified by the Treasury.

(3) In this paragraph references to responsibilities include in particular–
  (a) responsibilities in relation to the signing of accounts;
  (b) responsibilities for the propriety and regularity of the finances of the Commissioner's Office; and
  (c) responsibilities for the economy, efficiency and effectiveness with which the resources of the Commissioner's Office are used.

(4) The responsibilities which may be specified under this paragraph include responsibilities owed to–
  (a) the Assembly, the executive committee or the Audit Committee; or
  (b) the House of Commons or its Committee of Public Accounts.

(5) If requested to do so by the House of Commons Committee of Public Accounts, the Audit Committee may–
- (a) on behalf of the Committee of Public Accounts take evidence from the accounting officer for the Commissioner's Office; and
- (b) report to the Committee of Public Accounts and transmit to that Committee any evidence so taken.

(6) In this paragraph and paragraphs 11 and 12 'the Commissioner's Office' means the Commissioner and the members of his staff.

Examinations into use of resources

11.—(1) The Auditor General for Wales may carry out examinations into the economy, efficiency and effectiveness with which the Commissioner has used the resources of the Commissioner's Office in discharging his functions.

(2) Sub-paragraph (1) shall not be construed as entitling the Auditor General for Wales to question the merits of the policy objectives of the Commissioner.

(3) In determining how to exercise his functions under this paragraph, the Auditor General for Wales shall take into account the views of the Audit Committee as to the examinations which he should carry out under this paragraph.

(4) The Auditor General for Wales may lay before the Assembly a report of the results of any examination carried out by him under this paragraph.

(5) The Auditor General for Wales and the Comptroller and Auditor General may co-operate with, and give assistance to, each other in connection with the carrying out of examinations in respect of the Commissioner under this paragraph or section 7 of the National Audit Act 1983 (economy etc. examinations).

Examinations by the Comptroller and Auditor General

12.—(1) For the purpose of enabling him to carry out examinations into, and report to Parliament on, the finances of the Commissioner's Office, the Comptroller and Auditor General–
- (a) shall have a right of access at all reasonable times to all such documents in the custody or under the control of the Commissioner, or of the Auditor General for Wales, as he may reasonably require for that purpose; and
- (b) shall be entitled to require from any person holding or accountable for any of those documents any assistance, information or explanation which he reasonably thinks necessary for that purpose.

(2) The Comptroller and Auditor General shall–
- (a) consult the Auditor General for Wales; and
- (b) take into account any relevant work done or being done by the Auditor General for Wales,

before he acts in reliance on sub-paragraph (1) or carries out an examination in respect of the Commissioner under section 7 of the National Audit Act 1983 (economy etc. examinations).

Evidence

13. A document purporting to be duly executed under the seal of the Commissioner or to be signed by him or on his behalf is to be received in evidence and, unless the contrary is proved, taken to be so executed or signed.

Payments

14. The Assembly may make payments to the Commissioner of such amounts, at such times and on such conditions (if any) as it considers appropriate.

General

15. In the House of Commons Disqualification Act 1975, in Part III of Schedule 1 (certain disqualifying offices), the following entries are inserted at the appropriate places–

'Children's Commissioner for Wales.'
'Member of the staff of the Children's Commissioner for Wales.'

16. In the Northern Ireland Assembly Disqualification Act 1975, the same entries as are set out in paragraph 15 are inserted at the appropriate places in Part III of Schedule 1.

17.—(1) Regulations may provide that the office of Children's Commissioner for Wales shall be added to the list of 'Offices' in Schedule 1 to the Superannuation Act 1972 (offices etc. to which section 1 of that Act applies).

(2) The Assembly shall pay to the Minister for the Civil Service, at such times as he may direct, such sums as he may determine in respect of any increase attributable to provision made under sub-paragraph (1) in the sums payable out of money provided by Parliament under the Superannuation Act 1972.

18. In section 144 of the Government of Wales Act 1998 (accounts etc.), in subsection (8)(a), after 'the Welsh Administration Ombudsman' there shall be inserted 'the Children's Commissioner for Wales'.

SCHEDULE 3
CHILD MINDING AND DAY CARE FOR YOUNG CHILDREN

The following Schedule shall be inserted in the 1989 Act after Schedule 9–

'SCHEDULE 9A
CHILD MINDING AND DAY CARE FOR YOUNG CHILDREN

Exemption of certain schools

1.—(1) Except in prescribed circumstances, Part XA does not apply to provision of day care within sub-paragraph (2) for any child looked after in–
    (a) a maintained school;
    (b) a school assisted by a local education authority;
    (c) a school in respect of which payments are made by the Secretary of State or the Assembly under section 485 of the Education Act 1996;
    (d) an independent school.

(2) The provision mentioned in sub-paragraph (1) is provision of day care made by–
  (a) the person carrying on the establishment in question as part of the establishment's activities; or
  (b) a person employed to work at that establishment and authorised to make that provision as part of the establishment's activities.
(3) In sub-paragraph (1)–
  'assisted' has the same meaning as in the Education Act 1996;
  'maintained school' has the meaning given by section 20(7) of the School Standards and Framework Act 1998.

Exemption for other establishments

2.—(1) Part XA does not apply to provision of day care within sub-paragraph (2) for any child looked after–
  (a) in an appropriate children's home;
  (b) in a care home;
  (c) as a patient in a hospital (within the meaning of the Care Standards Act 2000);
  (d) in a residential family centre.
(2) The provision mentioned in sub-paragraph (1) is provision of day care made by–
  (a) the department, authority or other person carrying on the establishment in question as part of the establishment's activities; or
  (b) a person employed to work at that establishment and authorised to make that provision as part of the establishment's activities.

Exemption for occasional facilities

3.—(1) Where day care is provided on particular premises on less than six days in any year, that provision shall be disregarded for the purposes of Part XA if the person making it has notified the registration authority in writing before the first occasion on which the premises concerned are so used in that year.
(2) In sub-paragraph (1) 'year' means the year beginning with the day (after the commencement of paragraph 5 of Schedule 9) on which the day care in question was or is first provided on the premises concerned and any subsequent year.

Disqualification for registration

4.—(1) Regulations may provide for a person to be disqualified for registration for child minding or providing day care.
(2) The regulations may, in particular, provide for a person to be disqualified where–
  (a) he is included in the list kept under section 1 of the Protection of Children Act 1999;
  (b) he is included on the grounds mentioned in subsection (6ZA)(c) of section 218 of the Education Reform Act 1988 in the list kept for the purposes of regulations made under subsection (6) of that section;
  (c) an order of a prescribed kind has been made at any time with respect to him;
  (d) an order of a prescribed kind has been made at any time with respect to any child who has been in his care;

(e) a requirement of a prescribed kind has been imposed at any time with respect to such a child, under or by virtue of any enactment;

(f) he has at any time been refused registration under Part X or Part XA or any prescribed enactment or had any such registration cancelled;

(g) he has been convicted of any offence of a prescribed kind, or has been placed on probation or discharged absolutely or conditionally for any such offence;

(h) he has at any time been disqualified from fostering a child privately;

(j) a prohibition has been imposed on him at any time under section 69, section 10 of the Foster Children (Scotland) Act 1984 or any prescribed enactment;

(k) his rights and powers with respect to a child have at any time been vested in a prescribed authority under a prescribed enactment.

(3) Regulations may provide for a person who lives–

(a) in the same household as a person who is himself disqualified for registration for child minding or providing day care; or

(b) in a household at which any such person is employed,

to be disqualified for registration for child minding or providing day care.

(4) A person who is disqualified for registration for providing day care shall not provide day care, or be concerned in the management of, or have any financial interest in, any provision of day care.

(5) No person shall employ, in connection with the provision of day care, a person who is disqualified for registration for providing day care.

(6) In this paragraph 'enactment' means any enactment having effect, at any time, in any part of the United Kingdom.

5.—(1) If any person–

(a) acts as a child minder at any time when he is disqualified for registration for child minding; or

(b) contravenes any of sub-paragraphs (3) to (5) of paragraph 4,

he shall be guilty of an offence.

(2) Where a person contravenes sub-paragraph (3) of paragraph 4, he shall not be guilty of an offence under this paragraph if he proves that he did not know, and had no reasonable grounds for believing, that the person in question was living or employed in the household.

(3) Where a person contravenes sub-paragraph (5) of paragraph 4, he shall not be guilty of an offence under this paragraph if he proves that he did not know, and had no reasonable grounds for believing, that the person whom he was employing was disqualified.

(4) A person guilty of an offence under this paragraph shall be liable on summary conviction to imprisonment for a term not exceeding six months, or to a fine not exceeding level 5 on the standard scale, or to both.

Certificates of registration

6.—(1) If an application for registration is granted, the registration authority shall give the applicant a certificate of registration.

(2) A certificate of registration shall give prescribed information about prescribed matters.

(3) Where, due to a change of circumstances, any part of the certificate requires to be amended, the registration authority shall issue an amended certificate.

(4) Where the registration authority is satisfied that the certificate has been lost or destroyed, the authority shall issue a copy, on payment by the registered person of any prescribed fee.

(5) For the purposes of Part XA, a person is—

    (a) registered for providing child minding (in England or in Wales); or

    (b) registered for providing day care on any premises,

if a certificate of registration to that effect is in force in respect of him.

Annual fees

7. Regulations may require registered persons to pay to the registration authority at prescribed times an annual fee of a prescribed amount.

Co-operation between authorities

8.—(1) Where it appears to the Chief Inspector that any local authority in England could, by taking any specified action, help in the exercise of any of his functions under Part XA, he may request the help of that authority specifying the action in question.

(2) Where it appears to the Assembly that any local authority in Wales could, by taking any specified action, help in the exercise of any of its functions under Part XA, the Assembly may request the help of that authority specifying the action in question.

(3) An authority whose help is so requested shall comply with the request if it is compatible with their own statutory or other duties and obligations and does not unduly prejudice the discharge of any of their functions.'

SCHEDULE 4
MINOR AND CONSEQUENTIAL AMENDMENTS

National Assistance Act 1948 (c.29)

1.—(1) Section 26 of the National Assistance Act 1948 (provision of accommodation in premises maintained by voluntary organisations) shall be amended as follows.

(2) In subsection (1), for '(1B)' there shall be substituted '(1C)'.

(3) For subsections (1A) and (1B) there shall be substituted—

'(1A) Arrangements must not be made by virtue of this section for the provision of accommodation together with nursing or personal care for persons such as are mentioned in section 3(2) of the Care Standards Act 2000 (care homes) unless—

    (a) the accommodation is to be provided, under the arrangements, in a care home (within the meaning of that Act) which is managed by the organisation or person in question; and

    (b) that organisation or person is registered under Part II of that Act in respect of the home.'

(4) In subsection (1C), for the words from 'no' to 'person' there shall be substituted 'no

arrangements may be made by virtue of this section for the provision of accommodation together with nursing'.

Mental Health Act 1959 (c.72)

2. In section 128 of the Mental Health Act 1959 (sexual intercourse with patients)–

    (a) in subsection (1), in paragraph (a), for 'or mental nursing home' there shall be substituted ', independent hospital or care home' and in paragraph (b), for the words from 'a residential' to the end there shall be substituted 'a care home'; and

    (b) after subsection (5) there shall be inserted–

      '(6) In this section "independent hospital" and "care home" have the same meanings as in the Care Standards Act 2000.'

Children and Young Persons Act 1969 (c.54)

3. In section 23(12) of the Children and Young Persons Act 1969 (remands and committals to local authority accommodation)–

    (a) at the appropriate place, there shall be inserted–

      '"children's home" has the same meaning as in the Care Standards Act 2000;' and

    (b) in the definition of 'secure accommodation'–

      (i) for 'community home, a voluntary home or a registered children's home' there shall be substituted 'children's home in respect of which a person is registered under Part II of the Care Standards Act 2000'; and

      (ii) at the end there shall be inserted 'or the National Assembly for Wales'.

Local Authority Social Services Act 1970 (c.42)

4. In Schedule 1 to the Local Authority Social Services Act 1970 (enactments conferring functions assigned to social services committee), in the entry relating to the 1989 Act, for 'registered' there shall be substituted 'private' and for 'residential care, nursing or mental nursing homes or in independent schools' there shall be substituted 'care homes, independent hospitals or schools'.

Adoption Act 1976 (c.36)

5.—(1) The Adoption Act 1976 shall be amended as follows.

    (2) In section 1 (establishment of adoption service)–

    (a) in subsections (1), (3) and (4), for 'approved adoption societies' and 'approved adoption society', in each place where those words occur, there shall be substituted, respectively, 'appropriate voluntary organisation' and 'appropriate voluntary organisations'; and

    (b) after subsection (4) there shall be inserted–

      '(5) In this Act "appropriate voluntary organisation" means a voluntary organisation which is an adoption society in respect of which a person is registered under Part II of the Care Standards Act 2000.'

(3) In section 2 (local authorities' social services), in paragraph (a), for 'registered' there shall be substituted 'private' and for 'residential care, nursing or mental nursing homes or in independent schools' there shall be substituted 'care homes, independent hospitals or schools'.

(4) In section 4(3) of that Act (power of Secretary of State to make directions where approval of adoption society is withdrawn or expires), for the words from 'Where' to 'expires' there shall be substituted 'Where, by virtue of the cancellation of the registration of any person under Part II of the Care Standards Act 2000, a body has ceased to be an appropriate voluntary organisation'.

(5) In section 8 (inactive or defunct adoption societies)–

(a) in subsection (1), for the words from 'an approved' to 'expired' there shall be substituted 'a body which is or has been an appropriate voluntary organisation'; and

(b) for 'society', in each place where it occurs, there shall be substituted 'organisation'.

(6) In section 9 (regulation of adoption agencies)–

(a) in subsection (2), for 'an approved adoption society' there shall be substituted 'an appropriate voluntary organisation';

(b) after that subsection there shall be inserted–

'(2A) The power under subsection (2) includes in particular power to make in relation to an appropriate voluntary organisation any provision which regulations under section 22(2) or (7) of the Care Standards Act 2000 (regulation of establishments and agencies) may make in relation to a fostering agency (within the meaning of that Act).';

(c) after subsection (3) there shall be inserted–

'(3A) The power under subsection (3) includes in particular power to make in relation to the functions there mentioned any provision which regulations under section 48 of the Care Standards Act 2000 (regulation of the exercise of relevant fostering functions) may make in relation to relevant fostering functions (within the meaning of Part III of that Act).'; and

(d) in subsection (4), after '(2)' there shall be inserted 'or (3)'.

(7) In section 11 (restriction on arranging adoptions and placing of children)–

(a) in subsection (2), for 'approved under section 3 of this Act' there shall be substituted 'an appropriate voluntary organisation'; and

(b) in subsection (3)(a), for 'which is not an adoption agency' there shall be substituted 'which is not–

(i) a local authority; or

(ii) a voluntary adoption agency within the meaning of the Care Standards Act 2000 in respect of which he is registered;'.

(8) In section 32 (meaning of 'protected child')–

(a) in subsection (3)(a)(i), for 'community home, voluntary home or registered children's home' there shall be substituted 'children's home in respect of which a person is registered under Part II of the Care Standards Act 2000'; and

(b) in subsection (3A), for "community home', 'voluntary home', 'registered children's home'' there shall be substituted "children's home''.

(9) For section 51(3)(d)(i) there shall be substituted–

'(i) which is an appropriate voluntary organisation'.

(10) In section 58A(1) (information concerning adoption), for 'approved adoption society' there shall be substituted 'appropriate voluntary organisation'.

(11) In section 72(1) (interpretation), for the definition of 'approved adoption society' there shall be substituted–

'"appropriate voluntary organisation" has the meaning assigned by section 1(5);'

Adoption (Scotland) Act 1978 (c.28)

6. In section 11(2) of the Adoption (Scotland) Act 1978 (restriction on arranging adoptions and placing of children), for 'approved as respects England and Wales under section 3 of the Adoption Act 1976' there shall be substituted 'a person registered under Part II of the Care Standards Act 2000'.

Magistrates' Court Act 1980 (c. 43)

7. In Schedule 6 to the Magistrates' Court Act 1980 (fees), in the entry relating to family proceedings, in the paragraph relating to the 1989 Act, for 'Part X' there shall be substituted 'Part XA'.

Limitation Act 1980 (c.58)

8. In section 38 of the Limitation Act 1980 (interpretation)–
  (a) in subsection (3), for the words from 'within' to the end there is substituted 'is incapable of managing and administering his property and affairs; and in this section 'mental disorder' has the same meaning as in the Mental Health Act 1983'; and
  (b) in subsection (4)(b), after 'receiving treatment' there shall be inserted 'for mental disorder' and for 'or mental nursing home' within the meaning of the Nursing Homes Act 1975' there shall be substituted 'or independent hospital or care home within the meaning of the Care Standards Act 2000'.

Mental Health Act 1983 (c.20)

9.—(1) The Mental Health Act 1983 shall be amended as follows.

(2) In sections 12(3), 23(3), 24(3), 46(1), 64(1), 119(2), 120(1) and (4), 131(1), 132(1), (2) and (4) and 133(1), for 'mental nursing home' and 'mental nursing homes' in each place where they occur, there shall be substituted, respectively, 'registered establishment' and 'registered establishments'.

(3) In paragraph (b) of section 24(3) (visiting and examination of patients), for 'Part II of the Registered Homes Act 1984' there shall be substituted 'Part II of the Care Standards Act 2000'.

(4) In section 34–

(a) in subsection (1), after the definition of 'the nominated medical attendant' there shall be inserted–

> '"registered establishment" means an establishment–
> (a) which would not, apart from subsection (2) below, be a hospital for the purposes of this Part; and
> (b) in respect of which a person is registered under Part II of the Care Standards Act 2000 as an independent hospital in which treatment or nursing (or both) are provided for persons liable to be detained under this Act;' and

(b) in subsection (2), for the words from 'a mental' to '1984' there shall be substituted 'a registered establishment'.

(5) In section 116(1) (welfare of certain hospital patients), for 'or nursing home' there shall be substituted ', independent hospital or care home'.

(6) In section 118(1) (code of practice)–
(a) for the first 'and mental nursing homes' there shall be substituted ', independent hospitals and care homes'; and
(b) for the second 'and mental nursing homes' there is substituted 'and registered establishments'.

(7) In section 121 (Mental Health Act Commission)–
(a) in subsection (4), for 'and mental nursing homes' there shall be substituted ', independent hospitals and care homes'; and
(b) in subsection (5), in paragraphs (a) and (b), for 'a mental nursing home' there shall be substituted 'an independent hospital or a care home'.

(8) In section 127(1) (ill-treatment of patients), for 'or mental nursing home' there shall be substituted ', independent hospital or care home'.

(9) In section 135(6) (warrant to search for and remove patients) for 'a mental nursing home or residential home' there shall be substituted 'an independent hospital or care home'.

(10) In section 145(1) (interpretation)–
(a) after the definition of 'approved social worker' there shall be inserted–

> ' "care home" has the same meaning as in the Care Standards Act 2000';

(b) after the definition of 'hospital order' and 'guardianship order' there shall be inserted–

> ' "independent hospital" has the same meaning as in the Care Standards Act 2000;'

(c) in the definition of 'the managers', for paragraph (c) there shall be substituted–

> '(c) in relation to a registered establishment, the person or persons registered in respect of the establishment;' and

(d) after the definition of 'Primary Care Trust' there shall be inserted–

> ' "registered establishment" has the meaning given in section 34 above;'.

Public Health (Control of Disease) Act 1984 (c.22)

10. In section 7(4) of the Public Health (Control of Disease) Act 1984 (port health district and authority for Port of London), paragraphs (h) and (i) and the 'and' following paragraph (i) shall be omitted.

Disabled Persons (Services, Consultation and Representation) Act 1986 (c.33)

11. In section 2(5)(d) of the Disabled Persons (Services, Consultation and Representation) Act 1986 (rights of authorised representatives of disabled persons), for 'a residential care home within the meaning of Part I of the Registered Homes Act 1984' there shall be substituted 'a care home within the meaning of the Care Standards Act 2000'.

Adoption (Northern Ireland) Order 1987 (S.I. 1987/2203 (N.I.22))

12. In Article 11(2) of the Adoption (Northern Ireland) Order 1987 (restriction on arranging adoptions and placing children), for 'approved as respects England and Wales under section 3 of the Adoption Act 1976 or as respects Scotland' there shall be substituted 'in respect of which a person is registered under Part II of the Care Standards Act 2000 or which is approved as respects Scotland'.

Income and Corporation Taxes Act 1988 (c.40)

13. In section 155A(6) of the Income and Corporation Taxes Act 1988 (care for children), after 'section 71' there shall be inserted 'or Part XA'.

Children Act 1989 (c.41)

14.—(1) The 1989 Act shall be amended as follows.
    (2) In section 19 (review of provision of day care, child minding etc.)–
        (a) in subsection (1)(c), for 'section 71(1)(b)' there shall be substituted 'Part XA'; and
        (b) in subsection (5), for the definition of 'relevant establishment' there shall be substituted–

        ' "relevant establishment" means–
            (a)   in relation to Scotland, any establishment which is mentioned in paragraphs 3 and 4 of Schedule 9 (establishments exempt from the registration requirements which apply in relation to the provision of day care in Scotland); and
            (b)   in relation to England and Wales, any establishment which is mentioned in paragraphs 1 and 2 of Schedule 9A (establishments exempt from the registration requirements which apply in relation to the provision of day care in England and Wales);'.
    (3) In section 23 (provision of accommodation and maintenance by local authority for children whom they are looking after)–
        (a) in subsection (2), for paragraphs (b) to (e) there shall be substituted–

        '(aa) maintaining him in an appropriate children's home;';

(b) after subsection (2) there shall be inserted–

'(2A) Where under subsection (2)(aa) a local authority maintains a child in a home provided, equipped and maintained by the Secretary of State under section 82(5), it shall do so on such terms as the Secretary of State may from time to time determine.'; and

(c) after subsection (9) there shall be inserted–

'(10) In this Act–
"appropriate children's home" means a children's home in respect of which a
    person is registered under Part II of the Care Standards Act 2000; and
"children's home" has the same meaning as in that Act.'

(4) In section 24 (advice and assistance for certain children), as it has effect before the commencement of section 4 of the Children (Leaving Care) Act 2000–
(a) in subsections (2)(c) and (12)(a), for 'registered' there shall be substituted 'private'; and
(b) in subsections (2)(d)(ii) and (12)(c), for 'residential care home, nursing home or mental nursing home' there shall be substituted 'care home or independent hospital'.
(5) In section 24 (persons qualifying for advice and assistance) as it has effect after that commencement–
(a) in subsection (2)(c), for 'registered' there shall be substituted 'private'; and
(b) in subsection (2)(d)(ii), for 'residential care home, nursing home or mental nursing home' there shall be substituted 'care home or independent hospital'.
(6) In section 24C(2) (information)
(a) in paragraph (a), for 'registered' there shall be substituted 'private'; and
(b) in paragraph (c), for 'residential care home, nursing home or mental nursing home' there shall be substituted 'care home or independent hospital'.
(7) In section 51(1) (refuges for children at risk), for 'registered' there shall be substituted 'private'.
(8) In section 59 (provision of accommodation by voluntary organisations)–
(a) in subsection (1), for paragraphs (b) to (e) there shall be substituted–

'(aa) maintaining him in an appropriate children's home;'; and

(b) after that subsection there shall be inserted–

'(1A) Where under subsection (1)(aa) a local authority maintains a child in a home provided, equipped and maintained by the Secretary of State under section 82(5), it shall do so on such terms as the Secretary of State may from time to time determine.'

(9) In section 60 (registration and regulation of voluntary homes)–
(a) for the sidenote there shall be substituted 'Voluntary homes.'; and
(b) for subsection (3) there shall be substituted–

'(3) In this Act "voluntary home" means a children's home which is carried on by a voluntary organisation but does not include a community home.'

(10) In section 62 (duties of local authorities in relation to children provided with accommodation by voluntary organisations)–

    (a) in subsection (6)(c), for 'paragraph 7 of Schedule 5' there shall be substituted 'section 22 of the Care Standards Act 2000'; and

    (b) after subsection (9) there shall be inserted-

'(10) This section does not apply in relation to any voluntary organisation which is a school.'

(11) In section 63 (children not to be cared for and accommodated in unregistered children's homes)–

    (a) for the sidenote there is substituted 'Private children's homes etc.';

    (b) in subsection (11), after 'to' there shall be inserted 'private'; and

    (c) in subsection (12), after 'treated' there shall be inserted ', for the purposes of this Act and the Care Standards Act 2000,'.

(12) In section 64 (welfare of children in children's homes), in subsections (1) and (4), before 'children's home' there shall be inserted 'private'.

(13) In section 65 (persons disqualified from carrying on, or being employed in, children's homes)–

    (a) in subsections (1) and (2), for 'the responsible authority' and 'their' there shall be substituted 'the appropriate authority' and 'its' respectively;

    (b) in subsection (3), for the words from 'an' to 'they' there shall be substituted 'the appropriate authority refuses to give its consent under this section, it';

    (c) for subsection (3)(b) there shall be substituted–

'(b) the applicant's right to appeal under section 65A against the refusal to the Tribunal established under section 9 of the Protection of Children Act 1999'; and

    (d) after subsection (5) there shall be inserted–

'(6) In this section and section 65A "appropriate authority" means–

    (a) in relation to England, the National Care Standards Commission; and

    (b) in relation to Wales, the National Assembly for Wales.'

(14) After section 65 there is inserted–

'Appeal against refusal   65A.—(1) An appeal against a decision of an appropriate
of authority to give   authority under section 65 shall lie to the Tribunal established
consent under section 65.   under section 9 of the Protection of Children Act 1999.

          (2) On an appeal the Tribunal may confirm the authority's decision or direct it to give the consent in question.'

(15) In section 66 (privately fostered children)–

    (a) in subsection (1)(a) after 'accommodation' there shall be inserted 'in their own home'; and

(b) after subsection (4) there shall be inserted–

'(4A) The Secretary of State may by regulations make provision as to the circumstances in which a person who provides accommodation to a child is, or is not, to be treated as providing him with accommodation in the person's own home.'

(16) In section 80 (inspection of children's homes etc by persons authorised by Secretary of State)–
(a) in subsections (1)(a) and (5)(c), before 'children's' there shall be inserted 'private';
(b) in subsection (1)(i), after '71(1)(b)' there shall be added 'or with respect to which a person is registered for providing day care under Part XA';
(c) for subsection (1)(j) there shall be substituted–

'(j) care home or independent hospital used to accommodate children;' and

(d) in subsection (5), after paragraph (h) there shall be inserted–

'(hh) person who is the occupier of any premises–
(i)   in which any person required to be registered for child minding under Part XA acts as a child minder (within the meaning of that Part); or
(ii)   with respect to which a person is required to be registered under that Part for providing day care;'.

(17) In section 81(1) (inquiries)–
(a) in paragraph (d), after 'a' there shall be inserted 'private'; and
(b) in paragraph (e), for 'a residential care home, nursing home or mental nursing home' there shall be substituted 'a care home or independent hospital'.
(18) In section 82(6) (financial support by Secretary of State), in the definition of 'child care training', for 'residential care home, nursing home or mental nursing home' there shall be substituted 'care home or independent hospital'.
(19) In section 83 (research and returns of information), in subsections (1)(c), (2)(c) and (3)(a)(ii), for 'residential care home, nursing home or mental nursing home' there shall be substituted 'care home or independent hospital'.
(20) In section 86–
(a) for the sidenote there shall be substituted 'Children accommodated in care homes or independent hospitals.'; and
(b) in subsections (1) and (5), for 'residential care home, nursing home or mental nursing home' there shall be substituted 'care home or independent hospital'.
(21) For the sidenote to section 87 (welfare of children accommodated in independent schools) there shall be substituted 'Welfare of children in boarding schools and colleges.'.
(22) In section 102(6)(a) (power of constable to assist in exercise of certain powers to search for children or inspect premises), after '76,' there shall be inserted '79U,'.
(23) In section 105 (interpretation)–
(a) in subsection (1)–
(i)   after the definition of 'adoption agency' there shall be inserted–

'"appropriate children's home" has the meaning given by section 23;'

(ii)   after the definition of 'bank holiday' there shall be inserted-

"'care home" has the same meaning as in the Care Standards Act 2000;'

(iii) for the definition of 'children's home' there shall be substituted–

"'children's home" has the meaning given by section 23;'

(iv)   in the definition of 'day care', after 'care' there shall be inserted '(except in Part XA)';

(v)   in the definition of 'hospital', after 'hospital' there shall be inserted '(except in Schedule 9A)';

(vi)   after the definition of 'income-based jobseeker's allowance' there shall be inserted–

' "independent hospital" has the same meaning as in the Care Standards Act 2000;' and

(vii) after the definition of 'prescribed' there shall be inserted–

"'private children's home" means a children's home in respect of which a person is registered under Part II of the Care Standards Act 2000 which is not a community home or a voluntary home;'; and

(b) after subsection (5) there shall be inserted–

'(5A) References in this Act to a child minder shall be construed–
    (a) in relation to Scotland, in accordance with section 71;
    (b) in relation to England and Wales, in accordance with section 79A.'.

(24) In Schedule 3 (supervision orders), in paragraphs 4(2)(c)(ii) and 5(2)(c), for 'or mental nursing home' there shall be substituted ', independent hospital or care home'.

(25) In Schedule 6 (registered children's homes)–
    (a) in the heading, for 'Registered Children's Homes' there shall be substituted 'Private Children's Homes'; and
    (b) in paragraph 10(1)(a), for 'registered' there shall be substituted 'private'.

(26) In paragraph 5(1) of Schedule 7 (foster parents: limit on number of foster children), after 'treated' there shall be inserted ', for the purposes of this Act and the Care Standards Act 2000'.

(27) In Schedule 8 (privately fostered children)–
    (a) in paragraph 2, sub-paragraph (1)(b) shall cease to have effect, and in sub-paragraph (2), for '(1)(b)' there shall be substituted '(1)(c)'; and
    (b) in paragraph 9(1), for '2(1)(d)' there shall be substituted '2(1)(c) and (d)', and at the end there shall be inserted–

'But this sub-paragraph does not apply to a school which is an appropriate children's home.'.

(28) For paragraph 2(1)(f) of Schedule 8 (privately fostered children) there shall be substituted–

'(f) in any care home or independent hospital;'.

(29) In paragraph 4(1) of Schedule 9 (child minding and day care for young children)–
    (a) for paragraphs (a) to (c) there shall be substituted–

'(aa) an appropriate children's home;' and

    (b) for paragraph (d) there shall be substituted–

'(d) a care home;'.

National Health Service and Community Care Act 1990 (c.19)

15. In section 48(1) of the National Health Service and Community Care Act 1990 (inspection of premises used for the provision of community care), for 'the Registered Homes Act 1984' there shall be substituted 'Part II of the Care Standards Act 2000'.

Criminal Procedure (Insanity and Unfitness to Plead) Act 1991 (c.25)

16. In paragraph 4(2)(a) of Schedule 2 to the Criminal Procedure (Insanity and Unfitness to Plead) Act 1991 (supervision and treatment orders), for 'hospital or mental nursing home' there shall be substituted 'independent hospital or care home within the meaning of the Care Standards Act 2000 or in a hospital'.

Criminal Justice Act 1991 (c.53)

17. In section 61(2) of the Criminal Justice Act 1991 (provision by local authorities of secure accommodation), for the words from 'voluntary' to the end there shall be substituted 'persons carrying on an appropriate children's home for the provision or use by them of such accommodation'.

Water Industry Act 1991 (c.56)

18. In Schedule 4A to the Water Industry Act 1991 (premises that are not to be disconnected for non-payment of charges), for paragraphs 8 and 9 there shall be substituted–

'8.—(1) A care home or independent hospital.
    (2) In this paragraph–
        "care home" means-
        (a) a care home within the meaning of the Care Standards Act 2000;
        (b) a building or part of a building in which residential accommodation
            is provided under section 21 of the National Assistance Act 1948;
        "independent hospital" means an independent hospital within the meaning of the Care Standards Act 2000.

9. A children's home within the meaning of the Care Standards Act 2000.'

19. In Schedule 4A to the Water Industry Act 1991 (premises that are not to be disconnected for non-payment of charges), in paragraph 12 for 'section 71(1)(b)' there shall be substituted 'Part XA'.

Local Government Finance Act 1992 (c.14)

20. In paragraph 7 of Schedule 1 to the Local Government Finance Act 1992 (persons disregarded for purposes of discount)–
    (a) in sub-paragraph (1)(a), for 'residential care home, nursing home, mental nursing home' there shall be substituted 'care home, independent hospital';
    (b) in sub-paragraph (1)(b), after 'home' there shall be inserted ', hospital';
    (c) for sub-paragraph (2), there shall be substituted–

    '(2) In this paragraph–
      "care home" means–
        (a) a care home within the meaning of the Care Standards Act 2000; or
        (b) a building or part of a building in which residential accommodation is provided under section 21 of the National Assistance Act 1948;
      "hostel" means anything which falls within any definition of hostel for the time being prescribed by order made by the Secretary of State under this sub-paragraph;
      "independent hospital" has the same meaning as in the Care Standards Act 2000.' and

    (d) in sub-paragraph (3), for ''mental nursing home', 'nursing home' or 'residential care home'' there shall be substituted ''care home' or 'independent hospital''.

Tribunals and Inquiries Act 1992 (c.53)

21. In Schedule 1 to the Tribunals and Inquiries Act 1992 (tribunals under supervision of Council), paragraph 36A (inserted by paragraph 8 of the Schedule to the Protection of Children Act 1999) is renumbered as paragraph 36B and, in the first column of that paragraph, after 'Protection of children' there shall be inserted 'and vulnerable adults, and care standards'.

Criminal Justice and Public Order Act 1994 (c.33)

22. In section 2 of the Criminal Justice and Public Order Act 1994 (secure training orders: supplementary provisions as to detention)–
    (a) in subsection (5), for 'registered children's home' there shall be substituted 'private children's home'; and
    (b) in subsection (8), for 'registered children's home' there shall be substituted 'private children's home'.

Children (Scotland) Act 1995 (c.36)

23. In section 93 of the Children (Scotland) Act 1995 (interpretation of Part II)–

(a) in paragraph (b) of the definition of 'residential establishment', for 'registered' there shall be substituted 'private'; and

(b) in the definition of 'secure accommodation', for 'paragraph 4(2)(i) of Schedule 4 to the Children Act 1989' there shall be substituted 'section 22(8)(a) of the Care Standards Act 2000'.

Education Act 1996 (c.56)

24.—(1) The Education Act 1996 shall be amended as follows.

(2) In section 467(2) (provision of information about registered and provisionally registered schools), for 'Children Act 1989' there shall be substituted 'Care Standards Act 2000'.

(3) In section 469(4) (notice of complaint by Secretary of State), after 'school is' there shall be inserted 'unsuitable to work with children or is for any other reason'.

(4) In section 471(2)(a) (determination of complaint by Secretary of State), after 'school is' there shall be inserted 'unsuitable to work with children or is for any other reason'.

Police Act 1997 (c.50)

25.—(1) In section 113(3A) of the Police Act 1997 (criminal record certificates), for 'suitability for' there shall be substituted 'suitability to be employed, supplied to work, found work or given work in'.

(2) In section 115 of that Act (enhanced criminal record certificates)–

(a) in subsection (5)(e), for 'or' there shall be substituted 'registration for child minding or providing day care under Part XA of that Act or registration under'; and

(b) in subsection (6A), for 'suitability for' there shall be substituted 'suitability to be employed, supplied to work, found work or given work in'.

Protection of Children Act 1999 (c.14)

26.—(1) The Protection of Children Act 1999 shall be amended as follows.

(2) In section 2 (inclusion in list on reference to Secretary of State)–

(a) in subsection (2)(b), for 'or retired', in each place where those words occur, there shall be substituted ', retired or made redundant'; and

(b) in subsection (8)(a), for 'or retiring' there shall be substituted ', retiring or being made redundant' and for 'or retired' there shall be substituted ', retired or been made redundant'.

(2) In section 7 (effect of inclusion in the lists kept under section 1 of the 1999 Act and section 218(6) of the Education Reform Act 1988)–

(a) after subsection (1) there shall be inserted–

'(1A) Where a child care organisation discovers that an individual employed by it in a child care position is included in any of the lists mentioned in subsection (1) above, it shall cease to employ him in a child care position.

For the purposes of this subsection an individual is not employed in a child care position if he has been suspended or provisionally transferred to a position which is not a child care position.'; and

(b) in subsection (2), after 'employment agency' there shall be inserted 'or an employment business'.

(3) In section 9 (the Tribunal)–
  (a) in subsection (2), for the words from 'on an appeal' to the end there shall be substituted-

    '(a) on an appeal or determination under section 4 above;
    (b) on an appeal under regulations made under section 6 above;
    (c) on an appeal under section 65A of the Children Act 1989 or under, or by virtue of, Part XA of that Act; or
    (d) on an appeal or determination under section 21, 68, 86, 87 or 88 of the Care Standards Act 2000;'; and

  (b) after subsection (3), there shall be inserted–

    '(3A) The regulations may also include provision for enabling the Tribunal to make investigations for the purposes of a determination under section 87 or 88 of the Care Standards Act 2000; and the provision that may be made by virtue of subsection (3)(j) and (k) above includes provision in relation to such investigations.
    (3B) Regulations under this section may make different provision for different cases or classes of case.
    (3C) Before making in regulations under this section provision such as is mentioned in subsection (2)(c) or (d) above, the Secretary of State shall consult the National Assembly for Wales.'

(4) In section 12 (interpretation)–
  (a) in subsection (1)–
    (i) in the definition of 'employment agency', for 'has the same meaning' there shall be substituted 'and 'employment business' have the same meanings'; and
    (ii) after the definition of 'harm' there shall be inserted–

    '"local authority" has the same meaning as in the Children Act 1989;'; and

  (b) after subsection (3) there shall be inserted–

    '(3A) For the purposes of this Act, an individual is made redundant if–
    (a) he is dismissed; and
    (b) for the purposes of the Employment Rights Act 1996 the dismissal is by reason of redundancy.'

Adoption (Intercountry Aspects) Act 1999 (c.18)

27. In section 2 of the Adoption (Intercountry Aspects) Act 1999 (central authorities and accredited bodies)–
  (a) after subsection (2) there shall be inserted–

    '(2A) A voluntary adoption agency in respect of which a person is registered under Part II of the Care Standards Act 2000 is an accredited body for the purposes of the

Convention if, in accordance with the conditions of the registration, the agency may provide facilities in respect of Convention adoptions and adoptions effected by Convention adoption orders.'; and

(b) for subsection (5) there shall be substituted–

'(5) In this section in its application to England and Wales, 'voluntary adoption agency' has the same meaning as in the Care Standards Act 2000; and expressions which are also used in the Adoption Act 1976 ('the 1976 Act') have the same meanings as in that Act.'

Powers of Criminal Courts (Sentencing) Act 2000 (c.6)

28.—(1) The Powers of Criminal Courts (Sentencing) Act 2000 shall be amended as follows.

(2) In paragraph 5(3)(a) of Schedule 2 (additional requirements which may be included in probation orders), for 'a hospital or mental nursing home' there shall be substituted 'an independent hospital or care home within the meaning of the Care Standards Act 2000 or a hospital'.

(3) In paragraph 6(2)(a) of Schedule 6 (requirements which may be included in supervision orders), for 'a hospital or mental nursing home' there shall be substituted 'an independent hospital or care home within the meaning of the Care Standards Act 2000 or a hospital'.

Amendments of local Acts

29.—(1) Section 16 of the Greater London Council (General Powers) Act 1981 (exemption from provisions of Part IV of the Act of certain premises) shall be amended as follows.

(2) For paragraph (g) there shall be substituted–

'(g) used as a care home, or an independent hospital, within the meaning of the Care Standards Act 2000;'

(3) For paragraphs (gg) and (h) there shall be substituted–

'(gg) used as a children's home within the meaning of the Care Standards Act 2000 which is a home in respect of which a person is registered under Part II of that Act;'

(4) Paragraph (j) shall be omitted.

30.—(1) Section 10(2) of the Greater London Council (General Powers) Act 1984 (exemption from provisions of Part IV of the Act of certain premises) shall be amended as follows.

(2) For paragraph (c) there shall be substituted–

'(c) used as a care home, or an independent hospital, within the meaning of the Care Standards Act 2000;'

(3) For paragraph (d) there shall be substituted–

'(d) used as a children's home within the meaning of the Care Standards Act 2000 which is a home in respect of which a person is registered under Part II of that Act;'

(4) Paragraphs (f) and (l) shall be omitted.

SCHEDULE 5
TRANSITIONAL PROVISIONS AND SAVINGS

Fostering agencies

1. The appropriate Minister may by regulations provide that, if prescribed requirements are satisfied, section 11 shall apply, during the prescribed period, to a person running a fostering agency who has made an application for registration under section 12(1) as if that person were unconditionally registered under Part II of this Act.

Voluntary adoption agencies

2.—(1) Where an approval granted to a body, before the commencement of section 13, under section 3 of the Adoption Act 1976 (approval of adoption societies) is operative at that commencement, Part II of this Act shall, if prescribed requirements are satisfied, have effect after that commencement as if any person carrying on or managing the body were registered under that Part in respect of it, either–
  (a) unconditionally; or
  (b) subject to such conditions as may be prescribed.
(2) Any application made before the commencement of section 12 for approval under section 3 of the Adoption Act 1976 shall be treated after that commencement as an application made under section 12(1) to the registration authority for registration under Part II of this Act.
(3) The appropriate Minister may by order make such further transitional provision in relation to the repeal by this Act of provisions of the Adoption Act 1976 as he considers appropriate.

Children's Commissioner for Wales

3.—(1) The Part of this Act which relates to the Children's Commissioner for Wales has effect, in relation to times before the commencement of any other relevant provision of this Act, as if references–
  (a) to regulated children's services in Wales; and
  (b) to the provider of such services,
were or included references to services which would be regulated children's services in Wales, or (as the case may be) to the person who would be the provider, if that provision were in force.
(2) Sub-paragraph (1) has effect subject to any provision made under sections 118 or 119.

SCHEDULE 6
REPEALS

Chapter	Short title	Extent of repeal
1948 c. 29.	National Assistance Act 1948.	Section 26(1E).
1957 c. 16.	Nurses Agencies Act 1957.	The whole Act.
1958 c. 51.	Public Records Act 1958.	In Schedule 1, in the Table at the end of paragraph 3, in Part II, the entry relating to the Care Council for Wales.
1963 c. 33.	London Government Act 1963.	Section 40(4)(i).
1970 c. 42.	Local Authority Social Services Act 1970.	In Schedule 1, in the entry relating to the Mental Health Act 1959, the words 'and the Registered Homes Act 1984 so far as its provisions relate to mental nursing homes', and the entry relating to the Registered Homes Act 1984.
1970 c. 44.	Chronically Sick and Disabled Persons Act 1970.	Section 18.
1972 c. 70.	Local Government Act 1972.	In Schedule 29, paragraph 30.
1973 c. 35.	Employment Agencies Act 1973.	In section 13(7), paragraphs (b) and (c) and the proviso.
1976 c. 36.	Adoption Act 1976.	Section 3. Section 4(1) and (2). In section 4(3), the word 'concerned'. Section 5. Section 9(1).
1979 c. 36.	Nurses, Midwives and Health Visitors Act 1979.	In Schedule 7, paragraphs 8, 9 and 10.
1981 c. xvii.	Greater London Council (General Powers) Act 1981.	Section 16(j).
1983 c. 20.	Mental Health Act 1983.	In section 145(1), the definition of 'mental nursing home'.
1983 c. 41.	Health and Social Services and Social Security Adjudications Act 1983.	In Schedule 2, paragraph 29.
1984 c. 22.	Public Health (Control of Disease) Act 1984.	In section 7(4), paragraphs (h) and (i) and the 'and' following paragraph (i).
1984 c. 23.	Registered Homes Act 1984.	The whole Act.
1984 c. xxvii.	Greater London Council (General Powers) Act 1984.	Section 10(2)(f) and (l).
1989 c. 41.	Children Act 1989.	Section 54. In section 58(1), the word '54(2)'. In section 60, subsections (1) and (2), and in subsection (3)(a), the words '(other than a small home)'.

Chapter	Short title	Extent of repeal
		Section 63(1) to (10).
		In section 80(4), the word 'or' before paragraph (d).
		In section 104(1), the word '54(2)'.
		In section 105(1), the definitions of 'child minder', 'mental nursing home', 'nursing home', 'registered children's home' and 'residential care home'.
		In Schedule 4, in paragraph 4, sub-paragraphs (1)(b) and (c), (2) and (3).
		In Schedule 5, paragraphs 1 to 6, in paragraph 7, sub-paragraphs (1)(b) and (c) and (2) to (4), and paragraph 8.
		In Schedule 6, paragraphs 1 to 9 and in paragraph 10, sub-paragraphs (1)(b) and (c), (2)(a) to (k), (3) and (4).
		In Schedule 8, paragraph 2(1)(b) and in paragraph 9(1), the words 'which is not maintained by a local education authority'.
		In Schedule 13, paragraph 49, in paragraph 73, sub-paragraphs (2) and (3) and in paragraph 74, sub-paragraphs (2) and (4).
1990 c. 19.	National Health Service and Community Care Act 1990.	In Schedule 9, paragraph 27.
1991 c. 20.	Registered Homes (Amendment) Act 1991.	The whole Act.
1992 c. 53.	Tribunals and Inquiries Act 1992.	In Schedule 1, the entry relating to the Registered Homes Tribunals constituted under Part III of the Registered Homes Act 1984.
1993 c. 8.	Judicial Pensions and Retirement Act 1993.	In Schedule 5, the entry relating to a Chairman of a Registered Homes Tribunal constituted under the Registered Homes Act 1984.
		In Schedule 6, paragraph 55.
		In Schedule 7, paragraph 5(5)(xxxi).
1994 c. 19.	Local Government (Wales) Act 1994.	In Schedule 9, paragraph 5.
1996 c. 23.	Arbitration Act 1996.	In Schedule 3, paragraph 41.
1996 c. 56.	Education Act 1996.	In Schedule 37, paragraphs 58, 86, 88 and 89.
1997 c. 24.	Nurses, Midwives and Health Visitors Act 1997.	In Schedule 4, paragraph 3.

| 1999 c. 14. | Protection of Children Act 1999. | In section 2(9), the words 'or an agency for the supply of nurses'. In section 7(2), the words 'or an agency for the supply of nurses'. Section 10. In section 12(1), the definition of 'agency for the supply of nurses'. Section 13(3) and (4). |
| 1999 c. 18. | Adoption (Intercountry Aspects) Act 1999. | Section 10. |

Appendix 2

THE PROTECTION OF CHILDREN AND VULNERABLE ADULTS AND CARE STANDARDS TRIBUNAL REGULATIONS 2002

SI 2002/816

ARRANGEMENT OF REGULATIONS

PART I

Introductory

PART II

Constitution

PART III

Appeals, determinations and applications for leave

PART IV

Case management

SCHEDULE 1
APPEAL UNDER SECTION 21 OF THE 2000 ACT AGAINST A DECISION OF THE REGISTRATION AUTHORITY OR AN ORDER OF A JUSTICE OF THE PEACE

1. Initiating an appeal
2. Acknowledgement and notification of application
3. Response to application
4. Misconceived appeals etc.
5. Further information to be sent by the applicant and respondent
6. Changes to further information supplied to the Tribunal

SCHEDULE 2
APPEAL UNDER SECTION 79M OF THE 1989 ACT AGAINST A DECISION OF THE REGISTRATION AUTHORITY OR AN ORDER OF A JUSTICE OF THE PEACE

1. Initiating an appeal
2. Acknowledgement and notification of application
3. Response to application
4. Misconceived appeals etc.
5. Further information to be sent by the applicant and respondent
6. Changes to further information supplied to the Tribunal

SCHEDULE 3
APPEAL UNDER SECTION 65A OF THE 1989 ACT AGAINST A DECISION OF THE APPROPRIATE AUTHORITY REFUSING TO GIVE CONSENT UNDER SECTION 65 OF THAT ACT

1. Initiating an appeal
2. Acknowledgement and notification of application
3. Response to application
4. Misconceived appeals etc.
5. Further information to be sent by the applicant and respondent
6. Changes to further information supplied to the Tribunal

SCHEDULE 4
APPEALS AND APPLICATIONS FOR LEAVE TO APPEAL UNDER SECTION 4 OF THE 1999 ACT AND APPEALS UNDER REGULATION 13 OF THE EDUCATION REGULATIONS

1. Initiating an appeal

2. Applying for leave
3. Acknowledgement and notification of application
4. Response to application
5. Misconceived applications etc.
6. Grant or refusal of leave
7. Reconsideration of leave
8. Further information to be sent by the applicant and respondent
9. Changes to further information supplied to the Tribunal

SCHEDULE 5
APPEALS AND APPLICATIONS FOR LEAVE UNDER SECTION 86 OF THE 2000 ACT

1. Initiating an appeal
2. Applying for leave
3. Acknowledgement and notification of application
4. Response to application
5. Misconceived applications etc.
6. Grant or refusal of leave
7. Reconsideration of leave
8. Further information to be sent by the applicant and the respondent
9. Changes to further information supplied to the Tribunal

The Secretary of State, in exercise of the powers conferred upon him by section 9(2) to (4) of, and paragraph 2(4) of the Schedule to, the Protection of Children Act 1999 and of all other powers enabling him in that behalf, after consultation with the Council on Tribunals in accordance with section 8 of the Tribunals and Inquiries Act 1992, and with the National Assembly for Wales in accordance with section 9(3C) of the Protection of Children Act 1999, hereby makes the following Regulations:–

PART I
INTRODUCTORY

Citation, commencement and interpretation
1.—(1) These Regulations may be cited as the Protection of Children and Vulnerable Adults and Care Standards Tribunal Regulations 2002 and shall come into force–
    (a) for the purposes of–
        (i) an appeal under section 86(1)(a) or (b) of the 2000 Act;
        (ii) an application for leave to appeal under section 86(1)(b) of the 2000 Act;
        (iii) a determination, or an application for leave for a determination, under section 86(2) of the 2000 Act,
    on the first day on which sections 80 to 93 of the 2000 Act are in force;
    (b) for all other purposes, on 1st April 2002.
    (2) In these Regulations–

'the 1989 Act' means the Children Act 1989;

'the 1999 Act' means the Protection of Children Act 1999;

'the 2000 Act' means the Care Standards Act 2000;

'case' in Parts IV and VI means–

(a) an appeal under section 21 of the 2000 Act;

(b) an appeal under section 79M of the 1989 Act;

(c) an appeal under section 65A of the 1989 Act;

(d) an appeal under section 4(1)(a) or (b) of the 1999 Act;

(e) a determination under section 4(2) of the 1999 Act;

(f) an appeal under the Education Regulations;

(g) an appeal under section 86(1)(a) or (b) of the 2000 Act; or

(h) a determination under section 86(2) of the 2000 Act;

'application for leave' means an application to the Tribunal–

(a) for leave to appeal under section 4(1)(b) of the 1999 Act or section 86(1)(b) of the 2000 Act;

(b) for leave for a determination by the Tribunal under section 4(2) of the 1999 Act or section 86(2) of the 2000 Act;

'appropriate authority' means in relation to an appeal under section 65A of the 1989 Act the Commission or the Assembly;

'the Assembly' means the National Assembly for Wales;

'the Chief Inspector' means Her Majesty's Chief Inspector of Schools in England;

'the clerk' means, in relation to a hearing before the Tribunal, the person appointed by the Secretary to act as clerk to the Tribunal;

'the Commission' means the National Care Standards Commission;

'costs order' shall be construed in accordance with regulation 24;

'county court' has the same meaning as in the County Courts Act 1984;

'document' means information recorded in writing or in any other form;

'the Education Regulations' means the Education (Restriction of Employment) Regulations 2000;

'an institution within the further education sector' shall be construed in accordance with section 4(3) of the Education Act 1996;

'local authority' has the same meaning as in section 105 of the 1989 Act;

'local education authority' shall be construed in accordance with section 12 of the Education Act 1996;

'nominated chairman' means the chairman appointed by the President in accordance with regulation 5 to determine a case or an application for leave;

'a party' means either the applicant or the respondent;

'parties' means the applicant and the respondent;

'the POCA list' means the list kept under section 1 of the 1999 Act;

'the POVA list' means the list kept under section 81 of the 2000 Act;

'records' means the records of the Tribunal;

'registration authority' means–

(a) in relation to an appeal under section 21 of the 2000 Act, the Commission or the Assembly; and

(b) in relation to an appeal under section 79M of the 1989 Act, the Chief Inspector or the Assembly;

'relevant programme' means a programme included in a programme service within the meaning of the Broadcasting Act 1990;

'relevant social work' has the same meaning as in section 55(4) of the 2000 Act;

'the respondent' means–

    (a) in relation to an appeal under section 21 of the 2000 Act, the registration authority;

    (b) in relation to an appeal under section 79M of the 1989 Act, the registration authority;

    (c) in relation to an appeal under section 65A of the 1989 Act, the appropriate authority;

    (e) in relation to an appeal, an application for leave or a determination under section 4 of the 1999 Act, the Secretary of State for Health;

    (f) in relation to an appeal under the Education Regulations, the Secretary of State for Education and Skills or the National Assembly for Wales;

    (g) in relation to an appeal, an application for leave or a determination under section 86 of the 2000 Act, the Secretary of State for Health;

'residential family centre' has the same meaning as in section 4(2) of the 2000 Act;

'school' has the same meaning as in section 4 of the Education Act 1996;

'the Secretary' means the person for the time being acting as the Secretary to the Tribunal;

'vulnerable adult' means a person who is not a child and who–

    (a) suffers from mental disorder within the meaning of the Mental Health Act 1983, or otherwise has a significant impairment of intelligence and social functioning; or

    (b) has a physical disability or is suffering from a physical disorder;

'working day' means any day other than a Saturday, a Sunday, Christmas Day, Good Friday or a day which is a bank holiday within the meaning of the Banking and Financial Dealings Act 1971.

(3) In these Regulations, a reference–

    (a) to a numbered regulation is to the regulation in these Regulations bearing that number;

    (b) in a regulation to a numbered paragraph is to the paragraph of that regulation bearing that number;

    (c) to a numbered Schedule, is to a Schedule in these Regulations bearing that number;

    (d) in a paragraph to a numbered or lettered sub-paragraph is to the sub-paragraph of that paragraph bearing that number or letter.

PART II
CONSTITUTION

Powers and functions exercisable by the President and Secretary

2.—(1) Anything which must or may be done by the President (except under regulation 5(1), (2), (4) or (5) or 25(4)), may be done by a member of the chairmen's panel authorised by the President.

(2) Anything which must or may be done by the Secretary may be done by a member of the Tribunal's staff authorised by the Secretary.

Requirements for membership of lay panel

3.—(1) A person may be appointed a member of the lay panel if he satisfies the requirements of–

(a) paragraph (2);

(b) paragraphs (3) and (4); or

(c) paragraph (5).

(2) The requirements of this paragraph are–

    (a) experience in the provision of services–

        (i) which must or may be provided by local authorities under the 1989 Act or which are similar to such services;

        (ii) for vulnerable adults; or

        (iii) in a residential family centre; and

    (b) experience in relevant social work.

(3) The requirements of this paragraph are–

    (a) experience in the provision of services by a Health Authority, a Special Health Authority, a National Health Service trust or a Primary Care Trust;

    (b) experience in the provision of education in a school or in an institution within the further education sector; or

    (c) experience of being employed by a local education authority in connection with the exercise of its functions under Part I of the Education Act 1996.

(4) The requirements of this paragraph are–

    (a) experience in the conduct of disciplinary investigations;

    (b) experience as a member of an Area Child Protection Committee, or similar experience;

    (c) experience of taking part in child protection conferences or in child protection review conferences, or similar experience; or

    (d) experience in negotiating the conditions of service of employees.

(5) The requirements of this paragraph are–

    (a) experience in carrying out inspections under Part II of the 2000 Act;

    (b) experience in carrying out inspections under the Registered Homes Act 1984;

    (c) experience in carrying out inspections under the 1989 Act;

    (d) experience in managing an establishment or agency under Part II of the 2000 Act;

    (e) experience in managing a children's home under the 1989 Act;

    (f) experience in managing a nursing home, mental nursing home or residential care home under the Registered Homes Act 1984;

    (g) experience in managing the provision of local authority social services;

    (h) that the person is a registered nurse or registered medical practitioner who has experience of the provision of health care services;

    (i) experience in managing or inspecting child minding and day care provision for children under 8 years of age; or

    (j) experience in a professional, managerial or supervisory position in the provision of early childhood education or child development.

PART III
APPEALS, DETERMINATIONS AND APPLICATIONS FOR LEAVE

Procedure for appeals, determinations and applications for leave

4.—(1) In the case of an appeal under section 21 of the 2000 Act, the procedure set out in Schedule 1 shall apply.

(2) In the case of an appeal under section 79M of the 1989 Act, the procedure set out in Schedule 2 shall apply.

(3) In the case of an appeal under section 65A of the 1989 Act, the procedure set out in Schedule 3 shall apply.

(4) In the case of

    (a) an application for leave under section 4(1)(b) or (2) of the 1999 Act;

    (b) an appeal under section 4(1)(a) of the 1999 Act against a decision to include an individual in the POCA list;

    (c) an appeal under section 4(1)(b) of the 1999 Act against a decision not to remove an individual from the POCA list under section 1(3) of that Act;

    (d) a determination under section 4(2) of the 1999 Act as to whether an individual should be included in the POCA list;

    (e) an appeal under regulation 13 of the Education Regulations against a decision to give a direction under regulation 5 of those Regulations; or

    (f) an appeal under regulation 13 of the Education Regulations against a decision not to revoke or vary such a direction,

the procedure set out in Schedule 4 shall apply.

(5) In the case of–

    (a) an application for leave to the Tribunal under section 86(1)(b) or (2) of the 2000 Act;

    (b) an appeal under section 86(1)(a) of the 2000 Act against a decision to include an individual in the POVA list;

    (c) an appeal under section 86(1)(b) of the 2000 Act against a decision not to remove an individual from the POVA list; or

    (d) a determination under section 86(2) of the 2000 Act as to whether an individual should be included in the POVA list,

the procedure set out in Schedule 5 shall apply.

PART IV
CASE MANAGEMENT

Appointment of Tribunal

5.—(1) The President shall, at such time as he considers it appropriate to do so, nominate a chairman (who may be himself) and two members of the lay panel to determine the case.

(2) The President shall, at such time as he considers it appropriate to do so, nominate a chairman (who may be himself) to determine an application for leave.

(3) The President or the nominated chairman may determine any application made in relation to the case or any application for leave.

(4) The President may at any time before the hearing (or, if the case is to be determined without an oral hearing, before the case is determined) nominate from the appropriate panel another person in substitution for the chairman or other member previously nominated.

(5) The President shall nominate members of the lay panel who appear to him to have experience and qualifications relevant to the subject matter of the case.

Directions

6.—(1) If either party has requested that there shall be a preliminary hearing, or if the

President or the nominated chairman considers that a preliminary hearing is necessary, the President or the nominated chairman, as the case may be, shall fix a date for the preliminary hearing, as soon as possible after the expiry of the 5 working days referred to in paragraph 6 of Schedule 1, 2 or 3 or paragraph 9 of Schedule 4 or 5, as the case may be.

(2) At the preliminary hearing, or if a preliminary hearing is not to be held, as soon as possible after, and in any event not later than 10 working days after, the expiry of the 5 working days referred to in paragraph (1) the President or the nominated chairman–

(a) shall give directions as to the dates by which any document, witness statement or other material upon which any party is intending to rely shall be sent to the Tribunal, and, if the President or the nominated chairman considers it appropriate, to the other party;

(b) may give any other direction in exercise of his powers under this Part which he considers appropriate; and

(c) shall, where the applicant has requested that the case be determined without an oral hearing, give a direction as to the date, which shall be not less than 10 working days after the last date on which he has directed that any document, witness statement or other evidence be sent to the Tribunal, by which the parties shall send any written representations regarding their appeal to the Tribunal.

(3) The President or the nominated chairman may direct that exchange of witness statements or other material shall be simultaneous or sequential, as he considers appropriate.

(4) The Secretary shall notify the parties as soon as possible in writing of any directions the President or the nominated chairman gives in writing under paragraphs (2) and (3) above.

(5) The Secretary shall notify the parties as soon as possible, and in any event not less than 5 working days before the hearing of the date, time and place of any preliminary hearing.

(6) The parties may be represented or assisted at any preliminary hearing by any person.

Fixing and notification of hearing

7.—(1) The Secretary must, in consultation with the President or the nominated chairman, fix a date for the hearing of the case unless the applicant has requested in writing that the case be determined without a hearing.

(2) The date fixed for the hearing shall be the earliest practicable date having regard to any directions which have been made by the President or the nominated chairman with regard to the preparation of evidence but shall be no sooner than 15 working days after the latest date on which the President or the nominated chairman has directed that the evidence of the parties (including the statements of any witnesses or experts) shall be filed or exchanged.

(3) The Secretary must inform the parties in writing of the date, time and place of the hearing no less than 20 working days before the date fixed for the hearing.

(4) The Secretary may, in consultation with the President or the nominated chairman, alter the place of the hearing and, if he does, he must without delay inform the parties in writing of the alteration.

(5) Subject to paragraph (6), the President or the nominated chairman may adjourn the hearing, either on the application of either party or on his own initiative.

(6) The President or the nominated chairman shall not adjourn the hearing unless satisfied that refusing the adjournment would prevent the just disposal of the case.

(7) If the President or the nominated chairman adjourns the hearing, then the Secretary must, without delay, inform the parties in writing of the date, time and place at which the hearing will be resumed.

Multiple appeals

8.—(1) Subject to paragraphs (2) and (3), where two or more cases relate to the same person, establishment or agency, the President or the nominated chairman may, on the application of either party or on his own initiative, direct that such cases shall be heard together if he considers it appropriate to do so.

(2) Where a person ('the applicant') has by virtue of section 92(1) and (2) of the 2000 Act been included in the POVA list pursuant to a reference under section 2, 2A, or 2D of the 1999 Act or as a result of being named in a relevant inquiry within the meaning of section 2B of that Act, then subject to paragraph (4) any appeal against inclusion in the POVA list shall be joined with any appeal against inclusion in the POCA list and in that event the appeal against inclusion in the POCA list shall be heard first.

(3) Where a person ('the applicant') has by virtue of section 2C of the 1999 Act been included in the POCA list pursuant to a reference made under section 82, 83 or 84 of the 2000 Act or as a result of being named in a relevant inquiry within the meaning of section 85 of that Act, then subject to paragraph (4) any appeal against inclusion in the POCA list shall be joined with any appeal against inclusion in the POVA list and in that event the appeal against inclusion in the POVA list shall be heard first.

(4) The applicant may request the President or the nominated chairman in writing to give a direction that the appeals referred to in paragraph (2) or (3) shall be heard separately.

(5) Before making any direction under paragraph (1) the President or the nominated chairman shall—

  (a) where the direction which he proposes to give is at the request of either party, give the other party the opportunity to make written representations; or

  (b) where the direction which he proposes to give is on his own initiative, give both parties the opportunity to make written representations.

(6) In considering whether to give a direction under paragraph (1), the President or the nominated chairman shall take into account the following matters—

  (a) any written representations made by either party;

  (b) the increased cost of hearing the cases together or separately; and

  (c) any unreasonable delay in hearing any case which would be caused by hearing the appeals together or separately.

(7) In considering whether to give a direction under paragraph (4) the President or the nominated chairman shall take into account the following matters—

  (a) any representations from the applicant which show he would be significantly disadvantaged if the appeals were to be heard together;

  (b) the increased cost of hearing the appeals together or separately; and

  (c) any unreasonable delay in hearing either appeal which would be caused by hearing the appeals together or separately,

and shall give a direction that the appeals be heard separately where he is satisfied that it would be unfair in all the circumstances to hear the appeals together.

Further directions

9.—(1) The President or the nominated chairman may at any time on the application of either party or on his own initiative, vary any direction which he has given or give any further direction in exercise of any of his powers under this Part as he considers appropriate.

(2) Before making any further direction, or varying any direction under paragraph (1)—

(a) the President or the nominated chairman shall, where the variation or further direction which he proposes to give–
  (i) is at the request of either party, give the other party the opportunity to make written representations; or
  (ii) is on his own initiative, give both parties the opportunity to make written representations;
(b) the President or the nominated chairman may direct that there shall be a preliminary hearing in relation to any proposed variation or further direction if he considers it appropriate or if a preliminary hearing has been requested by either party.

Unless orders

10.—(1) The President or the nominated chairman may at any time make an order to the effect that, unless the party to whom the order is addressed takes a step specified in the order within the period specified in the order, the case may be determined in favour of the other party.

(2) The Secretary shall give written notification of the order to the party to whom it is addressed and to the other party and shall inform him of the effect of paragraph (3).

(3) If a party fails to comply with an order addressed to him under this regulation, the President or the nominated chairman may determine the case in favour of the other party.

Copies of documents

11.—(1) The President or the nominated chairman may give a direction as to the number of copies of relevant material, which each party must send to the Tribunal and relevant material means, all documents, witness statements and other material on which the parties intend to rely or which they have been ordered by the President or the nominated chairman to send to the Secretary under this Part.

(2) The President or the nominated chairman may, if he considers it appropriate to do so, direct the form and order in which relevant material shall be supplied to the Tribunal.

Disclosure of information and documents

12.—(1) Subject to paragraphs (3) to (5), the President or the nominated chairman may give directions–
  (a) requiring a party to send to the Secretary any document or other material which he considers may assist the Tribunal in determining the case and which that party is able to send, and the Secretary shall take such steps as the President or the nominated chairman may direct, to supply copies of any information or document obtained under this paragraph to the other party;
  (b) granting to a party the right to inspect and take copies of any document or other material which it is in the power of the other party to disclose, and appointing the date, time and place at which any such inspection and copying is to be done.

(2) Subject to paragraphs (3) to (5), the President or the nominated chairman may give a direction on the application of either party, requiring a person who is not a party to the proceedings to disclose any document or other material to the party making the application, if he is satisfied that–
  (a) the documents or other material sought are likely to support the applicant's case or adversely affect the case of the other party;
  (b) it is within the power of the person subject to the direction to disclose any document or other material; and

(c) disclosure is necessary for the fair determination of the case.

(3) It shall be a condition of the supply of any document or material under paragraph (1) or (2) that a party shall use it only for the purpose of the proceedings.

(4) Paragraphs (1) and (2) do not apply in relation to any document or material which the party could not be compelled to produce in legal proceedings in a county court.

(5) Before making a direction under paragraph (1) or (2), the President or the nominated chairman shall take into account the need to protect any matter which relates to intimate personal or financial circumstances, is commercially sensitive, or was communicated or obtained in confidence.

Expert evidence

13.—(1) The President or the nominated chairman may, if he thinks that any question arises in relation to the case on which it would be desirable for the Tribunal to have the assistance of an expert, appoint a person having appropriate qualifications to enquire into and report on the matter.

(2) The Secretary must supply the parties with a copy of any written report received under paragraph (1) in advance of the hearing (or, if the case is to be determined without an oral hearing, before the case is determined).

(3) If the President or the nominated chairman sees fit, he may direct that the expert shall attend the hearing, and give evidence.

(4) The Tribunal shall pay such reasonable fees as the President or the nominated chairman may determine to any person appointed under this regulation.

Evidence of witnesses

14.—(1) The President or the nominated chairman may direct that the parties send to each other by the date specified in the direction a copy of a witness statement in respect of each witness on whose evidence he wishes to rely.

(2) A witness statement must contain the words 'I believe that the facts stated in this witness statement are true', and be signed by the person who makes it.

(3) The President or the nominated chairman (before the hearing or, if the case is to be determined without an oral hearing, before the case is determined) or the Tribunal may direct that a document or the evidence of any witness other than the applicant shall be excluded from consideration because–

(a) it would be unfair in all the circumstances to consider it;

(b) the party wishing to rely on the document or evidence has failed to submit the document, or witness statement containing it, in compliance with any direction; or

(c) it would not assist the Tribunal in determining the case.

(4) Instead of excluding evidence under this regulation the President or the nominated chairman or the Tribunal may permit it to be considered on such terms as he or it thinks fit, including, subject to regulation 24, the making of a costs order.

(5) The President or the nominated chairman may direct that a witness (other than the applicant) shall not give oral evidence.

Withholding medical report from disclosure in exceptional circumstances

15.—(1) This regulation applies where the respondent wishes the Tribunal, in determining the case, to consider a medical report and the President or the nominated chairman is satisfied–

(a) that disclosure to the applicant of all or any part of the contents of the report would be so harmful to his health or welfare that it would be wrong to disclose it to him; and

(b) that in all the circumstances it would not be unfair if the report or that part of it is considered by the Tribunal.

(2) The President or the nominated chairman may appoint a person having appropriate skills or experience to–

(a) assess whether disclosure of the report to the applicant would be harmful to the applicant's health or welfare; and

(b) report on the matter to the President or the nominated chairman.

(3) The President or the nominated chairman may direct that–

(a) the report may be considered by the Tribunal; and

(b) all or any part of its contents must not be disclosed to the applicant.

Summoning of witnesses

16.—(1) The President or the nominated chairman may, on the application of either party or on his own initiative, issue a summons requiring any person–

(a) to attend as a witness at the hearing, at the date, time and place set out in the summons; and

(b) to answer any questions or produce any documents or other material in his possession or under his control which relate to any matter in question in the case.

(2) The summons must–

(a) explain that it is an offence under section 9(5)(c) of the 1999 Act to fail, without reasonable excuse, to comply with it; and

(b) explain the right to apply under this regulation to have it varied or set aside.

(3) A person summoned under this regulation may apply in writing to the Secretary for the summons to be varied or set aside by the President or the nominated chairman, and–

(a) the President or the nominated chairman may do so if he sees fit; and

(b) the Secretary must notify him and the parties in writing of the decision.

(4) No person shall be required to attend, answer questions or produce any document in obedience to a summons issued under this regulation unless–

(a) he has been given at least 5 working days' notice of the hearing; and

(b) the necessary expenses of his attendance are paid or tendered to him by the party who requested his attendance or by the Tribunal, as the President or the nominated chairman shall direct.

(5) No person shall be required under this regulation to give any evidence or produce any document or other material that he could not be required to produce in legal proceedings in a county court.

Child and vulnerable adult witnesses

17.—(1) A child shall only give evidence in person where–

(a) the President or the nominated chairman has given the parties an opportunity to make written representations before the hearing or representations at the hearing; and

(b) having regard to all the available evidence, and the representations of the parties, the President or the nominated chairman considers that the welfare of the child will not be prejudiced by so doing.

(2) If he directs that a child shall give evidence in person, the President or the nominated chairman shall–

(a) secure that any arrangements he considers appropriate (such as the use of a video link) are made to safeguard the welfare of the child; and

(b) appoint for the purpose of the hearing a person with appropriate skills or experience in facilitating the giving of evidence by children.

(3) Where the President or the nominated chairman believes that it might not be in the best interests of a vulnerable adult for the vulnerable adult to give oral evidence to the Tribunal, the President or the nominated chairman shall—

(a) give the parties the opportunity to make written representations before the hearing or representations at the hearing; and

(b) having regard to all the available evidence, including any written representations made by the parties consider whether it would prejudice the vulnerable adult's welfare to give oral evidence to the Tribunal—

(i) in any circumstances; or

(ii) otherwise than in accordance with paragraph (5).

(4) If the President or the nominated chairman considers that—

(a) it would prejudice the vulnerable adult's welfare to give oral evidence to the Tribunal in any circumstances, he shall direct that the vulnerable adult shall not do so; or

(b) it would prejudice the vulnerable adult's welfare to give oral evidence to the Tribunal otherwise than in accordance with paragraph (5) he shall direct that paragraph (5) shall apply in relation to the vulnerable adult.

(5) If he directs that this paragraph shall apply in relation to the vulnerable adult, the President or the nominated chairman shall—

(a) secure that any arrangements he considers appropriate (such as the use of a video link) are made to safeguard the welfare of the vulnerable adult; and

(b) appoint for the purpose of the hearing a person with appropriate skills or experience in facilitating the giving of evidence by vulnerable adults.

(6) The President or the nominated chairman shall pay such fees as he may determine to any person appointed under this regulation.

Restricted reporting orders

18.—(1) If it appears appropriate to do so, the President or the nominated chairman (or, at the hearing, the Tribunal) may make a restricted reporting order.

(2) A restricted reporting order is an order prohibiting the publication (including by electronic means) in a written publication available to the public, or the inclusion in a relevant programme for reception in England and Wales, of any matter likely to lead members of the public to identify the applicant, any child, any vulnerable adult or any other person who the President or the nominated chairman or the Tribunal considers should not be identified.

(3) An order that may be made under this regulation may be made in respect of a limited period and may be varied or revoked by the President or the nominated chairman before the hearing (or by the Tribunal at the hearing).

Exclusion of press and public

19.—(1) Where paragraph (2) applies, the President or the nominated chairman (or, at the hearing, the Tribunal) may on his (or its) own initiative, or on a written request by either party that the hearing or any part of it should be conducted in private, direct that—

(a) any member of the public specified in the direction;

    (b) members of the public generally; or

    (c) members of the press and members of the public,

be excluded from all or part of the hearing.

    (2) This paragraph applies where the President or the nominated chairman (or, at the hearing, the Tribunal) is satisfied that a direction under paragraph (1) is necessary in order to–

    (a) safeguard the welfare of any child or vulnerable adult;

    (b) protect a person's private life; or

    (c) avoid the risk of injustice in any legal proceedings.

PART V
HEARING

Procedure at the hearing

20.—(1) The Tribunal may regulate its own procedure.

    (2) At the beginning of the hearing the chairman must explain the order of proceedings which the Tribunal proposes to adopt.

    (3) The parties may be represented or assisted at the hearing by any person.

    (4) If either party fails to attend or be represented at the hearing, the Tribunal may hear and determine the case in that party's absence.

Hearing to be in public

21.—(1) The hearing must be in public except in so far as any person is excluded under regulation 19.

    (2) Whether or not the hearing is held in public–

    (a) a member of the Council on Tribunals;

    (b) the President;

    (c) the clerk; and

    (d) any person whom the President or the nominated chairman permits to be present in order to assist the Tribunal,

are entitled to attend the hearing.

    (3) Whether or not the hearing is held in public–

    (a) a member of the Council on Tribunals; and

    (b) the President,

may remain present during the Tribunal's deliberations, but must not take part in the deliberations.

Evidence

22.—(1) The Tribunal may consider any evidence, whether or not such evidence would be admissible in a court of law.

    (2) The applicant has the right to give evidence at the hearing in person, and any other witness may do so unless the President or the nominated chairman has directed otherwise.

    (3) No child may be asked any question except by the Tribunal or a person appointed under regulation 17(2).

    (4) Where a direction has been made under regulation 17 that paragraph (5) of that regulation shall apply to any vulnerable adult, the vulnerable adult may not be asked any question except by the Tribunal or a person appointed under regulation 17(5).

(5) The Tribunal may require any witness to give evidence on oath or affirmation which may be administered for the purpose by the chairman or the clerk.

PART VI
DECISION

The decision

23.—(1) The Tribunal's decision may be taken by a majority and the decision shall record whether it was unanimous or taken by a majority.

(2) The decision may be made and announced at the end of the hearing or reserved, and in any event, whether there has been a hearing or not, the decision must be recorded without delay in a document signed and dated by the chairman (or if as a result of his death or incapacity he is unable to sign, or if he ceases to be a member of the chairman's panel, by another member of the Tribunal).

(3) The document mentioned in paragraph (2) must also state—

(a) the reasons for the decision; and

(b) what, if any, order the Tribunal has made as a result of its decision.

(4) The Secretary must, as soon as reasonably possible, send to each party a copy of the document mentioned in paragraph (2) and a notice explaining to the parties any right of appeal which they may have against the Tribunal's decision and the right to apply for a review of the Tribunal's decision.

(5) Where the appeal was against an order made by a justice of the peace under section 20 of the 2000 Act or section 79K of the 1989 Act, the Secretary must, as soon as reasonably practicable, send a copy of the document mentioned in paragraph (2) to the justice of the peace who made the order.

(6) Except where a decision is announced at the end of the hearing, the decision shall be treated as having been made on the day on which a copy of the document mentioned in paragraph (2) is sent to the applicant.

(7) The decision shall be entered in the records.

Costs

24.—(1) Subject to regulation 31 and to paragraph (2) below, if in the opinion of the Tribunal a party has acted unreasonably in bringing or conducting the proceedings, it may make an order (a 'costs order') requiring that party ('the paying party') to make a payment to the other party ('the receiving party') to cover costs incurred by the receiving party.

(2) Before making a costs order against a party, the Tribunal must—

(a) invite the receiving party to provide to the Tribunal a schedule of costs incurred by him in respect of the proceedings; and

(b) invite representations from the paying party and consider any representations he makes, consider whether he is able to comply with such an order and consider any relevant written information which he has provided.

(3) When making a costs order, the Tribunal must—

(a) order the payment of any sum which the parties have agreed should be paid;

(b) order the payment of any sum which it considers appropriate having considered any representations the parties may make; or

(c) order the payment of the whole or part of the costs incurred by the receiving party in connection with the proceedings as assessed.

(4) Any costs required by an order under this regulation to be assessed may be assessed in a county court according to such rules applicable to proceedings in a county court as shall be directed in the order.

(5) A costs order may, by leave of a county court, be enforced in the same manner as a judgment or order of that court to the same effect.

Review of the Tribunal's decision

25.—(1) A party may apply to the President for the Tribunal's decision to be reviewed on the grounds that–

(a) it was wrongly made as a result of an error on the part of the Tribunal staff;

(b) a party, who was entitled to be heard at a hearing but failed to appear or to be represented, had good and sufficient reason for failing to appear; or

(c) there was an obvious error in the decision.

(2) An application under this regulation must–

(a) be made not later than ten working days after the date on which the decision was sent to the party applying for the Tribunal's decision to be reviewed; and

(b) must be in writing stating the grounds in full.

(3) An application under this regulation may be refused by the President, or by the chairman of the Tribunal which decided the case, if in his opinion it has no reasonable prospect of success.

(4) Unless an application under this regulation is refused under paragraph (3), it shall be determined, after the parties have had an opportunity to be heard, by the Tribunal which decided the case or, where that is not practicable, by another Tribunal appointed by the President.

(5) The Tribunal may on its own initiative propose to review its decision on any of the grounds referred to in paragraph (1) above, in which case–

(a) the Secretary shall serve notice on the parties not later than ten working days after the date on which the decision was sent to them; and

(b) the parties shall have an opportunity to be heard.

(6) If, on the application of a party or on its own initiative the Tribunal is satisfied as to any of the grounds referred to in paragraph (1)–

(a) it shall order that the whole or a specified part of the decision be reviewed; and

(b) it may give directions to be complied with before or after the hearing of the review.

(7) The power to give directions under paragraph (6) includes a power to give a direction requiring a party to provide such particulars, evidence or statements as may reasonably be required for the determination of the review.

Powers of Tribunal on review

26.—(1) The Tribunal may, having reviewed all or part of a decision–

(a) set aside or vary the decision by certificate signed by the chairman (or if as a result of his death or incapacity he is unable to sign, or if he ceases to be a member of the chairmen's panel, by another member of the Tribunal); and

(b) substitute such other decision as it thinks fit or order a rehearing before the same or a differently constituted Tribunal.

(2) If any decision is set aside or varied (whether as a result of a review or by order of the

High Court), the Secretary shall alter the relevant entry in the records to conform to the chairman's certificate or the order of the High Court and shall notify the parties accordingly.

(3) Any decision of the Tribunal under this regulation may be taken by a majority and the decision shall record whether it was unanimous or taken by a majority.

Publication

27.—(1) The President must make such arrangements as he considers appropriate for the publication of Tribunal decisions.

(2) Decisions may be published electronically.

(3) The decision may be published in an edited form, or subject to any deletions, if the President or the nominated chairman considers it appears appropriate bearing in mind–

    (a) the need to safeguard the welfare of any child or vulnerable adult;

    (b) the need to protect the private life of any person;

    (c) any representations on the matter which either party has provided in writing;

    (d) the effect of any subsisting restricted reporting order; and

    (e) the effect of any direction under regulation 15.

PART VII
SUPPLEMENTARY

Method of sending documents

28.—(1) Any document may be sent to the Secretary by post, by fax, electronically or through a document exchange, unless the President or the nominated chairman directs otherwise.

(2) Any notice or document which these Regulations authorise or require the Secretary to send to a party shall be sent–

    a) by first-class post to the address given for the purpose by that party in accordance with these Regulations;

    (b) by fax or electronically to a number or address given by that party for the purpose; or

    (c) where the party has given for the purpose an address which includes a numbered box number at a document exchange, by leaving the notice or document addressed to that numbered box at that document exchange or at a document exchange which transmits documents on every working day to that exchange.

(3) If a notice or document cannot be sent to a party in accordance with paragraph (2), the President or the nominated chairman may dispense with service of it or direct that it be served on that party in such manner as he thinks appropriate.

(4) Any notice or document sent by the Secretary to a party in accordance with these Regulations shall be taken to have been received–

    (a) if sent by post and not returned, on the second working day after it was posted;

    (b) if sent by fax or electronically, unless the Secretary has been notified that the transmission has been unsuccessful, on the next working day after it was sent;

    (c) if left at a document exchange in accordance with paragraph (2), on the second working day after it was left; and

    (d) if served in accordance with a direction under paragraph (3), on the next working day after it was so served.

Irregularities

29.—(1) An irregularity resulting from failure to comply with any provision of these Regulations or any direction given in accordance with them before the Tribunal has reached its decision shall not of itself render the proceedings void.

(2) Where any irregularity comes to the attention of the President or the nominated chair-man (before the hearing) or the Tribunal he or it may and, if it appears that any person may have been prejudiced by the irregularity, shall, before reaching a decision, give such directions as he or it thinks just to cure or waive the irregularity.

(3) Clerical mistakes in any document recording the decision of the Tribunal or a direction or decision of the President or the nominated chairman, or errors arising in such documents from accidental slips or omissions, may at any time be corrected by the chairman or, as the case may be, the President, or nominated chairman by means of a certificate signed by him.

(4) The Secretary shall as soon as practicable where a document is corrected in accordance with paragraph (3) send the parties a copy of any corrected document together with reasons for the decision to correct the document.

Application on behalf of person under a disability

30.—(1) A person may, by writing to the Secretary, request authorisation by the President or the nominated chairman to make any application to the Tribunal on behalf of any person who is prevented by mental or physical infirmity from acting on his own behalf.

(2) A person acting in accordance with an authorisation under this regulation may on behalf of the other person take any step or do anything which that person is required or permitted to do under these Regulations, subject to any conditions which the President or the nominated chairman may impose.

Death of applicant

31. If the applicant dies, before the case or application for leave is determined, the President or the nominated chairman may–

    (a) strike out the case or application for leave in so far as it relates to that individual without making a costs order;

    (b) appoint such person as he thinks fit to proceed with the appeal in the place of the deceased applicant.

Amendment of appeal, application for leave or response

32.—(1) The applicant may amend the reasons he gives in support of the case or application for leave as the case may be, but only with the leave of the President or the nominated chairman (or at the hearing, with the leave of the Tribunal).

(2) The respondent may amend the reasons he gives for opposing the applicant's case or application for leave, as the case may be, but only with the leave of the President or the nominated chairman (or at the hearing, with the leave of the Tribunal).

(3) Where the President, the nominated chairman or Tribunal gives leave to either party to amend the reasons given in support of his case, he may do so on such terms as he thinks fit (including, subject to regulation 24, the making of a costs order).

Withdrawal of proceedings or opposition to proceedings

33.—(1) If the applicant at any time notifies the Secretary in writing, or states at a hearing, that he no longer wishes to pursue the proceedings, the President or the nominated chairman (or at the hearing, the Tribunal) must dismiss the proceedings, and may, subject to regulation 24(2) and (3) make a costs order.

(2) If the respondent notifies the Secretary in writing, or states at a hearing, that he does not oppose or no longer opposes the proceedings, the President (or at the hearing, the Tribunal)–

    (a) must without delay determine the case or, as the case may be, the application for leave in the applicant's favour;

    (b) subject to regulation 24(2) and (3) may make a costs order; and

    (c) must consider making one.

Proof of documents and certification of decisions

34.—(1) A document purporting to be issued by the Secretary shall be taken to have been so issued, unless the contrary is proved.

(2) A document purporting to be certified by the Secretary to be a true copy of a document containing–

    (a) a decision of the Tribunal; or

    (b) an order of the President or the nominated chairman or of the Tribunal,

shall be sufficient evidence of the matters contained in it, unless the contrary is proved.

Time

35.—(1) The President or the nominated chairman may extend any time limit mentioned in these Regulations if in the circumstances–

    (a) it would be unreasonable to expect it to be, or to have been, complied with; and

    (b) it would be unfair not to extend it.

(2) Where the time prescribed by these Regulations, or specified in any direction given by the President or the nominated chairman, for taking any step expires on a day which is not a working day, the step must be treated as having been done in time if it is done on the next working day.

(3) This regulation does not apply to the time limits provided for initiating an appeal in paragraph 1 of Schedule 1 and paragraph 1 of Schedule 2.

PART VIII
MISCELLANEOUS

Revocation

36.—(1) The Protection of Children Act Tribunal Regulations 2000 ('the 2000 Regulations') are hereby revoked.

(2) Any application or appeal which–

    (a) was made to the Tribunal under the 2000 Regulations before 1st April 2002; and

    (b) the Tribunal has not determined before that date,

shall for the purposes of these Regulations be treated as having been made to the Tribunal under these Regulations.

(3) Any direction or notice given, or thing done, by the Tribunal before 1st April 2002 shall for the purposes of these Regulations be treated as having been given or done by the Tribunal under these Regulations.

SCHEDULE 1   Regulation 4(1)
APPEAL UNDER SECTION 21 OF THE 2000 ACT AGAINST A DECISION OF
THE REGISTRATION AUTHORITY OR AN ORDER OF A JUSTICE OF THE
PEACE

Initiating an appeal

1.—(1) A person who wishes to appeal to the Tribunal under section 21 of the 2000 Act against a decision of the registration authority under Part II of the 2000 Act, or an order made by a justice of the peace under section 20 of that Act, must do so by application in writing to the Secretary.

(2) An application under this paragraph may be made on the application form available from the Secretary.

(3) An application under this paragraph must–

   (a) give the applicant's name and full postal address, if the applicant is an individual his date of birth and, if the applicant is a company, the address of its registered office;

   (b) give the name, address and profession of the person (if any) representing the applicant;

   (c) give the address within the United Kingdom to which the Secretary should send documents concerning the appeal;

   (d) give, where these are available, the applicant's telephone number, fax number and e-mail address and those of the applicant's representative;

   (e) identify the decision or order against which the appeal is brought and give particulars of–

   (i) whether the appeal is against a refusal of registration, an imposition or variation of conditions of registration, a refusal to remove or vary any condition, or a cancellation of registration;

   (ii) whether the appeal is against a decision of the registration authority or an order made by a justice of the peace;

   (iii) where the appeal is in respect of a cancellation of registration, whether the establishment or agency in respect of which the appeal is made remains open and, in the case of an establishment, the number of residents in that establishment;

   (f) give a short statement of the grounds of appeal; and

   (g) be signed and dated by the applicant.

Acknowledgement and notification of application

2.—(1) On receiving an application, made within the period for bringing an appeal specified in section 21 of the 2000 Act, the Secretary must–

   (a) immediately send an acknowledgement of its receipt to the applicant; and

   (b) enter particulars of the appeal, and the date of its receipt in the records and send a copy of it, together with any documents supplied by the applicant in support of it, to the respondent.

(2) If in the Secretary's opinion there is an obvious error in the application–

   (a) he may correct it;

   (b) he must notify the applicant in writing that he has done so; and

   (c) unless, within five working days of receipt of notification under head (b) of this sub-paragraph the applicant notifies the Secretary in writing that he objects to the correction, the application shall be amended accordingly.

Response to application
3.—(1) The Secretary must send the information provided by the applicant under paragraph 1 to the respondent together with a request that it respond to the application within 20 working days of receiving it.

(2) If the respondent fails to respond as requested, it shall not be entitled to take any further part in the proceedings.

(3) The response must–
  (a) acknowledge that the respondent has received a copy of the application;
  (b) indicate whether or not the respondent opposes it, and if it does, give the reasons why it opposes the application;
  (c) provide the following information and documents–
  (i) the name, address and profession of the person (if any) representing the respondent and whether the Secretary should send documents concerning the appeal to the representative rather than to the respondent; and
  (ii) in the case of an appeal under section 21(1)(a) of the 2000 Act, a copy of the written notice of the decision (which is the subject of the appeal) served under section 19(3) of that Act, and the reasons for the decision; or
  (iii) in the case of an appeal under section 21(1)(b) of the 2000 Act, a copy of the order made by the justice of the peace.

(4) The Secretary must without delay send to the applicant a copy of the response and the information and documents provided with it.

Misconceived appeals etc.
4.—(1) The President or the nominated chairman may at any time strike out the appeal on the grounds that–
  (a) it is made otherwise than in accordance with paragraph 1;
  (b) it is outside the jurisdiction of the Tribunal or is otherwise misconceived; or
  (c) it is frivolous or vexatious.

(2) Before striking out an appeal under this paragraph, the President or the nominated chairman must–
  (a) invite the parties to make representations on the matter within such period as he may direct;
  (b) if within the period specified in the direction the applicant so requests in writing, afford the parties an opportunity to make oral representations;
  (c) consider any representations the parties may make.

Further information to be sent by the applicant and respondent
5.—(1) As soon as the respondent has provided the information set out in paragraph 3, the Secretary must write to each party requesting that he send to the Secretary within 15 working days after the date on which he receives the Secretary's letter the following information–
  (a) the name of any witness whose evidence the party wishes the Tribunal to consider (and whether the party may wish the Tribunal to consider additional witness evidence from a witness whose name is not yet known) and the nature of that evidence;

(b) whether the party wishes the President or the nominated chairman to give any directions or exercise any of his powers under Part IV of these Regulations;

(c) whether the party wishes there to be a preliminary hearing with regard to directions;

(d) a provisional estimate of the time the party considers will be required to present his case;

(e) the earliest date by which the party considers he would be able to prepare his case for hearing; and

(f) in the case of the applicant, whether he wishes his appeal to be determined without a hearing.

(2) Once the Secretary has received the information referred to in sub-paragraph (1) from both parties, he must without delay send a copy of the information supplied by the applicant to the respondent and that supplied by the respondent to the applicant.

Changes to further information supplied to the Tribunal

6.—(1) Either party, within 5 working days of receiving the further information in respect of the other party from the Secretary, may ask the Secretary in writing to amend or add to any of the information given under paragraph 5(1).

(2) If the Secretary receives any further information under sub-paragraph (1) from either party he must, without delay, send a copy of it to the other party.

SCHEDULE 2   Regulation 4(2)

APPEAL UNDER SECTION 79M OF THE 1989 ACT AGAINST A DECISION OF THE REGISTRATION AUTHORITY OR AN ORDER OF A JUSTICE OF THE PEACE

Initiating an appeal

1.—(1) A person who wishes to appeal to the Tribunal under section 79M of the 1989 Act, against the taking of any step mentioned in section 79L(1), or an order under section 79K, of that Act, must do so by application in writing to the Secretary.

(2) An application under this paragraph must be received by the Secretary no later than 28 days after service on the applicant of notice of the decision to take the step in question or the order.

(3) An application under this paragraph may be made on the application form available from the Secretary.

(4) An application under this paragraph must–

(a) give the applicant's name and full postal address, if the applicant is an individual his date of birth and, if the applicant is a company, the address of its registered office;

(b) give the name, address and profession of the person (if any) representing the applicant;

(c) give the address within the United Kingdom to which the Secretary should send documents concerning the appeal;

(d) give, where these are available, the applicant's telephone number, fax number and e-mail address and those of the applicant's representative;

(e) identify the decision against which the appeal is brought and give particulars of–

    (i) whether the appeal is against the refusal or cancellation of registration, or the imposi-
tion, removal or variation of any condition of registration, or a refusal to remove or
vary any condition;

    (ii) whether the appeal is against a decision of the registration authority or a justice of the
peace;

    (f) give a short statement of the grounds of appeal; and

    g) be signed and dated by the applicant.

Acknowledgement and notification of application

2.—(1) On receiving an application, the Secretary must—

    (a) immediately send an acknowledgement of its receipt to the applicant;

    (b) enter particulars of the appeal, and the date of its receipt in the records and send a
copy of it, together with any documents supplied by the applicant in support of it,
to the respondent.

(2) If in the Secretary's opinion there is an obvious error in the application—

    (a) he may correct it;

    (b) he must notify the applicant in writing that he has done so; and

    (c) unless within five working days of receipt of notification under head (b) of this
sub-paragraph the applicant notifies him in writing that he objects to the correction,
the application shall be amended accordingly.

Response to application

3.—(1) The Secretary must send the information provided by the applicant under paragraph 1
to the respondent together with a request that he respond to the application within 20 working
days of receiving it.

(2) If the respondent fails to respond as directed, he shall not be entitled to take any
further part in the proceedings.

(3) The response must—

    (a) acknowledge that the respondent has received a copy of the application;

    (b) indicate whether or not the respondent opposes it, and if he does, give the reasons
why he opposes the application;

    (c) provide the following information and documents—

    (i) the name, address and profession of the person (if any) representing the respondent
and whether the Secretary should send documents concerning the appeal to the representative rather than to the respondent; and

    (ii) a copy of the written notice of the decision to take the step in question (which is the
subject of the appeal) served under section 79L of the 1989 Act, and the reasons for
the decision; or

    (iii) where the appeal is against an order of a justice of the peace under section 79K of the
1989 Act, a copy of the order and a copy of the statement referred to in subsection
(5)(b) of that section.

(4) The Secretary must without delay send to the applicant a copy of the response and the
information and documents provided with it.

Misconceived appeals etc.

4.—(1) The President or the nominated chairman may at any time strike out the appeal on the
grounds that—

(a) it is made otherwise than in accordance with paragraph 1;

(b) it is outside the jurisdiction of the Tribunal or is otherwise misconceived; or

(c) it is frivolous or vexatious.

(2) Before striking out an appeal under this paragraph, the President or the nominated chairman must–

(a) invite the parties to make representations on the matter within such period as he may direct;

(b) if within the period specified in the direction the applicant so requests in writing, afford the parties an opportunity to make oral representations;

(c) consider any representations the parties may make.

Further information to be sent by the applicant and respondent

5.—(1) As soon as the respondent has provided the information set out in paragraph 3, the Secretary must write to each party requesting that he send to the Secretary, within 15 working days after the date on which he receives the Secretary's letter, the following information–

(a) the name of any witness whose evidence the party wishes the Tribunal to consider (and whether the party may wish the Tribunal to consider additional witness evidence where the name of the party is not yet known) and the nature of that evidence;

(b) whether the party wishes the President to give any directions or exercise any of his powers under Part IV of these Regulations;

(c) whether the party wishes there to be a preliminary hearing with regard to directions;

(d) a provisional estimate of the time the party considers will be required to present his case;

(e) the earliest date by which the party considers he would be able to prepare his case for hearing; and

(f) in the case of the applicant, whether he wishes his appeal to be determined without a hearing.

(2) Once the Secretary has received the information referred to in sub-paragraph (1) from both parties, he must without delay send a copy of the information supplied by the applicant to the respondent and that supplied by the respondent to the applicant.

Changes to further information supplied to the Tribunal

6.—(1) Either party, within 5 working days of receiving the further information in respect of the other party from the Secretary, may ask the Secretary in writing to amend or add to any of the information given under paragraph 5(1).

(2) If the Secretary receives any further information under sub-paragraph (1) from either party he must, without delay, send a copy of it to the other party.

SCHEDULE 3   Regulation 4(3)

APPEAL UNDER SECTION 65A OF THE 1989 ACT AGAINST A DECISION OF THE APPROPRIATE AUTHORITY REFUSING TO GIVE CONSENT UNDER SECTION 65 OF THAT ACT

Initiating an appeal

1.—(1) A person who wishes to appeal to the Tribunal under section 65A of the 1989 Act against a decision of the appropriate authority must do so by application in writing to the Secretary.

(2) An application under this paragraph must be received by the Secretary no later than the first working day after the expiry of three months from the date of the letter informing the applicant of the decision.

(3) An application under this paragraph may be made on the application form available from the Secretary.

(4) An application under this paragraph must–

(a) give the applicant's name and full postal address, if the applicant is an individual his date of birth and, if the applicant is a company, the address of its registered office;

(b) give the name, address and profession of the person (if any) representing the applicant;

(c) give the address within the United Kingdom to which the Secretary should send documents concerning the appeal;

(d) give, where these are available, the applicant's telephone number, fax number and e-mail address and those of the applicant's representative;

(e) give sufficient information concerning the decision appealed against to make it clear whether it falls within section 65(1) or (2) of the 1989 Act;

(f) give a short statement of the grounds of appeal; and

(g) be signed and dated by the applicant.

Acknowledgement and notification of application

2.—(1) On receiving an application, the Secretary must–

(a) immediately send an acknowledgement of its receipt to the applicant; and

(b) subject to the following provisions of this paragraph, enter particulars of the appeal and the date of its receipt in the records and send a copy of it, together with any documents supplied by the applicant in support of it, to the respondent.

(2) If the President is of the opinion that the applicant is asking the Tribunal to do something which it cannot do, he may notify the applicant in writing–

(a) of the reasons for his opinion; and

(b) that the appeal will not be entered in the records unless within five working days the applicant notifies the President in writing that he wishes to proceed with it.

(3) If in the Secretary's opinion there is an obvious error in the application–

(a) he may correct it;

(b) he must notify the applicant accordingly; and

(c) unless within five working days of receipt of notification under heading (b) of this sub-paragraph the applicant notifies the Secretary in writing that he objects to the correction, the application shall be amended accordingly.

Response to application

3.—(1) The Secretary must send the information provided by the applicant under paragraph 1 to the respondent together with a request that it respond to the application within 20 working days of receiving it.

(2) If the respondent fails to respond as requested it shall not be entitled to take any further part in the proceedings.

(3) The response must–

(a) acknowledge that the respondent has received a copy of the application;

(b) indicate whether or not it opposes it, and if it does, why; and

(c) provide the following information and documents–

(i) the name, address and profession of the person (if any) representing the respondent and whether the Secretary should send documents concerning the appeal to the representative rather than to the respondent; and

(ii) a copy of the written notice of the decision which is the subject of the appeal and the reasons for the decision.

(4) The Secretary must without delay send to the applicant a copy of the response and the information and documents provided with it.

Misconceived appeals etc.

4.—(1) The President or the nominated chairman may at any time strike out the appeal on the grounds that–

(a) it is made otherwise than in accordance with paragraph 1;

(b) it is outside the jurisdiction of the Tribunal or is otherwise misconceived; or

(c) it is frivolous or vexatious.

(2) Before striking out an appeal under this paragraph, the President or the nominated chairman must–

(a) invite the parties to make representations on the matter within such period as he may direct;

(b) if within the period specified in the direction the applicant so requests in writing, afford the parties an opportunity to make oral representations; and

(c) consider any representations the parties may make.

Further information to be sent by the applicant and respondent

5.—(1) As soon as the respondent has provided the information set out in paragraph 3 the Secretary must write to each party requesting that he send to the Secretary within 15 working days after the date on which he receives the Secretary's letter the following information–

(a) the name of any witness whose evidence the party wishes the Tribunal to consider (and whether the party may wish the Tribunal to consider additional witness evidence from a witness whose name is not yet known) and the nature of that evidence;

(b) whether the party wishes the President or the nominated chairman to give any directions or exercise any of his powers under Part IV of these Regulations;

(c) whether the party wishes there to be a preliminary hearing with regard to directions;

(d) a provisional estimate of the time the party considers will be required to present his case;

(e) the earliest date by which the party considers he would be able to prepare his case for hearing; and

(f) in the case of the applicant, whether he wishes his appeal to be determined without a hearing.

(2) Once the Secretary has received the information referred to in sub-paragraph (1) from both parties, he must without delay send a copy of the information supplied by the applicant to the respondent and that supplied by the respondent to the applicant.

Changes to further information supplied to the Tribunal

6.—(1) Either party, within 5 working days of receiving the further information in respect of the other party from the Secretary, may ask the Secretary in writing to amend or add to any of the information given under paragraph 5(1).

(2) If the Secretary receives any further information under sub-paragraph (1) from either party he must, without delay, send a copy of it to the other party.

SCHEDULE 4   Regulation 4(4)

APPEALS AND APPLICATIONS FOR LEAVE TO APPEAL UNDER SECTION 4 OF THE 1999 ACT AND APPEALS UNDER REGULATION 13 OF THE EDUCATION REGULATIONS

Initiating an appeal

1.—(1) A person who wishes to appeal to the Tribunal–

(a) under section 4(1)(a) of the 1999 Act, against a decision to include him in the POCA list;

(b) under regulation 13 of the Education Regulations, against a decision to give a direction under regulation 5 of those Regulations; or

(c) under regulation 13 of the Education Regulations, against a decision not to revoke or vary such a direction,

must do so by application in writing to the Secretary.

(2) An application under this paragraph must be received by the Secretary no later than the first working day after the expiry of three months from the date of the letter informing the applicant of the decision.

(3) An application under this paragraph may be made on the application form available from the Secretary.

(4) An application under this paragraph must–

(a) give the applicant's name, date of birth and full postal address;

(b) give sufficient information concerning the decision appealed against to make it clear whether it falls within sub-paragraph (1)(a), (1)(b) or (1)(c);

(c) give the reasons why the applicant believes he should not be included in the POCA list, or why he believes the direction should not have been given, or why that direction should be revoked or varied, as the case may be;

(d) give the name, address and profession of the person (if any) representing the applicant;

(e) give the address within the United Kingdom to which the Secretary should send documents concerning the appeal;

(f) give, where these are available, the applicant's telephone number, fax number and e-mail address and those of the applicant's representative; and

(g) be signed and dated by the applicant.

Applying for leave

2.—(1) An application for leave–

(a) to appeal to the Tribunal under section 4(1)(b) of the 1999 Act against a decision not to remove the applicant from the POCA list; or

    (b) to have the issue of the applicant's inclusion in the POCA list determined under
         section 4(2) of the 1999 Act by the Tribunal,
must be made in writing to the Secretary.

    (2) An application under sub-paragraph (1)(a) must be received by the Secretary no later than the first working day after the expiry of three months from the date of the letter informing the applicant of the decision.

    (3) An application under this paragraph may be made on the application form available from the Secretary.

    (4) An application under this paragraph must–

    (a) give the applicant's name, date of birth and full postal address;
    (b) give sufficient information to make it clear whether the application falls within sub-paragraph (1)(a) or (b);
    (c) give the reasons why the applicant believes the decision was wrong or, as the case may be, why he believes he should not be included in the POCA list;
    (d) give the dates of any previous appeal under the 1999 Act and (where applicable) application for leave the applicant has made to the Tribunal;
    (e) give details of any new evidence or material change of circumstances since that appeal and (where applicable) application for leave was determined which might lead the Tribunal to a different decision;
    (f) in the case of an application to have the issue of his inclusion in the POCA list determined by the Tribunal, give details of any civil or criminal proceedings relating to the misconduct of which the applicant is alleged to have been guilty;
    (g) give the name, address and profession of the person (if any) representing the applicant;
    (h) give an address within the United Kingdom to which the Secretary should send documents concerning the appeal and application for leave;
    (i) give, where these are available, the applicant's telephone number, fax number and e-mail address and those of the applicant's representative; and
    (j) be signed and dated by the applicant.

Acknowledgement and notification of application

3.—(1) On receiving an application, the Secretary shall–

    (a) immediately send an acknowledgement of its receipt to the applicant;
    (b) subject to the following provisions of this paragraph, enter particulars of the application and the date of its receipt in the records and send a copy of it, together with any documents supplied by the applicant in support of it, to the respondent.

    (2) If the President is of the opinion that the applicant is asking the Tribunal to do something which it cannot do, he may notify the applicant in writing–

    (a) of the reasons for his opinion; and
    (b) that the application will not be entered in the records unless within five working days the applicant notifies the President in writing that he wishes to proceed with it.

    (3) If in the Secretary's opinion there is an obvious error in the application–

    (a) he may correct it;
    (b) he shall notify the applicant accordingly; and
    (c) unless within five working days of receipt of notification under head (b) of this sub-paragraph the applicant notifies the Secretary in writing that he objects to the correction, the application shall be amended accordingly.

Response to application

4.—(1) The Secretary must send information provided by the applicant under paragraph 1 or 2, as the case may be, to the respondent together with a request that he respond to the application within 20 working days of receiving it.

(2) If the respondent fails to respond as requested, he shall not be entitled to take any further part in the proceedings.

(3) The response must–

    (a) acknowledge that the respondent has received a copy of the application;

    (b) indicate whether or not he opposes it, and if he does, why; and

    (c) provide the following information and documents–

        (i) the name, address and profession of the person (if any) representing the respondent and whether the Secretary should send documents concerning the application to the representative rather than to the respondent;

        (ii) copies of any letters informing the applicant of the decision which is the subject of the appeal or application for leave, as the case may be;

        (iii) copies of any information submitted with a reference under section 2, 2A, 2B or 2D of the 1999 Act and of any observations submitted on it by the applicant;

        (iv) copies of any evidence and expert evidence relied on by the respondent in making a decision under the Education Regulations.

(4) The Secretary must without delay send to the applicant a copy of the response and the information and documents provided with it (subject, in the case of any material provided in accordance with sub-paragraph (3)(c)(iv), to any direction of the President or the nominated chairman under regulation 15).

Misconceived applications etc.

5.—(1) The President or the nominated chairman may at any time strike out the appeal or, as the case may be application for leave, on the grounds that–

    (a) it is made otherwise than in accordance with paragraph 1 or 2 (as the case may be);

    (b) it is outside the jurisdiction of the Tribunal or is otherwise misconceived; or

    (c) it is frivolous or vexatious.

(2) Before striking out an appeal or, as the case may be, application for leave, under this paragraph, the President or the nominated chairman must–

    (a) invite the parties to make representations on the matter within such period as he may direct;

    (b) if within the period specified in the direction the applicant so requests in writing, afford the parties an opportunity to make oral representations; and

    (c) consider any representations the parties may make.

Grant or refusal of leave

6.—(1) The President or the nominated chairman shall grant or refuse leave in relation to an application under paragraph 2 without a hearing, as he sees fit.

(2) Subject to paragraph 7, if the President or the nominated chairman refuses leave the application shall be dismissed.

(3) The Secretary must without delay notify the parties in writing of the President or the nominated chairman's decision, and if he has refused leave–

    (a) must notify them of his reasons for doing so; and

(b) must inform the applicant of his right to request a reconsideration of the decision under paragraph 7.

Reconsideration of leave

7.—(1) The President or the nominated chairman must reconsider a decision to refuse leave if within ten working days after receipt of a notice under paragraph 6(3) the Secretary receives a written request to do so from the applicant.

(2) If in his request under sub-paragraph (1) the applicant has asked to make representations about leave at a hearing, the Secretary must fix a hearing for those representations to be heard.

(3) The Secretary must notify the respondent of any hearing fixed for the purpose of considering whether to grant leave, and the applicant and the respondent may appear or be represented by any person at that hearing.

(4) If the President or the nominated chairman again refuses leave after reconsideration–
(a) he must give his reasons for doing so in writing; and
(b) the Secretary must without delay send to the parties a copy of the President or the nominated chairman's decision and if he has refused leave, of his reasons for doing so.

Further information to be sent by the applicant and respondent

8.—(1) As soon as the respondent has provided the information set out in paragraph 4, or as soon as leave has been granted under paragraph 6 or 7, the Secretary must write to each party requesting that he send to the Secretary, within 20 working days after the date on which he receives the Secretary's letter, the following information–
(a) the name of any witness whose evidence the party wishes the Tribunal to consider (and whether the party may wish the Tribunal to consider additional witness evidence from a witness whose name is not yet known) and the nature of that evidence;
(b) whether the party wishes the President to give any directions or exercise any of his powers under Part IV of these Regulations;
(c) whether the party wishes there to be a preliminary hearing with regard to directions;
(d) a provisional estimate of the time the party considers will be required to present his case;
(e) the earliest date by which the party considers he would be able to prepare his case for hearing; and
(f) in the case of the applicant, whether he wishes his case to be determined without a hearing.

(2) Once the Secretary has received the information referred to in sub-paragraph (1) from both parties, he must without delay send a copy of the information supplied by the applicant to the respondent and that supplied by the respondent to the applicant.

Changes to further information supplied to the Tribunal

9.—(1) Either party, within 5 working days of receiving the further information in respect of the other party from the Secretary, may ask the Secretary in writing to amend or add to any of the information given under paragraph 8(1).

(2) If the Secretary receives any further information under sub-paragraph (1) from either party he must, without delay, send a copy of it to the other party.

SCHEDULE 5   Regulation 4(5)
APPEALS AND APPLICATIONS FOR LEAVE UNDER SECTION 86
OF THE 2000 ACT

Initiating an appeal

1.—(1) A person who wishes to appeal to the Tribunal under section 86(1)(a) of the 2000 Act, against a decision to include him in the POVA list must do so by application in writing to the Secretary.

(2) An application under this paragraph must be received by the Secretary no later than the first working day after the expiry of three months from the date of the letter informing the applicant of the decision.

(3) An application under this paragraph may be made on the application form available from the Secretary.

(4) An application under this paragraph must–

    (a) give the applicant's name, date of birth and full postal address;

    (b) give the reasons why the applicant believes he should not be included in the POVA list;

    (c) give the name, address and profession of the person (if any) representing the applicant;

    (d) give the address within the United Kingdom to which the Secretary should send documents concerning the appeal;

    (e) give, where these are available, the applicant's telephone number, fax number and e-mail address and those of the applicant's representative; and

    (f) be signed and dated by the applicant.

Applying for leave

2.—(1) An application for leave–

    (a) to appeal to the Tribunal under section 86(1)(b) of the 2000 Act against a decision not to remove the applicant from the POVA list; or

    (b) to have the issue of the applicant's inclusion in the POVA list determined under section 86(2) of the 2000 Act by the Tribunal,

must be made in writing to the Secretary.

(2) An application under sub-paragraph (1)(a) must be received by the Secretary no later than the first working day after the expiry of three months from the date of the letter inform-ing the applicant of the decision.

(3) An application under this paragraph may be made on the application form available from the Secretary.

(4) An application under this paragraph must–

    (a) give the applicant's name, date of birth and full postal address;

    (b) give sufficient information to make it clear whether the appeal falls within sub-paragraph (1)(a) or (b);

    (c) give the reasons why the applicant believes the decision was wrong or, as the case may be, why he believes he should not be included in the POVA list;

    (d) give the dates of any previous appeal under section 86 of the 2000 Act and (where applicable) application for leave, he has made to the Tribunal;

    (e) give details of any new evidence or material change of circumstances since that appeal and (where applicable) application for leave was determined which might lead the Tribunal to a different decision;

(f) in the case of an application to have the issue of his inclusion in the POVA list determined by the Tribunal, give details of any civil or criminal proceedings relating to the misconduct of which the applicant is alleged to have been guilty;

(g) give the name, address and profession of the person (if any) representing the applicant;

(h) give the address within the United Kingdom to which the Secretary should send documents concerning the appeal and the application for leave;

(i) give, where these are available, the applicant's telephone number, fax number and e-mail address and those of the applicant's representative; and

(j) be signed and dated by the applicant.

Acknowledgement and notification of application

3.—(1) On receiving an application, the Secretary must–

(a) immediately send an acknowledgement of its receipt to the applicant; and

(b) subject to the following provisions of this paragraph, enter particulars of the application and the date of its receipt in the records and send a copy of it, together with any documents supplied by the applicant in support of it, to the respondent.

(2) If the President is of the opinion that the applicant is asking the Tribunal to do something which it cannot do, he may notify the applicant in writing–

(a) of the reasons for his opinion; and

(b) that the application will not be entered in the records unless within five working days the applicant notifies the President in writing that he wishes to proceed with it.

(3) If in the Secretary's opinion there is an obvious error in the application–

(a) he may correct it;

(b) he shall notify the applicant accordingly; and

(c) unless within five working days of receipt of notification under head (b) of this sub-paragraph the applicant notifies the Secretary in writing that he objects to the correction, the application shall be amended accordingly.

Response to application

4.—(1) The Secretary must send the information provided by the applicant under paragraph 1 or 2, as the case may be, to the respondent together with a request that he respond to the application within 20 working days of receiving it.

(2) If the respondent fails to respond as directed, he shall not be entitled to take any further part in the proceedings.

(3) The response must–

(a) acknowledge that the respondent has received a copy of the application;

(b) indicate whether or not he opposes it, and if he does, why;

(c) provide the following information and documents–

(i) the name, address and profession of the person (if any) representing the respondent and whether the Secretary should send documents concerning the appeal or, as the case may be, application for leave, to the representative rather than to the respondent;

(ii) copies of any letters informing the applicant of the decision which is the subject of the appeal or, as the case may be, application for leave;

(iii) copies of any information submitted with a reference under section 82(1), 83(1), 84(1) or 85 of the 2000 Act and of any observations submitted on it by the applicant.

(4) The Secretary must without delay send to the applicant a copy of the response and the information and documents provided with it.

Misconceived applications etc.

5.—(1) The President or the nominated chairman may at any time strike out the appeal or, as the case may be, application for leave, on the grounds that–

    (a) it is made otherwise than in accordance with paragraph 1 or 2 (as the case may be);

    (b) it is outside the jurisdiction of the Tribunal or is otherwise misconceived; or

    (c) it is frivolous or vexatious.

(2) Before striking out an appeal or application for leave, as the case may be, under this paragraph, the President or the nominated chairman must–

    (a) invite the parties to make representations on the matter within such period as he may direct;

    (b) if within the period specified in the direction the applicant so requests in writing, afford the parties an opportunity to make oral representations; and

    (c) consider any representations the parties may make.

Grant or refusal of leave

6.—(1) The President or the nominated chairman shall grant or refuse leave in relation to an application under paragraph 2 without a hearing, as he sees fit.

(2) Subject to paragraph 7, if the President or the nominated chairman refuses leave the application shall be dismissed.

(3) The Secretary must without delay notify the parties in writing of the President or the nominated chairman's decision, and if he has refused leave–

    (a) must notify them of his reasons for doing so; and

    (b) must inform the applicant of his right to request a reconsideration of the decision under paragraph 7.

Reconsideration of leave

7.—(1) The President or the nominated chairman must reconsider a decision to refuse leave if within ten working days after receipt of a notice under paragraph 6(3) the Secretary receives a written request to do so from the applicant.

(2) If in his request under sub-paragraph (1) the applicant has asked to make representations about leave at a hearing, the Secretary must fix a hearing for those representations to be heard.

(3) The Secretary must notify the respondent of any hearing fixed for the purpose of considering whether to grant leave, and the applicant and the respondent may appear or be represented by any person at that hearing.

(4) If the President or the nominated chairman again refuses leave after reconsideration–

    (a) he must give his reasons for doing so in writing; and

    (b) the Secretary must without delay send to the parties a copy of the President or the nominated chairman's decision and if he has refused leave his reasons for doing so.

Further information to be sent by the applicant and the respondent

8.—(1) As soon as the respondent has provided the information set out in paragraph 4, or as soon as leave has been granted under paragraph 6 or 7, the Secretary must write to each party requesting that he send to the Secretary, within 20 working days after the date on which he receives the Secretary's letter, the following information–

(a) the name of any witness whose evidence the party wishes the Tribunal to consider (and whether the party may wish the Tribunal to consider additional witness evidence from a witness whose name is not yet known) and the nature of that evidence;

(b) whether the party wishes the President to give any directions or exercise any of his powers under Part IV of these Regulations;

(c) whether the party wishes there to be a preliminary hearing with regard to directions;

(d) a provisional estimate of the time the party considers will be required to present his case;

(e) the earliest date by which the party considers he would be able to prepare his case for hearing; and

(f) in the case of the applicant, whether he wishes his case to be determined without a hearing.

(2) Once the Secretary has received the information referred to in sub-paragraph (1) from both parties, he must without delay send a copy of the information supplied by the applicant to the respondent and that supplied by the respondent to the applicant.

Changes to further information supplied to the Tribunal

9.—(1) Either party, within 5 working days of receiving the further information in respect of the other party from the Secretary, may ask the Secretary in writing to amend or add to any of the information given under paragraph 8(1).

(2) If the Secretary receives any further information under sub-paragraph (1) from either party he must, without delay, send a copy of it to the other party.

Appendix 3

THE PROTECTION OF CHILDREN AND VULNERABLE ADULTS AND CARE STANDARDS TRIBUNAL (AMENDMENT) REGULATIONS 2003

SI No. 2003/626

Made	10th March 2003
Laid before Parliament	11th March 2003
Coming into force	1st April 2003

The Secretary of State, in exercise of the powers conferred upon him by section 9(2)(c) and (d), (3) and (3B) of the Protection of Children Act 1999[1] and of all other powers enabling him in that behalf, after consultation with the Council on Tribunals in accordance with section 8 of the Tribunals and Inquiries Act 1992[2], and with the National Assembly for Wales in accordance with section 9(3C) of the Protection of Children Act 1999, hereby makes the following Regulations:–

Citation, commencement and interpretation
1.—(1) These Regulations may be cited as the Protection of Children and Vulnerable Adults and Care Standards Tribunal (Amendment) Regulations 2003 and shall come into force on 1st April 2003.

(2) In these Regulations, 'the Tribunal Regulations' means the Protection of Children and Vulnerable Adults and Care Standards Tribunal Regulations 2002[3].

Amendment of regulation 1 of the Tribunal Regulations
2. In regulation 1(2) of the Tribunal Regulations (citation, commencement and interpretation)–

---

[1] 1999 c.14. Section 9(2) of the Protection of Children Act 1999 ('the 1999 Act') was amended by the Care Standards Act 2000 (c.14) ('the 2000 Act'), section 116 and Schedule 4, paragraph 26(1), (3)(a). Section 9(3A) to (3C) of the 1999 Act was inserted by the 2000 Act, section 116 and Schedule 4, paragraph 26(1), (3)(b), in the case of section 9(3A) on a date to be appointed.
[2] 1992 c.53. Schedule 1, paragraph 36A of the Tribunal and Inquiries Act 1992 was inserted by the Schedule to the 1999 Act, paragraph 8. Schedule 1, paragraph 36A of the Tribunals and Inquiries Act 1992 was renumbered as paragraph 36B and amended by the 2000 Act, Schedule 4, paragraph 21.
[3] S.I. 2002/816.

(a) in the definition of 'case'–
    (i) at the end of paragraph (g), the word 'or' shall be omitted;
    (ii) there shall be added at the end the following–

        '(i) an appeal under section 68 of the 2000 Act; or
        (j) an appeal under the Suspension Regulations;';

(b) at the end of the definition of 'the respondent' there shall be added the following–

        '(h) in relation to an appeal under section 68 of the 2000 Act, the Council;
        (i) in relation to an appeal under the Suspension Regulations, the Chief Inspector;';

(c) the following definitions shall be added at the appropriate places–

        ' "Council" means in relation to England, the General Social Care Council or in relation to Wales, the Care Council for Wales[4];
        "the Suspension Regulations" means the Child Minding and Day Care (Suspension of Registration) (England) Regulations 2003[5];'.

Amendment of regulation 4 of the Tribunal Regulations

3. In regulation 4 of the Tribunal Regulations (procedure for appeals, determinations and applications for leave), there shall be added at the end the following paragraphs–

    '(6) In the case of an appeal under section 68 of the 2000 Act against a decision of the Council under Part IV of the 2000 Act, the procedure set out in Schedule 6 shall apply.
    (7) In the case of–
        (a) an appeal under regulation 8(1)(a) of the Suspension Regulations against a decision to suspend the registration of a person acting as a child minder or providing day care; or
        (b) an appeal under regulation 8(1)(b) of the Suspension Regulations against a refusal to lift the suspension of such registration,
the procedure set out in Schedule 7 shall apply.'.

Amendment of regulation 6 of the Tribunal Regulations

4. In regulation 6 of the Tribunal Regulations (directions)–
    (a) there shall be added at the beginning the following paragraph–

    '(Z1) This regulation shall not apply in the case of an appeal under the Suspension Regulations.';
    (b) in paragraph (1), for the words 'in paragraph 6 of Schedule 1, 2 or 3', there shall be substituted the words 'in paragraph 6 of Schedule 1, 2, 3 or 6'.

Insertion of regulation 6A in the Tribunal Regulations

5. After regulation 6 of the Tribunal Regulations there shall be inserted the following new regulation–

---

[4] *See*: section 54 of the Care Standards Act 2000 (c.14).
[5] S.I. 2003/332.

'Directions: appeals under the Suspension Regulations

6A.—(1) This regulation shall apply in the case of an appeal under the Suspension Regulations.

(2) The President or the nominated chairman may, if he considers it necessary or expedient (and whether at the request of either party or otherwise)–

(a) give directions as to the dates by which any document, witness statement or other material upon which any party is intending to rely shall be sent to the Tribunal, and, if the President or the nominated chairman considers it appropriate, to the other party;

(b) give any other direction in exercise of his powers under this Part;

(c) where the applicant has requested that the case be determined without an oral hearing, give a direction as to the date by which the parties shall send any written representations, regarding the appeal, to the Tribunal.

(3) The President or the nominated chairman may direct that exchange of witness statements or other material shall be simultaneous or sequential, as he considers appropriate.

(4) The Secretary shall notify the parties as soon as possible in writing of any directions the President or the nominated chairman gives in writing under paragraphs (2) and (3).'.

Amendment of regulation 7 of the Tribunal Regulations

6. In regulation 7 of the Tribunal Regulations (fixing and notification of hearing)–

(a) at the beginning of paragraph (2), for the words 'The date' there shall be substituted the words 'Except in the case of an appeal under the Suspension Regulations, the date';

(b) after paragraph (2), there shall be inserted the following new paragraph–

'(2A) In the case of an appeal under the Suspension Regulations, the date fixed for the hearing shall be the earliest practicable date having regard to any directions which have been made by the President or the nominated chairman with regard to the preparation of evidence but shall be not later than 10 working days after the date on which the Secretary receives the written response from the respondent under paragraph 3 of Schedule 7.';

(c) at the beginning of paragraph (3), for the words 'The Secretary' there shall be substituted the words 'Except in the case of an appeal under the Suspension Regulations, the Secretary';

(d) after paragraph (3) there shall be inserted the following new paragraph–

'(3A) In the case of an appeal under the Suspension Regulations, the Secretary must inform the parties in writing of the date, time and place of the hearing–

(a) subject to sub-paragraph (b), by no later than 5 working days before the date fixed for the hearing, or by such later date as the parties may agree;

(b) where it appears to the President or the nominated chairman that it is necessary or expedient for the parties to be informed of the hearing at a date later than 5 working days before the date fixed for the hearing, by such date as the President or the nominated chairman may direct.'.

Amendment of regulation 8 of the Tribunal Regulations

7. In regulation 8 of the Tribunal Regulations (multiple appeals)–

(a) in paragraph (5), for the words 'to make written representations' on both occasions where they occur there shall be substituted the following–

'to make–
  (i) in the case of an appeal under the Suspension Regulations, oral representations at the commencement of the hearing; or
  (ii) in any other case, written representations';

(b) in paragraph (6), for sub-paragraph (a) there shall be substituted the following sub-paragraph–

'(a) any representations made by either party under paragraph (5);'.

Amendment of regulation 16 of the Tribunal Regulations

8. In regulation 16(4)(a) of the Tribunal Regulations (summoning of witnesses), there shall be added after the word 'hearing' the words 'or has consented to a shorter period of notice'.

Amendment of regulation 35 of the Tribunal Regulations

9. In regulation 35 of the Tribunal Regulations (time), for paragraph (3) there shall be substituted the following paragraph–

'(3) This regulation does not apply to the time limits provided for initiating an appeal mentioned in paragraph 1 of Schedule 2, 6 or 7.'.

Amendment of the Tribunal Regulations: Schedules 6 and 7

10. After Schedule 5 to the Tribunal Regulations (appeals and applications for leave under section 86 of the 2000 Act), there shall be added the Schedules set out in the Schedule to these Regulations.

Signed by authority of the Secretary of State for Health

Jacqui Smith
Minister of State, Department of Health

10th March 2003

SCHEDULE

Regulation 10

'SCHEDULE 6

Regulation 4(6)

APPEAL UNDER SECTION 68 OF THE 2000 ACT AGAINST
A DECISION OF A COUNCIL IN RESPECT OF REGISTRATION
UNDER PART IV OF THAT ACT

Initiating an appeal

1.—(1) A person who wishes to appeal to the Tribunal under section 68 of the 2000 Act against a decision of the Council under Part IV of the 2000 Act in respect of registration must do so by application in writing to the Secretary.

(2) An application under this paragraph may be made on the application form available from the Secretary.

(3) An application under this paragraph must be received by the Secretary no later than 28 days after the date of service on the applicant of notice of the decision.

(4) An application under this paragraph must–

(a) give the applicant's name, date of birth and full postal address;

(b) give the name, address and profession of the person (if any) representing the applicant;

(c) give the address within the United Kingdom to which the Secretary should send documents concerning the appeal;

(d) give the applicant's telephone number, fax number and e-mail address and those of the applicant's representative where these are available;

(e) identify the decision against which the appeal is brought and give particulars of whether the appeal is against–

    (i) the refusal of registration of the applicant as a social worker or, as the case may be, a social care worker in the relevant part of the register;

    (ii) the removal of the applicant from a part of the register;

    (iii) the suspension, or the refusal to terminate the suspension, of the applicant from a part of the register;

    (iv) the grant of an application for registration subject to conditions; or

    (v) the removal, alteration or restoration of an entry relating to the applicant in a part of the register;

(f) give a short statement of grounds for the appeal; and

(g) be signed and dated by the applicant.

(5) In this Schedule, 'register' means the register maintained by the Council under section 56(1) of the Act and 'relevant part' of the register means–

(a) in relation to a social worker, the part of the register for social workers; and

(b) in relation to a social care worker of a specified description, the part of the register for a social care worker of that description.

Acknowledgement and notification of application

2.—(1) On receiving an application, the Secretary must–

(a) immediately send an acknowledgement of its receipt to the applicant; and

(b) enter particulars of the appeal and the date of its receipt in the records and send a copy of it, together with any documents supplied by the applicant in support of it, to the respondent.

(2) If, in the Secretary's opinion, there is an obvious error in the application–

(a) he may correct it;

(b) he shall notify the applicant in writing accordingly; and

(c) unless within five working days of receipt of notification under head (b) the applicant notifies him in writing that he objects to the correction, the application shall be amended accordingly.

Response to application

3.—(1) The Secretary must send the information provided by the applicant under paragraph 1 to the respondent together with a request that he respond to the application within 20 working days of receiving it.

(2) If the respondent fails to respond as requested, he shall not be entitled to take any further part in the proceedings.

(3) The response must–

(a) acknowledge that the respondent has received a copy of the application;

(b) indicate whether or not he opposes it, and if he does, why; and

(c) provide the following information and documents–

(i) the name, address and profession of the person (if any) representing the respondent and whether the Secretary should send documents concerning the appeal to the representative rather than to the respondent;

(ii) a copy of the decision which is the subject of the appeal and the reasons for the decision; and

(iii) a copy of the relevant entry in the register.

(4) The Secretary must without delay send to the applicant a copy of the response and the information and documents provided with it.

Misconceived appeals etc.

4.—(1) The President or the nominated chairman may at any time strike out the appeal on the grounds that–

(a) it is made otherwise than in accordance with paragraph 1;

(b) it is outside the jurisdiction of the Tribunal or is otherwise misconceived; or

(c) it is frivolous or vexatious.

(2) Before striking out an appeal under this paragraph, the President or the nominated chairman must–

(a) invite the parties to make representations on the matter within such period as he may direct;

(b) if within the period specified in the direction the applicant so requests in writing, afford the parties an opportunity to make oral representations; and

(c) consider any representations the parties may make.

Further information to be sent by the applicant and the respondent

5.—(1) As soon as the respondent has provided the information set out in paragraph 3, the Secretary must write to each party requesting that he send to the Secretary, within 15 working days after the date on which he receives the Secretary's letter, the following information–

(a) the name of any witness whose evidence the party wishes the Tribunal to consider (and whether the party may wish the Tribunal to consider additional witness evidence from a witness whose name is not yet known) and the nature of that evidence;

(b) whether the party wishes the President or the nominated chairman to give any directions or exercise any of his powers under Part IV of these Regulations;

(c) whether the party wishes there to be a preliminary hearing with regard to directions;

(d) a provisional estimate of the time the party considers will be required to present his case;

(e) the earliest date by which the party considers he would be able to prepare his case for hearing; and

(f) in the case of the applicant, whether he wishes his appeal to be determined without a hearing.

(2) Once the Secretary has received the information referred to in sub-paragraph (1) from both parties, he must without delay send a copy of the information supplied by the applicant to the respondent and that supplied by the respondent to the applicant.

Changes to further information supplied to the Tribunal

6.—(1) Either party, within 5 working days of receiving the further information in respect of the other party from the Secretary, may ask the Secretary in writing to amend or add to any of the information given under paragraph 5(1).

(2) If the Secretary receives any further information under sub-paragraph (1) from either party he must, without delay, send a copy of it to the other party.

SCHEDULE 7

Regulation 4(7)

APPEALS UNDER THE SUSPENSION REGULATIONS

Initiating an appeal

1.—(1) A person who wishes to appeal to the Tribunal–

    (a) under regulation 8(1)(a) of the Suspension Regulations against a decision to suspend the registration of a person acting as a child minder or providing day care; or

    (b) under regulation 8(1)(b) of the Suspension Regulations against a refusal to lift the suspension of such registration,

must do so by application in writing to the Secretary.

(2) An application under sub-paragraph (1)(a) must be received by the Secretary no later than 10 working days after service on the applicant of a notice suspending his registration.

(3) An application under sub-paragraph (1)(b) must be received by the Secretary no later than 10 working days after service on the applicant of a notice informing him of the decision not to lift his suspension.

(4) An application under this paragraph may be made on the application form available from the Secretary.

(5) An application under this paragraph must–

    (a) give the applicant's name, full postal address and, if the applicant is an individual, his date of birth or, where the applicant is a company, the address of its registered office;

    (b) give the name, address and profession of the person (if any) representing the applicant;

    (c) give the address within the United Kingdom to which the Secretary should send documents concerning the appeal;

    (d) give, where these are available, the applicant's telephone number, fax number and e-mail address and those of the applicant's representative;

    (e) identify the decision against which the appeal is brought and give particulars of whether the appeal is made under sub-paragraph (1)(a) or (1)(b) or both;

(f) set out the reasons for and grounds upon which the applicant is appealing;

(g) state whether or not the applicant wishes the Tribunal to determine the appeal by way of an oral hearing;

(h) where the applicant wishes the Tribunal to determine the appeal by way of an oral hearing–

    (i) insofar as the applicant is able to identify them at that stage, give the names of any witnesses that the applicant will be calling or is likely to call to support his case and provide a statement as to the nature of the evidence to be given by those witnesses; and

    (ii) specify any working days within the 20 working days following the date of the application when the applicant or any such witnesses will not be available to attend a hearing before the Tribunal, and the reasons for which he or they (as the case may be) will not be so available; and

(i) be signed and dated by the applicant and must contain a statement as follows: 'To the best of my knowledge, information and belief, the facts contained in this application are true'.

(6) The applicant must, so far as it is practicable to do so, ensure that the application includes a copy of any documentary evidence (including any statements from witnesses) that the applicant intends to rely upon in presenting his case.

(7) At the same time as he sends the application to the Secretary, the applicant must send a copy of his application to the respondent.

Acknowledgement and notification of application

2.—(1) On receiving an application, the Secretary must–

(a) immediately send to the applicant an acknowlegement of its receipt;

(b) enter particulars of the appeal and the date of its receipt in the records and send a copy of it, together with any documents supplied by the applicant in support of the appeal, to the respondent.

(2) If in the Secretary's opinion there is an obvious error in the application–

(a) he may correct it;

(b) he must as soon as reasonably practicable and wherever possible, in advance of any determination of the appeal notify the applicant that he has done so; and

(c) amend the application accordingly unless, at any stage prior to the determination of the appeal by the Tribunal, the applicant notifies the Secretary that he objects to the correction.

Response to application

3.—(1) The respondent must, within 3 working days of the date of receipt of the application from the applicant or the Secretary (whichever is the earliest) send to the Secretary and to the applicant a written response to the application.

(2) Where the respondent fails to respond as directed under sub-paragraph (1), he shall not be entitled to take any further part in the proceedings.

(3) The response must–

(a) acknowledge that the respondent has received a copy of the application and any documentary evidence enclosed with it;

(b) indicate whether or not the respondent opposes the appeal;

(c) provide a copy of the notice referred to in paragraph 1(2) or (3) that was served on the applicant;

(d) provide a provisional estimate of the time the respondent considers he will require to present his case;

(e) state whether the respondent wishes the President or the nominated chairman to give any directions or exercise any of his powers under Part IV of these Regulations;

(f) provide the name, address and profession of the person (if any) representing the respondent and whether the Secretary should send any further documents relating to the appeal to the representative rather than the respondent;

(g) where the applicant has requested an oral hearing–

(i) insofar as the respondent is able to identify them at that stage, give the names of any witnesses that the respondent will be calling or is likely to call to support his case and provide a statement as to the nature of the evidence to be given by those witnesses;

(ii) specify any forthcoming working days within the period of 20 working days after the date of the application when the respondent or any such witnesses will not be available to attend a hearing before the Tribunal, and the reasons for which he or they (as the case may be) will not be so available.

(4) The respondent must, so far as it is practicable to do so, ensure that the response includes a copy of any documentary evidence (including any statements from witnesses) that the respondent intends to rely upon in presenting his case.

Further evidence

4.—(1) Subject to sub-paragraph (2), either party shall, at the earliest practicable date after he sent his application or response (as the case may be) to the Secretary, send to the Secretary and to the other party–

(a) any further documentary evidence which he intends to rely upon at the hearing (or wishes the Tribunal to take into consideration in otherwise determining the appeal); and

(b) the names of any witnesses or any further witnesses that he will be calling or is likely to call to support his case and a statement as to the nature of the evidence to be given by those witnesses.

(2) The evidence or information referred to in sub-paragraph (1)(a) or (b) must be received by the Secretary and the other party no later than 5 working days before the hearing or the determination of the appeal or, where it appears to the President or the nominated chairman that it is necessary or expedient for a later date to be substituted, by such date as the President or the nominated chairman may direct.

Misconceived appeals etc.

5.—(1) Subject to sub-paragraph (2), the President or the nominated chairman may at any time strike out the appeal on the grounds that–

(a) it is made otherwise than in accordance with paragraph 1;

(b) it is outside the Tribunal's jurisdiction or is otherwise misconceived; or

(c) it is frivolous or vexatious.

(2) Before striking out an appeal under this paragraph, the President or the nominated chairman must–

(a) invite the parties to make representations on the matter within such period as he may direct;

(b) if within the period specified in the direction, the applicant so requests in writing, afford the parties an opportunity to make oral representations; and

(c) consider any representations the parties may make.'.

EXPLANATORY NOTE

(This note is not part of the Regulations)

These Regulations amend the Protection of Children and Vulnerable Adults and Care Standards Tribunal Regulations 2002 (S.I. 2002/816) ('the Tribunal Regulations'). The Tribunal Regulations make provision about the proceedings of the Tribunal established by section 9 of the Protection of Children Act 1999 ('the 1999 Act') (c.14). The jurisdiction of the Tribunal has been extended by the Care Standards Act 2000 ('the 2000 Act') (c.14).

These Regulations amend the Tribunal Regulations so as to make provision for the conduct of the following appeals to the Tribunal–

appeals ('Part IV appeals') under section 68 of the 2000 Act, against decisions of the General Social Care Council and the Care Council for Wales in respect of registration under Part IV of the 2000 Act;

appeals ('suspension appeals') under regulation 8(1) of the Child Minding and Day Care (Suspension of Registration) (England) Regulations 2003, against decisions of Her Majesty's Chief Inspector of Schools in England–

to suspend the registration, under Part XA of the Children Act 1989, of a person acting as a child minder or providing day care; or

to refuse to lift the suspension of such registration.

Part XA was inserted in the Children Act 1989 by section 79 of the Care Standards Act 2000.

The amendments made by these Regulations relate in particular to the procedure for the appeals. Regulation 10 and the Schedule add two new Schedules to the Tribunal Regulations, in respect of Part IV appeals and suspension appeals respectively. The two new Schedules make provision in respect of the documents which the applicant must send to the Tribunal in order to initiate an appeal, the procedure for the Secretary to follow when an appeal is made, information which the respondent must send to the Tribunal, and the provision of further information by both parties.

The Regulations amend the Tribunal Regulations, for the purposes of suspension appeals, with respect to the giving of directions by the President or nominated chairman (regulation 5), the fixing and notification of the appeal hearing (regulation 6) and multiple appeals (regulation 7).

Regulations 2, 3, 4, 8 and 9 make minor consequential amendments.

Appendix 4

THE PROTECTION OF CHILDREN AND VULNERABLE ADULTS AND CARE STANDARDS TRIBUNAL (AMENDMENT NO. 2) REGULATIONS 2003

SI No. 2003/1060

Made	*8th April 2003*
Laid before Parliament	*9th April 2003*
Coming into force	*30th April 2003*

The Secretary of State, in exercise of the powers conferred upon him by section 9(2)(ca), (3) and (3B) of, and paragraph 2(4) of the Schedule to, the Protection of Children Act 1999[1], and of all other powers enabling him in that behalf, after consultation with the Council on Tribunals in accordance with section 8 of the Tribunals and Inquiries Act 1992[2], hereby makes the following Regulations:–

Citation, commencement and interpretation
1.—(1) These Regulations may be cited as the Protection of Children and Vulnerable Adults and Care Standards Tribunal (Amendment No. 2) Regulations 2003 and shall come into force on 30th April 2003.

(2) In these Regulations 'the Tribunal Regulations' means the Protection of Children and Vulnerable Adults and Care Standards Tribunal Regulations 2002[3].

Amendment of regulation 1 of the Tribunal Regulations
2. In regulation 1(2) of the Tribunal Regulations (citation, commencement and interpretation)–

(a) in the appropriate place there shall be inserted the following definition–

---

[1] 1999 c. 14. Section 9(2)(ca) of the Protection of Children Act 1999 ('the 1999 Act') was substituted by paragraph 6 of Schedule 14 to the Education Act 2002 (c. 32).
[2] 1992 c. 53. Schedule 1, paragraph 36A of the Tribunals and Inquiries Act 1992 ('the 1992 Act') was inserted by the Schedule to the 1999 Act, paragraph 8. Schedule 1, paragraph 36A of the 1992 Act was renumbered as paragraph 36B and amended by the Care Standards Act 2000 (c. 18) ('the 2000 Act'), Schedule 4, paragraph 21.
[3] S.I. 2002/816, amended by S.I. 2003/626.

' "the 1998 Act" means the School Standards and Framework Act 1998[4];';

(b) in the definition of 'case'–
   (i) at the end of paragraph (i) the word 'or' shall be omitted; and
   (ii) there shall be added at the end the following–
        'or
        (k) an appeal under paragraph 10(1A) of Schedule 26 to the 1998 Act[5];';
(c) at the end of the definition of 'the respondent' there shall be added the following–

   '(j) in relation to an appeal under paragraph 10(1A) of Schedule 26 to the 1998 Act, the Chief Inspector;'.

Amendment of regulation 3 of the Tribunal Regulations

3. In regulation 3 of the Tribunal Regulations (requirements for membership of lay panel)–
   (a) in paragraph (2)(a) after the words 'the 1989 Act' there shall be inserted the words 'or the Adoption Act 1976';
   (b) in paragraph (5)(c) after the words 'the 1989 Act' there shall be inserted the words 'or the Adoption Act 1976';
   (c) after paragraph (5)(e) there shall be inserted the following sub-paragraph–

   '(ee) experience in managing an adoption society approved under the Adoption Act 1976;';

   (d) in paragraph (5)(j) after the word 'education' there shall be inserted the words 'child minding or day care'.

Amendment of regulation 4 of the Tribunal Regulations

4. In regulation 4 of the Tribunal Regulations (procedure for appeals, determinations and applications for leave) there shall be added at the end the following paragraph–

   '(8) In the case of an appeal under paragraph 10(1A) of Schedule 26 to the 1998 Act against a decision of the Chief Inspector, the procedure set out in Schedule 8 shall apply.'.

Amendment of regulation 6 of the Tribunal Regulations

5. In regulation 6 of the Tribunal Regulations (directions) in paragraph (1), for the words 'in paragraph 6 of Schedule 1, 2, 3 or 6', there shall be substituted 'in paragraph 6 of Schedule 1, 2, 3, 6 or 8'.

---

[4]   1998 c. 31.

[5]   Paragraph 8(1) of Schedule 26 to the School Standards and Framework Act 1998 ('the Schedule') provides for the establishment of a register of nursery education inspectors for England and for Wales. Paragraph 10(1) of the Schedule provides for an appeal against certain decisions of the Chief Inspector of Schools in England and the Chief Inspector of Education and Training in Wales in relation to the registration of nursery education inspectors. Section 79P(1) of the Children Act 1989 (c. 41) provides for the establishment of a register of early years child care inspectors for England and subsection (3) provides that paragraph 10 of the Schedule (including the right to appeal) applies in relation to that register as it applies in relation to the register of nursery education inspectors maintained for England. Section 79P is in Schedule XA to the Children Act 1989 substituted by Part VI of the 2000 Act. By virtue of paragraph 10(1A) of the Schedule inserted by paragraph 5(2) of Schedule 14 to the Education Act 2002 appeals in relation to the registers maintained for England are to the Tribunal established under the 1999 Act.

Amendment of regulation 35 of the Tribunal Regulations
6. In regulation 35 of the Tribunal Regulations (time) in paragraph (3), for the words 'Schedule 2, 6 or 7', there shall be substituted the words 'Schedule 2, 6, 7 or 8'.

Amendment of Schedules 2, 4 and 5 to the Tribunal Regulations
7. In paragraph 5(1)(b) of Schedule 2, and paragraph 8(1)(b) of each of the Schedules 4 and 5, to the Tribunal Regulations after the word 'President' there shall be inserted the words 'or nominated chairman'.

Amendment of the Tribunal Regulations : Schedule 8
8. After Schedule 7 to the Tribunal Regulations (appeals under the Suspension Regulations) there shall be added the Schedule set out in the Schedule to these Regulations.

Signed by authority of the Secretary of State for Health

Jacqui Smith
Minister of State, Department of Health

8th April 2003

SCHEDULE

Regulation 8

'SCHEDULE 8

Regulation 4(8)

APPEAL UNDER PARAGRAPH 10(1A) OF SCHEDULE 26 TO THE
1998 ACT AGAINST A DECISION OF THE CHIEF INSPECTOR

Initiating an appeal
1.—(1) A person who wishes to appeal to the Tribunal under paragraph 10(1A) of Schedule 26 to the 1998 Act against a decision of the Chief Inspector must do so by application in writing to the Secretary.

(2) An application under this paragraph may be made on the application form available from the Secretary.

(3) An application under this paragraph must be received by the Secretary no later than 28 days after the date of service on the applicant of notice of the decision of the Chief Inspector.

(4) An application under this paragraph must–
  (a) give the applicant's name, date of birth and full postal address;
  (b) give the name, address and profession of the person (if any) representing the applicant;

(c) give the address within the United Kingdom to which the Secretary should send documents concerning the appeal;

(d) give the applicant's telephone number, fax number and e-mail address and those of the applicant's representative where these are available;

(e) identify the decision against which the appeal is brought and give particulars of whether the appeal is against–

(i)   the refusal of the Chief Inspector to renew the registration of the applicant as a nursery education inspector or an early years child care inspector;

(ii) the imposition or variation of any condition subject to which the applicant is registered; or

(iii) the removal of the name of the applicant from the register;

(f) give a short statement of grounds for the appeal; and

(g) be signed and dated by the applicant.

(5) In this Schedule, 'register' means the register maintained by the Chief Inspector under paragraph 8(1) of Schedule 26 to the 1998 Act or section 79P(1) of the 1989 Act[6], and 'registration' and 'registered' shall be construed accordingly.

Acknowledgement and notification of application

2.—(1) On receiving an application, the Secretary must–

(a) immediately send an acknowledgement of its receipt to the applicant; and

(b) enter particulars of the appeal and the date of its receipt in the records and send a copy of it, together with any documents supplied by the applicant in support of it, to the respondent.

(2) If, in the Secretary's opinion, there is an obvious error in the application–

(a) he may correct it;

(b) he shall notify the applicant in writing accordingly; and

(c) unless within five working days of receipt of notification under head (b) the applicant notifies him in writing that he objects to the correction, the application shall be amended accordingly.

Response to application

3.—(1) The Secretary must send the information provided by the applicant under paragraph 1 to the respondent together with a request that he respond to the application within 20 working days of receiving it.

(2) If the respondent fails to respond as requested, he shall not be entitled to take any further part in the proceedings.

(3) The response must–

(a) acknowledge that the respondent has received a copy of the application;

(b) indicate whether or not he opposes it, and if he does, why; and

(c) provide the following information and documents–

(i)   the name, address and profession of the person (if any) representing the respondent and whether the Secretary should send documents concerning the appeal to the representative rather than to the respondent;

(ii) a copy of the decision which is the subject of the appeal and the reasons for the decision; and

---

[6] Under section 79P (2) the register of early years child care inspectors may be combined with the register of nursery education inspectors.

(iii)   a copy of the relevant entry in the register.

(4) The Secretary must without delay send to the applicant a copy of the response and the information and documents provided with it.

Misconceived appeals etc.

4.—(1) The President or the nominated chairman may at any time strike out the appeal on the grounds that–

(a) it is made otherwise than in accordance with paragraph 1;

(b) it is outside the jurisdiction of the Tribunal or is otherwise misconceived; or

(c) it is frivolous or vexatious.

(2) Before striking out an appeal under this paragraph, the President or the nominated chairman must–

(a) invite the parties to make representations on the matter within such period as he may direct;

(b) if within the period specified in the direction the applicant so requests in writing, afford the parties an opportunity to make oral representations; and

(c) consider any representations the parties may make.

Further information to be sent by the applicant and the respondent

5.—(1) As soon as the respondent has provided the information set out in paragraph 3, the Secretary must write to each party requesting that he send to the Secretary, within 15 working days after the date on which he receives the Secretary's letter, the following information–

(a) the name of any witness whose evidence the party wishes the Tribunal to consider (and whether the party may wish the Tribunal to consider additional witness evidence from a witness whose name is not yet known) and the nature of that evidence;

(b) whether the party wishes the President or the nominated chairman to give any directions or exercise any of his powers under Part IV of these Regulations;

(c) whether the party wishes there to be a preliminary hearing with regard to directions;

(d) a provisional estimate of the time the party considers will be required to present his case;

(e) the earliest date by which the party considers he would be able to prepare his case for hearing; and

(f) in the case of the applicant, whether he wishes his appeal to be determined without a hearing.

(2) Once the Secretary has received the information referred to in sub-paragraph (1) from both parties, he must without delay send a copy of the information supplied by the applicant to the respondent and that supplied by the respondent to the applicant.

Changes to further information supplied to the Tribunal

6.—(1) Either party, within 5 working days of receiving the further information in respect of the other party from the Secretary, may ask the Secretary in writing to amend or add to any of the information given under paragraph 5(1).

(2) If the Secretary receives any further information under sub-paragraph (1) from either party he must, without delay, send a copy of it to the other party.'.

EXPLANATORY NOTE

(This note is not part of the Regulations)

These Regulations further amend the Protection of Children and Vulnerable Adults and Care Standards Tribunal Regulations 2002 ('the Tribunal Regulations') which make provision about the proceedings of the Tribunal established by section 9 of the Protection of Children Act 1999. The jurisdiction of the Tribunal has been extended by the Care Standards Act 2000 ('the 2000 Act') and the Education Act 2002.

These Regulations amend the Tribunal Regulations so as to make provision for the conduct of appeals ('relevant appeals') to the Tribunal against the following decisions of the Chief Inspector of Schools in England–

(a) a decision not to renew a person's registration as a nursery education inspector or early years child care inspector;

(b) a decision to impose or vary any condition subject to which a person is registered; or

(c) a decision to remove a person from the register of nursery education inspectors or early years child care inspectors.

The new Schedule 8 inserted by regulation 8 makes provision in respect of the procedure to be followed on these appeals. In particular, the Schedule makes provision about the documents which the applicant must send to the Tribunal in order to initiate an appeal, the procedure for the Secretary to follow when an appeal is made, information which the respondent must send to the Tribunal and further information to be supplied to the Tribunal by both parties to enable the Tribunal to give directions.

Regulation 3 also amends regulation 3 of the Tribunal Regulations to make minor changes to the requirements for the membership of the lay panel consequential upon the jurisdiction of the Tribunal being extended to include relevant appeals and appeals in relation to the registration of voluntary adoption agencies under Part II of the 2000 Act from 30th April 2003.

Appendix 5

USEFUL WEBSITES

Care Standards Tribunal (www. carestandardstribunal.gov.uk)
Chartered Institute of Personnel and Development (www.cipd.co.uk)
Commission for Health Improvement (www.chi.nhs.uk)
Criminal Records Bureau (www.crb.gov.uk)
Department of Health (www.doh.gov.uk)
Disclosure Service (www.disclosure.gov.uk)
General Social Care Council (www.gscc.org.uk)
National Care Standards Commission (www.carestandards.org.uk)
Ofsted (www.ofsted.gov.uk)
Welsh Assembly (www.wales.gov.uk)
Welsh Council (www.ccwales.org.uk)

National Minimum Standards
Accommodation of Students under Eighteen by Further Education Colleges
(www.doh.gov.uk/ncsc/fecollegesfinal.pdf)
Adoption (www.carestandards.org.uk/nation+min.+standards/nationalminstandards_adoption.pdf)
Boarding Schools (www.doh.gov.uk/ncsc/boardingschoolsfinal.pdf)
Care Homes for Adults 18-65 (www.doh.gov.uk/ncsc/carehomesadults18-65.pdf)
Care Homes for Older People (www.doh.gov.uk/ncsc/carehomesolderpeople.pdf)
Care Homes for Younger Adults and Adult Placements
(www.doh.gov.uk/ncsc/youngadult.pdf)
Children's Homes (www.doh.gov.uk/ncsc/childrenshomesregulations.pdf)
Domiciliary Care (www.doh.gov.uk/ncsc/domcarenmsregs.pdf)
Fostering Services (www.doh.gov.uk/ncsc/fosteringregs.pdf)
Independent Health Care (www.doh.gov.uk/ncsc/independenthealthcare.pdf)
Nurses Agencies (www.doh.gov.uk/ncsc/nursesagencies-standards.pdf)
Residential Family Centres (www.doh.gov.uk/ncsc/standardsregsrfcdec02.pdf)
Residential Special Schools (www.doh.gov.uk/ncsc/residspecialschools.pdf)

Regulations
Care Homes Regulations 2001 (www.hmso.gov.uk/si/si2001/20013965.htm)
Care Standards Act 2000 (Establishments and Agencies) (Miscellaneous Amendments)
Regulations 2002 (www.hmso.gov.uk/si/si2002/20020865.htm)
Children's Homes Regulations 2001 (www.doh.gov.uk/ncsc/childrenshomesregulations2001.pdf)

Domiciliary Care Regulations (www.doh.gov.uk/domiciliarycare/domcareregs02.pdf)
Fostering Services Regulations 2002 (www.doh.gov.uk/ncsc/fosteringregs.pdf)
Local Authority Adoption Service (England) Regulations 2003
  (www.hmso.gov.uk/si/si2003/20030370.htm)
National Care Standards Commission (Children's Rights Director) Regulations 2002
  (www.hmso.gov.uk/si/si2002/20021250.htm)
National Care Standards Commission (Fees & Frequency of Inspections) Regulations 2003
  (www.hmso.gov.uk/si/si2003/20030753.htm)
National Care Standards Commission (Fees & Frequency of Inspections) (Adoption
  Agencies) Regulations 2003 (www.hmso.gov.uk/si/si2003/20030368.htm)
National Care Standards Commission (Fees and Frequency of Inspections) (Amendment)
  Regulations 2002 (www.hmso.gov.uk/si/si2002/20021505.htm)
National Care Standards Commission (Inspections of Schools and Colleges) Regulations
  2002 (www.hmso.gov.uk/si/si2002/20020552.htm)
National Care Standards Commission (Registration) Regulations 2001
  (www.doh.gov.uk/ncsc/ncscregistrationregulations.pdf)
National Care Standards Commission (Registration) (Amendment) Regulations 2003
  (www.hmso.gov.uk/si/si2003/20030369.htm)
Nurses Agencies Regulations (www.doh.gov.uk/ncsc/nursesagencies-standards.pdf)
Private & Voluntary Health Care Regulations 2001 (www.doh.gov.uk/ncsc/
  privatevolhealthcareregulations.pdf)
Residential Family Centres Regulations (www.doh.gov.uk/ncsc/standardsregsrfcdec02.pdf)
Voluntary Adoption Agencies and the Adoption Agencies (Miscellaneous Amendment)
  Regulations 2003 (www.hmso.gov.uk/si/si2003/20030367.htm)

Index